The Modern Middle East

The Modern Middle East

A History

JAMES L. GELVIN
University of California, Los Angeles

FOURTH EDITION

New York   Oxford
OXFORD UNIVERSITY PRESS

Oxford University Press is a department of the University of Oxford.
It furthers the University's objective of excellence in research,
scholarship, and education by publishing worldwide.

Oxford   New York
Auckland   Cape Town   Dar es Salaam   Hong Kong   Karachi
Kuala Lumpur   Madrid   Melbourne   Mexico City   Nairobi
New Delhi   Shanghai   Taipei   Toronto

With offices in
Argentina   Austria   Brazil   Chile   Czech Republic   France   Greece
Guatemala   Hungary   Italy   Japan   Poland   Portugal   Singapore
South Korea   Switzerland   Thailand   Turkey   Ukraine   Vietnam

Published by Oxford University Press
198 Madison Avenue, New York, New York 10016
http://www.oup.com

Library of Congress Cataloging-in-Publication Data

Gelvin, James L., 1951–
    The modern Middle East: a history / James L. Gelvin (University of California,
Los Angeles). — Fourth edition.
        pages cm
    Includes bibliographical references and index.
    ISBN 978-0-19-021886-7 (paperback : acid-free paper) 1. Middle East—History.
2. Nationalism—Middle East—History. 3. Secularism—Middle East—History. 4. Islam
and politics—Middle East—History. 5. Middle East—Politics and government. I. Title.
    DS62.4.G37 2015
    956—dc23

                                                                                    2014042376

Printing number: 9 8 7 6 5 4 3

Printed in Canada on acid-free paper

CONTENTS

VIGNETTES AND MAPS

VIGNETTES

MAPS

PREFACE

New Coke. The 1970 Ford Mustang. *Godfather: Part III* (some would say *Godfather: Part II*). Sometimes it is a mistake to tinker with something that is already known and appealing. The fourth edition of this book does more than just tinker with the previous three editions. It offers a reconceptualization of the trajectory of the history of the modern Middle East and expands the geographic breadth covered in the previous editions. And unlike the aforementioned blunders, I am confident it is not a mistake.

I handed in the final version of the previous edition of *The Modern Middle East: A History* the day Zine al-ᶜAbidine bin ᶜAli, who had ruled Tunisia for a quarter century, was forced to step down as president in the wake of massive protests that had broken out less than a month earlier. Anyone who knows the publishing industry understands that it would have been impossible to reclaim the manuscript so that I might have included that event, or the subsequent uprising in Egypt, or the ones that broke out after that. But that was for the best: It would have been insufficient to integrate the uprisings into the preexisting historical narrative simply because they transformed the narrative. The revised narrative is the one you have before you.

Parts of this edition of *The Modern Middle East: A History* are based on work I have published elsewhere: Introduction to Part IV and the vignette, "Who Was Abdesslem Trimech?" draw from *The Arab Uprisings: What Everyone Needs to Know* (New York: Oxford University Press, 2015); Chapter 18 draws from "Reassessing the Recent History of Political Islam in Light of the Arab Uprisings," in Fahed Al-Sumait et al. (eds.), *Conceptualizing the Arab Uprisings: Origins, Dynamics, and Trajectories* (New York: Rowman & Littlefield, 2014); and Chapter 19 draws from "The Arab World at the Intersection of the Transnational and National," in David W. Lesch and Mark Haas (eds.), *The Arab Spring: Change and Resistance in the Middle East* (Boulder, Colo.: Westview Press, 2012).

ACKNOWLEDGMENTS

Every book is a group effort, mine no less than anyone else's. I would therefore like to use this space to thank those whose assistance has been invaluable to me in writing four editions of this book. First off, there are my former professors, particularly J. C. Hurewitz at Columbia and Zachary Lockman at Harvard, who showed me how it should be done. As the old saying goes, we stand on the shoulders of giants. Others gave direct encouragement, argued, offered advice and solace, and pointed out missteps: Ziad Abu-Rish, Joel Beinin, David Dean Commins, Kate Elizabeth Creasey, Howard Eissenstat, Katherine E. Fleming, Kristen Hillaire Glasgow, Carol Hakim, Alma Heckman, Matthew S. Hopper, Emine Rezzan Karaman, Dina Rizk Khoury, Fred Lawson, Pauline Lewis, Ussama Makdisi, Karla Mallette, Michael O'Sullivan, William B. Quandt, Chase Robinson, Sarah Shields, and Zeynep Turkyilmaz. Special thanks go to William L. Cleveland, a true gentleman and friend who is now sadly gone, and to Teo Ruiz at UCLA and Helen Sader at the American University of Beirut, who provided me with the time and support necessary to write the first edition of this book. T. M. Rollins of the Teaching Company inspired me to begin this project many years ago; Bruce D. Borland took an early interest in the manuscript and sold Oxford University Press on the idea; and Peter Coveney, my initial editor at Oxford University Press, saw the first edition of this book through to publication, with the assistance of his committed staff. The torch has now been passed to Charles Cavaliere and *his* committed staff and my thanks go to them as well. Many of the photographs in this book came from the private collection of Wolf-Dieter Lemke of the Orient-Institut der Deutschen Morgenländischen Gesellschaft in Beirut and the Fondation Arabe pour l'image, also in Beirut. I am grateful to Sara Scalenghe for apprising me of the latter resource, and Tamara Sawiya for walking me through its extensive collection.

Finally, there are the students I taught at Harvard University; Boston College; Massachusetts Institute of Technology; the University of California, Los Angeles; and the American University of Beirut who, over the years, forced me to distill the narrative and rethink many of the issues raised in this book. It is to them that I dedicate it.

A NOTE ON TRANSLITERATION

In this book I have tried to keep the number of foreign words—particularly words borrowed from Arabic, Persian, and Turkish—to a minimum. To a large degree I think I have succeeded, although, to paraphrase Sigmund Freud, sometimes a *timar* is just a *timar*. Although Arabic in particular contains sounds that do not exist in English (and vice versa), most words readers will confront should pose no problems in terms of pronunciation.

There are two sounds, however, that are represented in English by symbols that will appear strange to the average reader: the *hamza* (represented by ʾ) and the *ayn* (represented by ʿ). The hamza designates what linguists call a glottal stop, the sort of sound one associates with Cockney English, as in "'allo, guvner!" Thus, when used in the middle of a word, it indicates a breaking off, then a resumption of sound. The *ayn* is a sound produced when the muscles of the throat are constricted as a vowel is pronounced. While it may be difficult for someone who does not speak Arabic to hear the difference between ʿajal and ajal, for example, the absence of the *ayn* in the latter word alters its meaning significantly, transforming "hurrying" into "hesitating."

NEW TO THIS EDITION

- The Introduction has been entirely rewritten.
- New material has been added to Chapters 2, 4, 5, 7, 8, 9, 10, 11, 13, and 16.
- Chapter 6, Chapter 12, Chapter 14, Introduction to Part IV, Chapter 15, Chapter 17, and the Conclusion have been extensively revised.
- Chapters 18 and 19 are new.
- The "Suggested Readings" sections in Parts I, II, III, and IV have been revised and updated.
- One new document selection, "An Arab Soldier in the Ottoman Army," is provided in Part III.
- Two new document selections "Statement of the April 6 Movement Regarding the Demands of the Youth and the Refusal to Negotiate with Any Side" and "Yassir al-Manawahly: 'The International Monetary Fund,'" are provided in Part IV.
- Two new photographs, "French steamship *Carthage* docking in Tunis, 1910–1915" and "'The People Want the End of the Regime.' Sana, Yemen, March 2011," have been added.
- One new vignette, "Who Was Abdesslem Trimech?" has been added.
- Two new maps, "The Caliphate of the Islamic State (according to the Islamic State) at the end of 2014" and "The Caliphate of the Islamic State in 2019, according to the organization's predictions" have been added.
- The Biographical Sketches, Glossary, and Timeline have been revised and updated.

INTRODUCTION

On 17 December 2010, the world's most famous produce vendor, Muhammad Bouazizi, set himself on fire in front of the local government building in Sidi Bouzid, a town in rural Tunisia. Earlier in the day, a policewoman had confiscated his wares and publicly humiliated him. He tried to complain to local government officials, but to no avail. He then went to the market, bought a flammable liquid, poured it over himself in front of the municipality building, and lit himself aflame with a lighter. He died eighteen days later.

The day following Bouazizi's desperate act, other vendors held a demonstration. They were soon joined by other residents of Sidi Bouzid from all walks of life. Government highhandedness and lack of responsiveness and accountability were central to the complaints of the protesters, but so were a host of other issues, ranging from unemployment to pervasive corruption. Onlookers recorded video clips of the protests and posted them on the internet, and when the government shut internet service down they sent them directly to *al-Jazeera*, the most popular satellite television broadcaster in the Arab world. Spurred on by images of rebellion, the protests spread throughout Tunisia, while Arabs elsewhere watched the growing cracks in the edifice of authoritarianism first with astonishment, then admiration. The Arab uprisings of 2010–2011 had begun.

Between January and March 2011, it seemed the entire Arab world was in revolt. Before the protests and uprisings were over, militaries would remove autocrats in Tunisia and Egypt, self-styled revolutionaries (*thuwwar*) would overthrow an entire regime in Libya (with the help of a NATO bombing campaign), and international pressure would force the leader of Yemen to step aside. In all, protests and uprisings broke out not only in those states, but in Algeria, Bahrain, Iraq, Jordan, Kuwait, Mauritania, Morocco, Oman, the Palestinian Territories, Saudi Arabia, Sudan, and Syria.

Perhaps the most memorable images associated with the early days of the uprisings came from Tahrir Square in Cairo, the epicenter of the Egyptian uprising, which protesters occupied for eighteen days before the army forced President Husni Mubarak to step down. Those images, broadcast around the world, showed throngs of youths who had gathered in peaceful protest demanding not only that Mubarak resign, but human rights, democracy, and *karama* (dignity) as well. We know now that those images painted a selective and sanitized picture of what was really taking place on the streets of Egypt where, during those eighteen days, 850 Egyptians died, 6,000 were injured, 1,200 were "disappeared" by the army, and arsonists torched hundreds of buildings housing various offices of the regime they despised. Nevertheless, for a fleeting moment in post-9/11 America, Americans were not asking of Arabs and Muslims, "Why do they hate us?" but rather thinking, "They *are* us."

Then the bubble burst. First the uprisings in Libya and Yemen turned violent; then it was Syria's turn. The short-lived protest movement in Algeria, modeled on that of Egypt, was completely shut down when the three thousand demonstrators in Algiers found themselves squaring off against thirty thousand riot police who blocked their line of march. Protests in Bahrain ended in bloodshed and fierce repression by the Bahraini government, with the help of troops and police from Saudi Arabia and the United Arab Emirates. Egypt passed from post-Mubarak military rule to rule by the Muslim Brotherhood then back to military rule whose human rights record makes Mubarak look almost saintly. By the end of 2014, the image probably most closely associated with the uprisings was not of festive youths in Tahrir Square, but of fighters from a group called the Islamic State, or the beheadings and crucifixions they performed, or the lines of refugees fleeing from their cruel and genocidal reign of terror in Syria and Iraq. And after having extricated itself from more than a decade of war in Afghanistan and Iraq that cost the lives of close to seven thousand American servicemen and women (and that of well over 500,000 Afghans and Iraqis) and will end up costing the American taxpayer an estimated $4–$6 trillion, the United States once again went to war in the region, this time to "degrade and destroy" the Islamic State. Three years after Bouazizi's self-immolation, the only uprising that still inspired cautious optimism was the original—that of Tunisia.

It was not just the Arab world that seemed so out of joint during this period. When a popular Islamist party won elections in Turkey in 2002, 2007, and 2011, it defied the prevailing wisdom that electing Islamists would mean "one man, one vote, one time." It also seemed to prove wrong all those who argued that Islam and democracy are incompatible. Then the popular prime minister ran for and won the position of president so that he might continue to play the role of puppet master in spite of term limits that prevented him from running for a fourth term as prime minister. Many Turks fear "creeping Islamization" of their society: Veiling, previously banned, has returned to university campuses, and there are now restrictions on alcohol sales that might remind Americans of the "good old days" of America's blue laws. They also fear "creeping authoritarianism" from a man whose role model seems to be Russian president Vladimir Putin. In Iran, the election of the moderate president Hassan Rouhani seemed to promise a new era after the bizarre antics of his predecessor. Yet the Iranian political system remains so opaque that it is difficult to know exactly where the power lies. Perhaps it lies with those who are merely seeking for Iran recognition as a regional power to be taken seriously—an Iran that might be interested in relaxing tensions with the West. Or perhaps it lies with hardliners who are hell-bent on going full steam ahead with the Iranian nuclear program and on adding fuel to the Syrian and Iraqi fires.

For some social scientists and pundits, the current cataclysm through which the Middle East is going is only to be expected from a region they view as wracked by tribalism and a proclivity toward authoritarianism and violence, a region in which few states have borders that make any sense or are the natural outgrowth of popular will, a region in which ties of kinship and religious sect trump all other ties, a region which never fully progressed into the modern period. As one usually perceptive observer of the Arab and broader Middle Eastern worlds put it, "The jihadists of the Islamic State ... did not emerge from nowhere. They climbed out of a rotting, empty hulk—what was left of a broken-down civilization."

As baseball player and pundit Yogi Berra once put it, "It's déjà vu all over again." In the wake of the 9/11 al-Qaeda attacks on the World Trade Center, the Pentagon, and some undisclosed target in Washington, DC (the attack was foiled mid-air), social scientists and the chattering classes tried to come up with an explanation for the "roots of Muslim rage," as one historian of the region put it. Many found the answer by conjuring up something they call an "Islamic civilization," whose main characteristic seems to be an implacable hatred toward the West and modernity. Perhaps the most famous advocate of this position was Samuel P. Huntington, professor of government at Harvard University. According to Huntington, the world is divided into a number of distinct civilizations which are irreconcilable because they hold to entirely different value systems. Islamic civilization, Huntington asserted, is particularly dangerous because of its propensity for violence (Islam, in Huntington's words, has "bloody borders"). For Huntington and his disciples, the dramatic events of 11 September 2001 offered proof positive that Western and Islamic civilizations are doomed to engage in a fight to the death.

Huntington's "clash of civilizations" thesis found a wide audience in the aftermath of 9/11, and while Huntington's work does not quite have the cachet it once did his thesis remains very much on the table, as the above-cited comment about the "rotting, empty hulk ... of a broken-down civilization" makes clear. Nevertheless, the "civilizational critique" so favored by Huntington and his imitators is open to criticism on a number of grounds. First, Huntington and others fail to take into account the diversity of the Islamic world. There are, after all, numerous ways Muslims practice their Islam, and there are numerous cultures with which Islam has interacted. Furthermore, "cultures" or "civilizations" are not billiard balls that bounce off each other when they come into contact. Throughout history, what we think of as discrete "cultures" have borrowed from and influenced each other. During the Middle Ages, for example, Arab philosophers kept alive ancient Greek texts that later provided the foundation for the European Renaissance. Interactions such as this make one despair of ever drawing distinct boundaries for any "culture" or "civilization"—which is why many scholars have abandoned those concepts entirely. Finally, the notion of a "clash of civilizations" is ahistorical. For Huntington and his disciples, the values of Islamic civilization are unchanging and are spelled out in the foundational texts of Islam (such as the Qur'an). But why are we to assume that the meaning and social function of Islam have not changed over time as circumstances have changed? Why are we to assume that a Muslim of the twenty-first century would approach those foundational texts in the same way as a Muslim of the seventh century? And, come to think of it, why should we associate the problems of the Middle East with Islam or some innate cultural "flaw" at all? What about the fact that throughout modern history the Middle East has served as ground zero for proxy wars launched by foreign powers, or that the Middle East has been cursed by oil, which has had the effect of distorting economic, social, and political life throughout the region?

If we re-shift our focus away from the so-called failings of the region and instead return to the immediate aftermath of Bouazizi's self-immolation, we are left with one indisputable fact: During 2010–2011—and, as we shall see, during the decades before then—millions of Middle Easterners from Morocco to Iran have gone out onto the street demanding the same human and democratic rights and social and economic justice enjoyed by so many others throughout the world. They did this knowing they faced the full wrath of the regimes that oppressed them. And while some states broke down, leaving chaos in their wake, and autocrats held onto power or returned to power in others, those aspirations remain. In Libya, for example, where violence continued long after the overthrow of the regime and an American ambassador died during an attack on the American consulate in the city of Benghazi, tens of thousands marched to protest the attack, ransacked the headquarters of the group that did it, and drove those responsible out of town. In November 2013, twenty-one Egyptian women, including seven under the age of eighteen, who called themselves the "7 a.m. Movement" after the time of their protest against the military government, defied the government's ban on all demonstrations. Even though their protest was peaceful, they were convicted of belonging to a terrorist group and sabotage and received prison sentences of eleven years each—as they probably anticipated. And in the midst of the civil war and Islamic State-induced carnage in Syria, Syrians in more than seventy towns and cities continued holding peaceful vigils and demonstrations demanding the end of a regime whose brutality toward its own citizens knew no bounds. There is, in other words, more than one way to view contemporary events in the region.

The argument of this book is twofold: First, the only way to understand these contemporary events is to understand the history of the region that is the focus of so much attention. Specifically, this book argues that recent events cannot be understood unless one understands the social, economic, cultural, and political evolution of the Middle East, particularly during the modern period—the period that began in the eighteenth century but has roots that stretch back as far as the sixteenth. Second, this book contends that the Middle East does not stand outside global history, that the social, economic, cultural, and political evolution of the region parallels (but does not necessarily duplicate) developments in other regions of the world, and that therefore events in the Middle East cannot fully be understood unless placed within their international context. To put it another way, historians specializing in the Middle East certainly have a story to tell, but it is a global story told in a local vernacular. It is to that story that we now turn.

PART I

The Advent of the
Modern Age

This book is about the *modern* Middle East. The underlying argument of this book is that the eighteenth century marked a new phase in the evolution of world history. Two important characteristics distinguish modern history: a world economy unlike any that had existed before and a world system of nation-states. On the one hand, the modern period marks the emergence of an integrated world market, binding together nations in a global division of labor. On the other hand, during the modern period a new form of political association—the nation-state—appears on the world stage for the first time, spreads, and achieves primacy worldwide. These twin systems have affected economic, social, cultural, and political life everywhere in ways that were unprecedented in world history.

Neither the world economy nor the world system of nation-states appeared overnight. Both needed an incubation period, during which they could be refined and expand throughout the globe. This incubation period took place during an era called by historians the "early modern" period, which lasted from about the beginning of the sixteenth century through the first half of the eighteenth century. Thus, to understand the modern history of the Middle East or any other region, it is necessary first to understand its roots in the early modern period.

Three events occurred in the first decades of the sixteenth century that would redefine the Middle East forever. Only one of these events actually occurred in the Middle East. The other two occurred far away from the Middle East, but would define the global environment in which the Middle East would evolve.

The first event that took place at the dawn of the early modern period was the emergence of large-scale, long-lived empires in the Middle East and beyond. Three such empires emerged during this period. The largest and longest-lived of these great empires was the Ottoman Empire. The Ottoman Empire survived for more than four centuries until it was finally dismantled at the end of World War I in 1918. The Ottoman Empire thus provides us with a direct link from the early modern period through the modern period.

At its height, the Ottoman Empire governed a huge expanse of territory, not only in the Middle East, but in North Africa and southeastern Europe—Greece, Hungary, the Balkans, Romania, Bulgaria—as well. Indeed, there is reason for the famous quip by the nineteenth-century Austrian statesman Prince Klemens von Metternich that "Asia begins at the eastern gate of Vienna." The Ottomans, in fact, had laid siege to Vienna itself twice, the first time in 1529, the second in 1683. No wonder, then, that an English historian writing in the beginning of the seventeenth century called the Ottoman Empire "the present terror of the world."

The second empire to emerge at the beginning of the sixteenth century was the Safavid Empire. The Safavid Empire was centered in Persia but at its height included territories that stretched from the Caucasus Mountains in the north to eastern Iraq. The Safavid Empire lasted from 1501 to 1722, when it was overthrown by an invading army from Afghanistan. After a disastrous interregnum period, most noted for bringing Persia incessant war, depopulation, deurbanization, and intermittent famine, another Turkic dynasty took over from the Safavids. This was the Qajar dynasty, which ruled from 1796 to 1925. Although the Safavid dynasty itself lasted only half as long as the Ottoman Empire, its significance lies in its twofold legacy: The Safavid Empire established a state whose boundaries roughly coincided with the boundaries of present-day Iran and, under the Safavids, the population of Persia became adherents of the Shiʿi branch of Islam.

One other Muslim empire emerged during this period, which bears mentioning even though its history lies outside the scope of this book: the Mughal Empire of India. Founded in 1526, the Mughal Empire stretched, at its height, from Afghanistan in the north three-quarters of the way down the Indian subcontinent. The Mughal Empire ran afoul of British imperialism and, in 1858, was demolished by the British, who then made India into a British colony. The Mughal Empire resembled the Ottoman and Safavid empires in many ways: Like the other empires, it was founded by a people from Central Asia (the first Mughal emperor, Babur, claimed descent from the half-Mongol, half-Turkish conqueror, Tamerlaine) and it shared political and economic structures and intellectual traditions with the Ottomans and Safavids. Unfortunately, the Mughal Empire lies outside the artificial boundaries we set for ourselves in writing the history of the modern Middle East. Its history is instead commonly addressed by historians who focus on another artificial geographical division, historians of South Asia.

The second event that occurred at the dawn of the early modern period was the Commercial Revolution in Europe. During the early sixteenth century, trade among Europeans, on the one hand, and between Europe and other parts of the world, on the other, began to increase dramatically. A variety of factors encouraged the Commercial Revolution: technological breakthroughs, such as the use of the compass and adjustable sails and multiple masts on ships; new institutions for organizing trade and banking; the introduction of new crops—from tomatoes and potatoes to tobacco—from the New World; the introduction of massive quantities of New World gold and silver into Europe; and the establishment of overseas colonies, from the Persian Gulf to the newly discovered Americas. According to many historians, the Commercial Revolution set off a chain of events that would culminate in the establishment of the modern world economy. The impact of the Commercial Revolution on the Middle East is the topic of Chapter 3.

The final event that took place at the dawn of the early modern era was the Protestant Reformation. The Protestant Reformation is commonly dated from 1517, when Martin Luther nailed his ninety-five theses on the door of the Wittenburg Cathedral in present-day Germany. Luther's theses both protested various policies and doctrines of the Roman Catholic Church and advocated new ones. The Protestant Reformation split Europe into separate Protestant and Catholic kingdoms and principalities, thereby ending the idea of a universal Christian state. It culminated in a series of religious wars during the sixteenth and seventeenth centuries. The Europe that emerged from these wars was very different from the Europe that entered them. As a result of the religious wars, Europe divided into highly competitive and sometimes highly efficient political units. European history became marked by attempts of these states to gain advantage or achieve a balance among themselves. In effect, then, modern nation-states and the nation-state system might be traced to the Protestant Reformation. The spread of the modern state system would have a profound effect on the Middle East.

Of course, the ways in which the three aforementioned events affected the Middle East were to a large extent determined by their interaction with existing social structures, economic arrangements, and cultural norms. Thus, to understand the impact of this period on the Middle East, we have to understand the legacy of the earlier history of the region. That is where Part I of this book begins.

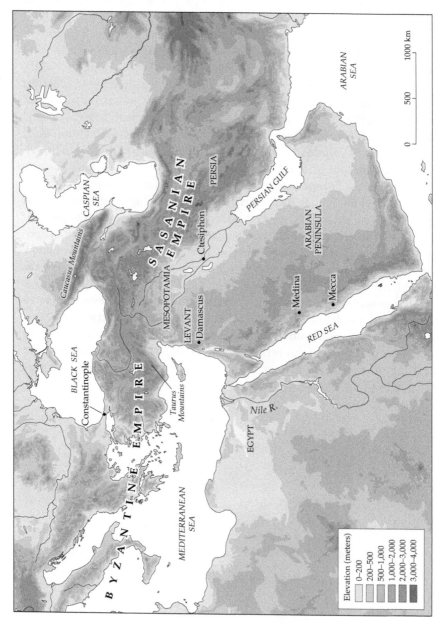

The Middle East in Late Antiquity

Elevation (meters)
0–200
200–500
500–1,000
1,000–2,000
2,000–3,000
3,000–4,000

BYZANTINE EMPIRE

SASANIAN EMPIRE

PERSIA

MESOPOTAMIA

LEVANT

EGYPT

ARABIAN PENINSULA

Constantinople

Ctesiphon

Damascus

Medina

Mecca

Nile R.

Taurus Mountains

Caucasus Mountains

MEDITERRANEAN SEA

BLACK SEA

CASPIAN SEA

RED SEA

PERSIAN GULF

ARABIAN SEA

0   500   1000 km

CHAPTER 1

From Late Antiquity to the Dawn of a New Age

That which might be called the Islamic "core area"—the area of the first Islamic conquests—is the area that stretches from the Nile River in the west to the Oxus River in the east. The Islamic core area consists of five parts. First, there is the area called the Levant. The word Levant is derived from the French word *lever*, to rise, as the sun does in the east. Accordingly, the Levant is the area that stretches from the Mediterranean coast as far east as the Euphrates River—the eastern Arab world. In the north, the Levant extends to the Taurus Mountains in the Anatolian peninsula (the site of present-day Turkey); in the south, it extends to the northern border of the Arabian peninsula.

To the south of the Levant lie Egypt and the Arabian peninsula. To the east lie Mesopotamia and Iran. The name Mesopotamia is derived from the Greek words meaning "middle of the rivers," much as the word hippopotamus is derived from the Greek words meaning "river horse." The term Mesopotamia refers not only to the territory between the Tigris and Euphrates Rivers, but to the areas immediately surrounding the two rivers as well. Iran is the name given to the territory that was once called Persia. In 1935, the shah (ruler) of Persia decreed that foreigners should use the word Iran, a word of ancient pedigree, when referring to his country. The story goes that the shah was so enamored of the racial theories popularized by Adolph Hitler that, at the suggestion of the Persian embassy in Berlin, he had the name Persia changed in diplomatic parlance to Iran to illustrate the "Aryan" roots of his nation. Needless to say, the name has stuck, and even the contemporary rulers of the country refer to their state as the Islamic Republic of Iran.

If you look closely at a map of the core area, you will see at the center a plain surrounded on all sides by mountains, deserts, and plateaus: to the north, in Anatolia, the Taurus Mountains; to the west, a range of mountains that divides the central plain from the coastal plain and the Mediterranean Sea; to the east, the Iranian plateau and the Zagros Mountains; and to the south, the Arabian

11

desert. The plain has been both prize and passageway for conquerors from both the east and the west for millennia.

Islam arose in an era known as Late Antiquity, a period that began in the fourth century and ended in the seventh. At the end of the sixth century, two empires contended for control of the central plain. To the west of the central plain lay the Roman Empire, also known as the Eastern Roman Empire or the Byzantine Empire. Its capital was Constantinople, a city built on the site of a previously existing village, Byzantium (hence, the name Byzantine Empire). It is now called Istanbul. Constantinople was founded by Emperor Constantine in A.D. 324. Toward the end of that same century, the Roman Empire was divided into two administrative parts, with capitals at Rome and Constantinople. With the fall of the Western Roman Empire in A.D. 476, Constantinople was, in effect, the sole capital of the Roman Empire. For most of Late Antiquity, the emperors ruling from Constantinople held sway over the Anatolian peninsula, the western Levant, and Egypt.

The Sasanian Empire lay to the east of the central plain. The Sasanian Empire had been founded in the early third century and lasted until the year A.D. 651. For most of its history, the Sasanian Empire actually controlled an area larger than contemporary Iran, incorporating parts of Central Asia, Afghanistan, Pakistan, eastern Anatolia, the southern Caucasus region, and Iraq. As a matter of fact, the Sasanian capital was Ctesiphon, in what is now Iraq, not far from present-day Baghdad.

Ancient empires were not like the nation-states we know. Imperial governments were mainly concerned with collecting taxes and tribute from their populations, expanding the territory from which they might collect taxes and tribute, and maintaining order in their empires to make that tax and tribute collection possible. Imperial governments did not attempt to impose a single language or ideology or culture on their populations. Nor did they much care that the peoples who lived in the territories they governed were of different ethnic backgrounds. Thus, although the state language of the Roman Empire in Late Antiquity was Greek and the state religion was Orthodox Christianity, the empire included diverse peoples—Greeks, Latins, Semites, and others—who spoke a variety of vernacular languages and practiced a variety of religions. These included non-Orthodox Christianity, Judaism, Greco-Roman paganism, and local cults. Likewise, the Sasanian Empire housed a variety of ethnic groups that spoke a variety of languages. Although the empire was governed by a Persian ruling class that spoke a language called Pahlavi (the forerunner of modern Persian), Kurds (mainly in the mountains), Aramaic-speaking Arabs (mainly in Iraq), and a variety of other peoples inhabited the empire. The Sasanian Empire sponsored a state religion, Zoroastrianism. Nevertheless, in many of the most densely inhabited places such as Iraq, Christianity overshadowed the official religion.

During the sixth century, energetic leaders in both the Sasanian and Roman empires sought to centralize control and expand their territories. The wars they fought against each other were fought mainly in the Middle East. In A.D. 602, the Sasanian emperor Chosroes II launched an offensive against the Roman Empire and conquered as far west as Syria and Egypt. He even laid siege to Constantinople before the Roman emperor, Heraclius, counterattacked. The war was devastating for both sides: The Sasanian Empire was, in effect, destroyed by the costs of incessant campaigning and by the loss of Iraq, which had provided more revenue than any other province. The Roman Empire survived, but in a truncated and weakened form. Both empires were thus vulnerable to a challenge from the south.

Islamic history begins in A.D. 622, when the prophet Muhammad fled to the western Arabian town of Medina from his hometown of Mecca, also in western Arabia. Muhammad was a merchant. According to Muslims, at the age of about forty he started receiving revelations from God brought by the archangel Gabriel. Persecuted in Mecca, Muhammad established the first lasting Islamic community in Medina. It is significant that, whereas Christians use the birth of Christ as the starting point of their calendar (A.D. 1), Muslims use the formation of the first Islamic community as the starting point of theirs: 1 A.H. (which stands for "after *hijra*," i.e., the year of Muhammad's migration) is, in the Christian calendar, A.D. 622. The notion of the community of believers is important in Islam, and the first community established by Muhammad is particularly important because, as we shall see later, it has provided many with a model for the ideal Islamic community.

Over the course of the next ten years, Muhammad's community continued to grow. By the time of Muhammad's death, much of the Arabian peninsula had joined or was affiliated with the Islamic community of Medina.

The period following Muhammad's death was one of vast Islamic expansion. Within a hundred years of Muhammad's death, Arab/Muslim armies had conquered all of Persia, Mesopotamia, Egypt, and the Levant. They had pushed back the frontier of the Byzantine Empire in the north, had traversed North Africa, and had crossed the Mediterranean. There is still a trace of this crossing in the name of the island between North Africa and Spain—Gibraltar—derived from the words *jabal Tariq*, the mountain of Tariq, the general who led the Muslim armies into Spain. In A.D. 732 a Muslim army even launched a foray into the territory that is now France, but was turned back. The Islamic conquests were followed by settlement of Arabs throughout the conquered territories. Different historians have given various reasons for the expansion of Arab settlement: Some claim it was the lure of booty or military pay, others religious or warrior zeal.

During the first century of Islamic history, the Islamic community was united in a single empire. Over time, most of the population of the empire converted to Islam. This did not occur overnight, nor did it occur at the same rate in every territory. Using as evidence the adoption of Arab/Muslim names—Persian children who would have once been named Ardeshir were now bearing the name Muhammad—historians have estimated that one hundred years after the Muslim conquests only about 8 percent of the Persian population was Muslim. By the tenth century, from 70 to 80 percent of the Persian population was Muslim. The rates of

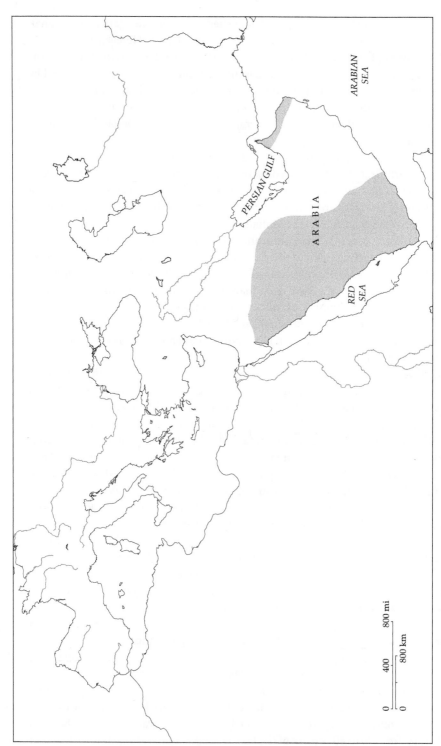

The Islamic World at the Time of Muhammad

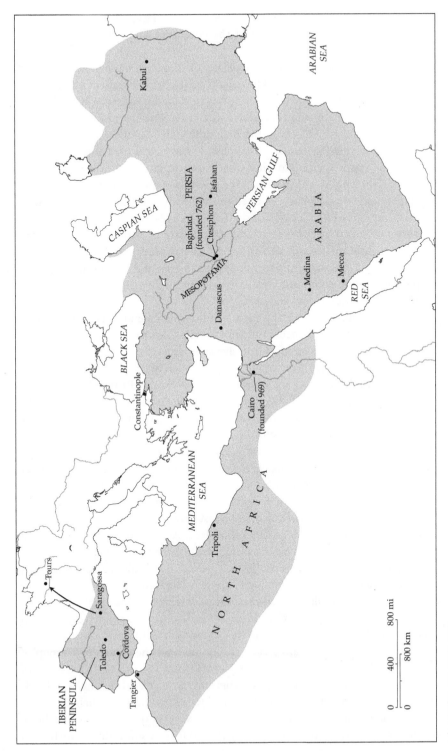

Islamic Conquests to 750

15

conversion were probably faster in Iraq and slower in Egypt. With the exception of Persia, most of the population of the core area adopted Arabic as their language.

Three other aspects of the early period of Islam are important for under-standing the subsequent history of the region. First, after the death of Muhammad, there was the question of whether or not there should be a leader of the Islamic community and, if so, who that leader should be. Prominent members of the community gathered and chose the first caliph, that is, the first successor to Muhammad. Unlike Muhammad, caliphs did not have a special religious role. Muhammad was, according to Islam, the "seal" (the last) of God's prophets. The function of the caliphs was to protect the interests of the community. Questions of religion and religious law remained in the hands of religious scholars called ulama (singular: ʿalim). They still do. Between 1924, when the last Ottoman caliph was deposed by the secularizing government of Turkey, and 2014, when an Islamic militant from Iraq, Abu Bakr al-Baghdadi, established what he claimed to be a caliphate in parts of Syria and Iraq and pronounced himself caliph, the Islamic community functioned quite well without one. It's only a matter of time before it does so again.

During its history, both the nature of the caliphate and its seat of power varied. At first, the caliph acted much like a tribal leader. He was "first among equals" who relied more on his persuasive abilities than on his coercive abilities to lead the community. Later, caliphs adopted much of the pomp and ceremony of the Byzantine and Sasanian courts, and even assumed the title "shadow of God on earth," a title originally used by Sasanian shahs. Over time, as caliphs increasingly lost political and military control to local princes, the role of the caliph became more and more symbolic.

The first four caliphs ruled from Medina. Their immediate successors ruled from Damascus. This was a logical development because the city lay on major trade routes linking Arabia with the north and Byzantine territories and pro-vided caliphs with access to reserves of warriors from Arabia. As the center of gravity of Islamic territories shifted to the east, and as more and more non-Arabs converted to Islam, the caliphs ruled from Iraq. As a matter of fact, the city of Baghdad was originally built as the administrative capital of the caliphate.

The second aspect of the early Islamic period that would have ramifications for later history was one of several splits in the Islamic community. The split was originally over who would act as successor to Muhammad. Some in the community thought that ʿAli, Muhammad's son-in-law and cousin, should have succeeded Muhammad. They became known as the partisans of ʿAli, or shiʿat ʿAli, and later just Shiʿis. Most of the Islamic community followed the choice of a group of leading notables, acquiring the name Sunnis (from the phrase "the people of [Muhammad's] example [sunna] and community"). Over time, the split hard-ened as each community developed its own traditions and sets of beliefs. Today, Shiʿis form a majority of the population in several of the states this book discusses: Iran, Iraq, and Bahrain. They also form a sometimes substantial minority in others, including Lebanon, Saudi Arabia, Kuwait, and Yemen. Sunnis are predominant in Turkey and, with the exception of Iraq, Bahrain, and Lebanon, the rest of the Arab world.

One aspect of Shiʿism merits further explanation. At its inception Shiʿism was an opposition party. During the early Islamic period, various Shiʿi sects arose that were united by a fundamental set of beliefs, even though they had political differences. At the center of these beliefs was the notion that the imam, the leader of the community, should be chosen from the house of ʿAli, Muhammad's closest male relative. Over time, the Shiʿi tendency adopted three other beliefs as well. First, Shiʿis came to believe that the imam alone was the community's teacher and religious leader. Furthermore, they believed that the imam had a special, esoteric (hidden) knowledge. This contrasted with the view of the Sunnis that proper Islamic belief was preserved by the community as a whole. Finally, Shiʿis came to believe that the next imam had to be designated by the previous imam.

The line of imams continued without interruption from ʿAli through six generations. The sixth imam named his son Ismaʿil as his successor. But Ismaʿil died before his father, and so his father selected his second son, Musa, to succeed him. For some Shiʿis, this could not be: After all, the imam had secret knowledge and so the father must have foreseen Ismaʿil's absence. These Shiʿis thus believed that Ismaʿil was not really dead, but instead had gone into what is called "occultation." In other words, Ismaʿil was around, they just did not know where. At the end of time he would return and establish justice and equity on earth. Because Ismaʿil was to have been the seventh imam, these Shiʿis were sometimes called Ismaʿilis. The contemporary Ismaʿili community in India, which is under the spiritual leadership of the Agha Khan, are their descendants.

Other Shiʿis, however, acknowledged the ʿAlid line as it ran through Musa and his descendants. But after the eleventh imam died without apparent heirs, they faced a problem similar to the one they had faced earlier. They came up with a solution similar to the solution at which the Ismaʿilis had arrived. They believed that the eleventh imam had had a son, but that he was in occultation. These Shiʿis came to be known as Twelvers, because they awaited the return of the twelfth imam. They represent the bulk of the Shiʿi population in Lebanon, Iraq, and parts of the Gulf today—and, of course, the home of the largest contemporary Twelver Shiʿi community, Iran. The idea of occultation raised two issues that would be of crucial importance to the Shiʿi community in the future: who should govern the community until the reemergence of the hidden imam and how the community should organize its affairs in the meantime.

The final aspect of the early period of Islam that is important for understanding later developments stems from the fact that the number of Arab conquerors was small in comparison with the number of those conquered. This disparity naturally created difficulties for the conquerors. The caliphs attempted to resolve these difficulties by borrowing administrative techniques from the Sasanians and Byzantines. For the most part, the conquerors allowed the inhabitants of

---

Vignette

From Nadir to Zenith

Benjamin Disraeli, the first (and only) Jewish-born prime minister of Great Britain, once dressed down an anti-Semitic detractor by reminding him that when his adversary's ancestors were swinging from trees, Disraeli's ancestors were priests in the temple of Solomon. A similar relationship held between the peoples of the Middle East and Europe during the Middle Ages. While Europe was dominated by unlettered men with axes, the caliphate was a world center for scientific inquiry and cultural enrichment. Through encounters in Spain, the Mediterranean, and, during the Crusades, the Middle East, Arabs introduced Europeans to a variety of ideas as well as foods and wares associated with the good life. Many of the Arab contributions to the societies of Europe can be traced through etymology—the study of the origin and development of words. It can be assumed that the introduction of words from Arabic occurred simultaneously with the introduction of ideas and commodities from the Middle East. Some of the following common English words originated in Arabic; others originated in ancient Greek, Persian, and Sanskrit—languages largely unknown in Europe—and were transmitted to English through Arabic:

admiral	almanac	aubergine	candy
adobe	amber	average	caper
albatross	amulet	azimuth	carat
alchemy	aniline	azure	caraway
alcohol	antimony	borax	carmine
alcove	apricot	cable	carob
alembic	arsenal	caliber	check
alfalfa	artichoke	camel	checkmate
algebra	assassin	camise	cipher
alkali	atlas	camphor	coffee

---

the territories they administered to retain their landed property and to maintain local governance. "People of the Book"—a category that included Christians and Jews—were, at least in theory, accorded the status of protected minorities and were allowed to continue practicing their religions. Pagans (polytheists) whom Muslims encountered were not so lucky, and Hindu parents on the Indian subcontinent still spook their children with stories of the eleventh-century Muslim conqueror Mahmud of Ghazna, whose plundering expeditions into India were accompanied by wholesale massacres. To prevent the conquering Arab/Muslims from being swallowed up by a much larger local population, Muslim generals in Egypt and Iraq often housed their armies and administrators in settlements outside towns. These settlements were called *amsar* (singular: *misr*), from which we get the Arabic name for Egypt (also *misr*). The custom of allowing local control would continue through Ottoman times.

Islam continued to spread long after the period of the first conquests. For example, it was not until the beginning of the sixteenth century that Islam

cork	giraffe	mohair	sirocco
cornea	gypsum	monsoon	soda
cotton	hashish	mufti	sofa
crimson	hazard	mummy	sugar
crocus	henna	muslin	syrup
cumin	jar	nadir	tabby
damask	lacquer	orange	talc
drub	lemon	popinjay	talisman
elixir	lilac	racket	tamarind
gala	lime	safari	tariff
garble	lute	saffron	tarragon
gauze	macabre	satin	zenith
gazelle	magazine	sequin	zero
genie	massacre	sherbet	zircon
gerbil	mattress	sheriff	
ghoul	mocha	sine	

Some words—like coffee, jar, and gazelle—were simply borrowed from Arabic. Others bear more colorful histories. Tabby comes from a street in Baghdad noted for its striped cloth. Assassin comes from hashish, which, according to legend, a Shiʿi group called the "hashishun" purportedly smoked before going out to kill Crusaders. Racket (as in tennis racket) is derived from the Arabic word for the palm of the hand—the original racket. Gala—as in a gala occasion—comes from the Arabic for a robe of honor or investing with a robe of honor. Satin refers to the city in China (called by Arabs "Zaytun") to which Arab merchants went to trade for the cloth. And checkmate comes from a Persian/Arabic phrase meaning the king (*shah*) is dead (*mat*). As chess aficionados know, a match ends with the trapping (and implied elimination) of the opponent's king.

became firmly established in Indonesia, today the most populous Muslim state. Nevertheless, at the beginning of the tenth century, the core area of the Islamic world began to fragment politically. Part of the reason for this political fragmentation was that the Islamic world was subjected to invasion from the outside.

A variety of groups came into the Middle East: crusaders from the West, Mongols from the Far East, and Mongol wannabes (like the legendary Tamerlaine) from Inner Asia. While most Westerners know about the Crusades, most of these military campaigns failed miserably. In fact, the Crusades might actually be considered a sideshow to the main event: invasions from the north and east. For example, the devastation wrought by the Mongols in the Middle East was enormous. According to contemporary accounts, between two hundred thousand and eight hundred thousand people died during the sack of Baghdad. Another city, Nishapur, one of the centers of learning in Persia, never recovered from the command of a Mongol general that "not even cats and dogs should be left alive." But the Mongol invasions brought more than doom and gloom to the Middle East.

Just as the Crusades exposed Europeans to the culture and products of their eastern neighbors, the Mongol invasions and subsequent "pax Mongolica" (Mongol peace) exposed the inhabitants of the Middle East to their eastern neighbors as well. The Mongol invasions introduced Middle Easterners to new forms of cultural expression, such as miniature painting and Far Eastern motifs still found in Middle Eastern carpets, and Middle Easterners were quick to take advantage of newly opened trade routes linking the eastern Mediterranean with China—as was Marco Polo, who traveled along the famed silk route on his journey from Venice to Cathay.

In spite of all this, it might be argued that the groups that had the most lasting impact on the Middle East were, in fact, Turkish-speaking peoples from Central Asia. Turkic peoples entered the lands of Islam in two ways. In the tenth century, bought or captured Turks were brought into Islamic lands to be used as imperial guards for caliphs or slave soldiers for local warlords. These military slaves were known as mamluks (literally, those who are "owned"). Caliphs and local warlords found mamluk warriors useful because they had no connections to any group in the region except their masters. It was therefore assumed that they would be entirely dependent on—and loyal to—those masters. Nevertheless, since mamluk armies often held the balance of power, they were known to seize it. For example, in 1250 slave soldiers of a local dynasty in Cairo pushed aside their former masters and began to rule in their own right. Replenishing their ranks with new mamluks, often from the Caucasus (who continued the tradition of overthrowing their masters when the opportunity arose), they ruled independently until 1517 and continued to exercise power in Egypt until the beginning of the nineteenth century. We shall thus meet up with the Egyptian mamluks again later in our story.

Starting in about the eleventh century, entire Turkic tribes began migrating from the Central Asian steppes into the Middle East. Tribes might be defined as groups of people who claim descent from a common ancestor, whether or not they are in reality related to that common ancestor or even to each other. The Turkic tribes that entered the region were, for the most part, pastoralists (think sheep and goats). No one knows for sure why they began migrating south and west. Some historians cite population pressures in their original homelands. Others cite climatic changes that affected all of Eurasia, a strengthening of the Chinese Empire, or the fact that the Middle East was a center of a flourishing civilization whose wealth would naturally attract the attention of outsiders: After all, how are you going to keep them down on the steppe after they've seen Baghdad?

In any case, the Turks who came in were dazzled by the superior civilization of Islam. For their part, many inhabitants of the Middle East had nothing but contempt for these uncouth tribesman and sheepherders. The great tenth-century Arab historian al-Mas⁽udi wrote of the Turks as follows:

> Because of their distance from the circuit of the sun when it rises and sets,
> there is much snow among the Turks, and cold and damp have conquered their

habitations; their bodies are slack and thick, and their backbones and neck-bones so supple that they can shoot their arrows as they turn and flee. Their joints form hollows because they have so much flesh; their faces are round and their eyes small because the warmth concentrates in their faces while the cold takes possession of their bodies. Those who dwell sixty miles beyond this latitude are Gog and Magog. They are in the sixth climate and are reckoned among the beasts.

The most powerful Turkic tribes that entered the Middle East took control of a given area and established principalities. There they adopted many of the local customs, including Islam. Some of these Turkish states covered large expanses of territory: The state established by a tribe called the Seljuks, for example, stretched from eastern Iran to Syria. Nevertheless, these Turkish states were, for the most part, short-lived. Not only was the size of tribes small in comparison to the populations they sought to control (there were only ten to fifteen thousand Seljuks, for example), but illiterate tribesmen are inherently better at conquest than at rule. There is the story of how one (apparently feisty) Chinese scholar chided a Mongol leader: "An empire can be conquered on horseback, but it cannot be governed on horseback." (We have no record as to how the Mongol leader took this criticism.) In addition, tribes are notoriously fractious, constantly dividing and reconstituting themselves and constantly warring on each other. As a result, the boundaries of the tribal states were continuously in flux. Often, there was no permanent seat of government. Instead, the capital was commonly situated wherever the army was camped. Hence, there could be no self-perpetuating bureaucracy to maintain the authority of the state over time. Thus it is that few readers of this book have ever heard of the Ghaznavids and Ghurids, the Saffarids and Samanids, and the Akkoyunlu and Karakoyunlu—the latter being the so-called white sheep and black sheep tribal confederations. All these tribes and tribal confederations established states in the Middle East between the tenth and the fifteenth centuries.

Two states that emerged at the beginning of the sixteenth century did leave a more lasting mark on the region, however: the Ottoman and Safavid empires. The Ottoman Empire began as many other Turkish states had begun. The Ottomans traced their history back to a legendary founder, Osman. Hence, their Turkish name: Osmanlis. Osman lived in the thirteenth century on the north-western tip of Anatolia. According to legend, Osman was divinely chosen to found a great empire. While a guest of a respected Muslim preacher, the story goes, Osman went to bed and had a dream:

A moon arose from the holy man's breast and came to sink in Osman's breast. A tree then sprouted from his navel, and its shade compassed the world. Beneath this shade there were mountains, and streams flowed forth from the foot of each mountain. Some people drank from these running waters, others watered gardens, while yet others caused fountains to flow.

According to the legend, when Osman awoke he told the story to the preacher. The preacher told him, "Osman, my son, congratulations for the imperial office bestowed upon you and your descendants by God, and take my daughter to be your wife." Apparently, Osman did so.

Sagas report that Osman was a leader of a band of warriors known as ghazis. Much of Anatolia at this time was a lawless frontier, sort of like the Wild West. The only law in town was the Byzantine Empire, which, by the thirteenth century, was a mere shadow of its former splendor. Ghazis made their living by plundering the wealth of their neighbors. Most ghazi principalities therefore consisted of little more than gangs of bandits. But the principality founded by Osman was different: Because it bordered on the Byzantine territories, Osman's state had more to loot and therefore attracted increasing numbers of ghazis. Because increasing numbers of ghazis led to increasing wealth, Osman's state could also attract artisans, merchants, religious scholars—all the elements necessary to establish a real state. Even peasants were attracted to the Ottoman state: Under the Byzantines, peasants had been serfs; that is, the property of their lords. The Ottomans never introduced serfdom into their domains. Under the Ottomans peasants were not property, although most were bound to the land.

The descendants of Osman began their conquests in the far west of Anatolia and in the Balkans, the mountainous territory of southeastern Europe. By the 1350s the Ottomans had a permanent foothold in Europe. In 1389, they defeated a coalition of Serbs, Hungarians, and Bulgarians at the Battle of Kosovo. Less than a hundred years later, the Ottomans finished off the Byzantine Empire by conquering Constantinople. For the next seventy years, they consolidated their position in Anatolia and the Balkans.

In the meantime, a threat to Ottoman power was arising to the east. During the first half of the fifteenth century, a band of Turkish pastoralists who lived in northern Persia gave their allegiance to another legendary figure, Safi al-Din, after whom the Safavid dynasty is named. Safi al-Din was the leader of a sufi order; that is, the leader of one of a variety of popular, often mystical Islamic movements. The followers of Safi al-Din were distinguished by their distinctive red headdress and, as a result, were called Qizilbash (red head) by the Ottomans.

Qizilbash missionaries spread throughout eastern Anatolia and northern Persia. By 1501, the Safavid leader Ismaᶜil, who claimed to be a descendant of Safi al-Din, entered the northern Persian city of Tabriz and proclaimed himself shah. He was fourteen at the time, putting Alexander the Great, who took his throne at the ripe old age of twenty, to shame. Within ten years all of Persia was under Ismaᶜil's control. Soon thereafter, Shah Ismaᶜil proclaimed Shiᶜism to be the official religion of his realm and imported Shiᶜi religious scholars from Lebanon and the Persian Gulf island of Bahrain to spread Shiᶜi doctrines.

The establishment of an expansionist Shiᶜi state on their borders was a strategic threat to the Ottomans. Ottoman sultans were fond of quoting the thirteenth-century Persian poet Saᶜdi, who wrote: "Ten dervishes can sleep in one blanket, but two kings cannot be contained on a continent." War soon erupted between the two states and, in 1514, at the Battle of Chaldiran, Ottoman gunners overwhelmed the Safavid cavalry and pushed back the Safavid army. In the wake of the battle, a frontier was established between the Safavid and Ottoman empires that roughly corresponds to the present-day border between the Republic of Turkey and the Islamic Republic of Iran. Perhaps even more important, to protect the southern flank of their new domains, the Ottomans began their conquest of the Arab Middle East. They did not stop until they reached the Iraqi-Persian border in the east, the Arabian peninsula in the south, and the borders of Morocco in North Africa in the west.

CHAPTER 2

Gunpowder Empires

Previous to the Ottomans and Safavids, Turkic and Mongolian rulers brought to the Middle East a new form of state that historians often refer to as the "military-patronage state." Numerous military-patronage states existed in the post-Turkic, post-Mongol Middle East. Nevertheless, they all shared three essential characteristics. First, military-patronage states were, like the name suggests, essentially military. At the head of society was a chief military leader who would rely on subleaders for local governance. Society was divided into two "classes": a ruling military class, which performed military and other services for the rulers, and the remainder of the population, which produced taxable surplus. The second characteristic of military-patronage states was that nearly all economic resources belonged to the chief military family or families. The ruling family or families could and did redistribute these resources as they wished. They often did so in return for the aforementioned services rendered by subchiefs or local notables; hence, the "patronage" in the "military-patronage state." Finally, the laws of military-patronage states combined dynastic law, local custom, and Islamic law (*shariʿa*).

As mentioned, the military-patronage states that arose before the Ottomans and Safavids were naturally unstable. While the family of a military or tribal chieftain might carve out such a state, it was dependent on other military leaders to control local areas. These leaders, often other tribal leaders, had little loyalty to the dynasties they were supposed to support. Furthermore, because the territory governed by a military or tribal chieftain was frequently large, it was difficult to rule. After all, military chieftains had none of the advantages of modern communications or transportation. Turkic and Mongolian chiefs therefore frequently divided their territories among their sons, thus splitting up empires after a single generation. Finally, the boundaries of the states were constantly in flux and were defined by incessant warfare. And because there was rarely a permanent seat of government in such a state, no permanent bureaucracy could be established to maintain the authority of the state over time.

The instability inherent to military-patronage states was ended by the introduction of a new technology into the Middle East: gunpowder weapons. Gunpowder weapons were a technological marvel and they gave their user an extraordinary advantage in warfare. But they were expensive and required a certain level of trade and industrial development to produce. Those dynasts who could harness gunpowder weapons could do a number of things that rival military chieftains had difficulty doing: They could subdue tribes and less technologically advanced military chiefs; they could protect their realms against invasion from other dynasts; they could build stable bureaucracies to collect revenue; and they could provide security for agriculture. This last factor was key: After all, in the early modern period almost all state revenues were derived from agriculture or pastoralism. Commerce, on the other hand, did not actually produce wealth; it merely rearranged it.

The Ottoman Empire was the first of the two empires to harness gunpowder weapons. Some historians claim that the Ottomans first learned of them from renegade Christians and used them, to devastating effect, to win the Battle of Kosovo in 1389. The Ottomans certainly used gunpowder weapons effectively during their siege of Constantinople—a siege that finished off the last remnants of the fifteen-hundred-year-old Roman Empire. Historian Edward Gibbon describes the final days of Constantinople in his famous *Decline and Fall of the Roman Empire* as follows:

> After a siege of forty days the fate of Constantinople could no longer be averted. The diminutive garrison was exhausted: the fortifications, which had stood for ages against hostile violence, were dismantled on all sides by the Ottoman cannon; many breaches were opened, and near the gate of St. Romanus four towers had been levelled with the ground. . . . From the lines, the galleys, and the bridge, the Ottoman artillery thundered on all sides; and the camp and city, the Greeks and the Turks, were involved in a cloud of smoke, which could only be dispelled by the final deliverance or destruction of the Roman Empire. The single combats of the heroes of history or fable amuse our fancy and engage our affections: the skilful evolutions of war may inform the mind, and improve a necessary, though pernicious science. But in the uniform and odious pictures of a general assault, all is blood, and horror, and confusion.

The Ottomans again used gunpowder weapons against the Safavids at the Battle of Chaldiran. Learning from their mistakes, the Safavids adopted the weapons soon thereafter.

It is interesting to note that the Ottoman conquest of Constantinople took place in 1453, the same year that the Hundred Years' War (which, in fact, lasted 116 years) ended. The group that turned the tide in that war and forced the British invaders to withdraw from all but a small foothold on the European continent was the Burgundians, the most advanced cannon makers in Europe. As of at least 1453, then, the use of gunpowder weapons had become essential for the survival of states. It also affected the internal dynamics of states.

Vignette

The Battle of Kosovo

In his famous essay, "What Is a Nation?" nineteenth-century French philosopher Ernest Renan wrote, "Where national memories are concerned, griefs are of more value than triumphs, for they impose duties, and require a common effort." No grief is more important to the Serbian national myth than the defeat inflicted on the Serbian leader Tsar Lazar by the Ottomans at the Battle of Kosovo in 1389. For Serbs, the memory of the battle was sustained through time by a tradition of epic poetry. One such poem, "Musitch Stefan," recounts Tsar Lazar's admonition to his followers on the eve of battle as follows:

> Whoso is a Serb, from Serbian mother,
> Who has Serbian blood and Serbian lineage,
> And comes not to battle, to Kosovo,
> May there never to his heart be granted
> Children, neither yet a maid or man-child.
> Underneath his hands shall nothing prosper,
> Neither vineyards nor the silver wheat fields,
> And from him shall misery be oozing
> Till his name and race die out and perish.

After the emergence of Serbian nationalism in the nineteenth century, Kosovo came to be regarded by many Serbs as "our Jerusalem." Unfortunately

---

Harnessing gunpowder weapons enabled the Ottoman and Safavid empires to adopt important features of the military-patronage model while at the same time avoiding many of the problems of their predecessors. Just as a military chief stood at the head of previous military-patronage states, at the top of Ottoman society was the sultan, a member of the house of Osman. At the top of Safavid society was the shah, a descendent of Isma'il. But, unlike their predecessors, the sultans and shahs did not divide their lands among their sons. They did not have to: Gunpowder weapons gave them the ability to establish a central government whose reach, when applied, could be felt throughout a vast empire.

While sultans and shahs remained at the center of imperial governments throughout the Ottoman and Safavid eras, the function each played in governance evolved over time. During the initial stages of conquest, the sultans and shahs were warriors-in-chief. They led campaigns of conquest and even met each other on the field of battle. When the two empires reached the limits of their expansion—which some historians place as early as the seventeenth century—the role of warrior-in-chief was no longer necessary. In fact, because continuous military campaigning brought no new sources of revenue and few other benefits to their empires, it could be downright detrimental. Sultans and shahs thus became less warriors-in-chief than ceremonial icons at the center of a well-oiled bureaucracy. The fact that they withdrew from public view, emerging for infrequent but spectacular religious or dynastic events, only enhanced their iconic status and the ability of the bureaucracy to function without disruption.

for Serbian nationalists, during the late seventeenth and early eighteenth centuries much of the ethnically Serbian population of the region had left and had been replaced by Albanian Muslims. In the aftermath of World War I, Serbia became a province of Yugoslavia, a state established as a homeland for southern Slavs. Because of its distinct history and ethnic composition, the Yugoslav government granted Kosovo autonomous status within the province of Serbia in 1974. Soon after the Serbian nationalist Slobodan Milosevic became leader of Yugoslavia in 1987, he revoked Kosovar autonomy, sparking resistance and calls for Kosovar independence. With the breakup of Yugoslavia in 1991, Milosevic began a campaign to end this resistance and, more ominously, to "protect" the ethnic Serbian population of the region by driving ethnic Albanians from their homes. In the resulting "ethnic cleansing," upwards of five thousand ethnic Albanian Kosovars were killed and nine hundred thousand displaced. Ethnic cleansing only ended after a NATO bombing campaign forced Milosevic to relent. Throughout it all, Milosevic exploited the potent symbol of the original battle. Standing on the battlefield, he exhorted Serbs to stand united: "The Kosovo heroism has been inspiring our creativity for six centuries and has been feeding our pride and does not allow us to forget that at one time we were an army, great, brave, and proud, one of the few that remained undefeated when losing."

Historians used to look at the loss of a warrior ethos among the leaders of the Ottoman and Safavid empires and call it "decline." It was not decline so much as a shift in the function of the sultan or shah. As a matter of fact, it might be argued that after states get established and stabilized, the more a leader interferes with their day-to-day operation the more trouble he will create. Think of how fortunate Americans are that many of our recent presidents have left well enough alone. On the other hand, one of the reasons for the longevity of the Ottoman Empire and the Persian empires of the Safavids and their successors, the Qajars, was that these empires could and did respond to changing circumstances. Thus, during the nineteenth century sultans and shahs once again sought to reassert themselves against an entrenched bureaucracy that opposed their plans to restructure their empires along the lines of European states.

Other factors link the Ottoman and Safavid empires to the military-patronage model as well. Both empires divided their populations into two categories (military and nonmilitary), much as their predecessors had done. Very often, the members of the military class were considered property of the sultan or shah. The Ottomans recruited potential soldiers and bureaucrats from among the children of their Balkan Christian subjects. This process of recruitment (*devshirme*) remains a sore spot in Balkan historiography: While many contemporary Turks prefer to look at the process of recruitment as purely voluntary, the word kidnapping is not unknown in histories written by Greek scholars. Although Islamic tradition forbade what was, in effect, the enslavement of Christians or, indeed, any People of the Book, the Ottomans were able to get around this injunction with an extraordinarily creative legal maneuver. Ottoman jurists argued that Balkan Christians were different from Christians encountered by Muslims previously. Balkan Christians, they argued, had converted to Christianity after the advent of Islam, not before, and therefore should have known better when choosing their religious preference. Besides, those enlisted in this way were not really slaves; they were "war booty." Regardless of the legalities, these recruits were converted to Islam, then underwent rigorous training. Some recruits remained soldiers, entering the elite Ottoman infantry as "janissaries." Others were siphoned off into the bureaucracy, where they could become scribes or even governors of provinces. In other words, former Christian subjects of the Ottoman Empire might rise to high imperial positions.

A similar process took place in the Safavid Empire. To break the power of the Qizilbash and strengthen the central government, Shah Abbas (r. 1588–1629) imported slaves from the Caucasus: Georgians, Armenians, Circassians, and so on. In one year alone (1616), his armies brought 130,000 Georgians back to Persia. In Persia, these slaves were called *ghilman* (singular: *ghulam*). Shah Abbas not only used these slaves in the bureaucracy and royal household, he made them into a forty-thousand-man standing army equipped with firearms. As in the Ottoman Empire, some were able to rise to high rank in Persia. By the end of Shah Abbas's reign, about half of the provincial governors were ghilman.

Overall, the use of slaves offered sultans and shahs a way out of perhaps the most serious problem of military-patronage states: their tendency to fragment. Sultans and shahs created an army and bureaucracy loyal to the central government alone. This enabled them to break the power of local warlords and potentates.

Two other aspects of the Ottoman and Safavid system link them with their predecessors. Like the rulers of previous military-patronage states, the ruling dynasties of the Ottoman and Safavid empires laid claim to the most important economic resource: land. Under this system, called prebendalism, land was considered to be the possession of the ruling dynasty, and the peasants who lived on the land enjoyed a number of freedoms. Peasants had the right to live on, work, and consume the fruits of their lands, in exchange for which they surrendered much of the surplus of their harvests in the form of taxes. But they did not own the lands they worked as "freehold" and could not sell them.

Sometimes, the Ottomans and Safavids bestowed on military leaders, governors, and local notables the right to keep the profits from parcels of land. In exchange, these select individuals had to provide military or administrative services. In the Ottoman Empire, these land grants were called *timars*, in the Safavid Empire, *tiyul*.

Unfortunately, the Ottoman and Safavid empires were early modern empires that attempted to govern huge expanses of land. The imperial governments were therefore not particularly adept at collecting revenues, especially revenues from far-flung provinces. This was not a problem for these empires alone: All early modern empires, from Europe to East Asia, were in the same boat. Different empires attempted to resolve this difficulty in various ways. Over time, to help with the collection of taxes, both the Ottoman and Safavid empires auctioned off to enterprising notables, merchants, civil servants, and the like the right to collect and keep the taxes owed from plots of land for a specified period of time. The amount for which this right went was (theoretically) based on competitive bidding and, when successful, enabled the Ottoman and Safavid governments to accumulate tax revenue upfront. This arrangement is known as tax farming.

Historians dispute whether this system was beneficial or detrimental to imperial governance. Some assert that tax farming, combined with imperial inefficiency and the increasing length of time tax farmers were allowed to maintain control of the revenues from their lands, alienated land and revenue from the central government. Others claim just the opposite. The latter assert that tax farming was actually a novel solution to a problem faced by all early modern empires and, in fact, might have been the best that an early modern empire could hope to do in order to collect the money it was owed, tap into privately held wealth, and thereby give local elites a stake in the imperial system. And it wasn't just the collection of taxes from land that the Ottomans and Safavids farmed out: They farmed out the right to collect customs duties from ports and other enterprises as well.

To expand the wealth of the central government or ruler, and to direct economic resources into vital areas, such as important cities, the Ottoman and Safavid governments sometimes created government monopolies over agricultural and industrial products. For example, because silk was the largest Persian export, Shah Abbas established a silk monopoly. He took one-third of all silk produced in Persia as tax, and paid the producers a fixed rate for the remainder. The Ottoman and Safavid governments also encouraged the formation of guilds. Guilds consisted of all practitioners of a given industry—from apprentices to master craftsmen—in a given city or region. There were guilds for those involved in metalwork, textiles, building, baking, transport, and even entertainment. Government sponsorship of guilds enabled the Ottomans and Safavids to regulate prices and help gather taxes. The government assigned each guild a certain amount of taxes that was to be collected from its members; the masters of each guild divided responsibility for its payment.

Finally, like earlier military-patronage states, law in the Ottoman and Safavid empires was derived from a combination of Islamic and dynastic law. This brings us to an important aspect of both empires: the role of religion.

Both the Ottoman and Safavid empires used religion to legitimate their rule. In the case of the Ottomans, it was Sunni Islam; in the case of the Safavids, it was Shiʿi Islam. Again, putting religion to use in this way was not unique to the Islamic world: Henry VIII of England, for example, established his own church (which most kings and queens of England have headed ever since), and other European monarchs claimed that they had a divine right to rule. In the early modern world, dynasties throughout Eurasia used religion to legitimate their rule in one of two ways. Sometimes, dynasties presented themselves as protectors of religion. The Ottoman sultans occasionally asserted their role as caliph, took part in religious ritual, sought legitimacy as protectors of Mecca and Medina, appointed judges in the Muslim courts, and sponsored religious endowments. Since making the trip

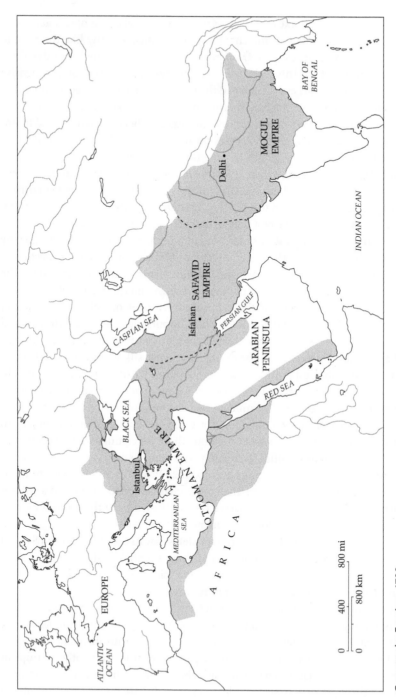

Gunpowder Empires, 1700

to Mecca and Medina (*hajj*) was a requirement for all Muslims who could do so, sultans even organized the hajj caravan from Istanbul to the Arabian holy cities. Each sultan took his religious responsibilities more or less seriously. Suleiman the Magnificent (r. 1520–1566), for example, attempted to demonstrate his religiosity by reconstructing and refurbishing Jerusalem, the third holiest city in Islam. He rebuilt the walls of the city (which exist to this day) and constructed aqueducts, fountains, hospitals, and schools there. Likewise, the Safavids claimed to be the protectors of Shi‘i Islam. In some cases, they went even further: They attempted to fit themselves into the Shi‘i narrative of history. For example, at various times, according to different sources, Shah Isma‘il represented himself as a descendent of ‘Ali, a representative of the hidden imam, the hidden imam, ‘Ali, or even God.

As had been the case earlier, religious minorities were allowed to organize many of their own affairs, including education, social services, charities, and law. Later—it is not known exactly when but probably varied from community to community— each minority religious community in the Ottoman Empire was represented in Istanbul by a religious dignitary from the sect. Each religious community came to be known as a *millet*, and this system of organizing the relationship between the state and religious communities came to be known as the millet system.

Before we can leave the discussion of the institutions of the Ottoman and Safavid empires, it is necessary to emphasize two points. What has so far been presented has been the ideal, which likely differed from the way things actually worked. Unfortunately, historians are forced to work mainly from official texts— which is like reading the *Federalist Papers* to understand how the United States government actually operates.

Second, both the Ottoman and Safavid empires began as early modern empires. Their ability to control events and territory waxed and waned over time. In the past, historians assumed that direct political control was a sign of imperial strength, while lack of direct political control was a sign of decline. We know better now: The Ottoman Empire lasted more than four hundred years. The Safavid Empire lasted more than two hundred. Each empire was either very lucky or was able to adapt. At times, adaptation demanded decentralization. As we shall see, during the eighteenth century the power of local warlords was greater than the power of the central government to control them. These local warlords, such as Dhahir al-‘Umar and Ahmad Jazzar in Palestine and ‘Ali Bey al-Kabir and Mehmet Ali (Muhammad ‘Ali) in Egypt, were able to take control of tracts of territory that were sometimes huge. We also shall see that, by applying techniques of political organization associated with modern states, the Ottoman Empire was able to reassert central control, albeit over a geographically diminished empire. In other words, the passage of the early modern Ottoman Empire to the modern Ottoman Empire entailed the progressive abandonment of structures and institutions associated with those the empire had adopted in the early modern period and their replacement by those more suitable for the modern age.

In terms of longevity, however, the Safavids were not so lucky: The power of the central administration began to decline following the death of Abbas the Great, and the Safavid dynasty was overthrown by Afghans in 1722.

CHAPTER 3

The Middle East and the Modern World System

The great University of Chicago historian Marshall G. S. Hodgson once wrote that if a visitor from Mars had come to Earth during the sixteenth century, he would have taken a look at the political, military, and cultural power of the Middle Eastern gunpowder empires and concluded that the entire world would shortly become Muslim. These empires not only ruled vast territories, they seemed to have resolved many of the problems of governance that had frustrated their predecessors. Yet, by the seventeenth century, Middle Eastern gunpowder empires were in deep crisis. In all fairness, these empires were not the only states in crisis at this time: States from Britain and France to China also entered into periods of difficulty. The problems these empires faced were so similar that historians even have a term for what was going on: the "crisis of the seventeenth century." Britain, France, China, and the Ottoman and Safavid empires all experienced the same problem: the inability of imperial governments to maintain their authority within their territories. Civil and religious wars wracked France and Britain. In China, the seventeenth century was marked by peasant insurrection and the collapse of the Ming Dynasty, which had ruled for almost three hundred years. The imperial Ottoman government faced popular rebellions, military revolts, and the appearance of warlords who challenged the central government from Anatolia in the north to Baghdad in the east and Yemen and Egypt in the south. The Safavid Empire was so weakened by numerous calamities that in 1722 it became easy prey for invaders from the north.

While there were probably multiple causes for the crisis of the seventeenth century, many historians have emphasized the role played by the general rise in prices that struck almost all of the Eurasian continent. Some have called this the "great inflation"; others, the "price revolution." Historians argue that inflation is the key to the crisis because the imperial governments that ruled in Europe and Asia at that time were, unlike the states that had preceded them, particularly dependent on a cash economy. There were two reasons for this. First, governments throughout Eurasia had attempted to displace the warlords and tame the aristocracies that had provided services to the crown by building armies and bureaucracies loyal to the central government alone. Building these armies and bureaucracies was expensive, and soldiers and bureaucrats had to be paid. Inflation raised the costs of maintaining them in the manner to which they had grown accustomed. Imperial states were, it appears, always short of money.

In addition, as newly centralized empires reached the limits of their expansion, rulers had to find new ways to legitimate their rule. As we have seen, the sultans and shahs of the Ottoman and Safavid empires could no longer claim a right to rule based on their position as warrior-in-chief or even on their personal magnetism or charisma. Imperial governments now entered a phase of their history that the great German sociologist Max Weber called the "routinization of charisma." This was a period in which rulers and bureaucrats had to focus on the mundane problems of running the day-to-day affairs of state. No longer riding at the head of armies, emperors, sultans, and shahs had to find new means to represent their authority to their subjects and outsiders alike. Many did so by building sumptuous palaces and capital cities or by staging elaborate ceremonials that displayed the splendor of their court. This was, after all, the era of Louis XIV of France (r. 1661–1715), the "Sun King," from whose magnificent court in Versailles power radiated. In a similar vein, a British traveler recorded the effect that Shah Abbas's capital city of Isfahan had on both Persians and foreigners:

> The City has no need of Walls, where so many Marble Mountains stand as a Guard, or Bulwark of Defence. . . . The Circumference of the Body of the City I guess may measure Seven Miles; but if the dispersed Gardens and Seats of the Great Men, with the Palace Royal be brought into that Computation, we must allow it as many Pharsangs [the distance a man can walk in one day]. . . . Its Founder (or at least, Adorner) *Shaw Abas* the Great, advisedly chose it for his Imperial Throne, that thence he might more readily disperse his Mandates to any suffering Part assaulted by the bold Incursions of his Enemies; irradiating like the Sun in the Firmament all within the Sphere of this Government: So that while the utmost of his Dominions are seasonably supplied with the comfortable Warmth of his Protection, he safely resides within, invulnerable.

Shah Abbas once proclaimed, "To know Isfahan is to know half the world." Such splendor cost money.

Historians do not agree on what sparked the inflation that led to the crisis of the seventeenth century. There are three main theories. Some historians claim inflation was caused primarily by demographic expansion. During the sixteenth century, they argue, the Eurasian continent experienced rapid population growth. It is estimated that during the sixteenth century alone, the population of Syria, Egypt, and Anatolia, for example, increased by 40 percent. Again, we are not really sure why this might have been the case. Some claim that the centralized states were able to provide better security for agriculturists than their predecessors had, and with better security came more agricultural production and population increase. Others maintain that the population of Eurasia naturally expanded in the aftermath of the Black Death that had devastated Eurasia during

Painting of the Safavid shah Suleiman and his courtiers by the Persian artist Ali Quli Jabbar, ca. 1660s or 1670s. Notice the Dutch supplicant to the left of the shah. *(From: Layla S. Diba and Maryam Ekhtiar, eds., Royal Persian Paintings: The Qajar Epoch, 1785–1925 (Brooklyn: Brooklyn Museum of Art in association with I.B. Tauris, 1988), p. 120.)*

the fourteenth century, or that populations were better able to control the spread of infectious diseases. Whatever the reason, historians argue that the increase in population put tremendous pressure on available resources and sparked an inflation as demand for goods began to exceed supply. They point to the fact that the crisis only began to abate after population growth stagnated during the seventeenth century.

Other historians argue that the unusual dependence of states on cash was reason enough for the inflation. States spent an enormous amount of money to sustain their employees. In Persia, for example, an estimated 38 percent of the state's expenditures went to the army. Another 41 percent went to the imperial harem, the royal family, and royal attendants. States competed with the private sector for resources, and this drove up prices. States frequently compounded their problems by debasing their currencies to meet their payrolls. This meant that they often mixed the gold or silver of their currencies with baser metals and attempted to pass these new currencies off as the real thing. Because debased currency was worth less, prices rose and government employees demanded higher salaries.

It seems obvious to us now that the debasement of currencies would inevitably lead to a vicious cycle: Debasement would induce price increases, which, in turn, would encourage shortsighted governments to undertake further debasement. But during the early modern period, notions of economics, where they existed at all, were even cruder than they are today. Sometimes, this guilelessness led to absurd consequences: Spain, for example, went bankrupt twice during the sixteenth century, first in 1557, then again in 1575. In the second instance, when King Philip II of Spain found himself overwhelmed by creditors, he simply called together church leaders who told him what he wanted to hear: Since usury (the charging of interest) was a sin, he was under no obligation to pay back his creditors. The king, finding within himself a wellspring of piety of which he had previously been unaware, obeyed. Spain was not alone in its folly: In the first half of the sixteenth century, the Netherlands, Portugal, and France, like Spain, spent almost twice as much to extract wealth from the New World and to make war on each other so that they might extract wealth from the New World than they actually wrested from the Americas.

This brings us to the third possible reason for the inflation of the sixteenth century: the Spanish conquest of the New World. When they arrived in Mexico and Peru, Spanish conquistadors found tons of precious metals in the Inca and Aztec empires. Huge amounts of gold and particularly silver flooded first into Europe, then into Asia. Wherever the precious metals hit, prices went up. In the six decades between the conquest of Mexico and Peru and 1575, prices in Western Europe increased between 300 and 400 percent. Historians, using the sudden increases in bread prices as their measure, have even timed the journey of precious metals from west to east: first Seville and Cadiz, then Paris, then Muscovy, then Istanbul and Delhi, then Beijing. Thus, in 1660 a European trader compared Persia to a huge caravansary—a stopping place and trading center for caravans—with a gate in the west and a gate in the east. Coins, he explained, entered Safavid domains from the Ottoman Empire in the west, circulated in Persia, driving up prices, and finally exited through the eastern gate of Persia to India.

While some historians remain skeptical about the circulation of New World gold and silver to points as far away as the Middle and Far East, others point out that even if the precious metals did not actually reach that far, the looting of the New World had momentous effects on economies throughout Eurasia. They argue that new stocks of precious metals increased the velocity of trade, first among the states of Western Europe, then between the states of Western Europe and the rest of the continent. According to economists, an increased velocity of trade naturally increases inflation. Even if we do not wish to take economists at their word (a good idea, in light of their more recent failings), the arrival of new stocks of precious metals into Europe and the resulting inflation certainly did produce dramatic effects throughout Eurasia. It is well known, for example, that the imperial Ottoman government was unable to halt the smuggling of huge amounts of such commodities as wood, metals, wheat, raw silk, and wool out of the Ottoman Empire and into Europe, where they fetched higher prices. This smuggling denied the Ottoman government precious customs revenues and inhibited its ability to buy social peace: After all, without an adequate supply of basic commodities, the imperial government could not guarantee that its cities would be adequately provisioned. At the same time, the smuggling denied to

Ottoman artisans the raw materials they needed to produce their wares and weakened the guilds that had been established in part to protect their members.

Whatever the role of Spanish silver, most historians agree that sometime during the sixteenth century the world economy began to undergo a revolutionary change. Among the historians who pioneered the research into this change were those who advocated something called "world systems analysis." In its most abstract form, world systems analysis runs something like this:

From the beginning of recorded time through the beginning of the sixteenth century, much of the world had been divided into what might be called "world empires." Taken together, these world empires made up what world systems analysts call the "system of world empires." The system of world empires had four characteristics. First, it was possible for several world empires to exist at the same time. For example, the early Ottoman Empire existed at the same time as did the Safavid, Habsburg (Austrian), and Chinese empires. Second, world empires spread through military conquest or the threat of military conquest. In other words, a world empire was no larger than the territory from which an imperial government might be able to extract taxes or tribute. In addition, each world empire provided for most of its economic needs independent of other world empires. Trade did take place, of course, and this trade was not just in luxury items. As a matter of fact, trade often involved bulk items such as cereals or wood. But in the system of world empires the economies of the trading partners were roughly equivalent and no economy was more "advanced" or dominated another. This is a far cry from the relationship among trading nations today, as we shall see. And this brings us to the final characteristic of the system of world empires: Each world empire was roughly equivalent to any nearby empire that existed at the same time. For example, no empire was technologically superior to any other, nor was any empire organized in a manner that gave it a particular advantage over any other. This stands to reason: If an empire fell behind economically or technologically, it would fall prey to its competitors.

Beginning about 1500, the system of world empires began to change into what is called the "modern world system" or "modern world economy." This change did not occur overnight—it required several centuries to complete. The crisis of the seventeenth century, described at the beginning of this chapter, might be seen as the birth pangs of the modern world system. (As we shall see, the strategies employed by rulers to address that crisis would, in many cases, come to define the future position of their states in that system.) Judging by the effects of the Depression of 1873, which affected every inhabited continent on the globe, we might say with assurance that by at least that year the modern world economy was in place. It has been with us ever since.

Like the system of world empires, the modern world economy possesses a number of distinguishing characteristics. Unlike the system of world empires, which was, for the most part, politically and economically fragmented, the modern world economy is politically fragmented but economically united. In other words, rather than consisting of independent empires that provided for most of their own needs, the modern world economy consists of independent states that participate in a single, integrated global economic system—a single market, if you will. Furthermore, while world empires spread their influence solely through conquest or the threat of conquest, the modern world system spread its influence by bringing outlying districts into a single economic structure. This has occurred through conquest as well, of course, but it also has occurred through the pull of the international market. Since the sixteenth century, agricultural producers throughout the world have discovered that they might profit more from producing goods for the international market than from producing merely for their own consumption. Where agriculturalists themselves did not take the initiative, governments often encouraged the transition in order to accumulate more revenue. Finally, while the system of world empires consisted of roughly equivalent states, some states in the world economy are more technologically and economically "advanced" than others and benefit more than others from the global marketplace. In effect, there are winners and losers in the modern world economy.

At first, Western European states acted as the engine that drove the modern world economy. These states brought other parts of the globe into the world market they dominated, but in a subordinate role. Thus, while states in Western Europe produced manufactured goods that they exported internationally, other parts of the globe bought the products produced in Western European factories and, in turn, produced the raw materials that fed those factories. As a result, the world economy came to be divided into distinct units: a developed core (first, states in Western Europe, then states in Western Europe and North America, then states in Western Europe, North America, and Japan) and what is called the periphery; that is, states at a lower technological and economic level. Some analysts have created a middle category, the semiperiphery, which includes states that share attributes with both the core and the periphery. The boundaries of the modern world economy expanded for centuries until it encompassed the entire globe. This process, which had an important effect on the Middle East, is known as integration and peripheralization.

Because states in Western Europe functioned as the core of the modern world economy at its inception, the modern world economy spread to outlying regions of the globe during periods in which the European economy expanded. One such period took place in the early nineteenth century, during the relatively peaceful years that followed the Napoleonic Wars (that is, after 1815). Not coincidentally, this is the period we associate with the industrial revolution. It was during this period that much of the Ottoman Empire became integrated into the modern world economy. Points further east—Iraq and Persia—had to wait until the second half of the nineteenth century.

To understand how the Middle East was integrated into the world economy in the status of periphery, we must go back to the sixteenth century. At their inception, both the Ottoman and Safavid empires stabilized and induced an expansion of the Middle Eastern economy. The Ottomans and Safavids, like all successful empire builders, encouraged economic self-sufficiency. They did this in a

---

Vignette

Coffee

During the sixteenth century, the European table was enriched with a multi-plicity of foods introduced from the New World, including corn (maize), potatoes, yams, peanuts, squash, chili peppers, tomatoes, pumpkins, chocolate, and manioc (tapioca). Between meals, Europeans could, for the first time, sit down with a pipe of tobacco (also introduced from the New World) or chew gum made from chicle— hence "Chiclets"—likewise a New World import. This was one side of what is called the "Columbian exchange." (In return, the inhabitants of the Americas got cattle, pigs, horses, German measles, and smallpox.)

One commodity, however, made the trip from another direction: Coffee, introduced into Europe about a century after the previously cited items, originated in the Middle East.

The history of coffee is enshrouded in legend. There is, for example, the tale of its origins: The story goes that coffee was first discovered in the ninth century when an Ethiopian goat herder noticed his goats got a bit frisky after they ate the berries of a local shrub. After sampling the berries himself, he, too, experienced the same effect, as did those who undertook coffee cultivation in Arabia when it was brought there three centuries later. There is the story of the first coffeehouse in Vienna: The emperor asked the man who acted as a guide for the Polish cavalry that raised the 1683 Ottoman siege of that city what he wanted as a reward. Rather than the usual "the hand of your daughter in marriage," he reportedly asked for the bulging sacks he saw in the abandoned Ottoman encampment, thinking they contained gold. In fact, they contained coffee beans. Thus, the first Viennese coffeehouse. (Strudel and *Linzertorten* would come later.) Then there is the story of the origin of tipping: In early British coffeehouses, coffeewenches placed cups for coins on each table. On the cups was inscribed "to insure prompt service"—abbreviated T.I.P.S.

Regardless of the truth of any or all of these stories, early travelers to the Middle East were amazed by coffee and the coffeehouses they found there. One Portuguese traveler, Pedro Teixeira, stopped off in Baghdad in the mid-1580s on his way to India and reported his first encounter with coffee as follows:

> Amongst other public buildings . . . is a *Casa de Kaoáh* [Teixeira's *kaoáh* is borrowed from the Arabic word for coffee, *qahwah*]. Coffee is a vegetable of the size and appearance of little dry beans, brought from Arabia, prepared and sold in public houses built to that end; wherein all men who desire it meet to

---

host of ways: by extending rural security, repairing and building infrastructure, making tax collection more efficient and less harsh, removing barriers to intra-regional trade, establishing government monopolies, ensuring that their principal cities received provisions, regulating labor practices in those cities, and combating piracy on the seas. In addition, because of their central location, the Ottoman and Safavid empires controlled and profited from most of the spice trade between the East Indies and Europe. They also controlled much of the trade in luxury items such as silk. During the seventeenth century, two-thirds of Persian silk

drink it, be they great or mean. They sit in order, and it is brought to them very hot, in porcelain cups holding four or five ounces each. Every man takes his own in his hand, cooling and sipping it. It is black and rather tasteless; and, although some good qualities are ascribed to it, none are proven. Only their custom induces them to meet here for conversation and use this for entertainment; and in order to attract customers there are here pretty boys richly dressed, who serve the coffee and take the money; with music and other diversions. These places are chiefly frequented at night in summer, and by day in winter. . . . There are others like it in the city, and many more throughout Turkey and Persia.

Teixeira was not the only European fascinated by coffee. When coffee was first introduced in Europe, it caused a sensation. Little wonder: Unlike the skeptical Teixeira, most Europeans believed coffee to have the power of an aphrodisiac. In 1732–1734, the composer Johann Sebastian Bach documented the sensation caused by coffee, as well as its purported aphrodisiac powers, in his "Coffee Cantata." In the cantata, a father confronts his daughter as follows:

You wicked child, you disobedient girl,
oh!, when will I get my way;
give up coffee!

To which she replies:

Father, don't be so severe!
If I can't drink
my bowl of coffee three times daily,
then in my torment I will shrivel up
like a piece of roast goat.

After the father promises his daughter to find her a husband if only she would give up coffee, she sings:

If it could only happen soon
that at last, before I go to bed,
instead of coffee
I were to get a proper lover!

(In the end, the ungrateful little vixen gets both a husband and her coffee.)

went to Europe. When the Portuguese attempted to horn in on the profitable Indian Ocean trade by establishing themselves in Aden (in contemporary Yemen) in 1513, the Ottomans swatted them away a quarter century later. While the world of uncontested and uncontestable European military supremacy might have been looming on the horizon, it had not yet arrived.

During the seventeenth and eighteenth centuries, there was a definite shift in the balance of power between Europe and the Ottoman and Safavid empires. This came about in the wake of the Commercial Revolution in Europe, which had

---

Vignette

Slaves, Opium, and the Course of World Trade

The modern world economy began to take shape in the early sixteenth century. Although Spain had access to New World gold and silver, Britain, France, and the Netherlands were soon able to surpass their rival in terms of economic power. And over the course of the next two centuries Britain would eclipse its rivals as well. Along with the institutional changes discussed in this chapter, the ability of the British to dominate international trafficking in a few choice commodities propelled their ascent to the heights of economic power. Among these commodities were slaves and opium.

In 1532, the first boatload of enslaved Africans landed in the New World. This event marks the inauguration of the so-called triangle trade. British merchants, carrying guns, ammunition, and manufactured goods to Africa, traded those goods for slaves, whom they then transported to the Caribbean and North America via the infamous "middle passage." There they sold those slaves, and with the proceeds bought sugar, tobacco, and cotton. The triangle trade generated huge profits for British banking houses (and British and North American merchants), enabling Britain to surpass its economic competitors. Britain continued to reap the surpluses from this trade until 1807—the year the British government (and the United States Constitution) declared the slave trade illegal. By that time, a new system for the circulation of commodities and capital was emerging.

Beginning in the early nineteenth century, the British East India Company began selling opium grown in India to China. The company did this to pay for its administrative apparatus in India and to offset its substantial trade imbalance with China. After all, the British had an unslakable thirst for Chinese tea and a boundless appetite for silk and *chinoiserie*, while the "Celestial Empire" had little use for the products of Britain. Not surprisingly, the Chinese government resisted

---

begun in the sixteenth century. As mentioned earlier, there were many aspects to this revolution, some of which spawned it, others that were spawned by it and further encouraged its progress. The Commercial Revolution was a period in which new technologies of direct benefit to trade were invented and applied. Alongside these technological breakthroughs were breakthroughs in finance and the organization of trade—joint stock companies, insurance, banking—which allowed participants to increase their profits and spread risk among investors. Technological and institutional breakthroughs enabled Europeans not only to embark on voyages of discovery but to exploit them to the fullest. In 1497, Vasco da Gama discovered the Cape Route, which allowed Europeans to reach India and the Spice Islands (present-day Indonesia) by heading south around Africa's Cape of Good Hope, that is, entirely by sea. This enabled European merchants to bypass the Ottoman and Safavid empires and monopolize long-distance trade. As a result, the Ottoman and Safavid governments lost vital customs revenues, and merchants from those empires lost access to the spice trade to their European competitors.

the British attempt to balance accounts by turning China into one large opium den. Twice during the nineteenth century Britain went to war with China—the "Opium Wars" of 1839–1842 and 1856–1860—to open up the Chinese market to their noxious export and to keep it open. As a result of the wars, the Chinese were forced to accept opium from India and make a number of their ports available for "free trade."

Like the triangle trade system, the India-China trade system that emerged in the wake of the opium wars provided a foundation upon which the worldwide circulation of commodities and capital during the mid-to-late Victorian era would rest. According to economic historian A. J. H. Latham,

> The sale of Bengal opium to China was a great link in the chain of commerce with which Britain had surrounded the world. The chain worked like this: The United Kingdom paid the United States for cotton by bills upon the Bank of England. The Americans took some of those bills to Canton and swapped them for tea. The Chinese exchanged the bills for Indian opium. Some of the bills were remitted to England as profit; others were taken to India to buy additional commodities, as well as to furnish the money remittance of private fortunes in India and the funds for carrying on the Indian government at home.

Besides supporting the global economic environment that the nineteenth-century Middle East economy inhabited, the Victorian-era system for the circulation of commodities and capital affected the region in other ways as well. For example, both the Ottoman Empire and Persia piggybacked onto the international trade in opium. Soon after the opium wars, the Ottoman Empire became one of the three largest producers of opium in the world (the other two being China and India), and as a result of the availability of opium in Persia, the ranks of drug smokers swelled as never before.

About two decades after Vasco da Gama's discovery, the Spanish conquered Mexico and Peru, flooding Eurasia with tons of precious metals. Over time, all of Eurasia came to be divided into different economic zones in which prices varied widely. Where the precious metals had hit, prices were high; where they had not, prices remained at their usual levels. The division of Eurasia into different economic zones opened up new possibilities for trade. It also affected the social organization of the various zones differently. For example, since the price of grain was initially higher in Western Europe than in Eastern Europe, Eastern European nobles could increase their wealth by expanding their production of grain and selling that grain in the west. Eastern European nobles thus did everything they could to extend their control over land and the peasantry, including reducing peasants to mere property. The result was what historians of Eastern Europe call the "second serfdom."

The Commercial Revolution was encouraged further by the rise of new political units in Europe. One such unit was a variation on an old theme: the merchant republic. Merchant republics had emerged in the Mediterranean region centuries before the Commercial Revolution. City-states like Venice and Genoa were highly efficient because merchants and bankers, not feudal landlords, controlled the institutions of state. Being at the helm of state, merchants and bankers ensured that the republic's foreign policy would coincide with its trade policy. By the seventeenth century, after the discovery of the Americas had shifted the center of gravity of world trade westward and the importance of the newly emergent Atlantic economy had surpassed the importance of the Mediterranean economy, Britain, France, and the Netherlands eclipsed their Mediterranean rivals.

These states possessed two attributes that other European states would seek to emulate. First, like the Mediterranean merchant republics, they possessed a strong central government that could maintain domestic order, guarantee commercial credit, and direct a national trade policy. Britain, France, and the Netherlands adopted the doctrine of mercantilism as their trade policy. Mercantilists believed that the more gold a state accumulated, the stronger it would be, and that if states encouraged trade, exported more than they imported, and protected their home industries, they would be able to accumulate more gold. Second, unlike their predecessors, Britain, France, and the Netherlands possessed an integrated internal market that united town and countryside. This ensured the state access to the resources necessary to maintain a high level of economic activity and protect its interests abroad.

In all, beginning in the seventeenth century, Britain, France, and the Netherlands were able to dominate and transform the world economic system. Why these states rose to dominance and not others is not entirely clear. Nor is it clear why this process would have taken place at all. Perhaps it was because these states were better situated to take advantage of the possibilities opened up by the Atlantic economy. Perhaps it had to do with the peculiar nature of that northwestern peninsula of the Eurasian continent where these states were located. On the one hand, Europe was small enough to allow for the rapid diffusion of the technologies and institutional breakthroughs associated with the Commercial Revolution. On the other hand, it was competitive enough to force states that wished to survive to explore new means of applying those technologies and institutional breakthroughs. Suffice it to say, there were European winners and losers (whatever happened to Spain, much less Venice and Genoa?), and the transformation of the world economy that the winners induced was hardly inevitable.

It was therefore not that the Ottoman and Safavid empires were necessarily doing something wrong that allowed for the emergence of the modern world system with its Western European core. Indeed, these empires did everything that one would have expected them to have done to deal with the crisis of the seventeenth century. Strapped for cash, they curtailed the *timar/tiyul* systems and increasingly depended on tax farming to make up shortfalls in revenues. As we have seen, this may have resulted in the long-term alienation of resources from the imperial governments. Both governments sold offices in the bureaucracy and even the military to the highest bidder. The Ottoman government allowed members of the elite janissary corps to take jobs and raise families in places where they were stationed, thereby decreasing their incentive to fight wars on the fringes of the empire. Both governments increased taxation, further alienating the peasants whose surplus provided revenue for the state. Both governments debased their currencies, and, when this did not resolve their economic woes, debased them again. In all, the Ottomans and the Safavids worked within the parameters of a system that had become out of date.

Ultimately, both the Ottoman Empire and Persia were integrated into the world system as periphery. Integration and peripheralization would have a profound effect on the future of the region. Agricultural lands that had once been used for subsistence farming were turned over to the cultivation of cash crops like cotton, opium, and tobacco. By 1880, 20 percent of Persia's exports consisted of opium; on the eve of World War I, cotton comprised 80 percent of Egyptian exports. To facilitate these exports, European and local governments financed and built railroads and expanded ports to handle steamships, in the process changing the face of the region. Throughout the Middle East, a market economy, in which people produced commodities for sale, came to replace local marketplace economies, in which people produced mainly for their own consumption and used whatever surplus was left over to buy those items they could not produce themselves. Land itself became a commodity like any other to be bought and sold, once independent peasants became wage laborers on other peoples' estates, and tribal leaders became landlords while fellow tribespeople worked their lands as tenant laborers. In sum, Europe cultivated a colonial-style trade with Middle Eastern empires, and this relationship affected not only economic relations in the region, but social relations as well.

CHAPTER 4

War, Diplomacy, and the New Global Balance of Power

The last of the three sixteenth-century events that defined the modern world was the Protestant Reformation. From 1517 (the year of Martin Luther's public denunciation of church doctrines and practices) through 1648 (the end of the Thirty Years' War), Europeans engaged in numerous conflicts pitting Catholics against Protestants. The Protestant Reformation ended the dream of a universal Christian empire in Europe. The Peace of Westphalia that ended the Thirty Years' War recognized fixed territorial boundaries among the states of Europe and established the principle that the religion of a state's ruler would be the religion of the state. Europe was now permanently divided into a number of highly competitive sovereign states which sought to defend themselves against each other, gain advantage over their adversaries, and, at times, establish a balance among themselves. In effect, both the modern state and the international political order assembled from those states—the modern state system—might be traced to the Protestant Reformation. We shall discuss the spread of the modern state system to the Middle East in a later chapter. First, however, it is necessary to see how the emergence of modern states in Europe affected the region in other ways.

The Middle East was one of the places where the competition among European states played itself out. In the eastern Mediterranean, this competition came to be known as the "Eastern Question." At first, the Eastern Question involved Britain and France. Over the course of the nineteenth century, it came to include Britain, France, and Russia, then, finally, Britain, France, Russia, and Germany. On the northern frontier of Persia, a related competition pit Great Britain against Russia. This competition was known as the "Great Game," a term popularized by the British writer Rudyard Kipling in his novel *Kim*. Both competitions are the subject of this chapter.

Let us begin by looking at how the Eastern Question evolved. From its founding in the sixteenth century, the Ottoman Empire played a role in the European balance of power. The sixteenth century was the glorious era of Ottoman expansion. The empire pushed forward its frontiers in southeastern Europe at the expense of the Habsburg Empire, the dominant power in much of central Europe and the Balkans. As mentioned before, the Ottomans even laid siege twice to the Habsburg capital of Vienna. On the seas, the Ottomans fought Venice for naval supremacy in the Mediterranean. By the last quarter of the sixteenth century, the Ottomans had conducted raiding expeditions in the Mediterranean as far west as Italy, and had even captured the western Mediterranean port city of Tunis from the Spanish.

To ease their military expansion at the expense of Venice and the Habsburg Empire, the Ottomans made alliances with anti-Habsburg states that were more than anxious to encourage Ottoman diplomatic interference in European affairs. Thus, in 1533 (four years after the first siege of Vienna), the Ottomans sent ten thousand gold pieces to Francis I of France so that he might join with Britain and some German states in an alliance against the Habsburgs.

The Protestant Reformation played a direct role in Ottoman strategies with regard to Europe. The Ottomans viewed the Protestant movement and Protestant states as natural allies in their common struggle against the pretensions of the Catholic Habsburgs. The Ottomans supported Protestant movements because they viewed them as a potential fifth column in Europe, and actually encouraged Calvinist missionaries to propagate their doctrines in the Ottoman-controlled area that is now Hungary and Transylvania (yes, that Transylvania), a region in contemporary Romania. Likewise, Protestant and anti-Habsburg monarchs of Europe were not blind to the strategic value of Ottoman friendship. When Henry VIII of England broke with the Catholic Church and established the Church of England, he confiscated church property. Brass church bells were melted down and the tin they contained found its way to the Ottomans. Tin was an essential ingredient in the manufacture of artillery. It was scarce in the Ottoman Empire but not in the place the ancient Romans had once called the "Tin Islands"—Great Britain.

The Ottomans took the offensive in trade policy as well. In 1569, they granted the first effective capitulations to the French. Capitulations were clauses attached to treaties that granted special economic, commercial, legal, and religious rights and privileges to representatives of foreign powers in the Ottoman Empire. For example, capitulations might grant European traders the right to establish commercial enclaves in the Ottoman Empire, to construct a church for their exclusive use, to have recourse to the courts of their own nations, or to be exempt from taxes. The granting of capitulations was an important weapon in the Ottoman diplomatic arsenal. It enabled the Ottomans to gain the favor of potential allies in the Christian world. At the same time, capitulations enabled the imperial government to increase customs revenues and obtain goods needed by the empire. Here we see a perfect correspondence between the economic policies of the mercantilist states of Europe and those of the Ottoman Empire: Mercantilist states wanted to accumulate gold by exporting more than they imported; the Ottomans were concerned with maintaining stocks of vital commodities for

---

Vignette

The Siege of Vienna Made Palatable

The second Ottoman siege of Vienna began in July 1683 and lasted for two months. For the inhabitants of the Austrian capital, the experience was horrific. According to one eyewitness account:

> After a Siege of Sixty days, accompanied with a Thousand Difficulties, Sicknesses, Want of Provisions, and great Effusion of Blood, after a Million of Cannon and Musquet Shot, Bombs, Granadoes, and all sorts of Fire Works, which has changed the Face of the fairest and most flourishing City in the World, disfigured and ruined most part of the best Palaces of the same, and chiefly those of the Emperor; and damaged in many places the Beautiful Tower and Church of St. Stephen, with many Sumptuous Buildings. After a Resistance so vigorous, and the Loss of so many brave Officers and Souldiers, whose Valour and Bravery deserve Immortal Glory. After so many Toils endured, so many Watchings and so many Orders so prudently distributed by Count Staremburgh, and so punctually executed by the other Officers. After so many new Retrenchments, Pallizadoes, Parapets, new Ditches in the Ravelins, Bastions, Courtins, and principal Streets and Houses in the Town: Finally, after a Vigorous Defence and a Resistance without parallel, Heaven favourably heard the Prayers and Tears of a Cast-down and Mournful People, and retorted the Terror on a powerful Enemy, and drove him from the Walls of Vienna.

---

which they were willing to pay. The capitulations provided both with the means to realize their economic strategies.

Since the capitulations encouraged European imports, European merchants and the governments that backed them used the capitulations to bring about the economic penetration of the Ottoman Empire. As a matter of fact, it might be said that during the sixteenth and seventeenth centuries, the capitulations provided *the* means by which Europeans were able to penetrate Ottoman markets. After the French, the Ottomans granted the Dutch, the British, and the Russians capitulatory privileges. Capitulations were not abolished in most of the Ottoman domains until 1914. The end of capitulations in Egypt had to wait until 1937. Well before that time, capitulations had become a major bone of contention between the Ottomans and Europeans, particularly because Ottoman merchants felt they had to operate at a disadvantage compared to their European counterparts, who could avoid taxes and customs duties.

During the seventeenth century, the nature of Ottoman-European relations began to change. The Ottomans were no longer the unbeatable foe they had once been. In 1656, the Venetians destroyed the Ottoman fleet not far off the coast of Istanbul, and in 1699 the Ottomans were forced out of the territories of contemporary Hungary, Croatia, and parts of Romania by the Habsburg Empire. But worse was yet to come. New, more powerful states supplanted the Habsburgs and Venetians as the main Ottoman adversaries, and as the new Atlantic economy

With all due respect to Count Staremburgh, the decisive factor in forcing the Ottomans to abandon their siege and withdraw their forces was the arrival of a detachment of Polish cavalry under the command of Jan III Sobieski. The Viennese, who shortly before the siege was raised had been contemplating the horrifying consequences of defeat, now reveled in their seemingly miraculous victory. In keeping with the triumphant sentiment, Viennese bakers decided to celebrate the victory by baking their bread in the shape of the Ottoman symbol—the crescent moon—which their customers then symbolically ate. Thus were croissants invented.

There is another story about the culinary effects of the siege of Vienna which, according to most historians, does not stand up to scrutiny. Nevertheless, it is a good story and deserves repeating. According to this story, the Jewish bakers of Vienna decided that they, too, would bake their bread in a celebratory shape. Wishing to memorialize the heroic exploits of Jan III Sobieski's cavalry, the bakers decided to bake their bread in the shape of a stirrup—round, with a hole in its center. The German word for stirrup is *bügel*. Hence, of course, the invention of bagels. (While a good story, most etymologists trace the word "bagel" to the German verb "biegen," "to bend.")

---

displaced the Mediterranean economy a wider area for conflict between the Ottomans and Europeans emerged.

The Ottomans were thus pushed onto the defensive, and as the eighteenth and nineteenth centuries progressed, the problem faced by European statesmen was no longer how to defend against Ottoman expansion. Instead, the problem became what to do about an increasingly enfeebled Ottoman Empire. Ottoman collapse or retreat from Europe would, after all, have a disruptive effect on the balance of power there. Thus, a series of new questions arose in international affairs. If the Ottoman Empire collapsed, what would become of the territory under its control, particularly the Turkish Straits (the narrow channel connecting the Black Sea with the Mediterranean)? If the Ottomans were pushed out of Europe, what would be the fate of its possessions in the Balkans, such as the territories that are now Greece, Bulgaria, and Serbia? What would be the role of Russia in the European balance of power, and since Russia was the strongest Orthodox Christian state, what would be Russia's relationship with Orthodox Christians in the Ottoman Balkans and Middle East? All these questions were elements of the Eastern Question.

These questions were not posed in a void. Over the course of the eighteenth and nineteenth centuries, three processes forced European statesmen to confront them time after time: the consolidation of the Russian imperial state under Peter the Great (r. 1689–1725) and Catherine the Great (r. 1762–1796) and its relentless drive to the south; the overflow of British-French rivalries into European, Mediterranean, and Indian affairs; and the internal fragmentation of the Ottoman Empire as a result of secessionist movements in the Balkans and attempts by leaders of Egypt and Tunisia to gain autonomy and, in the case of the latter, independence for their provinces. Over the course of two centuries, these processes created crisis after crisis for European and Ottoman diplomats.

During the eighteenth century, Russia became the principal antagonist of the Ottoman Empire. There were two reasons for this. First, the tsars and Orthodox establishment saw Russia as the center of Orthodox Christianity (after the Ottoman capture of Constantinople they called Moscow "the Third Rome") and protector of Orthodox populations outside its borders. Many of those populations lived within the Ottoman Empire. In addition—and probably more important—was the strategic factor that motivated Russian confrontation with the Ottoman Empire. Russia was landlocked for much of the year because freezing temperatures prevented use of its northern harbors. Russian governments therefore coveted the warm-water ports of the Black Sea and Turkish Straits as a commercial and naval outlet to the Mediterranean. Only one thing stood in the way of Russia's Mediterranean ambition: the Ottoman Empire.

Beginning in 1768 Russia and the Ottoman Empire became involved in a series of wars, all of which ended badly for the Ottomans. The first of these wars ended in 1774 with the signing of the Treaty of Kuchuk Kainarja. According to the terms of the treaty, the Ottomans ceded to the Russians parts of the Crimean peninsula, which gave Russia a foothold on the Black Sea. Just as bad for the Ottomans, the Russians won freedom of navigation on the sea and the right of their merchant ships to pass through the straits.

With Russia on the Black Sea and, after another war with the Ottomans, Russian influence guaranteed in the Caucasus, the Russians began to put pressure on Persia. In 1801, Russia incorporated the Kingdom of Georgia. Twelve years later, Russia won the exclusive right to have warships on the Caspian Sea. Nevertheless, the Russian drive south might have been of minimal concern to other European states, particularly Great Britain, had it not been for the second element of the Eastern Question: the British-French colonial rivalry.

In the eighteenth century the profitability of colonies established by France and Britain over the course of previous centuries declined. Each state sought to consolidate its possessions and frustrate the strategic ambitions of the other. Each state attempted to seize control of the other's colonies. The result was a series of long-forgotten wars, such as the War of the Spanish Succession and the War of the Austrian Succession, that dragged in most European powers and that were fought on several continents at the same time. The most important of these wars was the Seven Years' War (1756–1763), known in the United States as the French and Indian War. As a result of the war, France lost to Britain almost all its colonial possessions in North America east of the Mississippi and in India, retaining only a few scattered trading stations.

The Seven Years' War thus made Great Britain the dominant European power in India. For the next two centuries, protecting its position in India and protecting the route from Great Britain to India would be a primary concern for British governments.

With the virtual eradication of French power on the subcontinent, the greatest threat to that position came from the north—Russia. Hence, the Great Game, the competition between Russia and Britain for influence in Central Asia and Persia, considered by British strategists the gateway to India. George Nathaniel Curzon, British viceroy of India, wrote in 1892:

> Not content with a spoil that would rob Persia at one sweep of the entire northern half of her dominions, [Russia] turns a longing eye southwards, and yearns for an outlet upon the Persian Gulf and Indian Ocean. The movements . . . along the south and east borders of Khorasan, the activity of her agents in regions far beyond the legitimate radius of an influence restricted to North Persia, her tentative experiments in the direction of Seistan—are susceptible of no other interpretation than a design to shake the influence of Great Britain in South Persia, to dispute the control of the Indian Seas, and to secure the long-sought base for naval operations in the east.

On the other hand, at the end of the Seven Years' War France had few options to obtain raw materials and market finished goods. France lacked control of the seas, had a growing urban population, and had an inadequate food supply. With the Atlantic under British domination, France began to focus on the Mediterranean. Over time, policy makers in France began to look to western North Africa as a site for colonization and to Egypt as a source of grain to overcome their overcrowding and food supply problems.

French activity in North Africa took place in three waves. The first took place at the end of the eighteenth century. In 1798, Napoleon Bonaparte, then a general acting under the orders of the French Revolutionary Directorate, invaded Egypt. Some in the directorate had wanted Napoleon to attack Britain, but this seemed too risky to the diminutive general. Instead, he landed troops in Egypt to gain access to Egyptian grain and to threaten the British route to India from the Mediterranean. Napoleon did not think that his invasion would create difficulties between France and the Ottoman Empire. Under the latter-day mamluks, Egypt had been virtually independent, and Napoleon claimed he was willing to govern Egypt in the name of the sultan. But the French invasion created economic chaos in the Ottoman Empire. Prices of grain and coffee doubled in Istanbul within the year, and the Ottomans were not fooled by Napoleon's declarations of disinterest. Thus, the Ottomans allied themselves with the British (and the Russians). In the Battle of the Nile, the British destroyed Napoleon's communication lines with France and made Napoleon's position in Egypt risky. The British and Ottomans eventually forced the surrender of the French army in Egypt. By that time, Napoleon had already sailed back to France to seize power there.

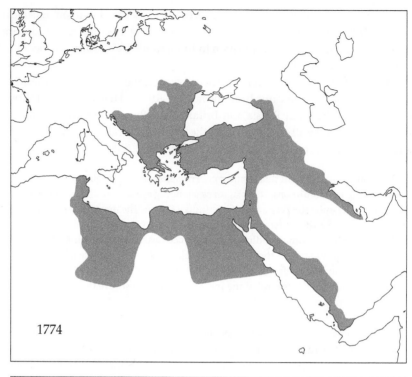

1774

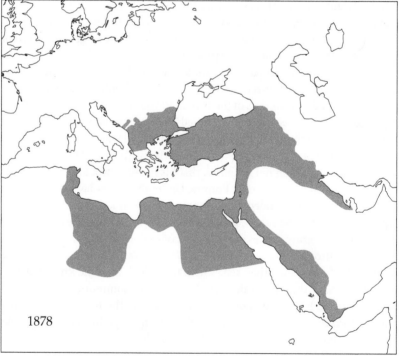

1878

The Ottoman Empire, 1774–1915

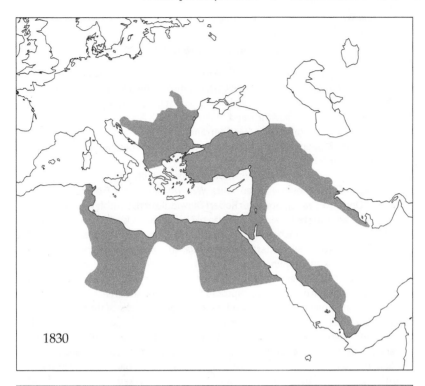

1830

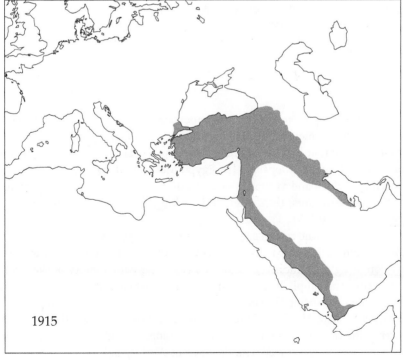

1915

Vignette

Provoking a Global War

During the eighteenth century, European powers fought a series of wars that were global in scope. For the Middle East, the most significant of these wars was the Seven Years' War (1756–1763), which was fought in Europe, the Mediterranean, the Caribbean, the Pacific, Africa, and North and South America. As a result of the war, the French adopted their "Mediterranean strategy" and Britain, now the undisputed European power in India, came to view the protection of the route to India as its overriding imperial interest.

As in the case of many other momentous conflicts throughout history, a minor incident sparked the Seven Years' War. Worried about French expansion into the Ohio River Valley, Governor Robert Dinwiddie of the British Virginia colony appointed an untested twenty-one-year-old surveyor to lead a detachment of troops to warn the French out of the area. Coming upon a French encampment in an area that is now western Pennsylvania, the Virginians surrounded their adversaries and opened fire. They killed ten of the French party and captured another twenty. The French protested, calling the incident an unprovoked attack on a diplomatic party. After they captured the surveyor, the French even got him to sign a statement in which he called the killing of the leader of the French party "*l'assassinat*," an assassination. Britain and France soon went to war. In the words of British statesman Horace Walpole, "The volley fired by a young Virginian in the backwoods of America set the world on fire." Perhaps the young Virginian panicked. Perhaps he was correct to assume that the French party was a war party. Whatever the case, the young Virginian whose action sparked a global war would later redeem himself to posterity. Acting in concert with the French, George Washington, as commander-in-chief of the Continental Army, went on to eliminate much of the British empire in North America—an empire built in the wake of his youthful impetuousness.

The French adventure in Egypt is important for two reasons. The first is the emergence of Mehmet Ali, the leader of an Albanian contingent attached to the Ottoman army that fought the French in Egypt. After the French, British, and most other Ottoman troops had left Egypt, Mehmet Ali took advantage of the chaos they had left and assumed power. He and his heirs would rule Egypt, first as Ottoman governors, then, after 1914, as kings. The Mehmet Ali dynasty of Egypt lasted until 1953.

In addition to the emergence of the Mehmet Ali dynasty in Egypt, the French adventure forced Britain to reassess its role in the eastern Mediterranean. Napoleon's invasion of Egypt demonstrated to the British the vulnerability of their communication and supply lines to India. For the most part, British policy would remain one of ensuring the survival, and sometimes the territorial integrity, of the Ottoman state, if only to prevent competition from one or another European power in the eastern Mediterranean. The occasional deviation notwithstanding, this policy was only reversed with the onset of World War I in 1914.

The second wave of French activity in North Africa began in 1830, when the French invaded Algeria. The French integrated Algeria into France, encouraged its settlement by European immigrants, and established a plantation economy based upon the export of cash crops (more on this in Chapter 6). It is worth emphasizing that the French did not establish a colony in Algeria—they literally made Algeria as much a part of France as Paris. (Beginning in 1911, the Italians would do the same with the territory that now comprises Libya, going so far as to call their conquest Italy's "fourth shore.") Algeria did not become independent until 1962.

The assimilation and settlement of Algeria was not the final chapter in the saga of France in North Africa. During the so-called Scramble for Africa (1881–1914), when mutual suspicions about each other's overseas ambitions induced European states to divide up the continent among themselves as formal colonies, France established Tunisia and Morocco as protectorates. This took place in 1881 and 1912, respectively. (Spain also established the northern and southern tips of Morocco as a separate protectorate in 1912.) While the French permitted the rulers of Tunisia and Morocco to set domestic policy and keep order, France "protected" them militarily and represented them in diplomatic councils. The French protectorate in both places lasted until they received independence in 1956. Interestingly, the establishment of the French protectorates came about as the result of the emergence of Germany as a major player on the international stage. Hoping to turn French attention away from retrieving the provinces it lost to Germany during the Franco-Prussian War (1870–1871), the Germans backed French ambitions in Tunisia at the Congress of Berlin, held seven years later. It was the French-German rivalry and the threat of the spread of German influence in Morocco that compelled the French to establish a protectorate there. Four years later, with the onset of World War I, France and Germany would play out their rivalry in a far more dramatic manner.

The third process that drove European statesmen to turn their attention to Middle Eastern affairs began at the close of the Napoleonic era. The internal fragmentation of the Ottoman Empire, mentioned earlier, redefined the nature of the Eastern Question. For the rest of the nineteenth century, the Eastern Question was concerned with the conflict between the Ottoman government and its Balkan subjects, on the one hand, and between the Ottoman government and its unruly governors in Egypt, on the other. When Balkan nationalists demanded independence, or when Mehmet Ali and his descendants demanded greater autonomy for Egypt, the Ottoman government resisted, as imperial governments are wont to do.

Added to the mix were continued British efforts to check Russian ambitions and to protect the route to India. Ironically, while the two goals often overlapped, they were sometimes at loggerheads. The former goal encouraged the British to intervene into Ottoman affairs to ensure the integrity of the empire, while the latter at times encouraged the British to intervene into Ottoman affairs at the expense of its territorial integrity. Hence, the British occupation of Egypt in 1882, its "leasing" of Cyprus from the Ottoman Empire in 1878, and its establishment of Kuwait as a British protectorate in 1899. All the while, European powers acting in concert worked to resolve each crisis in an attempt to find some solution that would protect the interests of each state while not upsetting the overall continental balance of power.

There were several reasons for the rise of Balkan nationalism during the immediate post–Napoleonic period. Most important was the consolidation and spread of the world system of nation-states. Starting in the nineteenth century, the nation-state became the gold standard for political organization worldwide. At the root of any modern nation-state lies the belief that because a given population shares (or can be made to share) certain identifiable characteristics— religion, language, history, and so on—it merits an independent existence. Any people that want to play in the big leagues of international politics has to join the world system of nation-states and be recognized as the local franchise of the system.

Nationalism emerged in the Balkans during the early nineteenth century for another reason as well. Nationalist movements need the proper conditions to take root. The appearance of these conditions does not guarantee a nationalist movement will materialize; rather, the appearance of these conditions merely makes the emergence of a nationalist movement possible. Three such conditions were at play in the Balkans. First was the emergence of new social classes, such as an intelligentsia that could articulate the doctrines and rationale for nationalist movements, along with a commercial bourgeoisie and professionals who consumed and disseminated the work of that intelligentsia. Such social classes emerged in the Balkans in large measure as a result of the post-Napoleonic expansion of trade, economic growth, and the spread of market relations—the second condition that often precedes the emergence of nationalist movements. Market relations unite the population economically and create a division of labor within proposed national boundaries. This, in turn, reinforces among a population an attitude that they belong to a distinct community and new conceptions of national/ economic space. Finally, there was the presence of a clearly identifiable "other" against which a nationalist movement might mobilize. This "other" might be anyone who does not share whatever distinguishing characteristics a nationalist movement credits to the nation. In the case of Balkan nationalisms, this "other" was usually the Turkish-speaking Muslim elites who governed them, although in some cases "Greeks" would do.

This is not to say that the Ottoman Empire was an alien power that imposed its presence on preexisting nations of Bulgarians, Greeks, Serbs, and so on. That would be the equivalent of saying that nations are timeless and natural entities rather than entities that are modern and fabricated. While some would argue that the former is the case, most scholars of nationalism working today do not agree. Instead, most would say that once the logic of nationalism is accepted—the oneness of a population on the basis of shared characteristics—those who do not share those characteristics become unabsorbable "others."

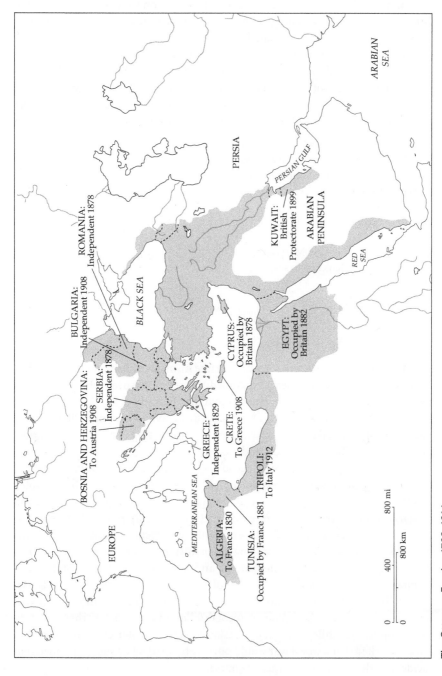

The Ottoman Empire, 1798–1914

BULGARIA:
Independent 1908

ROMANIA:
Independent 1878

BOSNIA AND HERZEGOVINA:
To Austria 1908

SERBIA:
Independent 1878

BLACK SEA

PERSIA

KUWAIT:
British
Protectorate 1899

ARABIAN
PENINSULA

PERSIAN GULF

ARABIAN
SEA

RED
SEA

CYPRUS:
Occupied by
Britain 1878

EGYPT:
Occupied by
Britain 1882

GREECE:
Independent 1829

CRETE:
To Greece 1908

TRIPOLI:
To Italy 1912

MEDITERRANEAN SEA

EUROPE

ALGERIA:
To France 1830

TUNISIA:
Occupied by France 1881

0   400   800 mi

0   800 km

55

The final reason for the emergence of Balkan nationalisms was that these nationalisms were encouraged from the outside. The Russians, for example, wanted allies in the Balkans. If independent states in the region were to emerge from the Ottoman Empire, those states would, more likely than not, want to use Russia as a counterweight to the Ottoman Empire (and, as often as not, the Habsburg Empire). In return, the Russians would be able to gain their strategic goal. The Russians were not alone in supporting Balkan nationalisms, however. Throughout Europe the cause of Greek independence, for example, became a *cause célèbre*, drawing in a diverse group of liberals and Romantics, including the English poet Lord Byron. He described the struggle of his idealized Greece thus:

> The isles of Greece, the isles of Greece!
> Where burning Sappho loved and sung,
> Where grew the arts of war and peace,
> Where Delos rose and Phoebus sprung!
> Eternal summer gilds them yet,
> But all, except their sun, is set. . . .
>
> The mountains look on Marathon—
> And Marathon looks on to sea;
>
> And musing there an hour alone,
> I dream'd that Greece might still be free;
> For standing on the Persians' grave,
> I could not deem myself a slave. . . .

And William Gladstone, the sometime prime minister of Britain during the last quarter of the nineteenth century, coined the term "unspeakable Turk" in his 1876 pamphlet, "The Bulgarian Horrors and the Question of the East." Gladstone used his pamphlet as a stick to beat his political rival, Benjamin Disraeli, who quite logically seemed more concerned about maintaining Britain's strategic position than about Bulgarian independence.

Thus, starting in the second decade of the nineteenth century a series of revolts took place against Ottoman control in the Balkans. From these revolts, a host of independent states emerged, from Serbia and Greece to Romania and Bulgaria. These states arose at the confluence of three empires: the Ottoman, the Habsburg, and the Russian. By the end of the nineteenth century, the Balkans had thus become a tinderbox, arraying nationalist movements against each other, empires against nationalist movements and newly formed nation-states, and empires against each other. On the eve of World War I, a coalition of Bulgaria, Serbia, Greece, and Montenegro defeated the Ottoman Empire in what became known as the First Balkan War. A second followed a year later when Bulgaria turned on its erstwhile allies. The Prussian foreign minister Otto von Bismarck once remarked that a world war would one day be sparked by some "damned fool incident in the Balkans." He was, of course, right.

The Greek revolt of 1821 is particularly important, for it endangered the balance of power in Europe by threatening the very integrity of the Ottoman Empire. To put down the revolt, the Ottomans called on their nominal vassal, Mehmet Ali, who had by this time built the best army in the empire. The Ottomans promised Mehmet Ali control over Syria if he suppressed the revolt. At first Mehmet Ali's army was successful in putting down the insurgents. But when reports reached Europe that Egyptian troops had conducted mass deportations—ethnic cleansing—the great powers intervened. At the Battle of Navarino a combined British/French/Russian fleet destroyed the Egyptian fleet and ultimately forced the Ottoman Empire to accept Greek autonomy, then Greek independence.

Nevertheless, for Mehmet Ali a deal was a deal, and Syria belonged to him. In 1831, his army invaded Syria and then, when the Ottomans protested, it began a march on Istanbul. To save themselves, the Ottomans initially threw themselves into the arms of Russia—an act which naturally worried the British. In response, the British for the first time officially committed themselves to protecting the integrity of the Ottoman Empire, issuing the following statement:

> His majesty's government attach great importance to the maintenance of the integrity of the Ottoman Empire, considering that state to be a material element in the general balance of power in Europe.

In 1840, the British and Ottomans together forced the Egyptians out of Syria. To ensure that Russian influence over the Ottoman Empire would be limited, the British organized a conference in London that made the concert of European powers—not any single power—the ultimate guarantor of the Ottoman Empire.

Overall, the concert of European powers managed both to protect the interests of the individual European nations in the Ottoman Empire and to diffuse crisis after crisis through diplomacy. Only once during the remainder of the century—during the Crimean War of 1853–1856—did European nations go to war to resolve a dispute involving the Ottoman Empire. But the establishment of a united Germany in 1871 disrupted the European balance of power, and thus disrupted the concert of Europe. And the end of the concert of Europe in 1914 heralded the end of the Ottoman Empire. But here we are getting ahead of ourselves.

DOCUMENTS

Evliya Chelebi: Seyahatanamé (1)

Evilya Chelebi (1611–1684?) was a Turkish traveler and travel writer. His *Seyahatanamé (Travelogue)* is an account of the various tours he took in the Ottoman Empire. In this selection, he describes the sprawling Topkapi Palace, the primary residence of the sultans. He served there as a page in the court of Sultan Murat IV. While the account is surely exaggerated, it does reflect the sense of awe which the palace was intended to inspire.

The Conqueror, having thus become possessed of so great a treasure (i.e., Constantinople), bethought himself that the most needful thing for a monarch was to build himself a permanent abode. He therefore expended the sum of three thousand purses on the erection of the New Palace. The best of several metrical dates (1) inscribed over the Imperial Gate is the one at the bottom, carved in conspicuous gold letters on a white marble tablet: 'Khállad Allâhu 'ázza sâhibiki.' (May God make the Glory of its Master eternal!)

Never has a more beautiful edifice been erected by the art of man; for, situated by the edge of the sea, having the Black Sea on the North and the White Sea (Sea of Marmora) on the East, it should rather be likened to a town placed at the confluence of two seas than to a palace.

Its founder was the second Solomon, Iskendér Zúlkarnéin. The Conqueror's palace was built upon the ruins of earlier edifices erected by former sovereigns to which he added seventy private, public and other well-appointed apartments such as a confectionary, bakery, hospital, armoury, mat-store, wood-shed, granary, inner and outer stables each one resembling the stable of Antar (2), several storerooms ranged round the garden delightful as the Garden of Irâm (3), and planted with twenty thousand cypresses, plane trees, weeping willows, thuyas, pines and box-trees, with an aviary and tulip bed which to this day may be compared to the garden of Jinns.

In the centre of this garden there stands a pleasant hill and slope on which the Conqueror erected forty private apartments wainscoted with tiles, a Hall of Audience (*Arz-Odasi*) inside the Gate of Felicity (*Báb-I Saadét*), and a fine horse-parade, to the east of which he built a bath close to the Privy Treasury. Adjoining this are the aviary, pantry, Treasurer's chamber, the senior and junior pages' quarters, the Seferlis' (4) and Külkhán (5) chambers, the mosque attached to the Büyük-Odá, and the gymnasium which adjoins the bath mentioned above. The privy chambers already mentioned were occupied by three thousand pages, fair as Joseph, richly attired in chemises fragrant as roses, with embroidered bonnets and robes smothered in gold and jewels, each one having his appointed place in the Emperor's service, where he must be ready at any moment to attend.

There were no women's quarters in the palace, and these were added later on in the reign of Sultán Suleymán. The latter also had quarters built for the black and white eunuchs, a recreation pavilion and a council chamber where the seven Vezírs of the Diván met four times a week.

Sultán Mehmét likewise surrounded this strongly fortified palace with a wall. This had 366 towers and 12,000 merlons, its total circumference being 6,500 paces, with sixteen gates, great and small.

Besides the officers already mentioned, there were 12,000 Bostanjis who lived within the precincts of the Palace. Forty thousand persons all told lodged within its walls.

Notes

1. A.H. 876–877, A.D. 1471–1472.
2. A legendary Arab hero.
3. The legendary garden of King Shaddâd of Arabia (cf. Rubáyat of Omar Khayyâm, Fitzgerald's translation), v. 'Iram indeed is gone with all his rose.'
4. These were pages who accompanied the Sultan when on campaign.
5. Heating-apparatus for the bath.

Alexander Pallis, *In the Days of the Janissaries: Old Turkish Life as Depicted in the "Travel-Book" of Evliya Chelebi* (London: Hutchinson and Co., 1951), pp. 103–104.

Evliya Chelebi: Seyahataname (2)

In this selection, Evliya Chelebi describes the casting of cannon in Topkhané (Tophané), a district of Istanbul. Not surprisingly, the name means "cannon foundry" in Turkish.

Topkhané in the time of the Infidels was a convent situated in the midst of a forest where now stands the mosque of Jihangír. It was dedicated to St. Alexander, and the infidels still visit it once a year on that Saint's feast day. A tradition says that Iskendér Zulkarnéin chained to this spot a number of magicians and witches from the country of Gog and Magog by heaping mountains upon them, with the injunction to go to sea during the forty winter days in brazen ships and keep watch over the waters surrounding Constantinople; but those demons having cut passage through the mountains enclosing the Black Sea, it broke through the Bosphorus engulfing the demons in the waters.

Mehmét II erected at this spot the gun-foundry which Bayazít II subsequently enlarged, adding the barracks. In the time of Suleymán I, who reigned forty-eight years, all kings and monarchs yielded peacefully to his sway with the exception of the Emperor of Germany who continued at war. Of these forty-eight years Suleymán spent four in waging war in Arabia, four in Persia, four against the Venetians, and thirty-six against the Emperor of Germany. These Germans be a race of strong, warlike, cunning, devilish, coarse infidels whom, excelling as they did in artillery, Sultán Suleymán endeavored to get equal with by recruiting gunners and artillerymen from all countries with the offer of rich rewards. He pulled down the gun foundry built by his predecessors and erected a new one; no one who has not seen it is able to judge of that which may be achieved by human strength and intelligence. . . .

On the day when cannon are to be cast, the masters, foremen, and founder, together with the Grand Master of Artillery, the Chief Overseer, Imâm, Muézzin and timekeeper, all assemble and, to their cries of 'Allâh! Allâh!,' the wood is thrown into the furnaces. After these have been heated for twenty-four hours, the founders and stokers strip naked, wearing nothing but their slippers, an odd kind of cap which leaves nothing but their eyes visible, and thick sleeves to protect their arms; for, after the fire has been alight in the furnaces twenty-four hours, no person can approach on account of the heat, save he be attired in the above manner. Whoever wishes to see a good picture of the fires of Hell should witness this sight.

The twenty-four hours having elapsed, the Vezirs, the Mufti and Sheikhs are summoned; only forty persons, besides the personnel of the foundry, are admitted all told. The rest of the attendants are shut out, because the metal, when in fusion, will not suffer to be looked at by evil eyes. The masters then desire the Vezirs and sheikhs who are seated on sofas at a great distance to repeat unceasingly the words 'There is no power and strength save Allâh!' Thereupon the master-workmen with wooden shovels throw several hundredweight of tin into the sea of molten brass, and the head-founder says to the Grand Vizier, Vezirs and Sheikhs: 'Throw some gold and silver coins into the brazen sea as alms, in the name of the True Faith!' Poles as long as the yards of ships are used for mixing the gold and silver with the metal and are replaced as fast as consumed.

As soon as the surface of the brass begins to bubble, the master workmen know that it is in a complete state of fusion. More wood is thrown into the furnaces, great care being taken that not a drop of water gets in, because a drop of water thrown into the molten brass would burst asunder the gun-mould and wipe out all those present. On both sides of the ovens forty to fifty sheep are kept in readiness. The whole company then rise to their feet, the timekeeper giving notice to the master of the furnace half an hour before it is time to open the mouth. The almoner recites the accustomed prayers, and the whole assembly cry aloud: 'Amen.' All are very fervent and zealous in their prayers, for it is a most dangerous business and one in which many master-workmen and vezirs have lost their lives.

The time-limit having expired and been announced by the timekeeper, the head-founder and master-workmen, attired in their clumsy felt dresses, open the mouth of the furnace with iron hooks exclaiming 'Allâh! Allâh!' The metal, as it begins to flow, casts a glare on the men's faces at a hundred paces' distance. The Vezirs and sheikhs, donning white shirts, sacrifice the sheep on either side of the furnace. The metal flows from channel to channel into the moulds, the largest taking half an hour to fill; the stream of brass is then stopped by a mass of oily clay and flows on to the next. Prayers are said once again, and so on till the end, when seventy robes of honour are distributed and increases of pay granted. The men doff their dresses of felt, and the Grand Master of Artillery gives a feast in honour of the Grand Vizier. . . .

Alexander Pallis, *In the Days of the Janissaries: Old Turkish Life as Depicted in the "Travel-Book" of Evliya Chelebi* (London: Hutchinson and Co., 1951), pp. 89–91.

Draft Treaty of Amity and Commerce between the Ottoman Empire and France, February 1535

The following commercial agreement between the Ottoman Empire and France was negotiated in 1535. Although never ratified, it demonstrates the sort of privileges sought by European powers in their dealings with the empire.

Be it known to everybody that in the year of Jesus Christ one thousand five hundred and thirty-five, in the month of February, and of Mohammed 941, in the moon of Chaban, Sire Jean de la Forest, privy councilor, and ambassador of the most excellent and most powerful prince Francis, by the grace of God most Christian King of France, accredited to the most powerful and invincible Grand Signior, Sultan Suleiman, Emperor of the Turks, and having discussed with the powerful and magnificent Signior Ibrahim, Serasker of the Sultan, the calamities and disadvantages which are caused by war, and, on the other hand, the good, quiet, and tranquillity derived from peace; and knowing how good it is to prefer the one (peace) to the other (war), each of them guaranteeing the above-mentioned monarchs, their superiors, they have negotiated and agreed upon the following chapters and conventions in the name and on the honor of the said monarchies which are the protectors of their component States and the bene-factors of their subjects:

I. They have negotiated, made, and concluded a valid and sure peace and sin-cere concord in the name of the above Grand Signior and King of France during their lives and for the kingdoms, dominions, provinces, castles, cities, ports, harbors, seas, islands, and all other places they hold and possess at present or may possess in the future, so that all subjects and tributaries of said sovereigns who wish may freely and safely, with their belongings and men, navigate on armed or unarmed ships, travel on land, reside, remain in and return to the ports, cities, and all other places in their respective countries for their trade, and the like shall be done for their merchandise.

II. Likewise, the said subjects and tributaries of the said monarchs shall, respect-ively be able to buy, sell, exchange, move, and transport by sea and land from one country to the other all kinds of merchandise not prohibited, by paying only the ordinary customs and ancient dues and taxes, to wit, the Turks, in the dominions of the King, shall pay the same as Frenchmen, and the said French-men in the dominions of the Grand Signior shall pay the same as the Turks, without being obliged to pay any other new tribute, impost, or storage due.

III. Likewise, whenever the King shall send to Constantinople or Pera or other places of this Empire a bailiff—just as at present he has a consul at Alexandria—the said bailiff and consul shall be received and maintained in proper authority so that each one of them may in his locality, and without being hindered by any judge, cadi, soubashi, or other, according to his faith and law, hear, judge, and determine all causes, suits, and differences, both civil and criminal, which might arise between merchants and other subjects of the King. . . .

J. C. Hurewitz, *The Middle East and North Africa in World Politics: A Documentary Record*, vol. 1: *European Expansion, 1535–1914* (New Haven, Conn.: Yale University Press, 1975), pp. 2–3.

The Travels of Sir John Chardin into Persia and the East-Indies (1)

> Sir John Chardin (1643–1713) was an Anglo-French traveler who began his travels to the East when he was twenty-one years old. In this selection, he describes the rival trade missions to the Ottoman Empire and the inflation-inducing trade in debased coins.

The English drive a great Trade at *Smyrna*, and over all the *Levant*. This Trade is driv'n by a Royal Company settled at *London*; which is Govern'd after a most prudent manner, and therefore cannot fail of success. It has stood almost these hundred Years, being first Confirm'd towards the middle of Queen *Elizabeth's* Raign. A Raign famous for having, among other Things, giv'n Life to several Trad-ing Companies, particularly those of *Hamborough, Russia, Greenland*, the *East-Indies* and *Turkie*, all which remain to this Day. Trade was then in its Infancy; and there is no greater Mark of the Ignorance of those Times, in reference to Countries, though a little remote, then the Association which those Merchants made: for they joyn'd several together in one Body, for mutual Conduct and Assistance. That Company which relates to the Turkish Trade, is of a particular sort: For it is not a Society, where every one puts in a Sum for one General and United Stock: It is a Body which has nothing in Common, but a peculiar Grant and Priviledge to Trade into the *Levant*. It assumes to it self the Name of *The Regulated Company*. None are admitted into it, but Sons of Merchants, or such as have served an Apprenticeship to the Trade, which in *England* is for Seven Years. They give to be admitted into the Society about an Hundred and Twenty Crowns, if under the Age of Twenty Five Years; and double if above that Age. The Company commits to any one single Person their Power, nor the sole Management of their Affairs, but manage their Business among themselves by the Plurality of Voices. So that who has sufficient to drive a Trade that will bear an Imposition of Eight Crowns, has as good a Vote as he that Trades for an Hundred Thousand. This Assembly, thus *Democratical*, sends out Ships, Levies Taxes upon all their Commodities, presents the Ambassador whom the King sends to the *Port*, Elects two Consuls, the one for *Smyrna*, the other for *Aleppo*, and prevents the sending of Goods which are not thought proper for the *Levant*. It consists at present of about Three Hundred Merchants, besides that they bring up in *Turkie* a great number of young Persons well descended, who learn the Trade upon the Place it self. This Trade amounts to about Five or Six Hundred Thousand Pounds yearly, and consists in Cloaths made in *England*, and Silver which they carry as well out of *England*, as out of *Spain, France*, and *Italy*: In exchange of which they bring back Wool, Cotton-Yarn, Galls, Raw Silk and Wov'n, together with some other Commodities of less value. . . .

The Hollanders also drive a great Trade at *Smyrna*, and more than any other Nation of *Europe*, but they have little to do elsewhere; all their Dealing in all the rest of the Cities in the *Levant* amounting to little or nothing. Their principal Profit consists in carrying the *Armenians* and the Goods into *Europe*, and carryin 'em back again. They also make great Advantage of their Money, of which *Turkie* is very full. This money of theirs is made of base Mettle, and notoriously intermix'd with Counterfeit pieces. It chiefly consists of Crowns, Half-Crowns, *Testons*, or Eighteen-penny pieces, and pieces of Fifteen *Sous*. The Crowns and Half-Crowns for the most part carry the Dutch Stamp. Which the Turks therefore call *Aslani*, that is to say *Lyons*; in regard of their being mark'd on both sides with the Figure of a Lyon. The Arabians, either out of Ignorance or otherwise, mistaking the Lyon for a Dog, give'em the Name of *Abou-Kelb*, or *Dogs*. The Quarter-Pieces are almost all Counterfeit; or at Best, but Half Silver. However the Turks are so void of Judgment and Understanding, that they esteem this Mony beyond that of *Spain*, which they call *Marsillies*, by reason that the Merchants of *Marseilles* first brought it in great Quantities into *Turkie*. . . .

The French are very numerous in *Smyrna*, and over all the *Levant*, there not being a Port of *Turkie* upon the *Mediterranean* Sea, wherein there are not several. They are for the most part all *Provençalls*. But the Trade which they drive is so inconsiderable, that one Merchant in each Place might dispatch all Business. . . . [T]he *Provençalls* have formerly had in *Turkie* those fortunate Chances and Luckie Opportunities, that it is highly to be wonder'd, that they did not fill their Country with Wealth in that happy Conjuncture. One of those Lucky Seasons began about the Year 1656, and lasted Thirteen Years, during which time they drove a Trade, by which they gain'd Fourscore and Ninety *per. Cent*.

This Trade which was really and truly a great piece of Knavery consisted in these *Five-Sous-Pieces* that have made such a Noise. For the Turks took the first that were brought at Ten Sous apiece; At which rate they held up for some time; tho afterwards they fell to Seven *Sous* and a half. There was no other Money Stirring: all *Turkie* was full of it; neither was there any other Mony to be had; for that the French carri'd all the other Money away. This good Fortune so intoxicated their Senses, that not content with such great Gains, they still thirsted after more; and to that purpose they set themselves to alter their own pieces of *Five Sous*, and made others of the same sort, but of base Mettle, which they Coin'd first at *Dombes*, then at *Orange*, and afterwards at *Avignon*. More then this, they Stampt far worse at *Monaco* and *Florence*: And lastly they made more of the same Stamp in the remote Castles belonging to the *State of Genoa*, and other private places, which were only Copper plated over. The Merchants of *Marseilles*, to utter this Money, brought down the price themselves, and put off their Pieces in payment, and to the Mony-Changers at a lower Rate then the Current Value. The Turks were a long time before they perceiv'd the Cheat that was put upon'em, though so palpable and of so great a Consequence; but so soon as they found it out, they were so incens'd, that they laid most heavy Impositions upon the *French*, using'em no better then Counterfeiters of Money, though the *Dutch* and *Genoeses* had a hand in it as well as they. Therupon they forbid'em to utter any of those Pieces which they call'd *Timmins*, but such as were stamp'd with the real Arms of *France*, which they also brought down and put at Five *Sous* apiece. So that all the *European* Merchants, except the *English*, were loaded at that time with great Quantities of those *Timmins*. Their Warehouses were full, whole Ships Loadings of 'em arriv'd daily, and they began to Coin'em in all parts. But soon after, this Money being cry'd down, several of those Money-Merchants lost all their Gains, and many much more then ever they got.

The *English* were the Procurers of this Decry. For had that Money continu'd Currant, their Trade had been ruin'd, which consisted chiefly in the purchase of Silks. And the reason was, because the *Timmin*-Merchants caus'd an advance to be made upon the price of Silks, not caring what they gave, provided the Sellers would take their Pieces of Five *Sous* in payment. I have seen above Fifty several sorts of Coins of this sort of Money. But the most common sort carri'd on the one side a Womans Head with this *Motto, Vera Virtutis Imago*: On the other, the Arms of *France*, with this Impresse, *Currens per totam Asiam*.

There are no People in the World that have been more frequently cheated, or that are more easily gull'd then the *Turks*; as being naturally very dull, and thick-skull'd, and apt to believe any fair Story: Which is the reason that the Christians have impos'd a Thousand Cony-catching-Tricks, and Cheats upon'em. But though you may deceive'em once or twice, yet when their Eyese are op'n, they strike home, and pay ye once for all. And those sort of Impositions which they lay upon Offenders in that Nature, are call'd *Avanies*; which are not always unjust Impositions neither; they being like the Confiscations so frequent in Custom-Houses: Where for the most part the Chief Ministers and their Officers devour the People, while the *Port* winks all thee first time, and only exhorts to Amendment. If the Complaints cease, the Offence is stifled; but if the Clamour grow too loud, the *Port* sends to take off the Head of the Party accus'd, and Confiscates his Estate. By which means the People are satisfied, the Treasury is fill'd, Justice is done, and the Example remains to terrifie others.

Sir John Chardin, *The Travels of Sir John Chardin into Persia and the East-Indies*, vol. 1 (London: Moses Pitt, 1686).

The Travels of Sir John Chardin into Persia and the East-Indies (2)

> Sir John Chardin traveled to Persia from the Ottoman Empire. Here he de-
> scribes the steps taken by the Safavid government to deal with famine in
> Isfahan.

All this while the Dearth encreas'd at *Ispahan*, and the poor people cry'd aloud
against the excessive price of it. And indeed there were many causes of this
Scarcity. First, the last Harvest did not amount scarce to the half of what they expected; for the Locust had devour'd the Ears. Then the whole Train of the Court
was come all together of a sudden to *Ispahan* before they were expected, so that
they had tak'n no care to lay in their Stores against Winter. Moreover, at the King's
first coming to the Crown, the greatest part of the Officers of the Empire coming
to present themselves before Him, and a vast number of private persons crouding
together about business, or for curiosity, the Multitude of Inhabitants was
encreas'd to above half as many again, so that of necessity the Price of Provisions
must be double in Proportion. But the chief Reason that all things were so dear
was the bad appearance of the Harvest at hand, which promis'd no better then
the last year. For in regard the Harvests in these Climates are generally reap'd in
the Months of *June* and *July*, it is easie to conjecture in *March* and *April* what the
year will produce. And therefore the Corn Merchants perceiving that there would
be an infallible scarcity of all sorts of Grain, enhans'd their Prizes, and would not
part with what they had, but staid till the Prizes were at the highest, so that the
probability of a dearth to come caus'd a present Famine. Lastly, the ill Government was in part a great cause of the scarcity, for that the Laws were not observ'd,
and the Magistrates neglected their duty, without fear of being punish'd. And this
was the Reason that the *Mochtesek*, or Chief of the Government, receiv'd Bribes of
those that sold the necessary Provisions, and therefore to gratifie'em he publish'd
every Week the Prizes of things as those people desir'd; that is to say, at an excessive rate, and three quarters higher then in the time of the deceas'd King. For we
are to observe, that it is a Custom in *Persia*, that every *Saturday* the Chief Justice
sets the Price of all Provisions for the Week following, which the Sellers dare not
exceed under great forfeitures. This Knavery then of the Judge of the City Government, who stood in no aw of the superior Government, was the cause that all
things were sold at double and treble the Rate they ought to have been.

The People therefore almost starv'd by this Scarcity, redoubl'd their Cries, so
that they reach'd the very Gate of the Palace Royal, which mov'd his Majesties
Compassion to that degree, that he committed the Affair to *Ali-Kouli-Kaan*, General
of all his Forces. Who began his first endeavours of redress with an Act of Generosity and Justice, which made him dreaded by all the Merchants and Corn-sellers.
He had commanded one of the most eminent Merchants in *Ispahan* to send him
in upon the place, the first day of the Market, two hundred Sacks of Wheat, and
not to sell'em at a dearer rate then they were sold the year before. Now the
Merchant thought that he expected a Bribe; and therefore upon the Market day,
thinking to exempt himself from obedience to his Command he sent him two
hundred *Tomans*, which amount to the value of about a thousand *Pistols*. Thereupon the *Generalissimo*, being highly offended, sent for him, and when he came,
Dog as thou art, said he, *is it thus thou goest about to famish a whole City? For
the Affront thou hast done me receive a hundred Drubs upon the soles of thy feet.*
Which were paid him at the same instant; and besides, the General condemned

him in a Fine of two thousand Crowns; which he took to himself, sending the thousand Pistols to the King.

Presently, he order'd a great Oven to be built in the Royal *Piazza*, and another in the publick *Piazza*, ordering the Criers to proclaim that those Ovens were fixed to bake those alive, that should sell their bread at a rate above the set price, or that should hide up their Corn. There was moreover a fire continually kept in these Ovens, but no body was thrown in; because no body would venture the pain of such a rigorous punishment of his Disobedience.

At the same time he also went himself to visit all the Granaries and Store-houses of Corn and Meal that were in *Ispahan*, and having taken an accompt in Writing of their Number, every Week he commanded the Merchants to send a certain quantity according to the Proportion of what the Store-houses contain'd, and not to sell but at a certain Price, and not to deliver their goods to any but such as brought a Note under his hand. He gave the same Command for Barley: so that almost for a whole years time there was neither Wheat or Barley to be had without a Ticket seal'd with his Signet. All the Bakers went for such a Ticket. And in regard the General knew full well what every one of 'em vented, he would not permit the Baker by vertue of his Ticket to buy any more then what he had occasion for. To that purpose he prohibited the Bakers to sell to any other then those of their own Precinct, nor to sell 'em any more then what was needful for their subsistence according to the usual rate of their spending, to the end that the Bakers should not pretend that persons came from abroad to buy their bread, or that those in their Precincts bought more one Week than they did another, and so that the vent could not be always equally proportion'd. And for the Price, he order'd that the *Batman-cha* of Bread (the Royal weight of *Persia*, consisting of eleven pounds three quarters) should be worth an *Abassi*, which makes four Groats.

By this good management he wonderfully eas'd the People, who before paid for eleven pound and three fourths of Bread an *Abassi* and a quarter, or twenty pence; whence it also came to pass, that there was Plenty sufficient. Thus the Complaints and Cries of the People ceas'd. For the Bakers being oblig'd to furnish those in their Precincts with as much bread as they stood in need of, no body was apprehensive of the scarcity, but only that he paid five farthings for that which cost not above four in time of plenty. And to the end that the same rate might continue, he sent to all the Burroughs, Towns, and Villages, from either to nine days journey round about, to send in such a number of Waggon-Loads of Corn and Meal to *Ispahan*, and there to sell it at the net price. By which means there came enough to supply the City for six Months. Moreover, when any considerable Quantity arriv'd, he order'd it to be brought in, as it were, in triumph; the People dancing before with their Instruments of Musick, and the horses being cover'd with Housses, and gingling an infinite number of little Bells, which together with the Acclamations of the Rabble made a strange, confused, and yet pleasing noise.

Some villages there were mutiny'd and refus'd to send in their Corn; but the punishment of the Inhabitants of *Ispahanim-cha* strook a terrour into the rest. For the General had sent to this Place, being a great Town consisting of four thousand Houses, two Leagues distant from *Ispahan*, one of his Officers with a Command from the King to send at the set Price two hundred Sacks of Meal to the Capital City for the present necessity. The Townsmen made answer, 'twas nothing to them if there were such a Famine in the City, for that they had paid all their duties and Impositions for the last Harvest: that they had something else to do then to send their Corn and the Meal to *Ispahan* Market, and that those that wanted might come to them, for that they were not bound to sell but in their own Town. Thereupon the Officer remonstrated to the Principal of the Village that it was the Kings pleasure, and shew'd 'em the Kings Warrant which he had in his hands; to which their answer not being with that becoming reverence which became 'em, the Officer laid his hand upon his Sword, thinking to have frighted 'em into obedience. But the Country fellows not understanding his hard words, fell upon the Officer, beat him almost blind, and tore the Kings Command, crying out, 'twas a Cheat and Counterfeit.

The General highly offended at this Insolence of the Countrymen, gave the King an account of it, who order'd him to inflict such punishment as the Offence deserv'd. Upon which he sent two hundred of his Guards, who Drubb'd to excess the Principal of the Ringleaders. He also set a Fine upon their heads of a hundred thousand Crowns; which was mitigated to a third part, tho after many Petitions and Submissions, with a Present to the General of a thousand Pistols, which was all paid down upon the nail.

Sir John Chardin, *The Travels of Sir John Chardin into Persia and the East-Indies*, vol. 1 (London: Moses Pitt, 1686).

SUGGESTED READINGS

General Works on Middle Eastern History

Abrahamian, Ervand. *A History of Modern Iran*. Cambridge, England: Cambridge University Press, 2008. Wonderful revisionist account of Iranian history during the nineteenth and twentieth centuries.

Beinin, Joel. *Workers and Peasants in the Modern Middle East*. Cambridge, England: Cambridge University Press, 2001. Very readable social history of labor in the modern Middle East.

Burke, Edmund III, ed. *Struggle and Survival in the Modern Middle East*. 2nd ed. Berkeley: University of California Press, 2005. Collection of biographies of lives of Middle Easterners—ranging from bedouin and peasants to workers and political activists—from the nineteenth century to the present.

Clancy-Smith, Julia, ed. *North Africa, Islam, and the Mediterranean World: From the Almoravids to the Algerian War*. New York: Frank Cass Publishers, 2001. This expansive set of essays traces the history of both North Africa and the wider Mediterranean through the centuries.

Cleveland, William. *A History of the Modern Middle East*. 5th ed. Boulder, Colo.: Westview Press, 2012. The best comprehensive history of the modern Middle East.

Daly, M. W., ed. *The Cambridge History of Egypt, vol. 2: Modern Egypt from 1517 to the End of the Twentieth Century*. Cambridge, England: Cambridge University Press, 2008. Excellent collection of essays on Egyptian politics, society, and culture from the beginning of the Ottoman period to the present day.

Faroqhi, Suraiya, et al., eds. *An Economic and Social History of the Ottoman Empire, vol. 2: 1600–1900*. Cambridge, England: Cambridge University Press, 1994. Detailed studies of three hundred years of Ottoman life written by top scholars in the field.

Findley, Carter. *The Turks in World History*. New York: Oxford University Press, 2004. Readable account tracing the history of Turks and Turkic peoples through five centuries.

Hodgson, Marshall G. S. *Rethinking World History: Essays on Europe, Islam, and World History*, edited by Edmund Burke, III. Cambridge, England: Cambridge University Press, 1993. Although the essays were written quite a while ago, this is a pioneering work situating Islam and the Middle East comparative and global history.

Hodgson, Marshall G. S. *The Venture of Islam: Conscience and History in a World Civilization*, 3 vols. Chicago: University of Chicago Press, 1961. Difficult reading and a bit dated, but a must for the serious student of Middle Eastern history.

Hourani, Albert, et al., eds. *The Modern Middle East*. Berkeley: University of California Press, 1993. An important collection of essays on the modern Middle East, most previously published elsewhere.

Lockman, Zachary. *Contending Visions of the Middle East: The History and Politics of Orientalism*. 2nd ed. Cambridge, England: Cambridge University Press, 2010. A study of how historians and social scientists have approached the study of the region from the mid-twentieth century through today.

Specialized Works

Barkey, Karen. *Empire of Difference: The Ottomans in Comparative Perspective*. Cambridge, England: Cambridge University Press, 2008. Barkey argues that one of the key elements contributing to the longevity of the empire was its policy of tolerance to its diverse elements.

Brown, Carl. *International Politics and the Middle East: Old Rules, Dangerous Game*. Princeton, N.J.: Princeton University Press, 1984. While the second half of this book deals with the cold war and is a bit dated, the first half provides a well-written synopsis of the relationship of the West and the Middle East during the "long nineteenth century."

Dale, Stephen F. *The Muslim Empires of the Ottomans, Safavids, and Mughals*. Cambridge, England: Cambridge University Press, 2010. An illuminating comparative history that deals not only with institutions and politics, but with culture and religion as well.

Foran, John. "The Long Fall of the Safavid Dynasty: Moving Beyond the Standard Views." *International Journal of Middle East Studies* 24 (1992): 281–304. A unique study that applies world systems analysis to Persia in the seventeenth and eighteenth centuries.

Gaonkar, Dilip Parameshwar. *Alternative Modernities*. Durham, N.C.: Duke University Press, 1999. A collection of essays outlining a useful approach to the problem of modernity.

Huntington, Samuel. "The Clash of Civilizations?" *Foreign Affairs* 72 (Summer 1993): 23–49. Influential article attempts to forecast the upcoming conflict between "the West" and "the rest."

Islamoglu-Inan, Huri, ed. *The Ottoman Empire and the World Economy*. New York: Cambridge University Press, 1987. Collection of essays applying world systems theory to the Ottoman Empire.

al-Jabarti, ᶜAbd al-Rahman. *Napoleon in Egypt: Al-Jabarti's Chronicle of the French Occupation, 1798*. Translated by Shlomo Moreh. Princeton, N.J.: Markus Wiener, 1993. An eyewitness account of Napoleon's campaign in Egypt, told from the Egyptian point of view.

Kafadar, Cemal. *Between Two Worlds: The Construction of the Ottoman State*. Berkeley: University of California Press, 1995. Accessible work on the history and historiography of Ottoman beginnings.

Kasaba, Resat. *The Ottoman Empire and the World Economy: The Nineteenth Century.* Albany: State University of New York Press, 1988. Examines why the Ottoman Empire became a peripheral part of the world economy in the nineteenth century.

Said, Edward. *Orientalism.* New York: Pantheon, 1978. This groundbreaking work analyzes the reasons for misperceptions of the Middle East in the West. A useful riposte to Huntington, although written a decade before.

Shannon, Thomas R. *Introduction to the World Systems Perspective.* Boulder, Colo.: Westview Press, 1989. Situates world systems theory in its historical context and analyzes its strengths and weaknesses.

PART II

The Question of Modernity

This section is about "modernity" and its effects on the Middle East. In 1964, when the United States Supreme Court was considering the question of the censorship of "obscene" materials, Associate Justice Potter Stewart remarked that he could not define pornography but he knew it when he saw it. The same might be said of modernity: Everyone thinks they know it when they see it, but getting a handle on the concept has not been easy.

The term "modernity" has been in the social science vocabulary since the dawn of the social sciences. Beginning in the eighteenth century, European and North American scholars came to believe there were societies that were "civilized"— that is, had reached the stage of modernity—and other societies that had not yet advanced along the path to civilization. Modern societies, they believed, were those that duplicated the European experience: These societies trusted in science, not superstition; secularism, not religion; freedom, not despotism. As far as the social sciences were concerned, European society was complex and dynamic, while "traditional" society was simple and stagnant. Scholars thus assumed that the evolution of European society and the European form of modernity could serve as a model that could be applied universally. They believed that there was a single path to modernity that every nonmodern society had to tread and from which they could not deviate.

This view of modernity had an unusually long run in the social sciences. It was only recently, when social scientists began questioning many of the assumptions that had guided them in the past, that the consensus about modernity broke down. Some voiced skepticism about some of the fundamental beliefs that had guided the social sciences in the past, such as the belief that there was progress in history or that societies evolve in the same way as biological organisms. Other social scientists pointed out that those who spoke about the scientific, secular, and free nature of Western societies were hopelessly naive, particularly because they idealized some aspects of Western society and disregarded those that were not so appealing. Still others pointed out that applying the European model of modernity universally was simply another example of European narcissism. After all, most social scientists had little or no acquaintance with societies outside Europe and North America—how could they presume to generalize about societies of which they had no knowledge?

But while many social scientists writing today scorn the assumptions of their predecessors, we should be careful not to throw out the baby with the bathwater. Although historians may disagree about a definition of modernity, or even the usefulness of such a concept, almost all would agree that the Middle East underwent widespread social, economic, and cultural changes during the nineteenth century and these changes propelled Middle Eastern societies in an entirely new direction.

The emergence of the contemporary world economic system, beginning in the sixteenth century, and the emergence of a world system of nation-states, beginning in the eighteenth century, fundamentally transformed the trajectory of world history. The world defined by these twinned systems is a world that we might call modern. This is not to say that societies were unchanging before the advent of modernity. There was plenty of change. Nor is it to say that the advent of modernity created a world that was homogeneous. Responses to the emergence of these twinned systems were hardly uniform throughout the world or even within the various states of the world. The attributes of "French modernity" have been, of course, different from the attributes of "Chinese modernity" or "Ottoman modernity." And the attributes of Ottoman modernity were different in Istanbul and Cairo, among rich and poor, town dwellers and their country cousins. Nevertheless, in the modern world the contemporary economic and state systems define the parameters in which every functioning society has to operate.

There were a number of ways in which the modern economic and state systems came to the Middle East. One way that the spread of the modern economic system—the process of integration and peripheralization—took place in the region was by the pull of the international market. Throughout the world, farmers, landlords, and merchants began to orient production and trade toward the international market, where there were profits to be made. But integration and peripheralization could not have taken place had there not been an accompanying political process that propelled the spread of the modern world economy. This political process had many dimensions. Sometimes, European states used diplomatic pressure and gunboat diplomacy to open up markets and keep them open. At other times, rulers of states outside Europe actively sought to participate in the new economic order and restructured their economies to do so.

A similar process encouraged the spread of the world system of nation-states. Sometimes, rulers and would-be rulers of states outside Europe copied European methods of governance and imposed them on their domains. They did this because those methods seemed to provide the most effective means to protect themselves and mobilize and harness the energies of their populations. Taken together, the application of these methods is known as "defensive developmentalism." At other times, European states imposed modern state institutions through bullying and the direct colonization, occupation, or administration of non-European territories. Bullying and the direct colonization, occupation, and administration of non-European territories by Europeans (and others) fit into the category of "imperialism." Both defensive developmentalism and imperialism took place in the Middle East. We are still living with the consequences.

CHAPTER 5

Defensive Developmentalism

As we have seen, the crisis of the seventeenth century had different effects in different regions of the Eurasian continent. Some states connected to the Atlantic economy, such as Britain, the Netherlands, and France, underwent a radical transformation that enabled them to eclipse states such as Spain and the Mediterranean merchant republics. In parts of Eastern Europe, a different transformation took place in the wake of the crisis: the second serfdom. The crisis of the seventeenth century had long-lasting effects in the Middle East as well. Imperial governments stumbled from financial crisis to financial crisis, often seeking cures that were worse than the disease. Warlords asserted themselves against weakened central governments, refused to send taxes or tribute to the imperial capital, and often waged war against representatives of the imperial government and against each other. By the end of the eighteenth century—even before the arrival of Mehmet Ali on the scene—the Ottomans had lost effective control of Egypt. Egypt would remain part of the Ottoman Empire until 1914, but its peculiar history and status within the empire, like that of Tunisia, demand that we treat both separately from our treatment of the rest of the empire. In Persia, the Safavid dynasty, weakened by tribal insurrection, collapsed under the impact of invasion from Afghanistan. Although the Qajars—a family of Turkic descent—established a dynasty that would rule Persia for a century and a half, their control outside their capital of Tehran was, according to many historians, never particularly impressive. All too often the Qajars had to balance off or bargain with local leaders. They were also at the mercy of the British and Russians who fought out the "Great Game" on their territory.

Middle Eastern sultans, shahs, and local dynasts such as Mehmet Ali were not blind to what was going on. Nor were they blind to the fact that the balance of international power had shifted to the West. Thus, beginning in the early nineteenth century, Ottoman sultans, Persian shahs, Egyptian dynasts (later accorded the title khedive in acknowledgment of the special status of Egypt in the empire), and even rulers in far off Tunisia undertook deliberate policies to reverse the process of fragmentation and to centralize and expand their authority. Their goal was to strengthen their states in the face of internal and external threats and to make their governments more proficient in managing their populations and their resources. This process is known as defensive developmentalism.

Once rulers adopted the policy of defensive developmentalism, the process took on a life of its own. In the abstract, the process of defensive developmentalism followed a number of predictable steps. The first step was military reform. This was a logical choice: In both the Ottoman and Qajar empires, leaders understood that they could preserve the independence and unity of their empires only if they were better able to project power internally and protect themselves from foreign aggression. Ottoman sultans and Persian shahs learned from successive military defeats that their military forces were overdue for an overhaul. They therefore sought to borrow recruitment, disciplinary, organizational, tactical, and technological strategies from European states, where armies were more professional and effective. This also stood to reason. Military reforms first introduced into France and Prussia around the turn of the nineteenth century diffused throughout Western Europe and Russia, making European armies not only formidable foes but models to be emulated. Mehmet Ali also began his program of defensive developmentalism with military reform, but for a different reason. The power from which he sought to protect his regime was not European, but the Ottoman Empire. Not only did he hope that military reform would help consolidate the position of his family in Egypt; he sought to use a reformed military to strengthen the position of Egypt in the region. In the case of Tunisia, the threat from both Europe and the Ottoman Empire spurred military reform.

The next steps in the process of defensive developmentalism derive directly from the policy of military reform. To build and support a modern army and defend their territories, Middle Eastern rulers needed to expand the sources of revenue under their control, their ability to coordinate the activities of their populations, and their ability to discipline their populations so that they might act in a manner advantageous to the state. To achieve the first goal, they encouraged the cultivation of cash crops, for example, and tried to restructure tax collection to increase tax revenues. As we shall see, encouraging the cultivation of cash crops may have been penny-wise but turned out to be pound-foolish: To protect their political independence, Middle Eastern rulers were, in effect, mortgaging their future economic independence.

To collect new taxes, man their new armies, and discipline and coordinate the activities of their populations, Middle Eastern rulers needed to eliminate tax farmers and other intermediaries who sapped resources from the state, augment their administrations, introduce uniform legal practice, and educate new administrators and soldiers. They therefore expanded access to education and standardized curricula, promulgated new legal codes, and experimented with centralized economic planning. In sum, defensive developmentalists sought, and often succeeded in building, a state apparatus capable of penetrating the lives of their populations in ways that could not have been implemented, much less imagined, a hundred years before.

Defensive developmentalism was not without its problems, however. All too often the achievements of defensive developmentalist rulers looked more impressive from the vantage point of their palaces in Istanbul, Tehran, or Cairo than they in fact turned out to be. Sometimes plans carefully worked out in the seat of government met with local resistance. Tax farmers, for example, were rarely enthusiastic about programs designed to speed their elimination. Defensive developmentalist policies also fostered the emergence of a new class of professional soldiers, intellectuals, and bureaucrats who were educated in Western techniques. Members of this new class frequently clashed with those who either had a stake in the old order or who believed that the new ways did more harm than good.

In a way, the old guard was correct to be suspicious of the ambitions of members of the new class. The members of the new class were frequently dissatisfied with their position in society. They were educated, but they held little effective power and were rarely consulted at the highest levels of government. During the latter part of the nineteenth century and early twentieth century, members of this new class led or participated in a series of revolts in an attempt to gain access to the corridors of power. Sometimes these revolts were led by civilians who demanded a greater role in governance. They often framed their complaints in the form of a demand for constitutional rule, which, they assumed, would limit the authority of the sultan or shah and delegate more power to them. Hence, intellectuals and bureaucrats led the agitation for an Ottoman constitution, which was granted in 1876, and members of the two groups played a significant role in the Persian Constitutional Revolution of 1905. At other times, professional military officers took matters into their own hands. During one such revolt, spearheaded by Colonel Ahmad ʿUrabi in 1881–1882, the khedive of Egypt felt so threatened that he sought refuge with a British fleet anchored nearby. Another military revolt, led by Turkish army officers in 1908, succeeded in restoring the Ottoman constitution, which had been suspended for thirty years.

Local resistance and the defection of military officers, intellectuals, and bureaucrats were not the only reasons why defensive developmentalist policies might fail. The law of unintended consequences derailed programs as well. The most famous example of this was the Ottoman Land Code of 1858. The code gave peasants the right to register the lands they were working in their own names as private property. The Ottoman government designed the code to increase accountability for taxation, expand agricultural production, and end tax farming. But peasants were, more often than not, suspicious of the motives of the Ottoman government. They feared that the government made this "gift" of land merely to increase their tax burden and that registration would lead to the conscription of their sons into the Ottoman army. As a result, some fled their land, or signed it over to urban-based notables, or soon lost it because they could not afford the registration fee or because they used it as collateral on loans to usurers. In the process, a law intended for entirely different purposes became the instrument by which peasants were frequently reduced to landless tenant farmers and absentee landowners came to possess huge agricultural estates.

As if these problems were not serious enough, defensive developmentalism repeatedly faced opposition from European states as well. Europeans opposed policies that did not serve their immediate economic or strategic interests. For example, many planners in the Middle East hoped to pay for their new armies or other institutions by fostering industry. European states, on the other hand, opposed two key components that defensive developmentalists thought necessary for industrial development: government monopolies and protective tariffs. The establishment of state monopolies in their territories would have allowed Middle Eastern governments to direct and set prices for raw materials used in government factories without the fear that competition from European merchants would drive prices up or deplete their supply. Protective tariffs would have allowed Middle Eastern governments to prevent European manufacturers from destroying local industry by dumping cheaper European products on their markets. Thus, in 1828 the Russians forced the Persians to agree to a ridiculously low 5 percent tariff on goods imported from Russia. At the dawn of the twentieth century, when Russian merchants were still paying their 5 percent tariff on Russian exports to Persia, Persian merchants were paying upward of 20 percent on select commodities. Likewise, in 1838, the British forced the Ottomans to sign a treaty abolishing monopolies in their territories and setting the same ridiculously low—5 percent— tariff on British imports.

Ultimately, the most significant problem with defensive developmentalism in the Middle East was that it was, in a way, counterproductive. For example, to accumulate money to pay for modern armies, rulers expanded the growth of cash crops (cotton, silk, tobacco) that were exported to Europe. They then borrowed money from Europeans to build expensive railroads and modern ports to get those crops to market. Thus, to resist European military expansion, Middle Eastern rulers actually encouraged European economic expansion into, and the further peripheralization of, their domains.

So much for an overview of defensive developmentalism. Let us now turn to the specifics of defensive developmentalism in Egypt and Tunisia, the heartland of the Ottoman Empire, and Persia.

DEFENSIVE DEVELOPMENTALISM IN EGYPT AND TUNISIA

The most striking examples of defensive developmentalism took place in Egypt under the dynasty established by Mehmet Ali and in Tunisia under Ahmad Bey and his successors. For Mehmet Ali, military reform was essential to consolidate his control over Egypt and to protect Egypt's near total autonomy in the Ottoman Empire for himself and his descendants. Furthermore, Mehmet Ali wanted to expand the area under his control to ensure the supply of raw materials crucial to Egypt's economy and development and to monopolize east/west trade routes. Under Mehmet Ali, Egyptian expansion took place in three directions. First, Mehmet Ali sent his armies south into the Sudan to obtain gold, slaves, and control of the west bank of the Red

Sea. When the Ottomans requested his aid in putting down a revolt in Arabia, Mehmet Ali was eager to comply: An Egyptian presence in Arabia would guarantee Egyptian control over the east bank of the Red Sea and thus the lucrative coffee trade (the importance of western Arabia in the coffee trade can be seen in the name of a port city in Yemen—Mocha—that is to this day frequently applied to coffee, with or without the suffix latté). Finally, in 1831, Mehmet Ali's son, Ibrahim, led an expedition into Syria. As discussed earlier, the Ottomans had promised Mehmet Ali control over Syria (present-day Syria, Lebanon, Jordan, Israel, and Palestine, also known as "Greater Syria") if he put down the rebellion in Greece. In reality, Syria was key to Mehmet Ali's plans for the Egyptian economy. Having control of Syria would give Mehmet Ali access to Levantine ports and long-distance trade routes as well as to raw materials such as timber and silk from Mount Lebanon.

While occupying Syria, Ibrahim introduced policies into the region based on those already in place in Egypt. These policies were typical of defensive developmentalists the world over: He conscripted Syrians into armies built on the French model, eliminated tax farming and introduced direct taxation, encouraged the cultivation of cash crops that could be sold abroad to earn foreign exchange, oversaw measures to increase security in the countryside, and ordered the construction of public works to expand agricultural revenues, get cash crops to market quickly, and strengthen central control. Egypt continued to occupy Syria for almost a decade. In 1840, the Ottoman government, with British assistance, was able to reassert its control. The price paid by the Ottomans for British assistance was a high one. In 1838, the Ottomans signed the Treaty of Balta Liman with the British—the treaty that forbade monopolies in Turkish territories and set low import tariffs for foreign goods. The treaty thus furthered the economic penetration of Ottoman territories, including Egypt, by the British.

To support his military adventures abroad, Mehmet Ali undertook new economic policies at home. For example, Mehmet Ali abolished tax farming. He literally destroyed the mamluk tax farmers by inviting them to dinner, killing those who attended, and hunting down the remainder in the provinces of Egypt. Mehmet Ali then confiscated their lands and placed those lands directly under the control of the Egyptian government. He did the same with properties that had been set aside as religious endowments: If the holders of an endowment could not provide the proper documents proving a right to the property, they lost it. Since many religious endowments dated back to the Middle Ages, many holders could not. To eliminate the threat posed by bedouin to settled communities, Mehmet Ali gave them a choice: settle on unused agricultural lands or suffer the same punishment as had the mamluks. Because agriculture was proving to be so profitable anyway, most chose the former.

At the same time, the Egyptian government attempted to control all aspects of agriculture. It encouraged the planting of cash crops, particularly cotton. It set up a government monopoly (abolished, of course, after the Treaty of Balta Liman) that bought cotton from the cultivators and sold it to European agents. It invested in industries associated with cotton, such as ginning and spinning. These changes had important social consequences. Women were put to work in factories spinning and weaving while their husbands were recruited to perform forced labor for the government, such as digging irrigation canals. As a result, government intervention into the economy ended up upsetting established family relations.

Mehmet Ali's encouragement of cotton cultivation further integrated Egypt into the world economic system, and Egyptian revenues became directly dependent on the price of cotton in the international marketplace. In 1800, for example, more than 50 percent of Egypt's trade was with the rest of the Ottoman Empire and 14 percent was with Europe. By 1823, these figures were reversed.

Cotton production proved to be both a blessing and a curse for Egypt. During the American Civil War, the Northern blockade of Southern ports cut off Europe's supply of Confederate cotton and drove prices up. This situation dramatically increased Egyptian revenues and dependency on cotton cultivation. Mehmet Ali's successors, anticipating a lasting boom, borrowed heavily from European bankers to finance internal improvements. One such improvement was the Suez Canal, which was opened in 1869. The Suez Canal was not only an engineering marvel, it reduced by half the distance that merchant ships traveled from London to Bombay. The Egyptian government also built prestige projects, such as an opera house in Cairo. After all, every "civilized" country had at least one opera house. When the American Civil War ended in 1865 and American cotton went on the market again, the price of cotton plummeted. Egyptian revenues collapsed. Then the Egyptian economy received a second shock: the international depression of 1873. By 1876 Egyptian debts had reached more than ninety million British pounds, most of

Ship passing through the Suez Canal soon after its opening. (*From: The Collection of Wolf-Dieter Lemke.*)

which was owed to foreigners. The Egyptian government was forced to declare bankruptcy that same year. European creditors then established a commission to supervise the Egyptian budget and oversee the repayment of Egyptian debt.

It is thus ironic that the policy originally intended to ensure political and economic independence had just the opposite effect. For Egypt, defensive developmentalism led to borrowing, borrowing led to bankruptcy, bankruptcy led to the ᶜUrabi Revolt in 1881, and the ᶜUrabi Revolt—which threatened the British position in the eastern Mediterranean and therefore Britain's route to India—led to British occupation in 1882. British occupation continued, in one form or another, until 1956. Well before that time, Egypt had become an economic satellite revolving around a British star. Adding to the irony was the fact that once they occupied Egypt, the British encouraged the continued cultivation of cotton to feed British textile mills. At the same time, they discouraged investment in industries that might compete with those in Britain.

Mehmet Ali's outsized ambitions for his dynasty and realm found their match in those of his counterpart in Tunisia, Ahmad Bey (1806–1855). Ahmad Bey came to power in 1837. Although nominally vassals of the Ottomans, Tunisian rulers did not pay much attention to orders from Istanbul. Ahmad Bey wanted to keep it that way. Worried about threats from both a potentially reinvigorated Ottoman Empire in the first throes of its defensive developmentalist moment and France, which was thoroughly ensconced in neighboring Algeria, Ahmad Bey, like Mehmet Ali, initiated a defensive developmentalist program of his own by investing heavily in military reform. Ahmad Bey built a 26,000-man conscript army, sent its officers to France for military training, and brought French military instructors to Tunis to drill his soldiers. He also purchased military equipment and ships from France, seeking to use his French connection as a counterweight to his Ottoman overlords, all the while remaining wary of French intentions. His new military received its trial by fire in the Crimean War, where it fought alongside French, British, and Ottoman forces against the Russians. This was not the only step taken by Ahmad Bey to win the favor of potential European predators: He ended the time-honored practice of privateering and, at British insistence, abolished chattel slavery in 1846.

The logic of defensive developmentalism led Ahmad Bey down a similar path as that taken by Mehmet Ali. For example, he overhauled Tunisia's tax system to pay for his military reforms, he invested in infrastructure, and he built a polytechnic university to train bureaucrats and military officers and sent educational missions to Europe. As in the case of Mehmet Ali, his policies proved so effective that he forced the Ottomans to recognize Tunisian autonomy and the hereditary right of his family to rule. And as in the case of Egypt, the cost of defensive developmentalism in Tunisia proved to be its Achilles heel: Measures he and his descendants undertook to build a strong state once again led to borrowing from European creditors, borrowing once again led to bankruptcy, and bankruptcy once again led to the takeover of Tunisia's finances by those creditors and, eventually, to the establishment of Tunisia as a French protectorate.

There is a postscript to the story of Mehmet Ali and Ahmad Bey that is of contemporary relevance. Both initiated state-building programs that were to continue for two centuries, even while their states were under foreign control. This makes Egypt and Tunisia unique among all the contemporary states of the region. In 2010–2011, structures and institutions established and reinforced for decades on end—the military, the judiciary, and later the security apparatus— would define the course of the uprisings there. These enduring structures and institutions, called by political scientists the "deep state," are difficult to dislodge or suppress. During the uprisings, the militaries of Egypt and Tunisia remained intact and deposed autocrats rather than let those autocrats drag down the entire regime with them. And in both places, the deep state not only remained intact, it put a brake on the sort of revolutionary change sought by many of the regime's opponents.

DEFENSIVE DEVELOPMENTALISM
IN THE OTTOMAN HEARTLAND

Defensive developmentalism in the remainder of the Ottoman Empire also produced mixed results. Historians commonly divide the attempts at defensive developmentalism in the Ottoman Empire into two periods. They call the first period the period of "liberal reform," or the *tanzimat* period (*tanzimat* means "regulations" in Turkish). Historians often date this period from 1839, but its roots go back further, as we shall see. The *tanzimat* culminated with the announcement of the short-lived Ottoman constitution of 1876. The second period of defensive developmentalism took place during the long rule of Sultan Abdulhamid II, who suspended the Ottoman constitution in 1878 and once again centered imperial governance in the palace. This period is commonly known as the period of "autocratic reform" and lasted until Abdulhamid II was deposed in 1909.

Unfortunately, the terms "liberal" and "autocratic" are a bit misleading. Actually, both periods were autocratic—constitutionalism should not be equated with democracy, after all, merely with the establishment of a written blueprint that would expand the role of "modernizing" intellectuals and bureaucrats in governance. It is true that during the first period bureaucrats and intellectuals made more of a conscious effort to mimic the institutions and ideas of Europe that were then fashionable. Of particular importance to them were the economic and political ideas associated with British Liberalism—individual rights (for society's elites), free market economics, and respect for private property. And it is true that the rhetoric of Abdulhamid II and his political allies drew from Islam, not Liberalism. But while the thin layer of Ottoman Westernizers may have thought it natural to couch their rhetoric in the rhetoric of British Liberalism, few others were convinced. Many embraced the idea of defensive developmentalism but found the principles of Liberalism to be distasteful. Others argued that Liberalism provided an insufficient basis for imperial revival. By the late 1870s, many Ottoman political elites had discovered a new model to emulate: the model provided by political developments in Germany and Italy after each had achieved unification in 1870–1871. This model emphasized governmental activism and change imposed from the top. And, if measured in terms of efficacy, far more development and government expansion took place in the latter period than in the former.

The Ottoman Empire that defensive developmentalists had inherited was hardly capable of swimming with the European sharks. Instead of power being concentrated in Istanbul, the influence of local notables often surpassed the power emanating from the central government. Even in those regions where the state could exercise power, however, it often did not do so, choosing instead to allow the population to organize its own affairs through informal networks. During the nineteenth century, the state not only attempted to curb the powers of local leaders, but also to expand its own authority into areas where government had never before intruded, such as education and social welfare.

Of course, military reform was of primary concern to the nineteenth-century Ottoman sultans. Sultan Selim III (r. 1789–1807) established a new military corps, known as the *nizam-i jedid* (new order), that adopted Western forms of drill and armament. By 1806, the corps included about twenty-four thousand trained soldiers. While Selim III was forced to abdicate by those opposed to his policies, including a jealous janissary corps, one of his successors, Mahmud II (r. 1808–1839) continued his efforts. In what became known as the "Auspicious Incident" (1826) to everyone but the janissaries, Mahmud II used the new corps to wipe out the janissaries in Istanbul and then hunt down remaining janissaries in the provinces. The achievements of Ottoman military reforms were such that they were mimicked in the Egypt of Mehmet Ali.

The creation of an effective army gave Mahmud II and his successors greater leeway in introducing new policies. Over the course of the nineteenth century, the Ottoman government legislated (unsuccessfully, as it turned out) against tax farming, restructured the central bureaucracy along European lines, and established provincial councils based on representative principles. It codified law and extended the authority of secular law. It established schools that took children after Qur'an training and prepared them for Western-style colleges. By the end of the nineteenth century, Istanbul hosted a school to educate bureaucrats, another to "civilize" the children of tribal leaders, and a third to train military officers. In all, by the beginning of the twentieth century more than thirty-five thousand Ottoman civil servants managed activities commonly associated with modern nation-states, from the administration of hospitals to the construction and maintenance of essential infrastructure.

As in the case of Egypt, the state increasingly assumed responsibility for directing the economy as well. Over the course of the nineteenth century, the Ottoman Empire backed away from the stranglehold of free trade that had done so much to integrate it into the world economy. The imperial government intervened directly to promote the economic development of the empire. Sometimes, government policy failed miserably. Attempts to establish state-run factories floundered not only because the Ottomans faced Western competition and shortages of skilled workers, but also because the empire suffered from a lack of investment capital. As a result, the state turned instead to programs that were intended to foster private industrial production. By the end of the century, the state had reorganized the guilds, assembled cooperative associations, offered tax breaks to entrepreneurs, set production standards, and raised customs duties. The Ottoman state attempted to attract foreign investment capital by offering concessions for building telegraph lines, railroads, and tramways and for expanding port facilities in Istanbul and Beirut. The Ottoman state also attempted to address the international agricultural crisis that began in the 1870s by establishing agricultural schools and issuing credits and seed to impoverished farmers. It even sent teams of agronomists out to the countryside to offer agricultural advice to peasants.

Whatever the efforts of the state, however, the effects of Ottoman defensive developmentalism were uneven. The nineteenth-century Ottoman Empire included Anatolia, the Balkans, parts of North Africa, and the Arab Middle East. The empire was so widespread that it was difficult for the power of the central government to radiate out through the provinces, even with the use of nineteenth-century technologies such as telegraphs and railroads. The diversity of the land and its peoples also obstructed the success of even the best-laid plans. Compare the Ottoman Empire with Egypt, a province that was relatively homogeneous both demographically and geographically. It was far easier for Cairo to dictate economic policy, especially because Egyptian soil and climate allowed it to base its economy on the cultivation and export of a few cash crops, particularly cotton. In contrast, the needs of Lebanese silk producers, as well as the organization of their communities, differed dramatically from those of the cotton producers of nearby Palestine, not to mention those of tobacco cultivators of the Balkans. Ottoman dependence on a variety of cash crops was hardly an effective economic strategy anyway. As in the cases of Egypt and Tunisia, the cost of defensive developmentalism combined with the international depression of 1873 eventually led to bankruptcy and to European supervision of Ottoman finances.

Furthermore, as might be expected, the Ottoman government faced resistance to its policies. In addition to the "losers" in the process of defensive developmentalism—janissaries and tax farmers—specific imperial policies were regarded by too many as a threat. Ultimately, defensive developmentalism meant centralization, and centralization threatened the pivotal role played by informal, local networks in Ottoman life. For peasants, the policies of the imperial government threatened to bring about more efficient taxation and conscription. For ulama who were not attached to the central bureaucracy, the policies threatened to bring about a loss of prestige and limit their educational and judicial functions. For local notables, the policies meant loss of power. Because of this local resistance, many of the regulations failed to achieve the intended goals.

One of the most glaring examples of how Ottoman policies yielded unanticipated results had to do with the attempt to redefine what it meant to be an Ottoman and to adjust the relationship among religious communities. During the *tanzimat*, the Ottoman government issued two decrees that many historians

---

Vignette

"What Hath God Wrought"

According to legend, in 1815 the financier Nathan Mayer Rothschild received news of the outcome of the Battle of Waterloo before his financial competitors. The news enabled him to secure his family's sizeable fortune with a timely investment in British, as opposed to French, government bonds. The means of communication between Belgium and Britain that gave Rothschild a jump on the competition? The carrier pigeon.

The story is apocryphal, but it speaks to a Britain in which long-distance communication was still carried on through semaphore relays. By 1851 Rothschild's ploy would have been impossible: He and his competitors would have received news of the outcome of the Battle of Waterloo within minutes, via the newly laid submarine telegraph cable linking France and Britain (France permitting, of course).

Samuel F. B. Morse invented the telegraph in 1837. The first words transmitted long distance provide the title for this vignette. The telegraph rapidly became as conventional a presence in the nineteenth century as the cell phone is today. And like other nineteenth-century inventions—steamboats and railroads and the Gatling gun—the telegraph proved to be an indispensable tool of imperialism. As a matter of fact, it was imperialism that provided the impetus for the construction of telegraph lines in the Ottoman Empire and Persia.

In 1857, India exploded in rebellion against the British. The subcontinent was nearly lost to Britain before anyone in London was even aware that trouble was brewing. So soon after, the British asked for, and were granted, concessions from the Ottoman and Persian governments to construct a telegraph line through their territories in order to connect Britain with its recalcitrant colony. For Britain, the

---

consider the cornerstones of the period of "liberal reform," the *Hatt-i Sharif* of Gulhane (1839) and the *Islahat Fermani* (1856). The documents promised all Ottoman subjects "perfect security for life, honor, and property," among other things, and offered religious liberty and equality for the non-Muslim inhabitants of the empire. In other words, the *Hatt-i Sharif* of Gulhane and the *Islahat Fermani* were attempts to promote a notion of Ottoman identity, *osmanlilik*. Henceforth, it was hoped, the empire would consist of a community of equal *citizens* (not just "subjects of the sultan") bound together by a common set of rights and responsibilities and an allegiance that transcended their religious allegiances.

Ottoman citizens quickly latched on to the idea that they were promised rights, and quite a number took advantage of that idea by petitioning the sultan whenever they felt those rights betrayed (most were not as keen on the idea of responsibilities, however). But for all its good intentions, a policy that attempted to establish equality among Ottoman citizens satisfied few Muslims or Christians. Muslim political and social elites resented a policy that threatened Muslim predominance and that was so obviously European in inspiration (in fact, the *Islahat Fermani* was dictated to the Ottoman government by the British ambassador to Istanbul, Stratford Canning, to make the Ottomans more sympathetic to a nation

upshot was predictable: enhanced imperial control. For Persia, it was less so, but nonetheless consequential: To allocate royalties and responsibilities, telegraph construction necessitated the demarcation of exact borders separating Persia from the Ottoman Empire, British India, and Afghanistan. The Indo-European Telegraph Department, a branch of the British government in India, surveyed and delineated those borders. As a result, the Persian piece was, at long last, fit into the jigsaw puzzle of the international state system, and the clear demarcation of Persia's territorial sovereignty—the hallmark of the modern state system—received international sanction. Persia's admission into the International Telegraph Union in 1869—the first such international coordinating body—followed, confirming Persia's place within the brotherhood of nations.

In the Ottoman Empire, the telegraph rapidly became an essential tool of state. By 1874, when there were approximately 17,000 miles of telegraph line in the empire, an American missionary hailed the Ottoman postal-telegraph for "enabling the central power in Constantinople to move the whole empire like a machine." But telegraph wires run both ways. Since the line to which the missionary was referring emanated from the palace, the telegraph came to symbolize for much of the populace a direct link to the sultan. Petitions poured into Istanbul from all over the empire complaining of mistreatment at the hands of local officials and landlords. Crowds even mobbed local telegraph stations demanding to be put in direct touch with a sultan who was responsible for ensuring their newly acquired rights. And the telegraph was a site for symbolic resistance as well: In remote corners of the empire, villagers expressed their disaffection by interrupting telegraph service, and bedouin and others estranged from Istanbul targeted for destruction the lines that symbolized, for both them and their government, imperial reach.

---

that had just fought on its behalf in the Crimean War). Muslim elites objected to the fact that the documents seemed to single out Christian communities for special consideration and opened the door to granting them economic and political privileges that Muslims did not enjoy. Many Christians were not pleased that the notion of equality was applied in such areas as military conscription—a privilege of citizenship most Christians would have just as readily forgone. Their protests once again enabled Christians to avoid military service through the payment of a fee, an option not open to their increasingly resentful Muslim fellow citizens. Other Christians, looking to developments in the Balkans, preferred the path of nationalist separation rather than equality within a predominantly Muslim empire. And the fact that the documents opened the door for would-be leaders of "aggrieved" minority communities to make claims on the sultan for rights real or imagined hardly served the cause of intercommunal harmony. It is thus ironic that the policy of promising equality to all inhabitants of the empire, regardless of religious affiliation, hardened communal boundaries and precipitated instances of intercommunal violence. In the process, it contributed to the distinctly modern phenomenon of sectarianism that is all too familiar to observers of the contemporary Middle East.

DEFENSIVE DEVELOPMENTALISM IN PERSIA

The Persian experience with defensive developmentalism was different from that of either Egypt or the Ottoman Empire. Historians commonly cite two reasons for this. The first was the nature of Qajar rule. The Qajar dynasty was of recent vintage, having established itself more than two centuries after the founding of the Ottoman Empire. Unlike the Ottoman Empire, it did not build an empire from scratch, but rather on the ruins of the Safavid Empire. An entirely new political and social order thus did not accompany conquest as it had with the Ottomans. In addition, the ruins upon which the Qajars established their rule were extensive. As a result of the Afghan invasion that finished off Safavid rule, it is estimated that approximately 20 percent of the population of the Safavid Empire died, while the cities of Persia lost upward of two-thirds of their population. And the Afghan invasion was hardly the only disaster to strike Persia during the eighteenth century.

Not only was the Qajar dynasty new, relatively untested, and heir to a devastated land, but Persia suffered from the ill fortune of being the site on which two stronger powers waged their struggle. Occasionally, Persia did benefit from the presence of rival imperialist powers on its borders. For example, Britain introduced the first telegraph line in Persia during the mid-1860s because it needed fast communications from India to London, and Persia happened to be situated in between. And sometimes the British-Russian rivalry itself left its trace on Persia: In 1891, three years after the British established the first modern bank in Persia, the Russians simply had to follow suit. But, for the most part, the "Great Game" blocked the introduction of nineteenth-century technologies and institutions into Persia. Both Britain and Russia discouraged the Persian government from seeking technical assistance or loans from their rival. For example, neither power was enthusiastic about the other building a north-south railroad in Persia for obvious reasons, so that project had to wait until 1927. There is a cruel irony here. For all its evils, in most of the world imperialism fostered institutions and infrastructure, if only to expand the reach of the imperialist power and integrate the colonized into the world economy. In Persia it all too often had the opposite effect.

If the Qajars did suffer from such internal and external challenges, then how were they able to rule for so long? The answer, according to many historians, was that they never quite ruled at all. Historians cite the fact that throughout Qajar history, governors were powerless outside the provincial capitals and local communities were virtually autonomous. The Qajars maintained their position, the argument goes, by balancing off various factions within society: tribe against tribe, province against province, region against region, social class against social class. Qajar rule was minimalist. Unlike the Safavids, the Qajars only intervened in the economy to prevent urban insurrections when prices rose too high or shortages threatened. They also allowed others to run the economy: They auctioned off governorships to the highest bidders, who then farmed out tax collection in districts and cities. They also auctioned off the right to collect customs

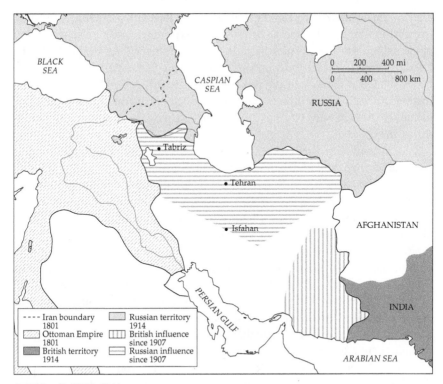

Qajar Persia, 1800–1914

and mint coins to the highest bidder. By 1850, the Qajars even lost control over the lands that had been granted as *tiyul*. This land became the virtual private property of merchants, ulama, and high officials. Their inability to project power meant that the Qajar shahs could only respond feebly to those religious scholars who resisted the government because it attempted to usurp their legal and educational functions, landowners who were unappreciative of government efforts to streamline tax collection and keep better track of titles to land, and merchants who feared they could not compete in international trade with foreigners backed by their governments.

This is not to say that the Qajar dynasty did not take a stab at defensive developmentalism. In fact, it tried twice, once during the mid-nineteenth century and a second time in the 1870s. Under the direction of two centralizing chief ministers, the government attempted to construct state-run factories, reform the budget, build a modern military based on conscription rather than tribal levies, and build modern educational facilities. Their efforts failed, with two notable exceptions. The first was the Dar al-Funun, a school founded in 1851 to train military officers and bureaucrats. At its peak at the end of the nineteenth century, the Dar al-Funun admitted roughly 250 students each year. Many of the graduates of the school chafed at what they considered Qajar despotism and inefficiency.

They would later participate in the Constitutional Revolution of 1905. The second institution founded during the brief Persian experiment with defensive developmentalism was the Cossack Brigade, an elite military force originally led by Russian officers. The brigade, under the leadership of Reza Khan, would overthrow the Qajar dynasty in the wake of World War I. Ironically, then, the two institutions with lasting impact that were founded during the defensive developmentalist periods were two institutions that weakened, then eventually overthrew, the Qajars.

Because of their limited control over the country, the Qajars attempted to generate revenues and hasten development by granting concessions to European financiers and adventurers. That is, the Qajars attempted to encourage "modernization," raise quick cash, or do both by selling select Europeans the right to produce, market, and export a commodity or commodities found in Persia. They also sold concessions for one or another infrastructural project that required capital and know-how unavailable domestically. The Qajars were not the only ones in the Middle East to grant concessions to Europeans. Both the Ottoman Empire and Egypt also did it: Germans built the railroads in Anatolia, for example, and French concessionaires did the same in Syria. The Suez Canal was also a concession. But the Persian case was different for two reasons. First, when it came to defensive developmentalism, there really wasn't much else going on. Second, there was the scope of the concessions granted.

In 1872, for example, the Persian shah granted Baron Julius de Reuter, a British subject, the exclusive rights to build streetcars and railroads, extract minerals, establish a national bank, and exploit the national forests in exchange for a

Members of the Cossack Brigade posing for photographer. Date unknown. (*From: The Collection of Wolf-Dieter Lemke.*)

modest down payment and the promise of future royalties. Lord Curzon called what came to be known as the Reuter Concession "the most complete and extraordinary surrender of the entire industrial resources of a kingdom into foreign hands that has probably ever been dreamed of, much less accomplished, in history." Because the Reuter Concession met opposition in Persia and was hardly pleasing to the Russians, the shah canceled it. Reuter retained the right to build the state bank of Persia, which financed the government, and, of course, did not walk away from an indemnity of forty thousand British pounds that the Persian government had to pay as a penalty. It should not be surprising, then, that after the Reuter Concession the Persian government never again granted a concession simply to foster modernization.

But this did not stop the Persian government from granting concessions altogether. In 1890, after bribing the right Persian officials, a British adventurer acquired from the shah the right to control the cultivation, sale, distribution, and export of all Persian tobacco and tobacco products for fifty years—all for an annual payment of fifteen thousand British pounds and a quarter of the anticipated profits. Soon afterward, he sold these rights to the Imperial Tobacco Company of Britain. The announcement of the concession aroused opposition from several layers of Persian society, particularly from merchants. By the time of the Tobacco Concession, merchants were already suffering. With the onset of the Depression of 1873, both trade and the price cash crops fetched on the international market had fallen. In addition, Persian merchants found it difficult to compete with European merchants, who had better organizational and financial backing and who paid lower customs duties. Soon after the government granted the concession, merchants in Tehran, then in other cities, began to protest and urge a boycott of tobacco. They were joined by the leading ulama of Isfahan, where merchant power was concentrated. Although the higher ranking ulama in Tehran were tied financially to the court and therefore initially opposed the merchants' actions, they could not stay out of the fray once merchants began to present their case in religious terms and circulate the rumor that the most important religious scholar in Persia had issued a ruling banning the consumption of tobacco. The cleric, seeing the strength of the protest, did not disavow it.

Once again, the shah canceled the concession. Once again, there was a penalty. This time, the cost of cancellation was 346,000 British pounds. To pay the indemnity, the shah contracted the first foreign loans ever borrowed by a shah of Persia, to the tune of 500,000 British pounds. This, of course, created huge deficits for the Persian government, which necessitated more foreign borrowing.

But there was another penalty to be paid by the Persian government as well. The popular mobilization against the tobacco concession set a precedent for future mobilizations against the government. In the future, all successful mobilizations would be built on alliances of various social classes united by a broad and vague ideology that often used religious symbols. Of course, none of these mobilizations were religious per se, nor were they actually led by clerics—until, that is, clerics seized control over the Iranian Revolution in 1979. Shiʿism was not a cause of these revolts. To the contrary, like most other revolts, these arose from a diverse set of grievances. Nevertheless, Shiʿism provided a unifying language and set of symbols, and the involvement of Shiʿi clerics would lend legitimacy to revolts in Persia for the next century.

Perhaps the concession that had the most significance for the future of Persia—and, indeed, for the rest of the Middle East—was granted to an Anglo-Australian adventurer, William Knox d'Arcy. In 1901 the Persian government granted d'Arcy the right to "obtain, exploit, develop, render suitable for trade, carry away and sell" petroleum and petroleum products from all of Persia (except for five northern provinces) in exchange for forty thousand pounds in cash and stock and 16 percent of his company's annual profits. The British admiralty, seeking to convert its navy from coal to oil, saw the strategic value of this concession. (When criticized in Parliament for acting against the traditions of the British navy, the vice lord of the admiralty, Winston Churchill, reportedly responded acidly that the only traditions of the British navy were "rum, sodomy, and the lash.") To prevent d'Arcy from selling the concession to the French, the British government bought the concession and created the Anglo-Persian Oil Company. This was the first oil concession granted in the Middle East and provided the model for all others that followed. By 1923, Winston Churchill would claim that the concession had earned Great Britain forty million British pounds, while the concession earned Persia a mere two million. Little wonder that it served Western oil companies as an archetype.

* * *

Overall, then, what were the effects of defensive developmentalism in Egypt and Tunisia, the Ottoman Empire, and Persia? If success in centralization and the spread of governmental authority into previously unregulated areas of society are the criteria, then it is possible to claim that defensive developmentalism succeeded best in Egypt and Tunisia, then the Ottoman Empire, but met with very modest success in Persia. However, the purpose of defensive developmentalism was to defend Middle Eastern states from Western political and economic intrusion, and in this the effort failed. During the nineteenth century, the Ottoman Empire lost most of its Balkan and North African territories, Egypt was subjected to British occupation, the French made Tunisia a protectorate, and in 1907 Britain and Russia conspired to divide Persia into spheres of influence. Economically, some measures—encouraging the cultivation of cash crops, foreign borrowing, and the construction of networks of communication and transportation—actually facilitated Western economic penetration of the region. Even the establishment of "modern" educational, legal, and governmental structures in the Middle East advanced the integration of the region into the modern world economy. After all, in the wake of Ottoman legal reforms European merchants doing business in Salonika or Alexandria could trust in the fact that they would be subject to a uniform set of regulations that often corresponded to those found in Europe.

But there was another lasting legacy of defensive developmentalism that bears mentioning as well. Even when they misfired, measures taken by defensive developmentalists—conscripting soldiers, standardizing education, nurturing economic development, and even promoting ideologies like *osmanlilik*—had important consequences. Defensive developmentalists engaged their populations in common activities, organized and disciplined those populations, and spread new conceptions about the role of the state in society and the responsibilities of the state and the populations it governed toward each other. Some defensive developmentalists were, of course, more successful in these endeavors than others. Nevertheless, by transferring the notion of the state first invented in eighteenth-century Europe to the Middle East, defensive developmentalists were instrumental in spreading the principles of the modern state and modern state system to the region.

CHAPTER 6

Imperialism

Defensive developmentalism and integration and peripheralization were not the only means by which the structures of governance and economics associated with the modern period were introduced into the Middle East. There was also imperialism. Historians and political scientists have yet to agree on a definition of imperialism. However, a good starting point is the definition provided by a scholar of the subject, Ronald Robinson. According to Robinson, "Imperialism . . . is a process whereby agents of an expanding society gain inordinate influence or control over the vitals of weaker societies by . . . diplomacy, ideological suasion, conquest and rule, or by planting colonies of its own peoples abroad." One of the key concepts in this definition is contained in the phrase "gain inordinate influence or control over the vitals of weaker societies." This differentiates modern imperialism from the acquisitions-of-land-through-conquest that took place in history prior to the modern period. True, pre-modern conquerors sometimes transformed social and economic relations in the societies they conquered. For example, once free populations might be reduced to slavery. But modern imperialism had a singular and inevitable effect: In the aftermath of the eighteenth-century industrial revolution, imperialism compelled the integration of targeted societies into the modern world economy. In the process, new economic and political structures and new forms of social organization compatible with the modern world economy emerged in those societies, whether as a result of conscious design on the part of imperialist powers or as an unforeseen consequence of their intrusion. In other words, wherever European imperialists set foot, they left behind market economies and the framework for modern states.

Europeans used all the methods identified by Ronald Robinson—diplomacy, ideological suasion, conquest and rule, planting colonies—at one time or another, in one place or another, in the Middle East. For the most part, European imperialism in the heartland of the Ottoman Empire and Persia was carried out in two ways. The first was by economic penetration carried out through investments, concessions, loans, and the creation of spheres of influence. The second was by diplomatic coercion, through which Europeans acquired capitulatory rights or forced treaties favorable to their interests on weaker states. The concessions extracted from the Persian government are a good example of the former, the Treaty of Balta Liman an example of the latter.

While the methods Europeans employed in the heartland of the Ottoman Empire and Persia might have been similar, the reasons they employed them differed. Since the mid-nineteenth century, the Ottoman Empire was part of the concert of Europe and, as such, enjoyed (at least in theory) the same sovereign rights as any other member of the concert, such as Britain, France, and Russia. While excuses could always be found to violate Ottoman sovereignty on the fringes of empire, European diplomats maintained the fiction that the Ottoman Empire was equal in status to other members of the concert. In the case of Persia, neither Britain nor Russia could acquire territory without violating the rules of the "Great Game." This did not, however, prevent Russia from continuing its conquest of the Caucasus and pushing the boundaries of its empire to the Persian frontier. On the whole, however, European penetration of the Ottoman heartland and Persia did not involve the formal acquisition of territory.

And here it is important to differentiate between two types of empire: informal and formal. While the former comes about as a result of economic penetration and diplomacy, for example, the latter comes about through conquest and annexation of territory, the implantation of colonies, and the like. In the end, though, both forms of empire set out to achieve the same goal; that is, to enable a stronger power to dominate a weaker one politically, economically, or both. Since an informal empire is cheaper to implement than a formal one, imperial powers prefer the former to the latter. Ronald Robinson and his collaborator, John Gallagher, masters of pithy aphorisms, once wrote that, as a rule of thumb, imperial powers obeyed the following maxim when expanding overseas: "Informally if possible and formally if necessary."

There are three conditions that make formal empire necessary. Informal empires only work if there are people abroad who are willing to collaborate voluntarily with the imperial power. They do so because it is in their interest. These people might be rulers or political elites, local merchants, or emigrants from the imperial power who set up shop elsewhere. When there are no willing collaborators, or when for some reason or other the collaborative relationship ends, imperial powers can only get what they set out to get by going in. The second reason imperial powers construct formal empires is to prevent a potential European rival from acquiring access to that territory for themselves. This was the main reason for the Scramble for Africa. Finally, there is what might be termed the "wild card" factor. Italy "needed" territory in North Africa to demonstrate it had reached the rank of a great power and to unify its quarrelsome citizens by undertaking a bold adventure abroad. Hence, their annexation of territory that would later become Libya. And come to think of it, why did the United States wake up one morning in 1898 and decide it had to wrest the Philippines, Puerto Rico, and Guam from the decaying Spanish Empire?

In the Middle East, formal empire took various forms. The British invaded and occupied Egypt in 1882, although they did not formally establish it as a colony or annex it. France and Italy annexed territories in North Africa (the future Algeria and Libya) and opened them up for settlement by Europeans. But strangely, there was only one formal colony in the entire Middle East: Aden, on the southern tip of the Arabian peninsula, which a local ruler ceded to the British in 1838. The British landed marines there the next year as part of their efforts to suppress piracy on the route to India; later on, it served them as a coaling station. Along with adjoining territories, it became independent in 1967 and joined with North Yemen in 1990 to become part of the Republic of Yemen.

In addition to informal and formal imperialism in the Middle East, there was a third way Europeans exerted their influence in the region that might be considered midway between the other two forms of imperialism: the protectorate. Europeans established protectorates on the fringes of the Ottoman Empire wherever inter-European rivalries prevented one or another state from establishing formal colonies or where an imperialist power's goals might be achieved without the expense of establishing a formal colony (to cite Robinson and Gallagher one final time, empire is not worth having unless it could be had "on the cheap").

We discussed the French and Spanish protectorates in North Africa in Chapter 4, but the British established protectorates as well, in the Gulf. Once again, their main motivation was to protect the route to India by suppressing piracy and by establishing special relationships with local rulers that would bind them to Britain. To this end, the British picked from among the prominent families of a given territory to establish a ruling dynasty. The fortunate families were more than happy to oblige the British, who demanded little in return but devotion. Hence, the British invented royal houses that still rule Kuwait, Qatar, and the United Arab Emirates (the UAE—called the Trucial States before their independence in 1971 because they pledged a "perpetual maritime truce" in the Gulf). The British also recognized the rulers of Bahrain, which they also made a protectorate, and Oman, which they didn't. If anyone were to wonder why there are so many kingdoms in the Gulf—six, to be exact—it is not because of oil, it is not because of tradition, and it is not because Arabs naturally follow patriarchal leaders. It's because British imperialism created them and the British (and later the Americans) guaranteed their sovereignty.

The remainder of this chapter will explore three case studies in imperialism in the region, chosen because they demonstrate how European imperialism integrated colonized space into the world economy, transplanted European-style institutions abroad, and transformed political and cultural relations among those who were on its receiving end. The cases are Algeria, Egypt, and Lebanon.

ALGERIA: A SETTLER PLANTATION COLONY

During the nineteenth century, Algeria was transformed from an Ottoman territory into a French one. Before the French sent their fleet to Algeria in 1830, Algeria had been virtually autonomous within the Ottoman Empire. It was ruled by locally chosen Ottoman governors called deys. For most of the Ottoman period, the main source of local revenue came from piracy. By the end of the eighteenth century, however, Mediterranean piracy had seen better days. Not only had European states become quite adept at projecting their power onto the seas, but they had become increasingly intolerant of what was, in effect, an extortion racket practiced by pirates and their North African sponsors.

As revenues from larceny, the ransoming of captives, and the sale of protection to European governments seeking to safeguard their merchants decreased, the authority of the dey and the dey's government weakened. Around the same time, the French adopted their Mediterranean strategy—the same strategy behind Napoleon's expedition to Egypt. As a matter of fact, although dead for almost a decade, Napoleon was in a way responsible for the French invasion and colonization of Algeria as well as the invasion and occupation of Egypt. While in Egypt, French forces had bought Algerian grain, and the French debt to Algeria remained a sore spot between the two governments for decades afterward. During one particularly grueling round of negotiations about the debt, the exasperated dey of Algeria hit the French consul with a flyswatter. The French government used the famous "fly-whisk incident" to launch a naval campaign against Algeria. The campaign began with a naval blockade and culminated in the French occupation of the Algerian capital, Algiers, in 1830. In 1848, the French integrated Algeria into France as three French *départements* (provinces). In the eyes of the French government, Algeria was France. It remained so for over one hundred years.

European settlers came to Algeria for both political and economic reasons. The French government used Algeria as a convenient place to dump political dissidents, particularly those who had fought in the French Revolution of 1848 or who had participated in the Paris Commune of 1871. But it would have been impossible to build a settler economy with political dissidents alone. During the nineteenth century, the population of southern Europe grew faster than its resource base, creating wide-scale impoverishment. Many from the region emigrated abroad, including numerous southern Italians, who came to the United States. Others—not only French, but Italians and Spanish as well—headed for Algeria.

In addition to impoverished peasants seeking a fresh start beyond the reach of their landlords, workers and artisans from southern Europe were drawn to Algeria by the lure of employment. Prospects for employment were good in Algeria because colonial outposts like Algeria provided lucrative investment opportunities for Europeans during the nineteenth century. Since risk was high and liquidity (the amount of money available locally) low in European colonies, the possibility that European investors would earn a sizable return on their investments was also high. Money flooded into those companies that promoted ventures associated with colonial economies, such as the construction of ports, roads, telegraph lines, and the like. The Algerian rail system dates from 1857—it was constructed at around the same time as the rail system in European France. These projects allowed colonizers to open up new areas of Algeria for cash cropping, speed crops to European markets, and maintain control over far reaches of the countryside. The construction of such projects required skilled and semiskilled workers. By the outbreak of World War I, there were approximately seven hundred thousand European settlers in Algeria—the vast majority of whom had actually been born there. They, rather than the almost five million Muslim inhabitants of the territory, controlled both political and economic institutions.

To accommodate these settlers and attract European capital to Algeria, the French government seized religious endowments, lands owned by the dey, pasture lands used by nomads, and abandoned urban property. Lands previously held by non-European inhabitants of Algeria became the property of European specula- tors and entrepreneurs who consolidated them into plantations for the cultivation of crops bound for the export market—grain, cotton (particularly during the American Civil War), tobacco, even flowers. (Plantations are large tracts of land that are devoted to a single crop [monoculture] grown for the market.)

During the 1870s, when the wine industry in France was virtually decimated by a parasite that ate the roots of grapevines, speculators and entrepreneurs with holdings in Algeria began expanding grape cultivation to take advantage of the shortfall. By 1914, one-third of Algerian exports was wine. The expansion of the plantation system squeezed out European settlers with small landholdings. At the same time, plantation owners hired the indigenous inhabitants of Algeria to work for low wages as seasonal laborers on their plantations. Others who had become landless or who owned plots that were too small for subsistence flocked to cities where they became day laborers or joined the ranks of the unemployed. Overall, then, French imperialism in Algeria encouraged the spread of market relations, disrupted rural life, and increased the population of towns and cities.

The integration of Algeria into the French political and economic system had other effects that no French policy maker could have foreseen in 1830. French poli- cies in Algeria resembled those of other imperial states elsewhere inasmuch as the French justified their activities by claiming that they brought civilization to the benighted natives—what the French called their civilizing mission (*mission civil- isatrice*). At the same time, however, European settlers and their descendants had access to rights of citizenship that no Muslim Algerian could hope to attain. As we shall discuss in Chapter 13, the integration of Algeria into the "civilized world"— what was, in fact, the integration of Algeria into the modern world economic and state systems—made the emergence of Algerian nationalism possible; the differen- tiation between European French citizens and Algerians on the basis of race or language or religion made the emergence of Algerian nationalism likely.

That likelihood was increased after the outbreak of World War I in 1914. During the war French industrial workers were conscripted into the French army. To take their place, seventy-six thousand Algerians went to metropolitan France to work in factories there. By 1950, their numbers had swelled to over six hundred thousand. Another 173,000 fought in the French army during World War I (about twenty-five thousand died). A number of these Algerians joined trade unions, communist organizations, and emigrant societies that nurtured political activists and introduced them to the latest techniques for political orga- nization and agitation. Beginning in the late 1920s, groups of emigrant workers in France and former emigrant workers in Algeria began to form associations that demanded Algerian independence. Between 1954 and 1962, Algerians, under the leadership of the FLN (*Front de libération nationale*, the National Liberation Front), fought an extremely bloody war for Algerian independence from France—a war in which over one million Algerians died. The FLN rules Algeria to this day. Its rule has hardly been unchallenged, however: In 1992, when the FLN annulled the results of elections it had lost to its Islamist opponents, Algeria once again descended into war.

Besides the economic and social repercussions of integrating Algeria into the global economy, the Algerian saga is important for a number of reasons. French administrators trained in Algeria provided expertise for the French in other parts of the Middle East, including Lebanon and Syria, which the French came to control after World War I. (India played a similar role for the British, and many a British administrator in Egypt, Iraq, and elsewhere in the Middle East had cut his teeth in the Indian civil service.) Algeria also provided the model for a second, less successful attempt to implant a settler-plantation colony in the Middle East. Seeking to replicate the Algerian example, the French financier and philanthropist Baron Edmund de Rothschild financed settler-plantation colonies in Palestine beginning in 1882. Rothschild's plan called for European Jews to emigrate to Palestine and establish and oversee plantations for the cultivation of citrus, almonds, and, particularly, grapes for wine. (Anyone who has drunk Levantine wine can only be thankful that Rothschild's experiment failed, even though he imported administrators who had gained experience in Algeria.) By 1900 Rothschild had lost patience with his experiment and withdrew his support, and within a few years about two-thirds of the Jewish agricultural workers had left Palestine. Although Jewish immigration to Palestine would expand over the course of the next century, the attempt to establish a plantation system in Palestine that would integrate Jewish and Arab labor was never attempted again.

Besides providing the model for settler-plantation colonies elsewhere, Algeria provided another model as well. During the 1950s and 1960s, the Algerian independence struggle became both a rallying point and a model for other revolutionary struggles throughout the world. Here's what Malcolm X had to say about Algeria in a speech to an African American audience in 1963:

> The Algerians were revolutionists, they wanted [their] land. France offered to let them be integrated into France. They told France, to hell with France, they wanted some land, not some France. And they engaged in a bloody battle. . . . Revolution is in Asia, revolution is in Africa, and the white man is screaming because he sees revolution in Latin America. How do you think he'll react to you when you learn what a real revolution is?

But if the Algerian struggle for independence provided the blueprint for revolutionary struggles throughout what became known as the "Third World" during the period of decolonization, its legacy was not without a downside. Sure, the Algerian struggle succeeded in removing foreign control from Algeria (although if the FLN had lost, that control would not have been considered foreign and what is now called a war of national liberation would have been called a French civil war). But at what cost? The Algerian war coarsened Algerian political culture. Other national liberation movements, like the Palestine Liberation Organization, adopted the "cult of armed struggle" from the Algerians, believing that national liberation could only come at the point of a gun. This sidelined the vast majority of the population while glorifying the fighters—their liberators—preventing the engagement of that population in the day-to-day spadework necessary for nation-building. The result in Algeria and elsewhere was what one might expect: To this day the military and those the military has brought into their inner circle make up what Algerians call "*le pouvoir*" (the power)—unelected powerbrokers who really run the show. It is no coincidence that Fatah—the largest of the Palestinian guerrilla factions whose leaders retired their revolutionary fatigues and adopted business suits—has done the same in the West Bank which it rules, while most of the population observes their power-brokering and deal-making from the outside.

We shall discuss the sad history of the revolutionary experience in the Middle East in later chapters.

EGYPT: BANKRUPTCY AND OCCUPATION

If Algeria presents an example of imperialism as settler-colonialism, Egypt presents a different example of imperialism: imperialism as occupation. While British administrators, under the protective gaze of British soldiers, ran most Egyptian affairs, Egypt never became the site of large-scale population transfer. Nor did Britain officially make Egypt part of its empire, as it did Canada and India. Egypt remained part of the Ottoman Empire until the outbreak of World War I.

The story of how the British ended up occupying Egypt begins, once again, with cotton. As we have seen, after the American Civil War the price of cotton collapsed. A second jolt to the cotton market came a few years later with the onset of the Depression of 1873. The Egyptian government, expecting the price of cotton to remain high, had borrowed heavily to finance internal improvements and, on more than one occasion, extravagances. In 1876, unable to pay back its debts, the Egyptian government declared bankruptcy. In response, the British, French, Italian, Austrian, and later the Russian governments came to the aid of their citizens who had invested in Egypt. The European governments set up an agency called the Caisse de la Dette, which oversaw Egyptian finances with an eye toward debt repayment (they would also set up an Ottoman Public Debt Administration for the same purpose in the wake of the Ottoman bankruptcy). The Caisse's administrators took control of over 50 percent of Egyptian revenues. The 1880 Law of Liquidation regularized the debt repayment. According to the law, the Caisse was to direct all net revenue from railroads, the telegraph, and the port of Alexandria to the repayment of Egypt's foreign creditors. The law also granted the Caisse the right to all income derived from customs and import taxes on tobacco and wrested from the government of Egypt control of all tax revenues from four Egyptian provinces. Finally, the Caisse demanded the reinstatement of taxes on land that had previously been exempted. The Caisse's actions infuriated a cross-section of the Egyptian population, from landowners who found their tax burden suddenly increased, to military officers who suffered as a result of government cutbacks, to religious, commercial, and political elites who found foreign control difficult to stomach.

Many in the military harbored other grievances as well. From the beginning of Ottoman rule through most of the nineteenth century, a Turkish-speaking elite dominated the highest rungs of Egyptian society. This elite, which at the beginning of the nineteenth century numbered no more than ten thousand members, was Ottoman in culture and outlook. Mehmet Ali, it must be remembered, hailed from Ottoman Albania, did not speak Arabic, and acted much like other Ottoman warlords who sought to carve out a privileged role for themselves and their families within the empire, not separate from it. Over the course of the nineteenth century, the gap between the ruling elite and the population narrowed. Political and military elites in Egypt increasingly came to speak Arabic and intermarry with the native inhabitants of Egypt. At the same time, those inhabitants came to penetrate the bureaucracy and officer corps of the military, once the exclusive preserve of the Ottoman elites. Nevertheless, the discrimination felt by many in Egyptian society stung, and officers who believed that their rise in the ranks had been blocked because of their background were in a position to do something about it. In 1881, the army under Colonel Ahmad ʿUrabi mutinied. The mutiny touched the exposed nerve that foreign interference and social cleavages had created in Egyptian society. ʿUrabi forced his way into the government and began preparing to defend Egypt from the assault from Europe that was sure to come.

And come it did. Historians disagree about the precise reasons for the British invasion and occupation of Egypt. Some attribute it to British fears for the Suez Canal. After all, the British felt that the canal was so important for preserving their interests in India that in 1875 they had bought a huge block of its shares from an Egyptian government on the verge of bankruptcy. While the French still held most of the shares of the canal, the British, it seems, held most of the anxiety. The British also feared for the repayment of the Egyptian debt, 25 percent of which was owned by British investors. In addition, they feared instability in the eastern Mediterranean, particularly since Europeans living in Egypt began sending back exaggerated reports of massacres of Christians. Probably all of these factors led to the British invasion and occupation. The British sent a flotilla to Egypt and established residence there that would last for three-quarters of a century.

Once in Egypt, the British exercised control through both military and political means. Although the size of the British occupation forces was small in comparison with the size of the population, its presence provided a reminder to the Egyptians of Britain's power in the territory. The British did not eliminate the Egyptian army, which had been the pride of Egyptian rulers since the time of Mehmet Ali, but they did reduce its size and place British officers in positions of command. At the same time, the British exercised political power through a local administration. Theoretically, of course, the Ottomans still ruled Egypt and invested its khedives. In reality, the most important political figure was the British consul general. The first consul general, Evelyn Baring, the Earl of Cromer (who was, coincidentally, a member of the family that had established the famous Barings Bank) replaced anti-British Egyptian ministers with British appointees. His high-handed attitude toward the Egyptians he ruled is reflected in the following passage from his memoirs:

> The European is a close reasoner; his statements of fact are devoid of ambiguity; he is a natural logician, albeit he may not have studied logic; he loves symmetry in all things; he is by nature skeptical and requires proof before he can accept the truth of any proposition; his trained intelligence works like a piece of mechanism. The mind of the Oriental, on the other hand, like his picturesque streets, is eminently wanting in symmetry. His reasoning is of the most slipshod description. Although the ancient Arabs acquired in a somewhat high degree the science of dialectics, the descendants are singularly deficient in the logical faculty. They are often incapable of drawing the most obvious conclusions from any simple premises of which they may admit the truth. Endeavour to elicit a plain statement of facts from an ordinary Egyptian. His explanation will generally be lengthy, and wanting in lucidity.

By 1908, the year Cromer wrote those lines, the British controlled all government ministries but one: the ministry that oversaw religious endowments. Egyptians held only 28 percent of high government posts.

The British invasion of Egypt in 1882 began with the shelling of the port city of Alexandria. On this page, Alexandria before bombardment. (*From: University of Chicago Library.*)

Over the course of their occupation, the British imposed policies in Egypt modeled on their experience at home or in India. At a time when municipal reform was of central concern to reformers in Britain and was just being implemented in India, British administrators in Egypt oversaw the establishment of municipal governments with responsibilities for taxation and public services. Five years after the colonial government in the Punjab region of India passed a law to prevent moneylenders from foreclosing on peasant-owned lands, the occupation government of Egypt did the same. As with many of the defensive developmentalist policies of the khedives, however, this law—the so-called Five Feddan Law—had unforeseen effects. The law forbade moneylenders from demanding land as collateral on loans if a peasant's holdings were five feddans or less (a feddan is about an acre). The law was intended to prevent peasants from losing their property to unscrupulous usurers. Instead, moneylenders simply refused to loan money to peasants covered by the law. Lacking money to buy seed, peasants with small plots of land were often worse off than ever.

British occupation had other long-term effects as well. The British encouraged the expansion of cotton cultivation to feed their textile mills and constructed infrastructure that would foster not only the cultivation, but the transport and sale of cotton as well. In the period between the onset of the British occupation and the beginning of World War I, almost one million additional acres of land came under cultivation and over four thousand kilometers of track for railroads were laid. At the same time, the British did everything they could to ensure the Egyptians would not establish a textile industry that might compete with their own. When Egyptian businessmen implored Cromer to impose tariffs

Alexandria after bombardment. (*From: Hume Family Collection, The University of Queensland, Australia.*)

on imported cloth so that they might establish textile factories free from competition from abroad, Cromer refused, citing the principle of free trade between Britain and its colonies (of which, of course, Egypt was not one). By the early twentieth century, the lesson that had been brought home to many political and economic elites in Egypt was that Egypt could never achieve full economic development under British rule.

Although the British discouraged investment in Egyptian industry to protect the interests of their manufacturers at home, this was not the only reason they did so. Many British policy makers believed that rapid economic development in Egypt would undermine the calm in their new acquisition and threaten their position there. British imperialists of the nineteenth and twentieth centuries were not alone in thinking that economic development brings social disruption and social disruption brings rebellion. After the Iranian Revolution of 1978–1979, many scholars in the United States likewise blamed rapid development under the previous regime for the revolutionary upsurge.

However one-dimensional such reasoning might be, British fears of turmoil and rebellion in Egypt led to what one economist has called the asymmetrical development of Egypt. From the beginning of the occupation through the outbreak of World War I, the Egyptian economy grew, but this growth could not be maintained because investment in education and industry lagged behind. As a matter of fact, per capita income among Egyptians actually declined over the course of the first half of the twentieth century. Investors—mainly Europeans and "foreigners" (Greeks, Jews, Syrians) living in Egypt—channeled their money into those areas of the economy that promised high returns on their investments. These areas were not necessarily ones that would ensure sustained, independent economic development. Egypt got its railways and its urban tramways, for sure, but by the time of World War I it had only sixty-eight publicly financed schools and spending on education took up no more than 1 percent of the government's budget. This was no accident: The British purposely restricted the enrollment in secondary schools and universities to a narrow group that could be absorbed into the economy. By doing so, they hoped to prevent the growth of a class of disaffected intellectuals.

The British were only partially successful, however. Disaffected intellectuals would go on to organize the first modern nationalist parties in the Arab world. As in the case of Algeria, it was the very presence of imperialists that encouraged the emergence of nationalism in Egypt. Building on the work of their khedival predecessors, the British engaged Egyptians in common activities and in a common marketplace. In the process, they instilled among Egyptians a sense of national community. At the same time, the British presence in Egypt provided the population with a clear target against which to mobilize. Because of this, the Egyptian national movement followed a trajectory that was different from that followed by nationalisms in the rest of the Ottoman domains. Over time, that difference would assure the emergence of a distinct Egyptian territorial identity and the dissemination of a national myth that would trace "Egyptianness" backward to antiquity.

British imperialism in Egypt had long-lasting effects. Fighting imperialism under the pyramids, ca. 1960. (*From: Fondation Arabe pour l'image, Beirut.*)

MOUNT LEBANON: MILITARY
AND POLITICAL INTERVENTION

So far, this chapter has discussed two instances of formal imperialism and its effects. Now it is time to turn our attention to an instance of informal imperialism, a form of imperialism just as intrusive but, to borrow a contemporary phrase, one that does not necessitate putting boots on the ground.

European powers supervised the administrative reorganization of Mount Lebanon and guaranteed its autonomy. European states intervened into the politics of Mount Lebanon to put an end to sectarian—inter-religious—conflict that pit Maronite Christians against their Muslim and Druze neighbors. Maronites are Christians who recognize the Catholic pope's authority but maintain their own traditions. The Druze are a religious sect that branched off from mainstream Islam in the eleventh century. Both groups live in Mount Lebanon. After European intervention, however, whatever differences that might have divided the two communities became etched in stone.

Sectarianism might be defined as a phenomenon whereby religious affiliation becomes the foundation for collective identity in a multireligious environment. Since there has been so much blather recently about sectarianism in the region—how Sunni-Shi'i animosity goes back nearly a millennium and a half, how Sunni-Shi'i animosity will define the battle lines in the Middle East in the future, and the like—it is necessary to clear up a few misconceptions before we begin our discussion of Mount Lebanon. Sectarian identities are not primordial or preordained. They emerge as a result of political circumstances, such as when a religious community is treated differently from others by another religious community, a colonial power, or a state as a matter of policy. Sectarianism also differs from nationalism. The object of nationalism is sovereignty. There is no demand for independence with sectarianism—only for autonomy or rights. When sectarians demand independence, they become nationalists.

Sectarian strife of the sort that took place in Mount Lebanon is a modern phenomenon. This is not to say that there were no clashes between religious communities before the modern period. Of course there were. It is to say, however, that sectarian clashes are very different because in the modern period both the nature of religious identity and the issues at stake are different. As discussed earlier, sectarian strife of the sort that took place in Mount Lebanon can be traced to the transformation of Middle Eastern society in the nineteenth century. It was then that the boundaries between Muslim and minority communities began to harden, the social and economic histories of those communities began to diverge, and religious affiliation became the platform from which imperial subjects asserted political claims.

Finally, sectarianism should not be thought of as the universal default position among religious groups in the Middle East. Sectarianism emerges when political entrepreneurs use it to advance a political agenda. Those entrepreneurs might be governments (the Saudis and Iranians are presently particularly adept at this game) or they might be aspiring politicians on the make. In the wake of uprisings in Syria and Bahrain in 2011, for example, governments dominated by religious minorities have maintained the loyalty of the communities of which they are members through what some scholars have called "legitimacy by blackmail." In other words, not only are regimes in both places bound together through ties of sect and kinship; they compel the religious communities from which they hail to circle their wagons to protect the regime when the regime is under threat. The communities do this because the regime is identified with them and they fear reprisals from opponents of the regime should those opponents come to power. In both cases the regimes have gone so far as to promote sectarianism by blaming dissent not on regime failures, but on the lust of the non-ruling majority sect for power. In Syria, the regime deliberately sparked tit-for-tat massacres, knowing that this would cement the bond between it and the increasingly terrified community from which it has sought support.

There were both economic and political factors that encouraged the rise of sectarianism in the eastern Mediterranean. During the nineteenth century, as the Ottoman Empire became increasingly integrated into the world economy, the prosperity of the Christian community along the Mediterranean coast increased dramatically. Christian (and Jewish) merchants acted as middlemen in the European trade. They frequently knew European languages, had contacts abroad, and could provide European merchants with information about local conditions. The local consulates of European states often granted these minority merchants special certificates, known as *berat*s. Merchants who obtained *berat*s were covered by the capitulatory agreements between the Ottoman Empire and the state that issued them. In other words, subjects of the sultan who happened to be members of minority groups obtained the same access to the commercial and legal rights the empire had accorded merchants of European states. Because they paid lower customs duties and received tax breaks, they were often more prosperous than their Muslim competitors.

The number of these *beratli*s, as these merchants and other foreign protégés were called, was not insignificant. By the turn of the nineteenth century, the Austrians had granted consular recognition to two hundred thousand Ottoman subjects. Around the same time, the Russians recognized an additional 120,000. Most of those recognized by the Russians were Greeks who shared religious affiliation with the Russians and who were employed by the Russians as "interpreters." Thus, one out of every one hundred Ottoman subjects was accorded the rights of Russian and Austrian citizens. And then there were the British, the French, the Prussians, and even the Americans. Each selected their favorite minority—Maronites for the French, Protestants for the British and Americans—and conferred on them the same privileges that were available to their own citizens.

But economic jealousy alone does not explain why Muslim/minority tensions would rise during the nineteenth century, nor does it explain why it would affect such a relatively isolated area as Mount Lebanon. For that, we must look at the promise of equality of citizenship offered by the *Hatt-i Sharif* of Gulhane and the *Islahat Fermani*, discussed in Chapter 5. Immediately after the announcement of the new Ottoman policy, local notables, clergymen, and even commoners began to assert claims for the political rights promised in the documents. But they asserted those claims in a novel way. Local notables, clergymen, and even commoners knew that they would gain support from European states and concessions from an Ottoman government that was vulnerable to those European states if they presented their claims in the name of one or another downtrodden religious community. By claiming that they were acting to protect the interests of their religious community, they were saying, in effect, that their religious community was a distinct social unit that had interests that differed from the interests of other religious communities. As a result, they made religious communities competitors in the political arena.

The mixture of religious affiliation and political identity had dangerous consequences. It became all too easy for the inhabitants of areas in which several religious communities lived side by side to interpret every indignity or act of exploitation they suffered as an assault on their religious community. And there were all too many leaders or would-be leaders in religious communities ready to exploit the occasion for their own political purposes. Thus, in 1858 a dispute between Maronite peasants and Maronite landlords in Mount Lebanon soon transmuted into a rebellion of Maronite peasants against Druze landlords. The Druze retaliated and the fighting spread. In various places in the eastern Mediterranean, Muslims, angered by the rising economic and political status of Christians, attacked them. In Damascus alone, they massacred between five and ten thousand Christians and they burned a number of European consulates. Other massacres took place in Aleppo, Syria and Nablus, Palestine. To protect their Maronite clients, the French landed a force in Beirut.

In the wake of these events, a conference of European representatives met in Istanbul in 1861 to impose a solution on the Ottoman government. Although the roots of the problem were complex, the European delegates saw it exclusively in religious terms. For them, the violence was the latest manifestation of an age-old problem: Muslim fanatics preying on oppressed non-Muslim communities. As a result, the Europeans stepped in to protect the Christians of Mount Lebanon. They insisted that the Ottomans grant Mount Lebanon autonomy and placed the region under the protection of all European powers acting in concert. Mount Lebanon became a special administrative district, a *mutasarrifiya*, governed by a non-Lebanese Ottoman Christian who was assisted by an elected representative council. That council consisted of four Maronites, three Druze, two members of the Greek Orthodox church, one Greek Catholic, one Sunni Muslim, and one Shiʿi Muslim. This arrangement fixed the connection between politics and religious allegiance and based political representation in Lebanon on the relative size of each religious community.

The arrangement reached in 1861, then amended in 1864, was the historical ancestor of the system of proportional representation that exists in Lebanon to this day. In 1943, the year Lebanon became independent, leading Christian and Muslim politicians in Lebanon reached an informal understanding called the National Pact. The purpose of the pact was to define the political spoils available to each religious community. The pact stipulated that the president, prime minister, and speaker of the lower house of parliament would be a Maronite, a Sunni, and a Shiʿi, respectively; that the lower house would be divided between Christians and Muslims in a ratio of six to five; and that even cabinet posts would be distributed according to a representational formula that, until 1990, was based on the last census taken in Lebanon—the census of 1932. After fifteen years of civil war, the representational formula was amended in 1989. This formula apportioned seats in the lower house of parliament equally between Muslims and Christians—this, at a time when it is estimated that Lebanese Muslims far outnumbered Lebanese Christians.

Sectarianism in the Middle East is not unusual wherever members of one sect rub shoulders with members of another. So far, this chapter has discussed the cases of Mount Lebanon, Syria, and Bahrain. To these we might add Algeria, Israel/Palestine, Iraq, and elsewhere. Once again, this has nothing to do with habits ingrained in the population of the region since the beginning of Islam; rather, imperial powers foster sectarianism by misreading what makes Middle Eastern societies tick, or someone at sometime feels there is advantage to be gained by promoting sectarian sentiments. French policy in Algeria is a good example of the former: In 1870 the French government issued the Crémieux Decree, which granted French citizenship to the forty thousand Jews of Algeria whom its author, Adolphe Crémieux, believed to be civilizable. Because no such privilege was granted to Algerian Muslims, French policy had the effect of separating and hardening the boundaries between the two communities. Again, the results were disastrous: In 1934, incited by anti-Semitic Nazi propaganda, elements of the Muslim community in the Algerian city of Constantine engaged in anti-Jewish riots, killing about two dozen Jews. In the wake of these riots, most Algerian Jews fled to European France.

The tragedy of contemporary Iraq represents a case where a combination of imperial blundering and political entrepreneurship encouraged sectarian conflict. After the American invasion of Iraq in 2003, a combination of "al-Qaeda in Mesopotamia" provocation and American missteps inflamed sectarian passions and brought the country to the brink of cataclysm. Soon after the American invasion in 2003, al-Qaeda in Mesopotamia, a Sunni group, began launching attacks against high-profile Shi'i targets, including celebrated mosques, Shi'is on pilgrimage, and Shi'is participating in rituals. The aim of the group was to spark tit-for-tat retaliations between Shi'is and Sunnis, leading to all-out civil war. In the mind of these al-Qaedists, this would both make the American position in Iraq untenable and mobilize Sunni Iraqis against their "heretical" rivals. The group's chances of achieving its aim were increased by the incompetence of the American occupation authority, which issued decree after decree that Sunnis believed showed favoritism toward the Shi'i community and hostility to the Sunni community to which Saddam Hussein had belonged. Along with other factors, the deliberate provocation and the blundering worked their magic. It took until the end of 2007 for relative calm to be restored, but that was not to last. Discriminatory policies of the post-occupation Shi'i government against the Sunni minority, along with massacres of government sympathizers and innocent Shi'is by an al-Qaeda-style group, the Islamic State of Iraq and Syria (ISIS), reignited sectarian conflict. This makes it difficult to remember that in contemporary Iraq close to one-third of all families come from mixed Sunni-Shi'i marriages.

There is one final aspect of sectarianism in the Middle East that is worth mentioning: Once sectarianism has been introduced into an area, it has never been eliminated. There are two reasons for this: geographic and political. Consider contemporary Syria (or Lebanon during its civil war). Before the uprising of 2011, Sunnis and Alawites (members of a branch of Shi'ism which has dominated the government of Syria since 1970) may have held negative feelings about each other and told jokes at the other's expense, but they shared public space. They shopped in the same markets, they sat together in the same public transportation, they relaxed in the same coffeehouses. There was, in other words, a form of civic tolerance. Since the outbreak of hostilities, however, space has become more and more segregated as each community has chosen or has been forced to wall itself off or move away from those it fears. It is unlikely that trust will ever be rebuilt or space reintegrated. And to get the minority communities in Syria to sign on to a political agreement to end their conflict—an unlikely scenario but worth mentioning nonetheless—they are likely to demand written guarantees of "set-asides" for minority representation, as happened in both Lebanon and Iraq. This, in effect, would freeze sectarian divisions in place.

CHAPTER 7

Wasif Jawhariyyeh and the Great Nineteenth-Century Transformation

By the late nineteenth century, integration and peripheralization, defensive developmentalism, and imperialism had established the ground rules for the subsequent economic, social, and political development of the Middle East. These processes did not operate in a vacuum, however, and when they intruded upon the social, economic, and cultural life of the region, the effects were dramatic. New social classes were created, while others were destroyed. Urban centers were demolished and reconstructed. The introduction of new agricultural methods, crops, property rights, and markets transformed rural life. The emergence of new groups of cultural producers and consumers and experimentation with novel forms of cultural expression reshaped cultural and political life. Governments and citizens renegotiated their mutual responsibilities.

This chapter looks at these changes through the eyes of a Jerusalem musician by the name of Wasif Jawhariyyeh. Jawhariyyeh left behind voluminous diaries that begin in 1904 and end in 1968. They describe in detail not only his life, but the social and cultural life of Jerusalem. These diaries were brought to light and edited by two Palestinian scholars, Salim Tamari and Issam Nassar. This chapter is based on their work.

Wasif Jawhariyyeh's diaries provide an ideal jumping-off point for understanding life in the Middle East in the late nineteenth and early twentieth centuries for other reasons as well. Jawhariyyeh was not a particularly important individual. This makes his diaries all the more interesting. We have many memoirs from political and cultural elites. These memoirs were written mostly to justify the political activities or to glorify the cultural achievements of their authors for posterity. Jawhariyyeh did not write for either purpose. And while Jawhariyyeh came from a fairly privileged background, his family was hardly at the pinnacle of Jerusalem life. Furthermore, Jawhariyyeh's diaries record daily life at a critical juncture in Jerusalem's history. When Jawhariyyeh began writing his diaries in 1904, Jerusalem was a relative backwater of the Ottoman Empire. As such, the city was a rather late entrant into what might be called the

106

"great nineteenth-century transformation," and Jawhariyyeh was a witness to that transformation.

To understand the position of Jerusalem among cities of the Ottoman Empire, it is worth comparing it with two other important cities in Palestine at the time: Jaffa and Nablus. Jaffa was a port city that grew in response to increased trade with Europe and the introduction of steamships into the Mediterranean. Between 1856 and 1880, the cultivation of citrus fruit shipped through Jaffa quadrupled and the value of Jaffa's exports increased 1,400 percent. The Jaffa orange—an orange that could survive long-distance shipment unscathed because of its thick skin—became a major export crop at that time. As Jaffa's importance as an export hub increased, so did the population of the city. At the beginning of the nineteenth century, the population of Jaffa ranged from five hundred to five thousand, depending on the state of the agricultural economy, security in the countryside, and the availability of urban employment for farmers immigrating into the city. By 1912, the population had reached fifty thousand. At that time, only about ten thousand inhabitants of the city were Jews recently arrived from Europe.

Nablus, on the other hand, was an inland commercial center under the sway of a few merchant families. Because it was dominated by merchants, the city of Nablus was more outward-looking than Jerusalem—it had industries such as soap manufacture and weaving, as well as a greater integration with both the outside world (Greater Syria, Egypt, and Europe) and its immediate hinterland, from which it derived raw materials for its manufactures.

Unlike Nablus, the major industries of Jerusalem were associated with its function as a religious center. Jerusalem catered to pilgrims and the European tourist trade that had emerged in the aftermath of the Napoleonic Wars. The city did not have a modern municipal water system until 1901, nor did it have a modern sewage system until about a decade later. The famous Jerusalem clock tower was constructed at the same time as the water system. The clock tower was an important symbol for the inhabitants of the city in the early twentieth century and an important signpost for historians. For the former, it represented an expanded imperial presence in the city as well as the Ottoman impulse for "modernization." For the latter, it represents what historian E. P. Thompson has called the intersection between "time and work discipline"; that is, for historians the clock tower exemplifies the attempt to regulate Jerusalem's labor force and make it submissive to a daily, nine-to-five type of schedule. In 1909, Jerusalem's wagon drivers went on strike to protest increased taxes. The strike shut the city down. Think of it: a modern form of social protest made effective because of the central economic role played by an antiquated technology.

Wasif Jawhariyyeh begins his diaries as follows:

> I was born on Wednesday morning the fourteenth of January 1897, according to the Western calendar, which happened to be the eve of the Orthodox New Year. At the moment my father was preparing a tray of knafeh [a sweet] for the occasion as was customary then in Eastern Orthodox households. I was named Wasif after the Damascene Wasif Bey al-Adhem, who was then my father's close friend and the sitting judge in Jerusalem's Criminal Court.

The Jerusalem clock tower. (*From: Fondation Arabe pour l'image, Beirut.*)

Wasif Jawhariyyeh's father was a prominent member of the Eastern Orthodox community, a member of Jerusalem's municipal council, and a lawyer. He spoke Greek, Turkish, and Arabic: Greek because of his membership in the Orthodox church, Turkish because that was the second language of upwardly mobile elites and aspiring elites throughout the Ottoman Empire who sought advancement in late Ottoman society. Neither Wasif nor his father lived in a monoglot world.

Wasif's father took up silk farming later in his life. Silk farming took off in Palestine during the 1850s, again as a result of expanded trade with Europe. The marriage between urban and rural life was typical in Ottoman/Arab society of the time. As discussed earlier, the Ottoman Land Code of 1858 enabled notable families and ambitious individuals with money to invest to gain access to rural property. The land code was one reason for the appearance of large landed estates in the Arab provinces of the empire. Such landed estates would remain part of the Arab Middle Eastern scene until the mid-twentieth century.

The consolidation of large landed estates had important social implications as well. During the second half of the nineteenth century, a new class of absentee urban landowners began to dominate local politics in Greater Syria. These urban landowners took advantage of the Ottoman Land Code of 1858 as well as the new forms of governance introduced into the empire. As a result, they made themselves indispensable both to the renovated Ottoman imperial system and local society. For example, by the close of the nineteenth century the imperial government had ordered the establishment of municipal councils in cities throughout the empire. The Jerusalem municipal council, of which Wasif's father was a member, was established in 1863. Before then, cities had no independent existence: They could not tax, nor could they commission the construction of municipal infrastructure. The establishment of municipal councils opened the way for the absentee landowners to gain access to positions of power and opportunities to enrich themselves further. Members of municipal councils were able to skim off taxes, register lands in their own names, and direct municipal resources to themselves and their friends. Like their contemporaries in the Tammany Hall political machine of New York, they "seen their opportunities and they took 'em." And like their contemporaries they attracted a devoted following of people who sought to take advantage of their social betters' access to power and their ability to bestow bounty on their followers. Wasif Jawhariyyeh's father thus attached himself to the Husseini family, the most prominent family in Jerusalem. He began his career looking after the extensive Husseini family estates in the villages to the west of Jerusalem.

Jawhariyyeh describes his youth with a great deal of nostalgia for the "good old days." While a bit romanticized, this description gives us a view of day-to-day life among people of his class in Jerusalem. Take, for example, the following entry into his diaries:

> During the summer months of 1904 [when Jawhariyyeh was seven years old] we would sit around the lowered table for the main meal. Food was served in enameled zinc plates. That year we stopped eating with wooden spoons imported from Anatolia and Greece and replaced them with brass ones. We replaced the common drinking bowl tied to the pottery jar with individualized crystal glasses. In 1906 my father acquired single iron beds for each of my siblings, thus ending the habit of sleeping on the floor. What a delight it was to get rid of the burden of having to place our mattresses into the wall enclaves every night.

As a youth, Jawhariyyeh received a rather eclectic education. Although Orthodox, his father had him memorize the Qur'an. At the age of nine, he entered a Lutheran school. There, he learned basic Arabic grammar, dictation, reading, arithmetic, German, and Bible recitation. After being beaten by an instructor whom he allegedly mocked, Wasif went to the "progressive" Dusturiyyeh (constitutional) National School, where corporal punishment was forbidden. At the Dusturiyyeh, he learned grammar, literature, mathematics, English, French, Turkish, physical education, and Qur'anic studies for Christians.

Two of these subjects are particularly noteworthy. First, physical education was associated with the cult of the body popular in Europe at the time and spreading into the Middle East. Physical education had become an important part of "Christian renewal"—what is known as muscular Christianity—and was, of course, of vital concern to nationalist movements throughout Europe. Educators, clerics, and politicians promoted physical education to prevent physical and moral weakness that were seen as detrimental to the "body politic." This tendency was later taken up in Egypt with the establishment of the Young Men's Muslim Association, modeled on the Young Men's Christian Association that had been founded

The cult of the body: student athletes at the American University in Cairo, 1924.
(*From: Fondation Arabe pour l'image, Beirut.*)

in England in 1844. Its spread to the Middle East demonstrates in a different form the impulse toward "renewal" that will be discussed in the next chapter.

The second item on the curriculum that bears scrutiny is Qur'anic studies for Christians. Christians studied the Qur'an because it was believed that the text was an important part of the literary and cultural tradition of the Middle East— their literary and cultural tradition. In other words, by the beginning of the twentieth century the Qur'an not only had a religious function but took on another function as well. For many in the region, the Qur'an had become part of a shared cultural heritage that distinguished the culture of the region from the culture of the West. One prominent scholar writing from Istanbul at the time explicitly linked the creation of a shared culture and efforts to revitalize the Middle East as follows:

> The Germans differed in religion in a manner similar to the way Persians and Afghans differ in religion. When this difference was manifested in politics, the Germans were weak. But when they returned to their authentic culture, when they heeded the call of national unity and the general interest, God returned their power and they became the rulers of Europe and dominated its politics.

Like this particular scholar, many Ottoman cultural elites of the time thought that the creation of a common culture that superseded sectarian, regional, or linguistic divisions was necessary for imperial revitalization.

Jawhariyyeh describes his education in the Qur'an in the following manner:

> I received my copy of the Qur'an from al-Hajjah Um Musa Kadhem Pasha al-Husseini . . . who taught me how to treat it with respect and maintain its cleanliness. [Um Musa was, of course, a woman.] My Qur'anic teacher was

Sheikh Amin al-Ansari, a well-known *faqih* [legal scholar qualified to rule on matters pertaining to shariʿa] in Jerusalem. The headmaster's idea was that the essence of learning Arabic lies in mastering the Qurʾan, both reading and in-cantation. My Muslim classmates and I would start with Surat al-Baqara and continue. . . . I can say in all frankness that my mastery of Arabic music and singing is attributable to these lessons—especially my ability to render classical poetry and *muwashahat* to musical form.

Jawhariyyeh was compelled to leave the school and enroll in another "in order to gain knowledge of the English language and build a solid base for my future." He remained in this school for another two years until it was closed at the beginning of World War I.

The story of Jawhariyyeh's education demonstrates the fluidity of boundaries in Ottoman Jerusalem during Jawhariyyeh's youth. In the contemporary world, peoples' identities and social and political roles are relatively fixed. In the world of Jawhariyyeh's youth, boundaries separating the lives of Christians or Jews from Muslims were more fluid, as were urban social boundaries and the boundaries separating so-called traditional and modern ways of life. The ceremonies and ritu-als of each religious group borrowed elements from the others, and the festivals celebrated by one group often marked the occasion for citywide revelry. Looking back from contemporary Jerusalem, it is hard to imagine a time when Muslim children would dress up in costumes alongside Jewish children to celebrate the Jewish feast of Purim (Jewish children joined their Muslim contemporaries as well in celebrating the festival of the prophet Muhammad), or when an Orthodox Christian musician like Jawhariyyeh would play at Jewish weddings, or when a native Palestinian would accompany an Ashkenazi (European Jewish) choral group on his oud (a popular Middle Eastern stringed instrument). Even gender roles and gender relations were less rigid during Jawhariyyeh's youth than they are today: The role of women in society varied from place to place, from city to coun-tryside, and from social class to social class. Although women, like men, faced social pressures to conform, no state or political movement forced women to dress in a manner that would make them walking billboards for either the "new nation-alist woman" or the "devout Islamic woman." It seems that for every set of bound-aries the modern world has broken down, it has created others.

One should not, of course, paint a picture of Jawhariyyeh's youthful world that is too rosy. Nevertheless, if one looks closely enough, over the course of the diaries one can detect a dramatic shift away from a world that appears remote to one that appears all too familiar. Take, for example, the spatial and cultural boundaries separating rich from poor. Although Jerusalem's rich and poor cer-tainly enjoyed different levels of creature comforts, before the mid-nineteenth century they lived side by side in urban quarters. During the late nineteenth and early twentieth centuries, notable families began to move out of densely packed urban areas and into suburban areas outside the city walls where life was cleaner and more spacious. The spatial separation of rich and poor was reflected in an emerging cultural separation as well. During Jawhariyyeh's youth what might be termed a genteel, cosmopolitan, bourgeois culture began to emerge among the wealthier families of Jerusalem. This genteel, cosmopolitan, bourgeois culture in many ways mimicked the dominant culture of Europe, not just in terms of the physical trappings of refinement—overstuffed couches and gaudy chandeliers—but in cultural terms as well.

In turn-of-the-century Jerusalem, both gentility and cosmopolitanism, on the one hand, and its bohemian opposition, on the other, were maintained and reproduced through a thriving salon culture. Wealthier Jerusalemites as well as their more fancy-free neighbors gathered nightly in homes and apartments to enjoy each other's company. Throughout his diaries, Wasif Jawhariyyeh describes nightly episodes of drinking, dancing, card playing, music, and hashish smoking in bachelor apartments kept by single men from notable families. Muslims, Christians, and Jews all participated in these entertainments, and Jawhariyyeh earned his living as a musician playing at such gatherings.

The music played by Jawhariyyeh reflected a mixture of conventional and Western styles and themes and typifies the culture of the educated urban elites of his time. Like many other children of relative privilege, Jawhariyyeh received a rigorous training in both classical Arabic poetry and contemporary writers associated with the *nahda*—the Arabic literary renaissance of the nineteenth century. The writers, playwrights, and poets of the *nahda* attempted to fuse Arabic and European forms of expression. Jawhariyyeh even tried his hand at creating a system of musical notation that would convert Ottoman/Arab music to a Western system of notation, much as *nahda* writers attempted to simplify the Arabic language and script so that it might be accessible to a wider audience.

The influence of *nahda* culture on Jawhariyyeh can also be seen from the themes he selected for his compositions. For his first public performance, Jawhariyyeh chose to play a work based on Salamah Hijazi's translation of *Romeo and Juliet*. Like Farah Antun (who rendered the Oedipus cycle into Arabic), Khalil Matran (who translated and produced the works of Sophocles, Molière, and Shakespeare), and ʿUthman Jalal (an actor who specialized in playing characters created by Molière), Hijazi cultivated a devoted following among educated audiences. The pinnacle of Hijazi's influence took place in June 1920, when he staged two outdoor performances of his *Romeo and Juliet* in Damascus as part of the ceremonies marking Syria's post–World War I declaration of independence. The performances were reportedly received with enthusiasm, and Hijazi's influence lasted longer than Syria's initial flirtation with independence, which was terminated by the French within a month.

Many in the Middle East saw the aping of Western ways among society's elites as just another aspect of Western corruption and imperialism. Some chose to fight this by espousing what might be termed a new Islamic orthodoxy. The new orthodoxy attempted to standardize and enforce rules for proper Islamic conduct. In Damascus, ulama led the campaign to shut down the city's only dance hall. In Basra, a city in the south of contemporary Iraq, other ulama protested the raising of a statue of a famous reformist governor. They argued that the statue would violate Islamic proscriptions against representational art. Throughout the Middle East, the issues of the veiling of women and the mixing of men and women in public took on a new urgency. For adherents to the new orthodoxy, the concern of Westerners and Westernizers about the status of Middle Eastern women in Middle Eastern society was part of an imperialist conspiracy against Islam. What made this conspiracy so insidious was that it was launched at women, a segment of society that, according to those adherents, was particularly vulnerable to foreign intrigue. One so-called orthodox periodical republished an article allegedly written in a French journal in which a French missionary stated, "The education of girls in convent schools leads to our gaining our true purpose and the arrival at our goal. In fact, I believe that the education of girls in this manner is the one means for finishing off Islam." It would not be a stretch to say that the roots of contemporary Islamic movements, with their obsession over issues of gender and personal conduct, lie in the attempts made by these early twentieth-century ulama and their followers to defend Islam against foreign influences.

The disputes between the adherents to the new, cosmopolitan culture and the adherents to the equally new orthodoxy actually boiled down to a single question: Who would control the new public sphere and determine how that public sphere was to be used? The public sphere is an imaginary space where citizens contest issues of common (that is, public) concern. These issues included everything from imperial politics to the role of women in society. While it would be a mistake to associate the emergence of a modern public sphere with democratization, it would not be a mistake to say that the emergence of a modern public sphere was essential for the emergence of mass political movements. In future

Musical ensemble, Aleppo, Syria, ca. 1900. (*From: The Collection of Wolf-Dieter Lemke.*)

chapters we shall see how the emergence of a modern public sphere allowed for the spread of constitutionalism and nationalism in the region.

One factor that set the stage for the emergence of a modern public sphere was the nineteenth-century print revolution in the region which made possible the widest possible circulation of ideas. The use of a printing press with movable type—Johannes Gutenberg's famous innovation—in the Ottoman Empire dates back as far as 1493, when two Jewish brothers, refugees from Spain, published a compendium of Jewish law. Over the years, others would try their hand at printing, including Ibrahim Muteferrika (1674–1745), a diplomat and scholar, who received the sultan's permission in 1726 to publish a two-volume Turkish-Arabic dictionary—the first book to use Arabic letters. Nevertheless, the print revolution in the Middle East had to wait until the nineteenth century, when technological breakthroughs imported from Europe rendered both printing and lithography cost effective. Then the dam burst. When Jawhariyyeh was just a schoolchild, for example, forty-one daily newspapers and seven journals competed for readership in Damascus, a significant increase from the three daily newspapers and two journals published in the city during the final three decades of the nineteenth century. The history of print in Persia follows a similar trajectory. Armenians operated the first presses in the Safavid Empire in the seventeenth century, publishing in Armenian. The Dar al-Funun housed the first press to publish in Persian in the early nineteenth century, and by the time of the Persian Constitutional Revolution of 1905 approximately ninety newspapers kept their readers informed of the latest developments.

Literacy was, of course, a rare commodity and most newspapers had only limited circulation (although this problem was partially overcome by reading them aloud in public spaces and by newsboys who shouted out headlines on street corners to attract customers). But there were exceptions: *al-Manar*, launched in Cairo in 1898, enjoyed an international circulation that stretched from the Dutch East Indies to British India to Muslim communities in Europe, and it printed letters and queries from Muslims around the globe. At the same time, newspapers reprinted each other's stories and even participated in a form of dialogue with one another. Thus it was that a polemic defending women's rights, originally written in Baghdad by poet, essayist, and law professor Jamil Sidqi al-Zahawi and published in an Egyptian newspaper in 1910, was critiqued one month later in a conservative Damascene journal that cited sociological data from Massachusetts, Pennsylvania, and California in its refutation.

Another factor that encouraged the emergence of a modern public sphere was the reconstruction of cities. There were a number of reasons why cities took on new attributes at this time. New technologies such as tramways were introduced into the region. These technologies broadened the territorial reach of urban environments and literally broke down the walls separating semiautonomous urban quarters from each other. Newly empowered municipal councils directed centralized planning and policing. Sultans, shahs, and khedives imported conceptions of municipal order from abroad. The new cities of Port Said and Isma'iliyya on the Suez Canal, for example, were laid out according to a checkerboard pattern, and the Egyptian khedive, Isma'il, and the shah of Persia, Nasr ed-Din Shah, were so impressed by late nineteenth-century Paris that they rebuilt parts of their capitals in imitation, with wide boulevards, public parks, and landscaped roads. The reconstruction of cities introduced new conceptions of space into urban areas and created spaces where public ceremonies could be held and individuals could meet and talk.

Then there were coffeehouses. Coffeehouses were not new to the Middle Eastern urban landscape. Indeed, the first coffeehouses in the region date from the fifteenth and sixteenth centuries. But in the nineteenth century coffeehouses were ubiquitous in Middle Eastern cities. Located both on main thoroughfares in the heart of cities and in market areas adjacent to semiprivate lanes, they were one of the main sites in which an expanding public sphere could be found. During Jawhariyyeh's lifetime, it was common for the more popular and centrally located coffeehouses to cater to several hundred clients a day. Coffeehouse patrons passed their time sipping coffee, playing backgammon (*tawula*), smoking water pipes (*narghiles*), and trading gossip. They also read aloud one or more of the seven newspapers published in Jerusalem at the time and watched shadow plays, which were frequently remade as political and social satire. In addition, coffeehouses served as centers for new entertainment technologies that catered to mass audiences. For example, phonographs were initially too expensive for private ownership, and Jawhariyyeh heard his first Edison recordings in a coffeehouse:

> I would take a matleek [small Ottoman coin] from my father and go to Ali Izhiman's café near the Damascus gate. A blind man by the name of Ibrahim al-Beiruti operated the phonograph. The machine was raised on a wooden cabinet full of 78 r.p.m. records and covered by red velvet to protect it from the evil eye. I used to throw my matleek in a brass plate and cry to the blind man: "Uncle, let us hear (such-and-such)." The blind man would immediately pull the requested record from the cabinet—only God knows how—and would play it on the phonograph. Later my music teacher would say, "Listening to this music is like eating with false teeth."

Wasif Jawhariyyeh's brother opened up one such coffeehouse in Jerusalem in 1918 called the Café Jawhariyyeh. Wasif's brother had learned how to tend bar in Beirut while stationed there during his enlistment in the Turkish army, putting the time he spent in the military to good use. It was at his brother's cafe that Jawhariyyeh honed the craft that would make him famous.

Phonographs were not the only imported marvel that Jawhariyyeh describes in his diaries. He saw his first movie at the Russian compound in Jerusalem soon after he experienced his first phonograph record. He saw his first car (a Ford) in 1912 when it passed through the streets driven by an American driver. He saw his first airplane in the summer of 1914 when it was flown to Jerusalem by two Ottoman pilots, and when the plane crashed he composed a eulogy on their behalf. To get a sense of the speed with which these technologies entered the lives of people like Jawhariyyeh, one need only compare Wasif's experiences with those of his father, which Jawhariyyeh also records in his diaries:

> When I was thirteen, in 1850 [the father states], I recall that we did all our travel on individual beasts: mules, donkeys, horses, and even camels. I did not see any animal driven carriages until a few years later when the French brought the "tambour"—a two wheel carriage driven by mules—to transport bricks for the roof of the French church in Abu Ghush. Boys of my generation used to run after this amazing new invention until we reached the approaches of Lifta.

Although Jawhariyyeh's diaries continue for a half century after the close of World War I in 1918, it is appropriate to end our discussion here. In the immediate decades following World War I, a new set of issues emerged that commanded Jawhariyyeh's attention. For example, the year 1936 lies at the exact midpoint of Jawhariyyeh's diaries. The year is significant because it was then that the first great uprising in modern Palestinian history broke out—the Great Revolt of 1936–1939—which will be discussed in Chapter 14. The revolt had two underlying causes: distress caused by the Great Depression of the 1930s and the dramatic rise of European Jewish immigration into Palestine. During the Great Depression, both international trade and the international market for agricultural products collapsed. This caused extreme economic hardship in an economy that was still, fundamentally, rural. Jewish immigration into Palestine sparked a resistance among non-Jewish Palestinians. The motivations that drove Palestinians to revolt ran the gamut from the desire to settle old scores to blind anger at what many considered an alien presence in their midst. But many of the rebels and their leaders were motivated by nationalist aspirations as well.

Overall, the Great Revolt of 1936–1939 was emblematic of a Palestine firmly entrenched in the modern world economic system and, as signified by the spread of nationalism in Palestine, a world political order defined by nationalism and nation-states. The Palestinian world of the 1930s was a world in which rapid demographic change and political instability had ravaged much of the genteel, bourgeois culture that had shaped Jawhariyyeh. It was a world in which hard-and-fast ideologies and exclusive loyalties would shortly become the norm. Palestine in the 1930s represented a very different world from the Palestine of Jawhariyyeh's youth.

Photo Essay: The Great Nineteenth-Century Transformation and Its Aftermath

A modernist reverie: Photo montage, Heliopolis (Cairo), 1910. (*From: The Collection of the author.*)

View of Galata Bridge, Istanbul, ca. 1910. (*From: The Collection of the author.*)

Place de l'Opera, Cairo, 1911. (*From: The Collection of Wolf-Dieter Lemke.*)

Damascus, Marja Square (with column commemorating the opening of the Istanbul-Hijaz telegraph line), 1911. (*From: The Collection of the author.*)

Damascus, Marja Square, 1922. (*From: The Collection of the author.*)

Train station, Isma⁣ᶜiliyya, date unknown. (*From: The Collection of the author.*)

Port Said, on the Suez Canal, laid out as a checkerboard. (*From: The Collection of Wolf-Dieter Lemke.*)

REMAPPING URBAN SPACE

Public garden, Beirut. (*From: The Collection of the author.*)

Covered market (Suq al-Hamidiyya), Damascus, after it was elongated and refurbished in the French arcade style in 1885. (*From: The Collection of Wolf-Dieter Lemke.*)

Street scene with tramway, Port Said, date unknown. (*From: The Collection of the author.*)

Outdoor café, Cairo, date unknown. (*From: The Collection of the author.*)

Smyrna (Izmir) market, early twentieth century. (*From: The Collection of the author.*)

The wharf, Smyrna (Izmir), 1903. (*From: The Collection of the author.*)

Waterfront, Algiers, French Algeria, 1915. (*From: The Collection of the author.*)

Italian commissioner's headquarters, Homs, Libya, 1936. (*From: The Collection of the author.*)

THE PULL OF THE MARKET

Merchant vessel in Muscat (Oman) harbor, early twentieth century. (*From: The Collection of the author.*)

Representatives of B. Altman & Co., New York, buying carpets in Tabriz, Persia, 1900-1910s. (*From: The Collection of the author.*)

Women sorting figs for Djanik Elmassian Exports, Smyrna, ca. 1900. (*From: The Collection of the author.*)

A Kodak moment on Prince Farouk Street, Port Said, date unknown. (*From: The Collection of the author.*)

Carpet weavers, Algeria, date unknown. (*From: The Collection of the author.*)

Silk thread factory, Brusa (Anatolia), date unknown. (*From: The Collection of Wolf-Dieter Lemke.*)

WORK

Porters loading the (appropriately named) coaling ship, *Vindictive*, Port Said, 1926. (*From: The Collection of the author.*)

Orphans learning cobbling, Damascus, date unknown. (*From: The Collection of the author.*)

DIVERSIONS

Coffeehouse, Cairo, late nineteenth century. (*From: The Collection of Wolf-Dieter Lemke.*)

Upscale coffeehouse, Istanbul, 1890s. (*From: The Collection of the author.*)

DIVERSIONS

Mozaffar ad-Din Shah shooting pigeons. (*From: The Collection of the author.*)

Studio photograph, Alexandria, 1927. (*From: Fondation Arabe pour l'image, Beirut.*)

DIVERSIONS

Ezbekiya Gardens, Cairo, ca. 1900. (*From: Fondation Arabe pour l'image, Beirut.*)

Sunbathing, Istanbul, ca. 1900. (*From: The Collection of Wolf-Dieter Lemke.*)

THE UPPER CRUST

An "Arab gentleman," 1905. (*From: The Gertrude Bell Collection, University of Newcastle.*)

Imperial princes, Istanbul, date unknown. (*From: The Collection of the author.*)

French steamship *Carthage* docking in Tunis, 1910-15. (*From: The Collection of the author.*)

The Zabadani station on the Beirut-Damascus Railway, 1916 (?). (*From: The Collection of the author.*)

Steamships on the Tigris River. (*From: The Collection of Wolf-Dieter Lemke.*)

Marking the opening of the Istanbul Tramway with a sacrifice of a lamb. (*From: Jacques Benoist-Méchin, La Turquie se dévoile, 1908-1938 [Paris: PML Editions, n.d.], p. 157.*)

Ottoman infantry, drilling: Iraq, 1911. (*From: The Gertrude Bell Collection, University of Newcastle.*)

Policeman on duty, Baghdad, post–World War I. (*From: The Collection of the author.*)

Governor (in white fez on left) distributing bread to the poor, Scutari (currently in Albania), early twentieth century. (*From: The Collection of the author.*)

Administrative center and staff in the northwest province of Zanjan, Persia, date unknown. (*From: The Collection of the author.*)

THE REACH OF IMPERIALISM

Headquarters of the Suez Canal Company, 1929. (*From:The Collection of the author.*)

"The (Italian) grenadiers evoke the admiration of the natives" (original caption), Tripoli, Libya, 1911. (*From: The Collection of the author.*)

Tourists enjoying the pyramids, date unknown. (*From: The Collection of the author.*)

Laying pipe for the Anglo-Persian Oil Company, date unknown. (*From: The Collection of the author.*)

THE CLASH OF CIVILIZATIONS AS IT WAS PRESENTED AT THE TURN OF A DIFFERENT CENTURY

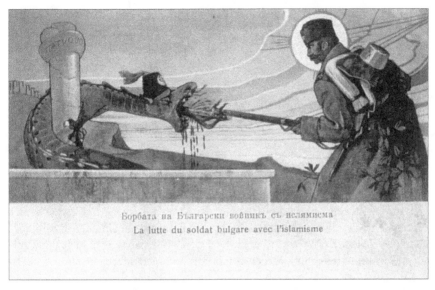

Bulgarian propaganda card with inscription: "A Bulgarian Soldier Struggles against Islam." (*From: The Collection of Wolf-Dieter Lemke.*)

Ottoman propaganda card showing Italian soldiers in Libya about to massacre women and children. Inscription reads: "Italian Civilization in Tripolitania." (*From: The Collection of Wolf-Dieter Lemke.*)

CHAPTER 8

The Life of the Mind

The previous chapter explored the great nineteenth-century transformation through the diaries of a Jerusalem musician, Wasif Jawhariyyeh. Jawhariyyeh's diaries both describe and situate the musician within the context of a rapidly changing Middle East. They locate Jawhariyyeh within a physical, social, and cultural world that his grandparents would not have recognized. It was a world in which urban spaces underwent radical changes, which allowed Ottoman (and Persian) citizens to enjoy greater mobility, amenities associated with modern urban life, and expanded contact with one another. It was a world in which new social classes appeared, such as urban absentee landowners who had been enriched by the Ottoman land law of 1858 and who came to dominate local and provincial politics. It was a world in which a secular intelligentsia also appeared, men and women who were schooled by missionaries or the state, who participated in a cosmopolitan, bourgeois culture, and who hankered after new ideas, imported creature comforts, the trappings of gentility, and the political rights to which they believed their station entitled them. It was a world in which new technologies—automobiles, sewing machines, the telegraph, gramophones, gas lamps, tramways, clock towers, electricity—had outsized effects, altering social and cultural life in unanticipated ways. And it was a world in which a wide and diffuse public sphere thrived. Within this public sphere new cultural, ideological, and religious movements emerged and often contended. Some of these movements faded into obscurity; others are with us to this very day.

One such movement was the *nahda*, or Arabic literary renaissance, described earlier. Poets, novelists, and playwrights of the *nahda* sought to rejuvenate Arabic literature to recover it from what they described as *inhitat* (decline). They experimented with techniques to simplify forms of expression, expand the reach of their works among Arabic speakers, and shatter literary conventions by infusing their works with new, sometimes borrowed, forms. Similar literary ventures were undertaken by belletrists writing in Turkish and Persian. The *nahda* and other literary movements might be seen as part of a generalized impulse for literary, political, and social reform that spread through the urban centers of the region.

More often than not, intellectuals who identified with the *nahda* were Syrian and Lebanese Christians from Beirut and Damascus. Syrian and Lebanese emigrants living throughout the region and in such far-flung places as Europe and the Americas also participated in the movement. And direct borrowings from the West did not end with them. Residents of seaport cities such as Istanbul, Alexandria, and Beirut rubbed shoulders with Italian expatriates who brought with them to the Middle East Italy's single largest export during the nineteenth century: anarchism. Darwinism (and free speech) became a public, contentious issue in the region in 1882 after an American chemistry professor teaching at Beirut's Syrian Protestant College (later the American University in Beirut) broached the subject in a commencement address. Reverberations from the incident reached as far as Egypt. And while it might be argued that feminism had indigenous roots, the modern feminist movement in the Arab world enjoyed its legendary founding moment in 1923 when three Egyptian women, returning from an international feminist conference in Rome, scandalized those of a more conservative bent by publicly unveiling. But while it was certainly the case that intellectuals and even laborers sometimes consciously borrowed forms of expression and ideas from the West, those borrowings represented only the tip of the iceberg when it came to ideas circulating in the public sphere. Focusing exclusively on them means losing sight of a much larger picture.

The intellectual currents that emerged during the eighteenth and nineteenth centuries sprang from a variety of sources and took a number of forms. In contrast to the endeavors of Westernizers, for example, some intellectual movements arose in direct opposition to Western imperialism or the influx of Western ideas. We have seen one example of this in the previous chapter: the attempt made by some late nineteenth-century ulama to formulate a new Islamic orthodoxy. As we shall see later, this attempt was hardly as untainted by ideas originally produced in the West as its adherents claimed.

Other intellectual and religious movements emerged as an indirect response to the effects of integration and peripheralization, defensive developmentalism, and imperialism. A good example of this sort of movement is the Baha'i movement in Persia. The roots of Baha'ism can be traced back to 1844, the one-thousandth anniversary of the occultation of the twelfth imam. That year, a merchant from Shiraz proclaimed himself to be the "gate" (*bab*) through which the hidden imam communicated. Then he revealed that he was, in fact, the hidden imam. For his efforts, he was executed by the Persian government. While the message of the *bab* was cloaked in what might be described as traditional religious garb, the movement he and his followers initiated was hardly traditional. Like other social/religious movements of the mid-to-late nineteenth century—the Taipings in China (1851–1864), who provoked a civil war that claimed more than thirty million lives, or the Native American Ghost Dance movement (1889–1895)—the Babi movement, as it was called, grew in response to the adverse conditions in which its members increasingly found themselves. The *bab*'s followers advocated the abolition of taxes and private property and supported equal rights for men and women—an understandable response in a society affected by the widespread economic and social dislocations associated with nineteenth-century developments. And, like other movements of the time, the Babi movement was supported by diverse layers of the population—in this case peasants, minor ulama, artisans, and guild members—all of which lost ground over the course of the century. After being suppressed by the Persian government, many in the Babi movement, apparently believing discretion to be the better part of valor, became pacifists and disavowed politics. These are the Baha'is who have been persecuted off and on in Persia/Iran ever since.

While the Babi/Baha'i movement situated a modern social movement within the framework of conventional religious images and language, there were numerous intellectual currents that cannot be traced, either directly or indirectly, to integration and peripheralization, defensive developmentalism, and imperialism. It was often the case that scholars contributed to fields of knowledge such as Islamic law and theology in seeming isolation from the outside world, much as academics claim to do today. These scholars were, in effect, holding a dialogue with their predecessors. They expressed their end of the dialogue in much the same way that Muslim scholars had fashioned their arguments for centuries. This is not to say that their arguments did not have implications for the world outside the walls of their schools and seminaries. Nor is it to say that there was no relationship between the most "convincing" arguments and the political, social, or economic circumstances of the time. We shall look at one such dispute between two schools of Shiʿi theology and its effects on subsequent developments later in this chapter.

This brings us to another important aspect of the intellectual and cultural movements of the eighteenth and nineteenth centuries: their implications for politics and political culture. Some of the movements discussed in this chapter had direct political ramifications; others did not. All the former movements had at least one thing in common: To be successful, their vision of political community had to be compatible with the international state system and the modern world economy. Those movements that were not initially compatible with both (such as the Sanusiyya movement of Libya or Wahhabism in Arabia, both of which will be discussed shortly) had to become compatible once their advocates achieved power. If not, these movements would simply not survive as a touchstone for political life. Thus, the state established by the Wahhabis in the early nineteenth century failed, but the state established by their descendants in the early twentieth century (Saudi Arabia) so far has not.

Although those intellectual and cultural movements with political implications needed to be compatible with the international state system and the modern world economy, they often used widely divergent arguments to justify their actions. For example, from 1878 until 1908 Sultan Abdulhamid II of the Ottoman Empire couched his policies of centralization and "modernization" within a rhetoric that drew from Islam. While the Young Turks who took over the Ottoman

Empire in 1908 initially couched their policies in a rhetoric that drew from the latest scientific theories and secular philosophies, they followed pretty much the same centralization and modernization policies as the sultan they would depose. There is nothing mysterious about this. As discussed throughout this book, the modern state is far more capable of harnessing the social power of its citizens than any of its precursors, and so any political movement that wants to survive has to adapt to the ways of the modern world, no matter what language it uses to justify its policies.

The intellectual and cultural movements that arose in the Middle East during the eighteenth and nineteenth centuries thus ran the gamut from those that directly borrowed from Western Enlightenment traditions to those that developed in isolation from those traditions, from those that drew from religious principles to those that adopted religious language for other purposes, not to mention those, like language reform, that had nothing to do with religion at all. It would be impossible to do justice to all these currents within the space of one chapter. Accordingly, this chapter will focus on just one type of movement: the sort that sought to reform society by reforming Islam. Other powerful currents, such as nationalism, will be taken up in later chapters.

During the eighteenth and nineteenth centuries, many in the Middle East looked around and concluded that Islam and the Islamic world had, indeed, fallen on hard times. Many attributed the predicament in which Islamic societies had found themselves to the fact that those societies had abandoned the original teachings and doctrines of Islam. These were, after all, the teachings and doctrines that allowed Muslims to establish a vast empire that had stretched from Spain to Afghanistan at a time when Europe was in its Dark Ages. In order to restore the glory of Islam—or at least stand up to the threat from the West—they felt that they had to eliminate from Islam everything that had contributed to its decline.

Several intellectual currents in the eighteenth and nineteenth centuries identified two sources of decline. First, many in the region questioned the tendency for Muslims to follow blindly the teachings of earlier generations of religious scholars who, they claimed, had contributed to Islam's decay. The harshest among them condemned their predecessors for misinterpreting or falsifying the original precepts of Islam. Others accused Islamic societies themselves of corrupting those precepts by mixing Islam with folk customs, such as saint worship, mysticism, and divination (prophesying the future by supernatural means). Movements that started from either of these two premises often encouraged Muslims to look to the first community established by Muhammad at Medina as a model for the moral and political regeneration of Islam. Because the first generation of Muslims was called al-salaf al-salih (the "pious ancestors"), those who advocated using this community as a model are called salafis and their movement is called salafism.

Most of the world was introduced to salafism during the Arab uprisings of 2010–2011. It was then that some salafis, who had previously shunned political participation as impious, jumped into the political fray. One salafist party, al-Nour in Egypt, shocked the world by garnering one-quarter of the seats in Egypt's first free parliamentary election. This was all the more shocking because Egypt's salafists, with their insistence on beards for men and veils for women, not only looked different from the image of the protesters in Tahrir Square popular in the West, but their views on women's rights, minority rights, and a strict interpretation and implementation of Islamic law had conflicted with those of the protesters as well. But nineteenth-century salafism was richer than salafism today, and nineteenth-century salafis were a more diverse lot than their heirs. They even included in their ranks members of groups today's salafis would not even consider Muslims, minority sects like the Zaydis of Yemen and the Ibadis of Oman and Zanzibar, who were attracted to salafism because in the original Islamic community of Muhammad there were no majority or (despised) minority sects, only Muslims.

Besides regarding the original community in Medina as the ideal community, all salafis share another characteristic: Since our knowledge of the Medinan community comes from two sources—the Qur'an and the hadith (reports of the sayings and activities of the prophet)—salafis rely exclusively on them, not on sources produced in later centuries. This, however, is easier in theory than in practice. After all, Islamic societies in the modern world confront situations that the first Islamic community never had to face. Is it legal to use the telegraph to transmit the sighting of the new moon marking religious holidays? Does the digging of artesian wells violate the injunction forbidding Muslims from drinking from standing pools of water? How should Muslims respond to the dictates of colonial rulers? To deal with new situations, salafis face two choices: restrict the domain of Islamic law to those issues that correspond to the issues faced by the first community, or somehow expand the range of issues Islamic law might deal with. Some have advocated the first approach, others the second. To expand the range of issues that Islamic law might deal with, a number of salafi scholars have argued that Muslims knowledgeable in the law should exercise independent judgment based upon reason—an established legal procedure called *ijtihad*. In the hands of some, *ijtihad* became a tool for preserving Islam in the face of modern conditions. In the hands of others, *ijtihad* became a tool for bringing in European ideas and the "spirit of the age" through the back door.

According to some historians, nineteenth-century salafism was foreshadowed by an eighteenth-century "moral reconstruction" movement. As discussed earlier, the eighteenth century was not a particularly auspicious period for Middle Eastern governments and the people they ruled. Local notables and warlords were effectively challenging the authority of imperial governments. Ottoman and Persian armies met with failure after failure in their confrontation with the armies of Europe. Peasants were unable to count on weak central governments to provide rural security and often sought shelter in inhospitable cities. Artisans were displaced by Europeans who dumped finished products on the Middle Eastern market. There was no lack of awareness of these problems among bureaucrats, scholars, and common people in the region. In fact, many were quite aware and searched for both the reasons for the malaise and ways to overcome it. One solution they came up with was to rebuild society from the ground up—that is, to rebuild society by reconstructing the social and moral fabric that bound its members to one another. There was no more accessible or appropriate model for this project than the one provided by the life and community of the prophet and the pious ancestors.

Moral reconstructionism was powerful in part because it was transmitted through networks of like-minded people. Sometimes the networks were confined to a single quarter of a city or to all the local practitioners of a trade. Sometimes the networks stretched for thousands of miles, joining like-minded Muslims from as far away as India and Indonesia with Muslims living in Persia, Egypt, Syria, and North Africa. Networks might take the shape of informal clubs or study groups, or they might be much more formal. And they were very popular. One historian has estimated that by the beginning of the nineteenth century, almost every male of every class in Cairo belonged to at least one such network.

These networks were called *turuq* (sing: *tariqa*). *Turuq* were not new to the Middle East. Sufis—those who adhered to popular, sometimes mystical forms of Islam—had used this structure for centuries to link initiates with their spiritual guides and with each other. But in the eighteenth century many mainstream Muslims, such as artisans and merchants, joined *turuq* to find solutions to common problems. To this end, members of these *turuq* went back to the Qur'an and hadith to see how the prophet and first community might have handled similar problems. (This phenomenon, called neo-sufism, has been hotly debated among scholars, so keep in mind this is only one side of the story.) While hadith had always been a pillar of Islamic law, the fact that sufis would turn to hadith to resolve day-to-day problems was hardly conventional. In other words, these *turuq* adopted the form of earlier *turuq* but used them for the very practical ends of reestablishing a sense of community and determining the rules for ethical/legal conduct.

Turuq thus became the vehicles for purification and revival. Since certain *turuq* and sufi masters were important in some cities, merchants, ulama, and the like would travel from city to city, cross-fertilizing ideas from one part of the Ottoman Empire or Persia with ideas from another—from Istanbul to Damascus to Mecca and Medina to Cairo, with its great Islamic university, al-Azhar.

At the same time, on the fringes of the Ottoman Empire where central control was particularly weak or the presence of imperialists was particularly strong, moral reconstruction based on the Medinan model took on a more overtly political form. The Sanusiyya *tariqa* that flourished in the territory that now constitutes Libya was typical. Founded by Muhammad ibn ʿAli al-Sanusi (1787–1859), who had studied in Egypt and Mecca and who preached a rigid puritanism, the *tariqa* spread throughout North and West Africa, uniting diverse tribes on the basis of a back-to-basics theology. Within a few years, there were approximately 140 Sanusiyya lodges across North Africa. These lodges participated

Students at al-Azhar, date unknown. (*From: The Collection of the author.*)

in religious study, agricultural settlement, and trade. Later, they would play a central role in the fight against the Italians who invaded North Africa in the beginning of the twentieth century, and a descendant of Muhammad ibn ʿAli al-Sanusi became the first and only king of the independent state of Libya, which was founded in 1951.

Another famous puritanical movement was founded by Muhammad ibn ʿAbd al-Wahhab in central Arabia. Ibn ʿAbd al-Wahhab rejected many of the folk practices of Arabia (worship of saints, pilgrimages to local cult centers, and so on) and what he regarded as the quibbling of medieval scholars. In fact, he rejected any authority but the Qurʾan and hadith. He joined forces with a local chieftain, Muhammad ibn Saʿud, and, as the official version of events puts it, the combination of sword and message proved unbeatable in Arabia. By 1803, ibn Saʿud's tribesmen had conquered Mecca, establishing a puritanical Islamic state based on the Medinan model there. This state was, however, soon suppressed by an Egyptian army under Mehmet Ali's son, Ibrahim, working at the behest of the Ottoman government. As we shall see in Chapter 12, this was not the final episode in the saga involving the descendants of ibn Saʿud.

Some intellectuals took salafism in a very different direction. Embracing the institutions and ideas brought to the region by integration and peripheralization, defensive developmentalism, and imperialism, many sought to reconstruct Middle Eastern society along Western lines. They argued that the true Islam which had preserved Greek philosophy during Europe's Dark Ages was not incompatible with science and reason. If Islam would shed its recent superstitious additions and root itself in the very reason that had given it its power, they argued, it could act as the foundation for a Middle Eastern scientific and industrial revolution. Those who argued that true Islam is compatible with Western notions of progress and other modern ideas are called "Islamic modernists."

Some Islamic modernists had been exposed directly to Western ideas and frequently were acquainted with either English or French. Others developed their ideas independently, as a result of their lifetime exposure to institutions and participation in practices prompted by defensive developmentalism, imperialism, or both. Unlike the pure Westernizers, who frequently blamed Islam for the so-called backwardness of the Middle East and promoted such Western ideas as secularism, Islamic modernists were more selective in what they chose to borrow from the West—although some were pickier than others. It is probable that most Islamic modernists honestly believed that Islam and Western ideas were reconcilable. Others, however, were more cynical or realistic (depending on your point of view). They wanted drastic change along the lines advocated by the Westernizers. However, they felt that the Middle Eastern population was too backward or the power of the government or religious establishment was too entrenched to allow a frontal assault to succeed. Realizing that their opinions were not held by the majority of the population, they sought to manipulate forces greater than themselves to effect change. They did this by masking their ideas in a conservative, even religious rhetoric. Many of those who did this belonged to secret societies or were members of minority groups or despised religious sects (such as the Babis).

Salafism was not the only source for Islamic modernism. In the heartland of the empire, close to the seat of power, for example, a diffuse group of intellectuals known as the Young Ottomans formed a secret society which was committed to revitalizing the empire. According to the Young Ottomans, the *tanzimat* had failed because it had been decreed from the top down and had done little to win the favor of the population or involve them in the political process. Although the changes it had brought about had strengthened the power of the sultan, this did not stop European imperial expansion at the expense of the empire. That, the Young Ottomans believed, could only be accomplished by rooting social and political reform in "Islamic principles." Since those principles were deeply embedded in Ottoman society, the Young Ottomans argued, they could, if adapted to the modern world, act as both a form of social "glue" that could unite society and inspire Ottoman patriotism. At the top of the list of Islamic principles advocated by the Young Ottomans was that of *shura*—government by consultation. Although the concept of *shura* originally referred to such convocations as that held by the elders of the early Islamic community to choose the successor to Muhammad, the Young Ottomans adopted it to argue for an Ottoman constitution and parliament. Their argument—borrowed by disciples or developed independently by later generations of like-minded revolutionaries and political reformers—can be found in the rhetoric of the Ottoman constitutional movement of 1876, the ʿUrabi rebellion in Egypt, and the Persian Constitutional Revolution of 1905.

Islamic modernism also found a home in Persia. Since Persia did not provide an environment conducive to salafism—Shiʿis believe in the religious authority of their imams as well as the Qurʾan and hadith—here, too, we must look elsewhere for its origins. Beginning in the mid-nineteenth century, a new class of intellectuals arose in Persia, many of whom had been educated in the Dar al-Funun in Tehran. Others received their education abroad, often in Europe. Both groups were affected by intellectual currents that traversed the region (by 1889, 16,000 Persians resided in Istanbul, a number of them political refugees) and both were repulsed by the same cultural and political "degeneration" in Persia that inspired others elsewhere in the region to turn to Islamic modernist ideas. But because of their position in society, and because of their aspirations for themselves and for a regenerated Persia, both groups also had a natural affinity with European political and social ideas of the time—particularly the thought of two European thinkers.

Auguste Comte (1798–1857) was a French intellectual who formulated a philosophy called Positivism. Positivism had many adherents in Europe, as it had in the Ottoman Empire and Persia. As a matter of fact, the Committee of Union and Progress that took over the Ottoman government in 1913 derived its name from two watchwords of Comte's philosophy: unity and progress. Positivism contained two ideas that were particularly appealing to intellectuals in the Middle East, which is why they gravitated to it. Comte believed that societies evolve through stages, like biological species: from religious-based societies through philosophically-based societies to scientifically-based societies. Thus, even though a society like Persia might be stuck at the first level, there was no reason why it might not rise to a higher level, as had European societies. Comte also believed that society should be guided by a class of technocrats known as *savants*. These were people who understood the scientific principles upon which society should be based. Of course, a Persian intellectual who thought of himself as a *monavvar al-fekr* (enlightened thinker), or, for that matter, an Arab intellectual who thought of himself as *mutanawwir* (enlightened), identified with this role.

The second European philosopher to whose ideas Persian (and Ottoman) intellectuals gravitated was Henri Comte de Saint-Simon (1760–1825). Saint-Simon's philosophy was similar to Comte's in many ways, but he envisioned the establishment of a planned, socialist-style economy run by benevolent industrialists—the sort of people many of the graduates of the Dar al-Funun wanted to become.

In all, many Persian intellectuals thought of themselves as a privileged enlightened class that was united by its opposition to royal despotism, religious fanaticism, and foreign imperialism. It was difficult for graduates of the Dar al-Funun and their allies to organize against these problems openly. After all, royalty and clerics do not appreciate being told they are despotic and fanatic. Thus, many joined together in secret societies called *anjumanha* (sing.: *anjuman*), where they could engage in political conspiracy. Others simply masked their ideas.

While there were numerous participants in *anjumanha*, historians have highlighted the careers and influence of two in particular. Mirza Malkom Khan was an Armenian Christian who may or may not have converted to Islam. He grew up and was educated in Paris, then returned to Persia, where he taught at the Dar al-Funun. Malkom Khan had an ambivalent relationship with religion.

Like Comte, Malkom Khan thought that religion would be superseded by "humanity" and "reason." But Malkom Khan also thought that religion in general and the ulama in particular could be enlisted to build a new Persia. He was particularly enamored by the idea of *ijtihad*, whose application, he believed, might be harnessed to advance society. Malkom Khan organized several secret societies that included intellectuals, guild leaders, ulama, and, on occasion, members of the Qajar family. Many of those who participated in the Constitutional Revolution of 1905 were affiliated with Malkom Khan's secret societies and may have been introduced to the idea of a constitution through Malkom Khan's *Book of Reform*. The *Book of Reform*, in turn, presented constitutionalist ideas picked up from the Young Ottomans.

Jamal al-Din al-Afghani was a second political conspirator of importance. In spite of his name (which means Jamal al-Din, the Afghan), Jamal al-Din was probably born in Persia and sought to obscure his Shiʿi origins so that he might be more influential in the Sunni world. During his lifetime, he traveled widely, living in Paris, Cairo, and Istanbul, among other places. Like Malkom Khan, al-Afghani was drawn to European and Ottoman ideas about social evolution and the special role for an intellectual elite in society. Like Malkom Khan, al-Afghani sought to harness religion to the cause of social change. And, like Malkom Khan, al-Afghani organized secret societies that would become politically influential. One of al-Afghani's followers took political activism to a whole new level by assassinating Nasr ed-Din Shah in 1896. Many others participated in the Persian Constitutional Revolution of 1905.

The sources from which Malkom Khan and al-Afghani drew were not just those within the European philosophical tradition. To the contrary, both they and their followers grew up in an environment enriched by the Persian legal tradition as well, particularly the debates between two schools of legal thought. Up until the early nineteenth century, there had been no consensus among the ulama of Persia regarding their role in society. On the one hand, followers of the Akhbari school claimed that the ulama were limited in their legal and doctrinal decisions to the traditions of the prophet and the teachings of the twelve imams. In contrast, members of the Usuli school asserted that select religious scholars— called *mujtahids*—could act as representatives of the hidden imam. *Mujtahids* were chosen informally from among the ulama because of their piety and learning. They had the right to give fresh interpretations to the law—to practice *ijtihad*—in order to make the law compatible with real-life conditions.

During the nineteenth century, the Usulis came out on top. They remained on top, at least in part, because they filled a necessary niche in Qajar society. Remember, the power of the Qajars was limited and their legitimacy was always suspect. Because the Usulis believed that ulama should be actively engaged in society by performing educational, judicial, and even legitimation functions for the Qajars, the Usuli tendency was perfectly consistent with the Qajar style of rule. Usuli ulama held a monopoly over the educational apparatus and over civil law (laws not related to state administration and criminal activity). Thus, unlike ulama in the Ottoman Empire and Egypt whose power was usurped by the state, the victory of the Usulis over the Akhbaris guaranteed that the ulama of Persia would retain a direct and necessary role in society. As a result, the participation or aloofness of the ulama could make or break such political movements as the Tobacco Protest, the Constitutional Revolution, and the revolution of 1978–1979.

Like the Usulis, Malkom Khan and al-Afghani believed that ulama had a key role to play in society, that Islam constantly had to be revised to be applicable to contemporary conditions, and that *ijtihad* could be harnessed for that revision. And like the Young Ottomans, both believed that Islam was ingrained in Eastern society and that any reform of that society had to take this into account. At the same time, both preached that Muslims had much to learn from the West, particularly in the realm of science and technology.

But how could religion and science be made compatible? Could Islam—or, indeed, any religion—be used to promote modernity? From the Enlightenment through Comte and beyond, Western social philosophers have pronounced secularism to be a prime attribute of modernity and religion to be either the primitive ancestor of modernity or its mortal enemy. Whether or not this is the case is the subject of the next chapter.

CHAPTER 9

Secularism and Modernity

On 25 April 2013, Kholoud Sukkarieh married Nidal Darwish in Beirut, Lebanon. Since both were young, unmarried, and in love, their story might seem commonplace. What makes it uncommon is that Sukkarieh is Sunni and Darwish is Shiʿi, and their marriage was the first civil (i.e., non-religious) marriage in Lebanese history. When their son Ghadi was born on 30 September 2013 (don't do the math), the English language media referred to him as Lebanon's first "sect-less baby."

In the contemporary Middle East, there are only two states—Turkey and Lebanon (as of 2013)—that perform civil marriages. If, for example, Middle Easterners in other states want to get married, they must go to their local clergyman and not to a nondenominational marriage license bureau. This, in effect, both discourages and obstructs interfaith marriages in the region. (Interestingly, Iraq has allowed—and recently has encouraged—intermarriage between Sunnis and Shiʿis, in part to build an inclusive Iraqi identity, in part because Iraqi law defines both Sunnis and Shiʿis as Muslim. As discussed in Chapter 6, 30 percent of families in Iraq are rooted in both sects—an embarrassing statistic for those who decry the 1,400-year-old animosity between Sunnis and Shiʿis.)

Issues of personal status such as marriage are not the only ones in which religion matters. Article 2 of the Egyptian constitution of 1973 states that "Islam is the religion of the State and Arabic is its official language. The principles of Islamic law are the main source of legislation." In 2012 Egypt adopted a new constitution which retained the identical wording. That's not surprising, considering the committee which drafted the constitution was dominated by the Egyptian Muslim Brotherhood, a group that had been devoted to "Islamizing" Egyptian society. What is surprising is that the same wording shows up again in the constitution adopted in 2013, after the military overthrew the Muslim Brotherhood government and banned the organization. Then there is Tunisia's post-uprising constitution, hailed as the most liberal in the Arab world because, among other stipulations, it guarantees equal rights for women unconditionally. That constitution does not even mention Islamic law. On the other hand, Article 1 defines Tunisia in the following way: "Tunisia is a free, independent and sovereign state. Its religion is Islam, its language is Arabic and its system the Republic."

Many in the West look at the Middle East and decry the role religion plays in the public sphere. They claim that secularism is an essential part of modernity and that states that are not secular cannot be considered modern. Those who do this, however, assume that the attributes of *Western* modernity can be generalized for the entire world. Another interpretation of the relationship between secularism and modernity is possible, however. It might be argued that secularism developed in the West as a result of idiosyncrasies associated with that region's historical experience. Europe suffered from bloody religious wars in the sixteenth and seventeenth centuries. Over the course of the centuries that followed, many in the West came to believe that the way to prevent a recurrence of that bloodshed was by severing the connection between politics and religion. In the process, they made the state, not religion, the ultimate source of authority. And since European modernity became the gold standard for "civilization" throughout the world, secularism tagged along for the ride.

The historical experience of Middle Eastern states was quite different from that of European states. As a result, their evolution was also quite different. The prominent role religion plays in politics and political discourse of Middle Eastern states does not mean these states are not modern; rather, it means these states subscribe to an alternative form of modernity.

The role religion plays in contemporary Middle Eastern life emerged during the second half of the nineteenth century. The transformation of the Middle Eastern state in the nineteenth century fostered a corresponding transformation of religious institutions and doctrines. As the region was integrated into the modern state system, the meaning and function of religion in society changed. Those Islamic institutions and beliefs that political and religious elites and non-elites found appropriate for changing circumstances grew stronger. Others diminished in value.

The influence of nineteenth-century events on religion was not restricted to Islam or to the Middle East. A similar institutional and doctrinal transformation occurred in the Roman Catholic Church as a result of its competition with the nineteenth-century European state, the emergence of mass politics, and the spread of market relations. After the Vatican Council of 1869, popes became infallible on issues of faith and morals (but not, significantly, on other issues that were consigned to the state). The church sanctioned the formation of mass-based Catholic political parties, and church institutions were redesigned to parallel or complement those of the modern state. In other words, both church structures and church doctrines came to reflect the social and political world in which the church functioned.

In the Ottoman Empire, where the "church" was not as centralized as in Catholic Europe, the transformation of religious institutions and doctrines occurred in two ways. Sometimes it occurred as a result of state initiative. At other times it emerged from below, as citizens of the empire reacted to new state structures or to European models.

As discussed in Chapter 5, historians have commonly divided the responses of the nineteenth-century Ottoman state to European economic, political, and military expansion into two periods. During the first, the so-called *tanzimat* period, the Ottoman state attempted to foster a notion of a political community made up of equal citizens bound together by their commitment to a common set of legal norms. This form of *osmanlilik* failed for a number of reasons, also described earlier. Under Sultan Abdulhamid II, the state introduced a new form of *osmanlilik*. In place of the idea that all Ottoman citizens were to be equal regardless of their religion, the Ottoman state under Abdulhamid II promoted an ideology that gave pride of place to an Ottoman/*Islamic* identity.

There were two reasons why the new interpretation of *osmanlilik* became feasible. First, the new interpretation would have been impossible had it not been for the intellectuals and political activists who had laid the foundation for it over the course of the nineteenth century. Islamic modernists and others discussed in the previous chapter picked up on European social theories and applied them to understand their own history and current circumstances. One of the first Middle Easterners to do this was Rifaʿa Rafiʿ al-Tahtawi, an Egyptian ʿalim. In 1826, Mehmet Ali sent al-Tahtawi to Paris at the head of an educational mission. When al-Tahtawi returned to Egypt five years later, Mehmet Ali appointed him director of the School of Languages, an institution where European books were translated into Arabic. Under al-Tahtawi's directorship, the school not only translated European military manuals, but works on geography and history as well. As a result, the concepts and vocabulary of European philosophy and social theory entered the lexicon of the region. (A similar phenomenon took place in Persia, which sent its first educational mission to Britain in 1815.)

Take, for example, the concept of "civilization." Before al-Tahtawi, Arabic books used the term "civilization" to indicate the high culture, refined manners, and luxurious trappings of urban life. Borrowing from the writings of the fourteenth-century scholar and traveler Ibn Khaldun, they contrasted civilization with the harshness and rusticity of desert and rural life. In the nineteenth century, the concept of "civilization" began to take on a new meaning in the region. Upon his return from Paris, al-Tahtawi introduced the notion of separate "Western" and "Eastern" civilizations then in vogue in Europe (as it is in the United States after 9/11). Like his European contemporaries, al-Tahtawi believed that each civilization possessed a distinguishing characteristic that differentiated it from the other: While science defined Western civilization, Islam and Islamic law defined its counterpart. Later writers developed this notion of "civilization" further, and even introduced the notion of a "clash of civilizations." Thus, according to al-Afghani,

> The problem facing the "East" is its struggle with the "West." Both cloak themselves in the armor of religion. The Westerner is an adherent of Christianity and the Easterner of Islam, and the people of the two religions are like a hard projectile in the hands of their throwers.

For both al-Tahtawi and al-Afghani, then, Islam was not only a divine message but also an expression of a culturally and geographically distinct civilization. Since the Ottoman Empire was the preeminent Muslim power of its time, it was logical that Sultan Abdulhamid II and his associates would link Islam and imperial identity. As the semiofficial newspaper *La Turquie* put it, "Islam is not only a religion, it is a nationality."

The second factor that made an Islamic *osmanlilik* feasible was the changing religious composition of the empire. The steady retreat of the Ottoman Empire from Europe during the nineteenth century naturally decreased the number of Christians under imperial rule. In addition, as Balkan nationalisms spread in southeastern Europe and Russian expansionism continued to the north and east, Muslim immigrants from Europe and the Caucasus flooded into the empire. As a result, the proportion of Muslims to Christians within the empire increased decidedly. In the 1860s and 1870s, more than two million Circassian, Chechen, Bosnian, Bulgarian, Romanian, and Greek Muslims immigrated into the empire. The Ottoman government dispersed these immigrants throughout its domains. It encouraged Circassian and Chechen immigrants to settle and pacify the unruly frontier that is now Jordan, and so many Muslims from outside the empire took up residence in Damascus that one of the districts of the city is still known as Muhajirin (literally, "emigrants"). Identified by their persecutors outside the Ottoman Empire as members of an inassimilable minority group, many of these immigrants themselves had come to associate religious affiliation with national identity. After all, why would displaced Chechens and Bosnians be consigned to the same fate except that members of both groups were Muslims? And why should the Ottoman Empire take them in, except for the fact that it was the foremost Muslim power?

Taking all this into account, it should be obvious that it was not a stretch for Abdulhamid II to champion an Islamic *osmanlilik*. Abdulhamid II asserted his role as caliph in a manner that was rare among Ottoman sultans. His government attempted to standardize Islamic belief, intermix state and religious institutions, and associate loyalty to the state with loyalty to Islam. Among the activities the Ottoman government undertook to achieve these goals during the Hamidian period were the following:

1. *Missionary Activity within the Empire*: During the late nineteenth century, the Ottoman government worried about the threat posed by Christian missionaries operating in the empire and about Wahhabism, which had established a foothold in the Arabian peninsula. It also worried about the rapid spread of Shiʿism among the tribes of southern Iraq. Shiʿism was, after all, the state religion of Persia, the Ottoman's rival to the east, and its spread in Iraq endangered Ottoman control there. The Ottoman government thus sought to reduce the threat posed by potentially subversive sects housed in the empire by sending out missionaries to convert members of those sects—Alawites in Syria and eastern Anatolia, Yazidis in Iraq, select sufi groups throughout the empire—to a form of Islam it regarded as orthodox.

2. *Dissemination of Propaganda and Official Islamic Texts*: In an attempt to make Islamic doctrine uniform and foster the idea of a unified Islamic "culture," the Ottoman state made the printing of the Qur'an a state monopoly and established a Commission for the Inspection of Qur'ans. The state also supported the publication of over four thousand books and pamphlets in the first fifteen years of Abdulhamid II's reign alone. These books not only included "classic" Islamic legal and religious texts, but books and pamphlets depicting the exploits of Muslim heroes such as Saladin, who had fought the enemies of Islam.

3. *Imperial Patronage and Employment of Religious Scholars*: In addition to expanded imperial patronage, ulama of all ranks from throughout the empire were integrated into imperial institutions, from municipal and provincial councils to the network of imperial schools. Ulama thus participated in the Military Council, the Council of Public Works, the Council of Finance, the Council of Agriculture, the Council of the Navy, the Council of Police, the Council of the Arsenal, and the Council of State, the central legislative body of the empire.

4. *Support for Religious Endowments and Infrastructure*: To bolster the Islamic credentials of the Ottoman government and the caliphal pretensions of the Ottoman sultan, the imperial government undertook the construction and restoration of Islamic monuments and expanded its contributions to religious endowments. For example, the imperial government supervised the reconstruction of the famous Umayyad Mosque in Damascus, partly destroyed by fire in 1893. These activities received extensive coverage in the official gazettes published in provincial capitals.

The most famous building project during the Hamidian period was the Hijaz Railroad. The government intended the railroad to connect Istanbul with the holy cities of Mecca and Medina (it eventually reached the latter but not the former). Since the railroad was built to assist Muslims in making the annual pilgrimage to the two holy cities, the government presented the Hijaz Railroad as an *Islamic* railroad and financed it by encouraging Muslims throughout the world to underwrite its costs.

The Islamic *osmanlilik* promoted by Abdulhamid II survived beyond his reign. The Young Turks deposed Abdulhamid II in 1909. Once in power they attempted to restore the secular *osmanlilik* of the *tanzimat* to bind together what remained of the empire. They did this not only to differentiate themselves from Abdulhamid II, but because they believed that the "constraints imposed by the modern age had made religiosity a weaker influence in building social and political nations over time," as a Syrian newspaper put it a few years later. Eventually, they returned to the Islamic *osmanlilik* of the deposed sultan. Policies and institutions created over the course of the previous three decades were not easily abandoned, particularly since the goals of the Young Turks—development and centralization—so closely matched those of Abdulhamid II.

There was another reason why the Young Turks had to change course: Abdulhamid II's policies had struck a chord with many in the empire. Soon after the Young Turk Revolution, soldiers, religious students, and others in such cities as Istanbul and Damascus went out into the streets in support of a countercoup on behalf of the sultan launched by an association called the Muhammadan Union. Inhabitants of the Maydan district of Damascus, for example, decorated and illuminated their streets in honor of the occasion, and marched through the streets of their quarter chanting, a bit prematurely, "God has granted victory to the sultan." Echoing the sentiments of *La Turquie*, a spokesman for the Muhammadan Union defended the failed countercoup by reaffirming his association's commitment to Abdulhamid II's Islamic *osmanlilik*: "The strongest bond of Arab, Turk, Kurd, Albanian, Circassian, and Laz [a people originally from the Caucasus inhabiting the Black Sea area]—and their nationhood—is nothing other than Islam." In the end, the countercoup failed.

Members of the short-lived Muhammadan Union were not the only ones who attempted to take the Hamidian blend of Islam and politics to the street. Two years after the Young Turks deposed Abdulhamid II, a group of ulama in Damascus began publishing a periodical, *al-Haqa'iq*, that urged both the Young Turks and the citizens of the empire not to abandon the policies of the former sultan. The members of this group were neither Westernizers nor Islamic modernists. They did not seek to reform Islam, nor did they seek to throw out the work of Islamic scholars who had interpreted the law for centuries. In fact, they claimed to be upholding religious tradition. Nevertheless, the Islam for which these ulama agitated was in fact an Islam that had been retooled for the modern age. Like the Young Turks and their Westernizing and Islamic modernist supporters, the ulama who wrote for *al-Haqa'iq* embraced such European notions as the progress of nations, universal standards of civilization, and the division of the world into an "East" and a "West." They integrated these notions into their polemics. Unlike their opponents, however, they distinguished themselves by their defense of "traditional values" and by their incessant denunciations of "the corruption of morals," which, they maintained, their opponents encouraged by attempting to separate religion and politics.

Nations could only be strong and progress, these ulama claimed (in words reminiscent of those used by Young Ottoman modernists), if they remained true to the religion and customs that engendered and defined them and that bound together their citizens in a common struggle. "If one thinks that religion orders inactivity and laziness," one contributor to *al-Haqa'iq* wrote, "he is a base, bigoted, ignoramus, or a treacherous Westernizer. Does he not understand that religion is our path to civilization and progress?" The ulama associated with *al-Haqa'iq* thus called on their fellow citizens to safeguard the empire's Islamic character and to shun foreign influences that could only lead to its weakening. At the same time, they demanded that the Young Turk government continue Abdulhamid II's policies of defensive developmentalism to safeguard Islam from European imperialism. To accomplish both these goals, these self-proclaimed traditionalists called for the establishment of an Islamic political party to compete in the arena of the new mass politics.

Constantinople. L'armée libératrice conduit à la caserne du Harbié les soldats mutinés qui viennent de se rendre le 25 avril 1909

Istanbul, 1909: Soldiers loyal to the Young Turks march "mutineers"—participants in the Muhammadan Union uprising—off to prison. (*From: The Collection of Wolf-Dieter Lemke.*)

That the ulama associated with *al-Haqa'iq* would even think of founding an Islamic political party to guarantee the "progress" of the "nation" demonstrates the extent to which the nineteenth-century cultural, social, and political transformation had influenced religious doctrines and institutions in the Ottoman Empire. And since this transformation was not limited to one city or region of the empire, associations such as the Muhammadan Union and the *al-Haqa'iq* group could be found throughout the empire. In the aftermath of World War I, when a collection of independent states came to replace the Ottoman Empire, associations and political parties committed to ideas similar to those recounted here forced their way into the political fray and extracted concessions from the new rulers. Thus, while many of the states that emerged from the Ottoman Empire did so under the supervision of European imperial powers, they did not produce a simple duplication of the public/private, religious/secular boundaries found in most states of Europe or North America.

CHAPTER 10

Constitutionalism

On 11 December 1905, the governor of Tehran ordered the beating of two sugar merchants whom he accused of price gouging. The merchants claimed that they could not reduce the price they charged for sugar to levels demanded by the government. They argued that, unlike foreign merchants who paid only a 5 percent tariff on imported sugar, they had to pay 20 percent. They had to pass this additional cost on to their customers.

Word of the beating spread throughout Tehran. Two days later, about two thousand angry tradesmen, merchants, ulama, and theology students took refuge at the Shah Abd al-Azim Shrine in Tehran. Taking refuge, or *bast*, in a sanctuary—a shrine, a mosque, or even a government telegraph office—was a time-honored ritual of political protest in Persia, much as one-day strikes are in France.

During the month-long *bast*, the protesters drew up a list of demands, which they submitted to the prime minister. Their first two demands related directly to the incident that sparked the protest in the first place. The protesters demanded the dismissal of the governor of Tehran who had ordered the beatings of the merchants, as well as the dismissal of Joseph Naus, one of several Belgian administrators whom the shah had hired in 1899 to reorganize the collection of customs. As a foreigner, Naus had become a lightning rod for popular anger. For the protesters, he symbolized both the privileges the Persian government had accorded foreigners and imperialist designs on their country.

The third demand made by the protesters was more far-reaching. Moving beyond the immediate events that precipitated their *bast*, the protesters demanded the establishment of something they called a "House of Justice." Although the term "House of Justice" is ambiguous, it was widely interpreted to mean a parliament. That parliament, called a *majlis*, convened in October 1906, and representatives immediately began drafting a "Fundamental Law"—a constitution—to secure the gains the protests had brought. Thus began the Persian Constitutional Revolution of 1905.

Persia was not the only place in the Middle East where the desire for constitutional and parliamentary rule inspired political action, nor was it the first. That distinction belongs to Tunisia, whose ruler (Muhammad III al-Sadiq) promulgated a constitution in 1861. That constitutional experiment, inspired by Islamic modernists and secular reformers who had been trained at the polytechnic established by Ahmad Bey, ran afoul of conservatives, Muhammad III (who stymied its implementation), and European governments (which, among other things, found dealing directly with Tunisia's ruler without interference from a Supreme Council much easier). Although the experiment was short-lived—Muhammad III suspended the constitution three years later and Tunisia would not have another for close to a century—the struggle between pro- and anti-constitutionalists foreshadowed events elsewhere in the region.

In Istanbul, bureaucrats and army officers, supported by popular protest, twice compelled the sultan to adopt a constitution and convene a parliament. The first instance occurred in 1876, when the empire was in the midst of crisis. Drought and famine had brought widespread suffering to peasants, the government had found itself unable to pay its external debt or its army and navy, and, in the wake of revolts by Bosnian Serbs and Bulgarians, a conference of European powers had convened in Istanbul to impose a Balkan settlement on the empire. Roused by the multiple failures of the Ottoman government, theological students rioted in Istanbul, demanding the dismissal of the grand vizier (the sultan's chief minister) and the chief mufti (the highest ranking Muslim religious official in the empire). According to the British ambassador, who was a witness to the unfolding events,

> The word "Constitution" was in every mouth; that the softas [religious students], representing the intelligent public opinion of the capital, knowing themselves to be supported by the nation—Christian as well as Mahometan—would not, I believed, relax their efforts till they obtained it, and that, should the Sultan refuse to grant it, an attempt to depose him appeared almost inevitable; that texts from the Koran were circulated proving to the faithful that the form of government sanctioned by it was properly democratic, and that the absolute authority now wielded by the Sultan was an usurpation of the rights of the people and not sanctioned by the Holy Law; and both texts and precedents were appealed to, to show that obedience was not due to a Sovereign who neglected the interests of the state.

Soon after these events, constitution-minded bureaucrats deposed Sultan Abdulaziz I, replaced him with his alcoholic nephew, and then replaced the replacement with Abdulhamid II, another nephew of Abdulaziz I. Before they threw their support to Abdulhamid II, however, they extracted from him a promise that he would rule in accordance with a constitution.

The first Ottoman constitutional period was even shorter than Tunisia's, lasting a mere two years. In 1878, Sultan Abdulhamid II, using the outbreak of war with Russia as a pretext to break his promise, suspended the Ottoman constitution, dismissed the elected parliament, and concentrated power in his own hands. Not until thirty years later, when a mutiny of Young Turk military officers stationed in Macedonia sparked a wider rebellion, was the constitution restored. That constitution remained in effect until World War I.

As we have seen in previous chapters, the transformation of society during the late nineteenth century laid the foundations for the emergence of a modern public sphere in the Middle East. In cities throughout the Ottoman Empire and Persia, all sorts of new ideas germane to new social, political, and economic realities emerged and competed with each other. The new Islamic orthodoxy that inspired the Muhammadan Union and the *al-Haqa'iq* group represented one intellectual current that attracted a following. Constitutionalism represented another. Accordingly, between the final quarter of the nineteenth century and the first decade of the twentieth, a significant group of Westernizing intellectuals and Islamic modernists, working in alliance with urban crowds and political reformers, devoted their political energies to the realization of constitutional rule. Ottoman civil servants and soldiers, socialists in the northern Persian city of Tabriz, and even the partisans of Ahmad ʿUrabi who demanded a charter from the Egyptian khedive in 1881–1882 all viewed constitutionalism as a panacea for the ills that beset their states.

Both local and international factors inspired the rise of constitutionalist movements in the region during this period. As we have seen, local factors—the beating of sugar merchants in Persia, a crisis of legitimacy in the Ottoman Empire, an army mutiny in Egypt—provided the spark that touched off constitutionalist movements in the Middle East. But this spark was, in turn, touched off

Crowd in Istanbul listening to the announcement of the restoration of the Ottoman constitution, July 1908. (*From: The Collection of Wolf-Dieter Lemke.*)

in a context defined by growing pains in the world economy, the consolidation of territorial states, intensified imperialist pressure and interimperialist rivalry, and the emergence of new social classes whose role in politics and society had yet to be determined. These conditions were not exclusive to the Middle East. They influenced events throughout the globe. Thus, any explanation for constitutionalism in the Middle East must take into account the fact that constitutionalist movements also emerged in such places as Japan (1874), Russia (1905), Mexico (1910), and China (1911). In each of these places, constitutionalists thought that the key to solving the predicament their states found themselves in was political reform, and political reform meant constitutional and parliamentary rule.

The first Ottoman constitutional revolution, the ʿUrabi Revolt, and the Persian Constitutional Revolution took place during periods of global economic crisis. Of course, in none of these cases did the economic crisis define the direction political protest would take. It did, however, prompt widespread dissatisfaction, and this dissatisfaction often found expression in constitutional movements.

In 1873, the collapse of the Viennese stock market precipitated a period of world depression that, according to some economists, lasted until 1896. The Depression of 1873 may not have been the first truly worldwide depression. Some economists give that honor to the "panic" of 1856–1857. And, of course, attributing such a cataclysmic event to the collapse of a stock market in Vienna would be as glib as attributing the Great Depression of the 1930s to the collapse of the New York Stock Exchange. Economists have, as economists tend to do, given numerous reasons for the Depression of 1873. Some have credited rampant stock speculation. Others, the emergence of the United States and Germany as new industrial powers. Still others, the spread of cash-cropping to the far reaches of the globe and the introduction of new technologies, such as refrigeration and railroads, which glutted markets with agricultural products and mineral wealth. But whatever the actual cause of the depression, its magnitude and breadth were unprecedented. The 1873–1896 depression affected countries from Argentina to the Dutch East Indies. In Europe, the price of wheat declined 30 percent. In the United States, two-thirds of all railroads went under. In the Middle East, the collapse of international trade and commodity prices bred discontent among merchants and farmers. It also resulted in Ottoman and Egyptian bankruptcy and foreign supervision of the finances of each. Money that had gone into public works, military salaries, and the expansion of services vital to the functioning of modern states now went to repaying European creditors. Many in the region were resentful.

In every country hit by depression, popular movements emerged. The ideologies expressed by these movements reflected local conditions and conventions: thus, communism, trade unionism, and anarchism in the cities and factories of Western Europe and North America, populism on the Great Plains of North America, and anti-Semitism in any place in Europe where Jews could be found. In the Middle East, discontent was often channeled into constitutionalism. And why not? Governments that seemed to have brought such disaster to the region,

Persian parliamentarians in session. (*From: The Collection of Wolf-Dieter Lemke.*)

that were unresponsive and did not allow those best fit for governance any role in decision making needed to be more representative and held responsible to their citizens. Constitutions and parliaments, many believed, would guarantee that broadening of representation and assumption of responsibility.

The economic background for the Persian Constitutional Revolution was a bit different from that which stimulated constitutionalism in the Ottoman Empire. During the late nineteenth and early twentieth centuries, the Persian economy was hit by a double whammy. First, there was the depression of 1873–1896, which affected Persia just as it did every other economy locked into the world system. Then, just as much of the world was climbing out of depression, another shock hit the economies of China, Japan, India, and Persia. Unlike the economies of the West, which used a gold standard, the economies of these states were silver-based. During the late nineteenth century, two events occurred that caused the silver-backed currencies of these countries to lose value. Both events bear a striking resemblance to those which many historians argue took place in the sixteenth century. First, as more and more countries bound themselves to the gold standard, silver flooded east, where it had a higher value. Second, the discovery of new deposits of silver, such as the Comstock Lode in Nevada and the Albert Silver Mine in South Africa, flooded the international market with the precious metal. This, too, affected economies and politics around the world. Cash-strapped, indebted farmers in the United States demanded that the United States Mint coin silver so that they not be "crucified on a cross of gold," as the 1896 Democratic presidential candidate, William Jennings Bryan, put it. In Persia, where coining silver was already the practice, prices skyrocketed 600 percent between 1850 and 1890. The Persian government borrowed heavily as a result of this inflation, and soon had to take out additional loans to pay back previous ones.

At the same time as the collapse of the international economy, both the Ottoman Empire and Persia experienced increasing political pressures that threatened their sovereignty and stimulated an anti-imperialist response. Many historians trace the increase in interimperialist rivalries directly to the Depression of 1873. After the onset of the depression, protectionist sentiments challenged free market liberalism, and Europeans and North Americans sought to establish overseas empires from which they could exclude foreign competition. Both Middle Eastern empires felt the sting of the "new imperialism" in forms that ranged from debt commissions to increased competition for concessions. In both empires, constitutionalists blamed autocratic government for the weak response to the threats to national sovereignty and demanded constitutional reform to strengthen their states. Constitutionalists also hoped that constitutions and parliaments would demonstrate to European powers that their empires were civilized members of the world community rather than carcasses to be picked clean by various imperialist vultures or nationalist movements.

However much they might have protested European imperialism, those who led constitutional movements were the products of the world created by imperialism and defensive measures taken by non-European states in response to imperialism. For example, Midhat Pasha, the chief engineer of Ottoman constitutionalist intrigue in 1876, had studied briefly at a palace school established by an early *tanzimat* sultan, Mahmud II. Designed to prepare students to participate in a renovated bureaucracy, the school encouraged students to stay abreast of the latest intellectual trends in Europe. Midhat Pasha also participated in an Istanbul salon dedicated to discussing such topics as Western literature and philosophy. Taking advantage of Ottoman provincial reorganization, Midhat Pasha went on to organize "model" provinces in Bulgaria, Baghdad, and Syria. These provinces might be considered laboratories in which *tanzimat* ideas were applied and tested.

Like Midhat Pasha, the military officers, bureaucrats, and intellectuals who formed the nucleus of constitutional movements throughout the region—and, indeed, throughout the world—had often received advanced educations that included a good dose of Western social science and technical know-how. The core group of army officers that founded the Committee of Union and Progress and restored the Ottoman constitution in 1908 were graduates of the military medical school in Istanbul, and many of the intellectuals who organized the *anjumanha*—the building blocks of the Persian Constitutional Revolution—had either been educated in the West or at the Dar al-Funun in Tehran. Their ideas drew from both Western and indigenous sources. Thus, the Ottoman constitution was modeled on the constitution of Belgium and justified by the ideas of the Young Ottomans. Because of their advanced education, leaders of constitutionalist movements demanded a greater role in determining the future of their states. They thought that that role would be guaranteed through constitutions and parliaments.

Constitutionalists also felt perfectly at ease in a world where newspapers could spread ideas and where the railroads and telegraph lines that connected the countryside with capital cities could mobilize popular support. The introduction of modern communications technologies, the formation of émigré communities outside the view of imperial surveillance, and labor migration played a key role in making constitutionalism an international movement. Constitutionalist movements were mutually reinforcing. Many of the Egyptians who joined the ʿUrabi movement in 1881 were influenced by the doctrines of the Young Ottomans and by the example of the Ottoman constitution, which had been announced only five years earlier. Emigré Persians in Istanbul followed closely the Ottoman constitutional movement as well as the ʿUrabi rebellion. Ottoman military officers knew what was going on in Persia in 1905 before they launched their own constitutional rebellion in 1908. And constitutionalists throughout the region took heart from the Russo–Japanese War of 1904–1905. Here, for the first time in modern history, an Asiatic power had defeated a European one. Could this have happened because the Asiatic power had a constitution while the European one did not? The Russo–Japanese War precipitated Russia's own constitutional revolution, which observers to the south also followed closely before embarking on theirs.

The close proximity of Russia affected constitutionalism in Persia in another way as well. Just as news spread from one state to another, so did techniques for mass political organizing. In the Persian case, laborers from northern Persia who had gone to Russia to work in the oil fields of Baku brought those techniques back with them when they returned home. By 1905, there were approximately three hundred thousand Persians in Russia, making up about a quarter of the oil field workers. About 80 percent of these workers eventually returned to Persia, bringing back with them ideas about trade unionism and socialism. Some organized an affiliate to the Russian Social Democratic Workers' Party called Hemmat, which promoted a combination of Islamic modernist and socialist ideas. This is one of the reasons why the northern city of Tabriz became a hotbed of pro-constitutionalist and social democratic ideas. Constitutionalists in Tabriz built a mass movement by infusing their political program with a social and economic program that advocated, among other things, an eight-hour workday, free public education, an expansion of women's legal rights, and the ownership of land by those who tilled it. After the shah launched a counterattack against the constitutionalists and closed the Persian *majlis*, Tabrizis established a pro-constitutionalist commune while an army composed of social democrats and Armenian and Muslim radicals marched from the northern city of Rasht to Tehran to restore the parliament.

In the end, constitutionalism failed in both the Ottoman Empire and Persia. In the former case, constitutional rule was replaced by the rule of a triumvirate of military leaders who took over the reins of government in 1913. They ruled the Ottoman Empire until the end of World War I. Although the constitution theoretically remained in effect in Persia, the Russians invaded from the north, destroyed the Tabrizi experiment, and dismissed the *majlis* in Tehran. The fact that elections for another *majlis* took place in 1914 is as much a testament to the inconsequence of government structures in Persia as it is evidence for the survival of constitutionalism there. Thus, the era of constitutionalism ended not so much with a bang as with a whimper. Why, then, bother with it at all?

There are two reasons constitutionalism in the Middle East is important for subsequent developments. First, constitutional movements, to a greater or lesser extent, brought about a change in the political culture of the Middle East. They made the state the site of political contestation. In other words, in the wake of the constitutional movements, control of the state apparatus became the focus of political activity. They spread the representative principle—the idea that individuals had the right to participate in governance and to select those who stood for their interests. They reinforced among the inhabitants of the Ottoman Empire and Persia the notion that they were citizens, not subjects. And they made ideology—not dynasty—the foundation for political legitimacy.

Furthermore, constitutionalist movements both embodied and spread mass politics. Even in the Ottoman Empire, where constitutionalism was twice put in place by means other than mass movements, there were widespread demonstrations in support of—as well as against—the constitutionalists. Here is how one (obviously unsympathetic) observer described demonstrations held in Damascus in support of the restoration of the Ottoman constitution:

> Imagine some five hundred illiterate young men, some with swords in their hands, others with revolvers and many with prohibited rifles stolen from the government, this whole crowd followed by a great multitude pass through the streets and the bazaars shooting and shouting. On the 8th instant, the orations in general were exceptionally liberal. A "Young Turk" having the grade of "Usbashy" stood on the platform, took out his sword and asked the people to stand up and repeat after him an oath to the meaning that if tyranny shall reign again, they would overthrow it no matter how dear it might cost them. They solemnly declared that they were ready to sacrifice for liberty their wives, their children and their blood! After this solemn oath three times three cheers were given for liberty, the Army and the sultan.

Damascus, it should be remembered, was also one of the centers for the anti-constitutionalist, anti–Young Turk Muhammadan Union demonstrations described in the previous chapter. While the success of constitutional movements in spreading the gospel of constitutions and parliaments may thus have been less than sweeping, constitutional movements were instrumental in fostering a new style of politics in the Middle East.

DOCUMENTS

Commercial Convention (Balta Liman): Britain and the Ottoman Empire

> As a price for assisting the Ottomans in expelling Mehmet Ali from Syria, the British insisted that the sultan sign the 1838 Treaty of Balta Liman. By lowering customs duties and abolishing monopolies in Ottoman territories, the treaty opened up the Ottoman Empire to British free trade policy.

Art. I. All rights, privileges, and immunities which have been conferred on the subjects or ships of Great Britain by the existing Capitulations and Treaties, are confirmed now and for ever, except in as far as they may be specifically altered by the present Convention: and it is moreover expressly stipulated, that all rights, privileges, or immunities which the Sublime Porte now grants, or may hereafter grant, to the ships and subjects of any other foreign Power, or which may suffer the ships and subjects of any other foreign Power to enjoy, shall be equally granted to, and exercised and enjoyed by, the subjects and ships of Great Britain.

Art. II. The subjects of Her Britannic Majesty, or their agents, shall be permitted to purchase at all places in the Ottoman Dominions (whether for the purposes of internal trade or exportation) all articles, without any exception whatsoever, the produce, growth, or manufacture of the said Dominions; and the Sublime Porte formally engages to abolish all monopolies of agricultural produce, or of any other articles whatsoever, as well as all *Permits* from the local Governors, either for the purchase of any article, or for its removal from one place to another when purchased; and any attempt to compel the subjects of Her Britannic Majesty to receive such *Permits* from the local Governors, shall be considered as an infraction of Treaties, and the Sublime Porte shall immediately punish with severity any Vizirs and other officers who shall have been guilty of such misconduct, and render full justice to British subjects for all injuries or losses which they may duly prove themselves to have suffered.

Art. III. If any article of Turkish produce, growth, or manufacture, be purchased by the British merchant or his agent, for the purpose of selling the same for internal consumption in Turkey, the British merchant or his agent shall pay, at the purchase and sale of such articles, and in any manner of trade therein, the same duties that are paid, in similar circumstances, by the most favoured class of Turkish subjects engaged in the internal trade of Turkey, whether Mussulmans or Rayahs.

Art. IV. If any article of Turkish produce, growth, or manufacture, be purchased for exportation, the same shall be conveyed by the British merchant or his agent, free of any kind of charge or duty whatsoever, to a convenient place of shipment, on its entry into which it shall be liable to one fixed duty of nine per cent. *ad valorem*, in lieu of all other interior duties.

Subsequently, on exportation, the duty of three per cent., as established and existing at present, shall be paid. But all articles bought in the shipping ports for exportation, and which have already paid the interior duty at entering into the same, will only pay the three per cent. export duty.

Art. V. The regulations under which Firmans are issued to British merchant vessels for passing the Dardanelles and the Bosphorus, shall be so framed as to occasion to such vessels the least possible delay.

Art. VI. It is agreed by the Turkish Government, that the regulations established in the present Convention, shall be general throughout the Turkish Empire,
whether in Turkey in Europe or Turkey in Asia, in Egypt, or other African possessions belonging to the Sublime Porte, and shall be applicable to all the subjects,
whatever their description, of the Ottoman Dominions: and the Turkish Government also agrees not to object to other foreign Powers settling their trade upon
the basis of this present Convention.

Art. VII. It having been the custom of Great Britain and the Sublime Porte, with
a view to prevent all difficulties and delay in estimating the value of articles imported into the Turkish Dominions, or exported therefrom, by British subjects, to
appoint, at intervals of fourteen years, a Commission of men well acquainted with
the traffic of both countries, who have fixed by a tariff the sum of money in the
coin of the Grand Signior, which should be paid as duty on each article; and the
term of fourteen years, during which the last adjustment of the said tariff was to
remain in force, having expired, the High Contracting Parties have agreed to
name conjointly fresh Commissioners to fix and determine the amount in money
which is to be paid by British subjects, as the duty of three per cent upon the value
of all commodities imported and exported by them; and the said Commissioners
shall establish an equitable arrangement for estimating the interior duties which,
by the present Treaty, are established on Turkish goods to be exported, and shall
also determine on the places of shipment where it may be most convenient that
such duties should be levied.

The new tariff thus established, to be in force for seven years after it has been
fixed, at the end of which time it shall be in the power of either of the parties
to demand a revision of that tariff; but if no such demand be made on either
side, within the six months after the end of the first seven years, then the tariff
shall remain in force for seven years more, reckoned from the end of the pre-
ceding seven years; and so it shall be at the end of each successive period of
seven years.

J. C. Hurewitz, *The Middle East and North Africa in World Politics: A Documentary Record, vol. 1:
European Expansion, 1535–1914* (New Haven, Conn.: Yale University Press, 1975), pp. 265–66.

The Hatt-i Sharif of Gulhane

The two cornerstones of the *tanzimat* were the *Hatt-i Sharif* of Gulhane
(1839) and the *Islahat Fermani* (1856), imperial edicts that set out an agenda
for Ottoman administrative reform and defined the rights of Ottoman citizens. The latter document reaffirmed and expanded on the promises and
program of the former.

All the world knows that since the first days of the Ottoman State, the lofty
principles of the Kuran and the rules of the Şeriat were always perfectly observed.
Our mighty Sultanate reached the highest degree of strength and power, and
all its subjects [the highest degree] of ease and prosperity. But in the last one
hundred and fifty years, because of a succession of difficulties and diverse causes,
the sacred Şeriat was not obeyed nor were the beneficent regulations followed;
consequently, the former strength and prosperity have changed into weakness
and poverty. It is evident that countries not governed by the laws of the Şeriat
cannot survive.

From the very first day of our accession to the throne, our thoughts have been devoted exclusively to the development of the empire and the promotion of the prosperity of the people. Therefore, if the geographical position of the Ottoman provinces, the fertility of the soil, and the aptitude and intelligence of the inhabitants are considered, it is manifest that, by striving to find appropriate means, the desired results will, with the aid of God, be realized within five or ten years. Thus, full of confidence in the help of the Most High and certain of the support of our Prophet, we deem it necessary and important from now on to introduce new legislation to achieve effective administration of the Ottoman Government and Provinces. Thus the principles of the requisite legislation are three:

1. The guarantees promising to our subjects perfect security for life, honor, and property.
2. A regular system of assessing taxes.
3. An equally regular system for the conscription of requisite troops and the duration of their service.

Indeed there is nothing more precious in this world than life and honor. What man, however much his character may be against violence, can prevent himself from having recourse to it, and thereby injure the government and the country, if his life and honor are endangered? If, on the contrary, he enjoys perfect security, it is clear that he will not depart from the ways of loyalty and all his actions will contribute to the welfare of the government and of the people.

If there is an absence of security for property, everyone remains indifferent to his state and his community; no one interests himself in the prosperity of the country, absorbed as he is in his own troubles and worries. If, on the contrary, the individual feels complete security about his possessions, then he will become preoccupied with his own affairs, which he will seek to expand, and his devotion and love for his state and his community will steadily grow and will undoubtedly spur him into becoming a useful member of society.

Tax assessment is also one of the most important matters to regulate. A state, for the defense of its territory, manifestly needs to maintain an army and provide other services, the costs of which can be defrayed only by taxes levied on its subjects. Although, thank God, our Empire has already been relieved of the affliction of monopolies, the harmful practice of tax-farming [iltizam], which never yielded any fruitful results, still prevails. This amounts to handing over the financial and political affairs of a country to the whims of an ordinary man and perhaps to the grasp of force and oppression, for if the tax-farmer is not of good character he will be interested only in his own profit and will behave oppressively. It is therefore necessary that from now on every subject of the Empire should be taxed according to his fortune and his means, and that he should be saved from further exaction. It is also necessary that special laws should fix and limit the expenses of our land and sea forces.

Military matters, as already pointed out, are among the most important affairs of state, and it is the inescapable duty of all the people to provide soldiers for the defense of the fatherland [vatan]. It is therefore necessary to frame regulations on the contingents that each locality should furnish according to the requirements of the time, and to reduce the term of military service to four or five years. Such legislation will put an end to the old practice, still in force, of recruiting soldiers without consideration of the size of the population in any locality, more conscripts being taken from some places and fewer from others. This practice has been throwing agriculture and trade into harmful disarray. Moreover, those who are recruited to lifetime military service suffer despair and contribute to the depopulation of the country.

In brief, unless such regulations are promulgated, power, prosperity, security, and peace may not be expected, and the basic principles [of the projected reforms] must be those enumerated above.

Thus, from now on, every defendant shall be entitled to a public hearing, according to the rules of the Şeriat, after inquiry and examination; and without the pronouncement of a regular sentence no one may secretly or publicly put another to death by poison or by any other means. No one shall be allowed to attack the honor of any other person whatsoever. Every one shall possess his property of every kind and may dispose of it freely, without let or hindrance from any person whatsoever; and the innocent heirs of a criminal shall not be deprived of their hereditary rights as a result of the confiscation of the property of such a criminal. The Muslim and non-Muslim subjects of our lofty Sultanate shall, without exception, enjoy our imperial concessions. Therefore we grant perfect security to all the populations of our Empire in their lives, their honor, and their properties, according to the sacred law.

As for the other points, decisions must be taken by majority vote. To this end, the members of the Council of Judicial Ordinances [Meclis-i Ahkam-I Adliyye], enlarged by new members as may be found necessary, to whom will be joined on certain days that we shall determine our Ministers and the high officials of the Empire, will assemble for the purpose of framing laws to regulate the security of life and property and the assessment of taxes. Every one participating in the Council will express his ideas and give his advice freely.

J. C. Hurewitz, *The Middle East and North Africa in World Politics: A Documentary Record, vol. 1: European Expansion, 1535–1914* (New Haven, Conn.: Yale University Press, 1975), pp. 269–70, 315–18.

The Islahat Fermani

Let it be done as herein set forth.

To you, my Grand Vizier Mehemed Emin Aali Pasha, decorated with my imperial order of the medjidiye of the first class, and with the order of personal merit; may God grant to you greatness and increase your power.

It has always been my most earnest desire to insure the happiness of all classes of the subjects whom Divine Providence has placed under my imperial sceptre, and since my accession to the throne I have not ceased to direct all my efforts to the attainment of that end.

Thanks to the Almighty, these unceasing efforts have already been productive of numerous useful results. From day to day the happiness of the nation and the wealth of my dominions go on augmenting.

It being now my desire to renew and enlarge still more the new institutions ordained with a view of establishing a state of things conformable with the dignity of my empire and the position which it occupies among civilized nations, and the rights of my empire having, by the fidelity and praiseworthy efforts of all my subjects, and by the kind and friendly assistance of the great powers, my noble allies, received from abroad a confirmation which will be the commencement of a new era, it is my desire to augment its well being and prosperity, to effect the happiness of all my subjects, who in my sight are all equal, and equally dear to me, and who are united to each other by the cordial ties of patriotism, and to insure the means of daily increasing the prosperity of my empire.

I have therefore resolved upon, and I order the execution of the following measures:

The guarantees promised on our part by the Hatti-Humayoun of Gulhané, and in conformity with the Tanzimat, to all the subjects of my empire, without distinction of classes or of religion, for the security of their persons and property, and the preservation of their honor, are to-day confirmed and consolidated, and efficacious measures shall be taken in order that they may have their full entire effect.

All the privileges and spiritual immunities granted by my ancestors *ab antiquo*, and at subsequent dates, to all Christian communities or other non-Mussulman persuasions established in my empire, under my protection, shall be confirmed and maintained.

Every Christian or other non-Mussulman community shall be bound within a fixed period, and with the concurrence of a commission composed *ad hoc* of members of its own body, to proceed, with my high approbation and under the inspection of my Sublime Porte, to examine into its actual immunities and privileges, and to discuss and submit to my Sublime Porte the reforms required by the progress of civilization and of the age. The powers conceded to the Christian patriarchs and bishops by the Sultan Mahomet II and to his successors shall be made to harmonize with the new position which my generous and beneficent intentions insure to these communities. . . . My Sublime Porte will take energetic measures to insure to each sect, whatever be the number of its adherents, entire freedom in the exercise of its religion. Every distinction or designation pending to make any class whatever of the subjects of my empire inferior to another class, on account of their religion, language, or race, shall be forever effaced from administrative protocol. The laws shall be put in force against the use of any injurious or offensive term, either among private individuals or on the part of the authorities.

As all forms of religion are and shall be freely professed in my dominions, no subject of my empire shall be hindered in the exercise of the religion that he professes, nor shall he be in any way annoyed on this account. No one shall be compelled to change their religion.

The nomination and choice of all functionaries and other employees of my empire being wholly dependent upon my sovereign will, all the subjects of my empire, without distinction of nationality, shall be admissible to public employments, and qualified to fill them according to their capacity and merit, and conformably with rules to be generally applied.

All the subjects of my empire, without distinction, shall be received into the civil and military schools of the government, if they otherwise satisfy the conditions as to age and examination which are specified in the organic regulations of the said schools. Moreover, every community is authorized to establish public schools of science, art, and industry. Only the methods of instruction and the choice of professors in schools of this class shall be under the control of a mixed council of public instruction, the members of which shall be named by my sovereign command.

All commercial, correctional, and criminal suits between Mussulmans and Christians, or other non-Mussulman subjects, or between Christian or other non-Mussulmans of different sects, shall be referred to mixed tribunals.

The proceedings of these tribunals shall be public; the parties shall be confronted and shall produce their witnesses, whose testimony shall be received without distinction, upon an oath taken according to the religious law of each sect.

Suits relating to civil affairs shall continue to be publicly tried, according to the laws and regulations, before the mixed provincial councils, in the presence of the governor and judge of the place.

Special civil proceedings, such as those relating to successions or others of that kind, between subjects of the same Christian or other non-Mussulman faith, may, at the request of the parties, be sent before the councils of the patriarchs or of the communities.

Penal, correctional, and commercial laws, and rules of procedure for the mixed tribunals, shall be drawn up as soon as possible and formed into a code. Translations of them shall be published in all the languages current in the empire.

Proceedings shall be taken, with as little delay as possible, for the reform of the penitentiary system as applied to houses of detention, punishment, or correction, and other establishments of like nature, so as to reconcile the rights of humanity with those of justice. Corporal punishment shall not be administered, even in the prisons, except in conformity with the disciplinary regulations established by my Sublime Porte, and everything that resembles torture shall be entirely abolished.

Infractions of the law in this particular shall be severely repressed, and shall besides entail, as of right, the punishment, in conformity with the civil code, of the authorities who may order and of the agents who may commit them.

The organization of the police in the capital, in the provincial towns and in the rural districts, shall be revised in such a manner as to give to all the peaceable subjects of my empire the strongest guarantees for the safety both of their persons and property.

The equality of taxes entailing equality of burdens, as equality of duties entails that of rights, Christian subjects, and those of other non-Mussulman sects, as it has been already decided, shall, as well as Mussulmans, be subject to the obligations of the law of recruitment.

The principle of obtaining substitutes, or of purchasing exemption, shall be admitted. A complete law shall be published, with as little delay as possible, respecting the admission into and service in the army of Christian and other non-Mussulman subjects.

Proceedings shall be taken for a reform in the constitution of the provincial and communal councils in order to insure fairness in the choice of the deputies of the Mussulman, Christian, and other communities and freedom of voting in the councils. My Sublime Porte will take into consideration the adoption of the most effectual means for ascertaining exactly and for controlling the result of the deliberations and of the decisions arrived at.

As the laws regulating the purchase, sale, and disposal of real property are common to all the subjects of my empire, it shall be lawful for foreigners to possess landed property in my dominions, conforming themselves to the laws and police regulations, and bearing the same charges as the native inhabitants, and after arrangements have been come to with foreign powers.

The taxes are to be levied under the same denomination from all the subjects of my empire, without distinction of class or of religion. The most prompt and energetic means for remedying the abuses in collecting the taxes, and especially the tithes, shall be considered.

The system of direct collections shall gradually, and as soon as possible, be substituted for the plan of farming, in all the branches of the revenues of the state. As long as the present system remains in force all agents of the government and all members of the medjlis shall be forbidden under the severest penalties, to become lessees of any farming contracts which are announced for public competition, or to have any beneficial interest in carrying them out. The local taxes shall, as far as possible, be so imposed as not to affect the sources of production or to hinder the progress of internal commerce.

Works of public utility shall receive a suitable endowment, part of which shall be raised from private and special taxes levied in the provinces, which shall have the benefit of the advantages arising from the establishment of ways of communication by land and sea.

A special law having been already passed, which declares that the budget of the revenue and the expenditure of the state shall be drawn up and made known every year, the said law shall be most scrupulously observed. Proceedings shall be taken for revising the emoluments attached to each office.

The heads of each community and a delegate, designated by my Sublime Porte, shall be summoned to take part in the deliberations of the supreme council of justice on all occasions which might interest the generality of the subjects of my empire. They shall be summoned specially for this purpose by my grand vizier. The delegates shall hold office for one year; they shall be sworn on entering upon their duties. All the members of the council, at the ordinary and extraordinary meetings, shall freely give their opinions and their votes, and no one shall ever annoy them on this account.

The laws against corruption, extortion, or malversation shall apply, according to the legal forms, to all the subjects of my empire, whatever may be their class and the nature of their duties.

Steps shall be taken for the formation of banks and other similar institutions, so as to effect a reform in the monetary and financial system, as well as to create funds to be employed in augmenting the sources of the material wealth of my empire. Steps shall also be taken for the formation of roads and canals to increase the facilities of communication and increase the sources of the wealth of the country.

Everything that can impede commerce or agriculture shall be abolished. To accomplish these objects means shall be sought to profit by the science, the art, and the funds of Europe, and thus gradually to execute them.

Such being my wishes and my commands, you, who are my grand vizier, will, according to custom, cause this imperial firman to be published in my capital and in all parts of my empire; and you will watch attentively and take all the necessary measures that all the orders which it contains be henceforth carried out with the most rigorous punctuality.

The d'Arcy Oil Concession

The first Middle Eastern oil concession was granted by the Qajar government of Persia to William Knox d'Arcy in 1901. It became the prototype for subsequent oil concessions in the region.

Between the Government of His Imperial Majesty the Shah of Persia, of the one part, and William Knox d'Arcy, of independent means, residing in London at No. 42, Grosvenor Square (hereinafter called "the Concessionnaire"), of the other part;

The following has by these presents been agreed on and arranged—viz.:

Art. 1. The Government of His Imperial Majesty the Shah grants to the concessionnaire by these presents a special and exclusive privilege to search for, obtain, exploit, develop, render suitable for trade, carry away and sell natural gas petroleum, asphalt and ozokerite throughout the whole extent of the Persian Empire for a term of sixty years as from the date of these presents.

Art. 2. This privilege shall comprise the exclusive right of laying the pipe-lines necessary from the deposits where there may be found one or several of the said products up to the Persian Gulf, as also the necessary distributing branches. It shall also comprise the right of constructing and maintaining all and any wells, reservoirs, stations and pump services, accumulation services and distribution services, factories and other works and arrangements that may be deemed necessary.

Art. 3. The Imperial Persian Government grants gratuitously to the concessionnaire all uncultivated lands belonging to the State which the concessionnaire's engineers may deem necessary for the construction of the whole or any part of the above-mentioned works. As for cultivated lands belonging to the State, the concessionnaire must purchase them at the fair and current price of the province.

The Government also grants to the concessionnaire the right of acquiring all and any other lands or buildings necessary for the said purpose, with the consent of the proprietors, on such conditions as may be arranged between him and them without their being allowed to make demands of a nature to surcharge the prices ordinarily current for lands situate in their respective localities.

Holy places with all their dependencies within a radius of 200 Persian archines are formally excluded.

Art. 4. As three petroleum mines situate at Schouster, Kassre-Chirine, in the Province of Kermanschah, and Daleki, near Bouchir, are at present let to private persons and produce an annual revenue of two thousand tomans for the benefit of the Government, it has been agreed that the three aforesaid mines shall be comprised in the Deed of Concession in conformity with Article 1, on condition that, over and above the 16 per cent mentioned in Article 10, the concessionnaire shall pay every year the fixed sum of 2,000 (two thousand) tomans to the Imperial Government.

Art. 5. The course of the pipe-lines shall be fixed by the concessionnaire and his engineers.

Art. 6. Notwithstanding what is above set forth, the privilege granted by these presents shall not extend to the provinces of Azerbadjan, Ghilan, Mazendaran, Asdrabad and Khorassan, but on the express condition that the Persian Imperial Government shall not grant to any other person the right of constructing a pipe-line to the southern rivers or to the South Coast of Persia.

Art. 7. All lands granted by these presents to the concessionnaire or that may be acquired by him in the manner provided for in Articles 3 and 4 of these presents, as also all products exported, shall be free of all imposts and taxes during the term of the present concession. All material and apparatuses necessary for the exploration, working and development of the deposits, and for the construction and development of the pipe-lines, shall enter Persia free of all taxes and Custom-House duties.

Art. 8. The concessionnaire shall immediately send out to Persia and at his own cost one or several experts with a view to their exploring the region in which there exist, as he believes, the said products, and in the event of the report of the expert being in the opinion of the concessionnaire of a satisfactory nature, the latter shall immediately send to Persia and at his own cost all the technical staff necessary, with the working plant and machinery required for boring and sinking wells and ascertaining the value of the property.

Art. 9. The Imperial Persian Government authorises the concessionnaire to found one or several companies for the working of the concession.

The names, "statutes" and capital of the said companies shall be fixed by the concessionnaire, and the directors shall be chosen by him on the express condition that, on the formation of each company, the concessionnaire shall give official notice of such formation to the Imperial Government, through the medium of the Imperial Commissioner, and shall forward the "statutes", with information as to the places at which such company is to operate. Such company or companies shall enjoy all the rights and privileges granted to the concessionnaire, but they must assume all his engagements and responsibilities.

Art. 10. It shall be stipulated in the contract between the concessionnaire, of the one part, and the company, of the other part, that the latter is, within the term of one month as from the date of the formation of the first exploitation company, to pay the Imperial Persian Government the sum of £20,000 sterling in cash, and an additional sum of £20,000 sterling in paid-up shares of the first company founded by virtue of the foregoing article. It shall also pay the said Government annually a sum equal to 16 per cent of the annual net profits of any company or companies that may be formed in accordance with the said article.

Art. 11. The said Government shall be free to appoint an Imperial Commissioner, who shall be consulted by the concessionnaire and the directors of the companies to be formed. He shall supply all and any useful information at his disposal, and he shall inform them of the best course to be adopted in the interest of the undertaking. He shall establish, by agreement with the concessionnaire, such supervision as he may deem expedient to safeguard the interests of the Imperial government.

The aforesaid powers of the Imperial Commissioner shall be set forth in the "statutes" of the companies to be created.

The concessionnaire shall pay the Commissioner thus appointed an annual sum of £1,000 sterling for his services as from the date of the formation of the first company.

Art. 12. The workmen employed in the service of the company shall be subject to His Imperial Majesty the Shah, except the technical staff, such as the managers, engineers, borers and foremen.

Art. 13. At any place in which it may be proved that the inhabitants of the country now obtain petroleum for their own use, the company must supply them gratuitously with the quantity of petroleum that they themselves got previously. Such quantity shall be fixed according to their own declarations, subject to the supervision of the local authority.

Art. 14. The Imperial Government binds itself to take all and any necessary measures to secure the safety and the carrying out of the object of this concession of the plant and of the apparatuses, of which mention is made, for the purposes of the undertaking of the company, and to protect the representatives, agents and servants of the company. The Imperial Government having thus fulfilled its engagements, the concessionnaire and the companies created by him shall not have power, under any pretext whatever, to claim damages from the Persian Government.

ART. 15. On the expiration of the term of the present concession, all materials, buildings and apparatuses then used by the company for the exploitation of its industry shall become the property of the said Government, and the company shall have no right to any indemnity in this connection.

ART. 16. If within the term of two years as from the present date the concessionnaire shall not have established the first of the said companies authorised by Article 9 of the present agreement, the present concession shall become null and void.

ART. 17. In the event of there arising between the parties to the present concession any dispute or difference in respect of its interpretation or the rights or responsibilities of one or the other of the parties therefrom resulting, such dispute or difference shall be submitted to two arbitrators at Teheran, one of whom shall be named by each of the parties, and to an umpire who shall be appointed by the arbitrators before they proceed to arbitrate. The decision of the arbitrators or, in the event of the latter disagreeing, that of the umpire shall be final.

ART. 18. This Act of Concession, made in duplicate, is written in the French language and translated into Persian with the same meaning.

But, in the event of there being any dispute in relation to such meaning, the French text shall alone prevail.

J. C. Hurewitz, *The Middle East and North Africa in World Politics: A Documentary Record, vol. 1: European Expansion, 1535–1914* (New Haven, Conn.: Yale University Press, 1975), pp. 483–84.

Algeria: The Poetry of Loss

The following poetry, transmitted orally and later written down by a French anthropologist, was composed by a young Algerian Qur'an-school student who bore witness to the French invasion of Algeria in 1830.

The days, my brothers, place diversity into the hours,
The century turns around and brusquely swerves
(Algiers), The Splendid, has had its flag, its wujak*
Nations have trembled before her on the continent and on two seas
But when God wanted it to be, the appointed time came upon her.
She was delivered by Allah's men, by the Saints.
The Frenchman marched against her and took her.
It was not one hundred ships that he had, nor two hundred;
He proudly had his flotilla defile before her,
Surging forth from the high seas, with powerful armies,
We were unaware of how many they were, their numbers becoming
embroiled, lost to our eyes.
Fiercely the Rumis† came against the Splendid city.
   Regarding al-Jazair,‡ Gentlemen, my heart is mourning!...
   Conquering her without fighting, he took her, the dog.
They carried away her treasures, those brothers of demons.
After having gone to Stawali and having seized it,

---

* *wujak*: corps of janissaries, Turkish military unit.
† *Rumis*: Algerian term to refer to Frenchmen and other Europeans.
‡ *al-Jazair*: Transliteration of the Algerians' own name for Algiers.

With their drums, their soldiers and their flags,
They secured the cafe of al-Biar and its villas
And they climbed toward Buzareah in a moment.
They brought down their forces in front of the "Pines"
And they took the Fort of My Lord Maulay Hussain.
In the night, the Rumis advanced: they made their drums resound:
And the Believers shed tears, O Muslims!
Some left the city; others waited resolutely.
They held the enemy in the gardens for about two days.
They left for adventures abandoning their homeland,
And they dispersed into diverse countries, poor exiles.
Be patient, people of Muhammad, endure the days the foreigners bring you!
It is the test the Master of the Universe has decreed for you.
Who would have said of al-Jazair, of its fortifications,
Of its wujak, that even the evil eye would have come to it?
Alas! Where is the place of its sultan and of its people?
They have gone and other faces have taken their places.
Alas! Where are their beys and their qaids?
Who knows what has become of those famous qasbajis*
And the Bailiff's guards of the station house?
And those militia men?
Alas! Where is the palace of the council and its dignitaries?
And the places of justice full of majesty?
Alas! Where are those shawush-es and their arrogance?
Alas! Where are those haughty Turks? . . .
May your servants regain peace, may all their grief be ended
And may this oppression which crushes the Muslims cease!
Let us cry over the muftis, over the qadis,
Over the ulama of the city, those guides of the religion.
Let us cry over the mosques and their sermons
And over their pulpits of elevated marble.
Let us weep over their minarets†; and the calls of the muezzins†;
and over the classes of their teachers and over their cantors of the Qur'an.
Let us lament the private chapels whose doors have been locked
And which have sunk today, yes Sir, into oblivion.
Alas where are the precious trinkets of the city, where are its houses?
Where are their low apartments and the elevated rooms for the eunuchs?
They are no longer but a parade ground and their traces have disappeared.
So much does that cursed one breathe to plague us!
The Christians have installed themselves in the city;
Its appearance has changed;
It no longer has seen anything but impure people.
The janissaries' houses! They have razed their walls;
They have torn down its marble and its sculptured balustrades,

---

* *qasbaji*: officer of the qasabah or fort.
† *minaret*: slender tower attached to mosques. Balconies on the minaret are the place from which people are called to prayer.
‡ *muezzin*: Muslim official who calls the faithful to prayer (from the minaret).

The iron grills which protected the windows
Have been put to pieces by those impious ones, enemies of the Religion.
Likewise, they have named that Qaisariya "the Square",
Where the Books and their binders were formerly found.
The Magnificent Mosque which was next to it
Has been destroyed by them simply in order to spite the Muslims....

Alf Andrew Heggoy, *The French Conquest of Algiers, 1830: An Algerian Oral Tradition* (Athens, Ohio: Ohio University Center for International Studies/Africa Studies Program, 1986), pp. 32–36.

Huda Shaarawi: A New Mentor and Her Salon for Women

Men such as Wasif Jawhariyyeh were not the only ones to participate in the salon culture of the late nineteenth- and early twentieth-century Middle East. Women did as well. In this selection, Egyptian feminist Huda Shaarawi describes her experiences at one such salon in Cairo.

Eugénie Le Brun, a Frenchwoman, was the first wife of Husain Rushdi Pasha. I met her for the first time at a wedding reception and was immediately taken by her dignity, sensitivity and intelligence. In spite of my extreme youth I attracted her attention as well. We were introduced by Rushdi Pasha's sister and spent most of the evening in delightful conversation. Some time later, my brother arranged for me to take a day's excursion on the Nile to the Delta Barrage with Mme Rushdi and a number of other European women. The hours I spent in her company on that occasion were the beginning of a close relationship. She soon became a dear friend and valued mentor. She guided my first steps in 'society' and looked out for my reputation....

Mme Rushdi not only guarded my reputation, but also nourished my mind and spirit. She took it upon herself to direct my reading in French. She would assist me over difficult passages in a book and when I had finished it she would discuss it with me. In that way, she helped me perfect my French and expand my learning.

Soon, at her request, I began to attend her Saturday salon during the hours set aside for women. She would tell me, 'You are the flower of my salon.' On the days when I was unable to attend I used to send flowers. Once she responded with a sweet note saying that the flowers I had sent could not make up for the absence of her 'beloved flower'. She begged me to lessen the number of bouquets so I would not diminish her joy. Her growing affection toward me made some of her friends jealous but others applauded her devotion to me.

As mistress of the salon, Mme Rushdi adroitly guided the discourse from issue to issue. There were debates about social practices, especially veiling. She confessed that although she admired the dress of Egyptian women, she thought the veil stood in the way of their advancement. It also gave rise to false impressions in the minds of foreigners. They regarded the veil as a convenient mask for immorality. Plenty of lurid tales were circulated by ignorant outsiders about Egyptian morals. Foreigners not infrequently departed from Egypt under the mistaken impression they had visited the houses of respectable families when, in truth, they had fallen into the hands of profiteers who, under the guise of introducing them into the harems of great families, had in fact led them merely to gaudy brothels.

The conversation would move to another topic such as offspring and immorality. Mme Rushdi believed that people who had children never died, as their children were extensions of themselves who kept their memories alive. 'I have no children to perpetuate my memory,' she would say, 'but I shall remain alive through my books.' She once revealed that she had provided for a burial plot in the cemetery of Imam al-Shafai. In answer to our surprised looks she said, 'You didn't know that I embraced Islam after my marriage? I wish to be buried in the Muslim cemetery next to my husband so we shall never be separated in this world or the next.'

Speaking of her books, she said, 'I have signed them, as I have written them— Niya Salima ('In Good Faith'). My purpose in *Harem et les musulmanes* (*The Harem and Muslim women*) was to describe the life of the Egyptian woman, as it really is, to enlighten Europeans. After it appeared in Europe, I received many letters saying my book had cleared up false impressions of life in Islamic countries. They said it had corrected outsiders' images of Egyptians. In fact, they said Egyptians seemed not unlike themselves.' That restored her peace of mind, she said. She had been very upset when she heard that many Egyptians had thought she had criticized the condition of women in Egypt.

'However,' she continued, 'my second book is different. I decided to attack the problem of the backwardness of Egyptian women, demonstrating it arose from the persistence of certain social customs, but not from Islam, as many Europeans believe. Islam, on the contrary, has granted women greater justice than previous religions. While working on the book I attended sessions of the *Shariah* Courts (religious courts where personal status or family law cases are heard) to find out for myself how women fared. I was aghast to see the blatant tyranny of men over women. My new book will be called, *Les Repudiées* (*The Divorcees*).' Mme Rushdi read me portions of the book as she completed them, asking for my reactions.

Huda Shaarawi, *Harem Years: The Memoirs of an Egyptian Feminist (1879–1924)*, trans. and ed. Margot Badran (New York: The Feminist Press at the City University of New York, 1986), pp. 76–81.

===

Rifaʿa Rafiʿ al-Tahtawi: The Extraction of Gold or an Overview of Paris

Mehmet Ali sent Rifaʿa Rafiʿ al-Tahtawi to Paris as the head of the first Egyptian educational mission. Upon his return, al-Tahtawi became head of the School of Languages, where he developed his ideas based upon his experiences in Europe and in Mehmet Ali's Egypt. Here is al-Tahtawi on patriotism and the responsibilities of citizenship.

Patriots who are faithful in their love of homeland redeem their country with all their means, and serve it by offering all they possess. They redeem it with their soul, and repel anyone who seeks to harm it the same way a father would keep evil away from his child. The intentions of the children of the country must always be directed toward the country's virtue and honor, and not toward anything that violates the rights of their country and fellow countrymen. Their inclination should be toward that which brings benefit and goodness. Likewise, the country protects its children from all that harms them, because of its possession of those characteristics. The love of homeland and the promotion of the public welfare are among the beautiful characteristics that get inculcated into each person, constantly, throughout one's life, and make every one of them loved by the others. No one could be happier than the human beings who are naturally inclined to keep evil away from their homeland, even if they must harm themselves to do so.

The quality of patriotism requires not just that humans demand the rights they are owed by their homeland. They must also carry out their obligations toward the country. If the children of the homeland fail to earn the rights of their country, then the civil rights to which they are entitled will be lost.

In olden times, the Romans used to force citizens who reached twenty years of age to give an oath that they would defend their country and their government. They required a pledge to this effect, the text of which is:

"May God be my witness that I shall carry the sword of honor to defend my country and its people whenever there is a chance I would be able to assist it. May God be my witness that I am willing to fight with the army or on my own for the protection of the country and religion. May God be my witness that I shall not disturb the serenity of my country, nor betray it or deceive it, and that I shall sail on the seas whenever necessary in all conquests that the government orders, and that I pledge to follow present and future laws and customs in my country. May God be my witness that I shall not tolerate anyone who dares violate them or undermine their order."

Based on this, it is understood that the Roman nation firmly adhered to the love of country, and that is the reason it reigned over all the countries of the world. When the quality of patriotism was removed, failure beset the members of this nation, its affairs were ruined, and the order of its system disintegrated by the numerous disagreements of its princes and the multiplicity of its rulers. After being ruled by one Caesar, it was divided between two Caesars in the east and the west, the Caesar of Rome and the Caesar of Constantinople. Power that had belonged to one mighty force was split into two minor forces. All its wars ended in defeat, and it retreated from a perfect existence to nonexistence. This is the fate of any nation whose government is in disarray, and whose state is disorganized.

Charles Kurzman, ed., *Modernist Islam, 1840–1940: A Sourcebook* (Oxford: Oxford University Press, 2002), p. 35.

Muhammad ʿAbduh: The Theology of Unity

The Islamic modernist Muhammad ʿAbduh (1849–1905), an Egyptian associate of Jamal al-Din al-Afghani, sought to make Islam compatible with the dogmas and doctrines of nineteenth-century rationalism. In this selection, he argues that Muslims cannot simply rely on the authoritative interpretation of texts handed down from medieval clerics (a procedure known as *taqlid*); rather, they must use reason to keep up with changing times.

Islam will have no truck with traditionalism, against which it campaigns relentlessly, to break its power over men's minds and eradicate its deep-seated influence. The underlying bases of *taqlid* in the beliefs of the nations have been shattered by Islam.

In the same cause, it has alerted and aroused the powers of reason, out of long sleep. For whenever the rays of truth had penetrated, the temple custodians intervened with their jealous forebodings. 'Sleep on, the night is pitch dark, the way is rough and the goal distant, and rest is scant and there's poor provision for the road.'

Islam raised its voice against these unworthy whisperings and boldly declared that man was not created to be led by a bridle. He was endowed with intelligence to take his guidance with knowledge and to consider the signs and tokens in the universe and in events. The proper role of teachers is to alert and to guide, directing men into the paths of study.

The friends of truth are those 'who listen to what is said and follow its better way.' (Surah 39.18.) as the Qur'an has it. It characterizes them as those who weigh all that is said, irrespective of who the speakers are, in order to follow what they know to be good and reject what gives evidence of having neither validity nor use. Islam threw its weight against the religious authorities, bringing them down from the dominance whence they uttered their commands and prohibitions. It made them answerable to those they dominated, so that these could keep an eye on them and scrutinize their claims, according to their own judgement and lights, thus reaching conclusions based on conviction, not on conjecture and delusion.

Further, Islam encouraged men to move away from their clinging attachment to the world of their fathers and their legacies, indicting as stupid and foolish the attitude that always wants to know what the precedents say. Mere priority in time, it insisted, is not one of the signs of perceptive knowledge, nor yet of superior intelligence and capacity. Ancestor and descendant compare closely no doubt in discrimination and endowment of mind. But the latter has the advantage over his forebears in that he knows events gone by and is in a position to study and exploit their consequences as the former was not. It may be that such traceable results which men of the present generation can turn to profit will also illustrate the ill-effects of things done in earlier times and the dire evils perpetrated by the men of the past. 'Say: Go through the world and see what was the fate of those who disbelieved.' (Surah 6.11.) The doors of the Divine favour are not closed to the seeker: His mercy which embraces everything will never repel the suppliant.

Islam reproves the slavish imitation of the ancestors that characterizes the leaders of the religions, with their instinct to hold timidly to tradition-sanctioned ways, saying, as they do: 'Nay! We will follow what we found our fathers doing.' (Surah 31.21.) and 'We found our fathers so as a people and we will stay the same as they.' (Surah 43.22.)

So the authority of reason was liberated from all that held it bound and from every kind of *taqlid* enslaving it, and thus restored to its proper dignity, to do its proper work in judgement and wisdom, always in humble submission to God alone and in conformity to His sacred law. Within its bounds there are no limits to its activity and no end to the researches it may pursue.

Hereby, and from all the foregoing, man entered fully into two great possessions relating to religion, which had for too long been denied him, namely independence of will and independence of thought and opinion. By these his humanity was perfected. By these he was put in the way of attaining that happiness which God had prepared for him in the gift of mind. A certain western philosopher of the recent past has said that the growth of civilisation in Europe rested on these two principles. People were not roused to action, nor minds to vigour and speculation until a large number of them came to know their right to exercise choice and to seek out facts with their own minds. Such assurance only came to them in the sixteenth century AD—a fact which the same writer traces to the influence of Islamic culture and the scholarship of Muslim peoples in that century.

Islam through its revealed scripture took away the impediment by which the leaders of the religions had precluded rational understanding of the heavenly books on the part of their possessors or adherents, in that they arrogated the exclusive right of interpretation to themselves, withholding from those who did not share their habit or go their way the opportunity of acquiring that sacred role.

Muhammad ʿAbduh, *The Theology of Unity*, trans. Ishaq Masaʿad and Kenneth Cragg (London: Allen and Unwin, 1966), pp. 126–28.

Namik Kemal: Extract from the Journal Hürriyet

Namik Kemal (1840–1888) was an Islamic modernist and, as a member of the Young Ottomans, an avid supporter of constitutionalism in the Ottoman Empire. He wrote this article defending the idea of consultation between ruler and ruled for *Hürriyet* (*Liberty*), a journal he and like-minded exiles published while in London.

As for the imagined detrimental effects that would stem from the adoption of the method of consultation, in reality these have no basis. First, it is said that the establishment of a council of the people would violate the rights of the sultan. As was made clear in our introduction, the right of the sultan in our country is to govern on the basis of the will of the people and the principles of freedom. His title is "one charged with kingship" [*sahib al-mulk*], not "owner of kingship" [*malik al-mulk*], a title reserved for God in the Qur'an. [Sura 3, Verse 26.] His Imperial Majesty the sultan is heir to the esteemed Ottoman dynasty, which established its state by protecting religion. It was thanks to this fact that the [Ottoman sultan] became the cynosure of the people and the caliph of Islam. The religion of Muhammad rejects the absolutist claim to outright ownership [of the state] in the incontrovertible verse: "Whose is the kingdom today? God's, the One, the Omnipotent." [Qur'an, Sura 40, Verse 16.]

Second, it is argued that the religious and cultural heterogeneity of the Ottoman lands and the ignorance of the people are reasons against this [the adoption of consultation]. In the gatherings of highly important personages, it is asked how a people speaking seventy-two different tongues could be convened in one assembly, and what kind of response would be given if [some of] the deputies to be convened opposed dispatching troops to Crete because they wished to protect the Greeks, or raised an objection to appropriations for holy sites and pious foundations.

O my God! In all provinces there are provincial councils. Members from all denominations serve in these councils, and all of them debate issues in the official language [Turkish]. How can anybody speak of linguistic heterogeneity in light of this obvious fact? Is it supposed that a council of the people is a seditious assembly whose members are absolutely independent, and whose administration is not based on any rules? Once the fundamental principles and the internal regulations of the assembly are issued, who would dare to protect those, like the rebels of Crete, who desire to separate themselves from the integral nation? Who would dare to say a word about [Islamic] religious expenditures [purchasing non-Muslim land], in return for which [non-Muslim communities] have acquired real estate valued several times more?

Let us come to the matter of ignorance. Montenegro, Serbia, and Egypt each have councils of the people. Why should [our people's] ignorance prevent us [from having a council], if it did not prevent these lands? Are we at a lower level of culture than even the savages of Montenegro? Can it be that we could not find people to become deputies, whose only necessary qualification will be attaining the age of majority, when we can find people in the provinces to become members of the State Council, membership in which is dependent upon possessing perfected political skills?

O Ottoman liberals! Do not give any credit to such deceptive superstitions. Give serious thought to the dangerous situation in which the nation finds itself today. While doing so, take into consideration the accomplishments that the opposition has already achieved. It will be obvious that the salvation of the state today is dependent upon the adoption of the method of consultation, and upon continuing the opposition aimed at achieving this method of administration. If we have any love for the nation, let us be fervent in advancing this meritorious policy. Let us be fervent so that we can move forward without delay.

Charles Kurzman, ed., *Modernist Islam, 1840–1940: A Sourcebook* (Oxford: Oxford University Press, 2002), pp. 147–48.

The Supplementary Fundamental Law of 7 October 1907

The Fundamental Law of 1906 and the Supplementary Fundamental Law of 1907 provided the foundation for the Persian constitution. The following excerpts come from the latter document.

In the Name of God the Merciful, the Forgiving

The Articles added to complete the Fundamental Laws of the Persian Constitution ratified by the late Shahinshah of blessed memory, Muzaffaru'd-Din Shah Qajar (may God illuminate his resting-place!) are as follows:

General Dispositions

Article 1. The official religion of Persia is Islam, according to the orthodox Jafari doctrine of the *Ithna Ashariyya* (Church of the Twelve Imams) which faith the Shah of Persia must profess and promote.

Article 2. At no time must any legal enactment of the Sacred National Consultative Assembly, established by the favor and assistance of His Holiness the Imam of the Age (may God hasten his glad Advent!), the favor of His Majesty the Shahinshah of Islam (may God immortalize his reign!), the care of the Proofs of Islam [the *mujtahids*] (may God multiply the like of them!), and the whole people of the Persian nation, be at variance with the sacred principles of Islam or the laws established by His Holiness the Best of Mankind [the Prophet Muhammad] (on whom and on whose household be the Blessings of God and His Peace).

It is hereby declared that it is for the learned doctors of theology (the *ulama*)—may God prolong the blessing of their existence!—to determine whether such laws as may be proposed are or are not conformable to the principles of Islam; and it is therefore officially enacted that there shall at all times exist a Committee composed of not less than five *mujtahids* or other devout theologians, cognizant also of the requirements of the age, [which committee shall be elected] in this manner: The ulama and Proofs of Islam shall present to the National Consultative Assembly the names of twenty of the ulama possessing the attributes mentioned above; and the members of the National Consultative Assembly shall, either by unanimous acclamation, or by vote, designate five or more of these, according to the exigencies of the time, and recognize these as Members, so that they may carefully discuss and consider all matters proposed in the Assembly, and reject and repudiate, wholly or in part, any such proposal which is at variance with the Sacred Laws of Islam, so that it shall not obtain the title of legality. In such matters the decision of this Ecclesiastical Committee shall be followed and obeyed, and this article shall continue unchanged until the appearance of His Holiness the Proof of the Age (may God hasten his glad Advent!).

Article 3. The frontiers, provinces, departments and districts of the Persian Empire cannot be altered save in accordance with the Law.

Article 4. The capital of Persia is Teheran.

Article 5. The official colors of the Persian flag are green, white, and red, with the emblem of the Lion and the Sun.

Article 6. The lives and property of foreign subjects residing on Persian soil are guaranteed and protected, save in such contingencies as the laws of the land shall except.

Article 7. The principles of the Constitution cannot be suspended either wholly or in part.

Rights of the Persian Nation

Article 8. The people of the Persian Empire are to enjoy equal rights before the Law.

Article 9. All individuals are protected and safeguarded in respect to their lives, property, homes, and honor, from every kind of interference, and none shall molest them save in such case and in such way as the laws of the land shall determine.

Article 10. No one can be summarily arrested, save *flagrante delicto* in the commission of some crime or misdemeanor, except on the written authority of the President of the Tribunal of Justice, given in conformity with the Law. Even in such case the accused must immediately, or at latest in the course of the next twenty-four hours, be informed and notified of the nature of his offense.

Article 11. No one can be forcibly removed from the tribunal which is entitled to give judgment on his case to another tribunal.

Article 12. No punishment can be decreed or executed save in conformity with the Law.

Article 13. Every person's house and dwelling is protected and safe-guarded, and no dwelling-place may be entered, save in such case and in such way as the Law has decreed.

Article 14. No Persian can be exiled from the country, or prevented from re-siding in any part thereof, or compelled to reside in any specified part thereof, save in such cases as the Law may explicitly determine.

Article 15. No property shall be removed from the control of its owner save by legal sanction, and then only after its fair value has been determined and paid.

Article 16. The confiscation of the property or possessions of any person under the title of punishment or retribution is forbidden, save in conformity with the Law.

Article 17. To deprive owners or possessors of the properties or possessions controlled by them on any pretext whatever is forbidden, save in conformity with the Law.

Article 18. The acquisition and study of all sciences, arts and crafts is free, save in the case of such as may be forbidden by the ecclesiastical law.

Article 19. The foundation of schools at the expense of the Government and the Nation, and compulsory instruction, must be regulated by the Ministry of Sciences and Arts, and all schools and colleges must be under the supreme control and supervision of that Ministry.

Article 20. All publications, except heretical books and matters hurtful to the perspicuous religion [of Islam] are free, and are exempt from censorship. If, however, anything should be discovered in them contrary to the Press law, the publisher or writer is liable to punishment according to that law. If the writer be known, and be resident in Persia, then the publisher, printer and distributor shall not be liable to prosecution.

Article 21. Societies (*anjumans*) and associations (*ijtimaat*) which are not productive of mischief to Religion or the State, and are not injurious to good order, are free throughout the whole Empire, but members of such associations must not carry arms, and must obey the regulations laid down by the Law on this matter. Assemblies in the public thoroughfares and open spaces must likewise obey the police regulations.

Article 22. Correspondence passing through the post is safeguarded and exempt from seizure or examination, save in such exceptional cases as the Law lays down.

Article 23. It is forbidden to disclose or detain telegraphic correspondence without the express permission of the owner, save in such cases as the Law lays down.

Article 24. Foreign subjects may become naturalized as Persian subjects, but their acceptance or continuance as such, or their deprivation of this status, is in accordance with a separate law.

Article 25. No special authorization is required to proceed against government officials in respect of shortcomings connected with the discharge of their public functions, save in the case of Ministers, in whose case the special laws on this subject must be observed.

Powers of the Realm

Article 26. The powers of the realm are all derived from the people; and the Fundamental Law regulates the employment of those powers.

Article 27. The powers of the Realm are divided into three categories:

First, the legislative power, which is specially concerned with the making or amelioration of laws. This power is derived from His Imperial Majesty, the National Consultative Assembly, and the Senate, of which three sources each has the right to introduce laws, provided that the continuance thereof be dependent on their not being at variance with the standards of the ecclesiastical law, and on their approval by the Members of the two Assemblies, and the Royal ratification. The enacting and approval of laws with the revenue and expenditure of the kingdom are, however specially assigned to the National Consultative Assembly. The explanation and interpretation of the laws are, moreover, amongst the special functions of the above-mentioned Assembly.

Second, the judicial power, by which is meant the determining of rights. This power belongs exclusively to the ecclesiastical tribunals in matters connected with the ecclesiastical law, and to the civil tribunals in matters connected with ordinary law.

Third, the executive power, which appertains to the King—that is to say, the laws and ordinances—is carried out by the Ministers and State officials in the august name of His Imperial Majesty in such manner as the Law defines.

Article 28. The three powers above mentioned shall ever remain distinct and separate from one another.

Article 29. The special interests of each province, department and district shall be arranged and regulated, in accordance with special laws on this subject, by provincial and departmental councils (*anjumans*).

Rights of the Persian Throne

Article 39. No King can ascend the Throne unless, before his coronation, he appears before the National Consultative Assembly, in the presence of the Members of this Assembly and of the Senate, and of the Cabinet of Ministers, and repeat the following oath:

"I take to witness the Almighty and Most High God, on the glorious Word of God, and by all that is most honored in God's sight, and do hereby swear that I will exert all my efforts to preserve the independence of Persia, safeguard and protect the frontiers of my Kingdom and the rights of my People, observe the Fundamental Laws of the Persian Constitution, rule in accordance with the established laws of Sovereignty, endeavor to promote the Jafari doctrine of the Church of the Twelve Imams, and will in all my deeds and actions consider God Most Glorious as present and watching me. I further ask aid from God, from Whom alone aid is derived, and seek help from the holy spirits of the Saints of Islam to render service to the advancement of Persia."

W. Morgan Shuster, *The Strangling of Persia: A Personal Narrative. Story of the European Diplomacy and Oriental Intrigue That Resulted in the Denationalization of Twelve Million Mohammedans* (New York: The Century Co., 1920), Appendix.

SUGGESTED READINGS

ʿAbduh, Muhammad. *The Theology of Unity.* Translated by Ishaq Musa and Kenneth Cragg. New York: Books for Libraries, 1980. Seminal work by one of the luminaries of the modernist movement in Islam.

Afary, Janet. *The Iranian Constitutional Revolution, 1906–1911: Grassroots Democracy, Social Democracy, and the Origins of Feminism.* New York: Columbia University Press, 1996. Revisionist account of the Persian Constitutional Revolution, with an emphasis on the processes and effects of popular mobilization.

Campos, Michelle. *Ottoman Brothers: Muslims, Christians, and Jews in Early Twentieth-Century Palestine.* Stanford, Calif.: Stanford University Press, 2010. Case study of what it meant to be an Ottoman citizen and of intercommunal relations.

Clancy-Smith, Julia. *Mediterraneans: North Africa and Europe in an Age of Migrations, c. 1800–1900.* Berkeley: University of California Press, 2012. Looking at the northern and southern shores of the Mediterranean as a single unit, Clancy-Smith traces the social and cultural impact of the two regions on each other.

Cole, Juan. *Colonialism and Revolution in the Middle East: Social and Cultural Origins of Egypt's ʿUrabi Movement.* Princeton, N.J.: Princeton University Press, 1993. Comprehensive study of the background to the ʿUrabi Revolt, along with a comparative analysis of revolution in the region.

Commins, David Dean. *Islamic Reform: Politics and Social Change in Late Ottoman Syria.* New York: Oxford University Press, 1990. Wonderfully written account of the development of Islamic modernist currents in Syria.

Deringil, Selim. *The Well-Protected Domains: Ideology and the Legitimation of Power in the Ottoman Empire, 1876–1909*. London: I. B. Tauris, 1998. Path-breaking study looks at the changing sources for Ottoman legitimacy during the nineteenth century, including new sources of religious legitimation.

Dumont, Paul. "Said Bey—the Everyday Life of an Istanbul Townsman at the Beginning of the Twentieth Century." In *The Modern Middle East*, edited by Albert Hourani et al., 271–88. Berkeley: University of California Press, 1993. Said Bey's life shows an interesting parallel to that of Wasif Jawhariyyeh.

Fahmy, Khaled. *All the Pasha's Men: Mehmed Ali, His Army and the Making of Modern Egypt*. Cambridge, England: Cambridge University Press, 1997. Revisionist work on Mehmet Ali and state formation in Egypt, focusing on the central institution for that effort: the military.

Gelvin, James L., and Green, Nile, eds. *Global Muslims in the Age of Steam and Print, 1850–1930*. Berkeley: University of California Press, 2013. A collection of essays that examine how new technologies and global interconnections affected the Muslim world.

Hanioglu, M. Sukru. *The Young Turks in Opposition*. New York: Oxford University Press, 1995. Detailed examination of the conspirators who took power in the Ottoman Empire in 1908 and the evolution of their ideas.

Hourani, Albert. *Arabic Thought in the Liberal Age: 1798–1939*. Cambridge, England: Cambridge University Press, 1983. Classic account of *nahda*, *salafi*, and Westernizing Arab intellectuals and intellectual trends of the long nineteenth century.

Jawhariyyeh, Wasif. *Storyteller of Jerusalem: The Life and Times of Wasif Jawhariyyeh, 1904–1948*, edited by Salim Tamari and Issam Nassar. Northampton, Mass.: Interlink Publishing, 2013. Wonderful account of a musician and composer whose diary gives contemporary historians of the Middle East access to daily life in Jerusalem over the course of six decades.

Karpat, Kemal H. *The Politicization of Islam: Reconstructing Identity, State, Faith, and Community in the Late Ottoman State*. Oxford: Oxford University Press, 2001. Dense but authoritative account of the transformation of the state and its impact on Islamic beliefs and institutions during the last half-century of Ottoman rule.

Khuri-Makdisi, Ilham. *The Eastern Mediterranean and the Making of Global Radicalism, 1860–1914*. Berkeley: University of California Press, 2010. Groundbreaking foray into intellectual history, placing the intellectual life of Beirut, Cairo, and Alexandria within the context of the global spread of ideas.

Kurzman, Charles. *Modernist Islam, 1840–1940: A Sourcebook*. Oxford: Oxford University Press, 2002. Good collection of documents from thinkers and activists who sought to make Islam compatible with the ideas of the modern age.

Makdisi, Ussama. *The Culture of Sectarianism: Community, History, and Violence in Nineteenth-Century Ottoman Lebanon*. Berkeley: University of California Press, 2000. Marvelous examination of the role played by European imperialism, Ottoman state policies, and local actors in creating religious boundaries and sparking violence in mid-century Lebanon.

Mikhail, Alan. *Nature and Empire in Ottoman Egypt: An Environmental History*. Cambridge, England: Cambridge University Press, 2012. Pioneering study in a cutting-edge field of historical scholarship.

Mitchell, Timothy. *Colonising Egypt*. Berkeley: University of California Press, 1991. Complex but rewarding analysis of the transformation of worldview in Egypt brought about by the combination of imperialism and the "self-colonization" of defensive developmentalism.

Owen, Roger. *The Middle East in the World Economy, 1800–1914*. London: Methuen, 1993. The gold standard of Middle East political/economic history in the nineteenth century.

Quataert, Donald. *The Ottoman Empire, 1700–1922*. Cambridge, England: Cambridge University Press, 2000. Concise yet excellent history of the empire after its initial expansion, particularly strong on economic and social history.

Robinson, Ronald. "Non-European Foundations of European Imperialism: Sketch for a Theory of Collaboration." In *Studies in the Theory of Imperialism*, edited by Roger Owen and Bob Sutcliffe, 117–42. London: Longman, 1972. This essay not only presents persuasive definition of imperialism, but also analyzes the reasons why imperialism took the various forms it did.

Rogan, Eugene. *Frontiers of State in the Late Ottoman Empire: Transjordan, 1850–1921*. Cambridge, England: Cambridge University Press, 1999. Excellent study of the application of defensive developmentalist policies in one of the frontier provinces of the Ottoman Empire.

Sohrabi, Nader. "Historicizing Revolutions: Constitutional Revolutions in the Ottoman Empire, Iran, and Russia, 1905–1908." *American Journal of Sociology* 100 (May 1995): 1383–447. Thoughtful, theoretical comparison of three turn-of-the-century constitutional revolutions.

al-Tahtawi, Rifaʿa Rafiʿ. *An Imam in Paris: Al-Tahtawi's Visit to France, 1826–1831*, translated by Daniel L. Newman. London: Saqi Books, 2011. Memoirs of the scholar who accompanied a group of students to France in Egypt's first educational mission there.

Voll, John Obert. *Islam: Continuity and Change in the Modern World*. Boulder, Colo.: Westview Press, 1982. Probably the best overview of Islam throughout the world from the eighteenth century through the present day.

PART III

World War I and the Middle East State System

On 28 June 1914, the heir to the Austrian throne, Archduke Franz Ferdinand, was shot by a Serbian nationalist while visiting the city of Sarajevo. With the backing of its ally, Germany, Austria presented an ultimatum to Serbia. The Austrians demanded that the Serbs rein in nationalist and anti-Austrian movements in their territory. Then, even after the Serbian government conditionally agreed to the ultimatum, the Austrians declared war.

While Germany was allied with Austria, Russia was allied with Serbia. The Russians feared that they would be at a disadvantage if war broke out and Germany had completed its military preparations before them. The Russian tsar thus ordered a general mobilization. Germany also mobilized and, to avoid fighting both Russia and France at the same time, decided to launch a knockout blow against France by striking at France through Belgium. Because Britain was committed by treaty to Belgian independence, it declared war on Germany. World War I had started.

When we think of World War I, we generally think of trench warfare on the Western Front in France. It is important to understand, however, that World War I was truly a world war. As a matter of fact, although the British and French referred to the war as the "Great War" until World War II, the Germans coined the phrase "world war" early on to describe the conflict. German strategists understood that the war was being waged among rival empires with worldwide interests. These empires depended on their colonial possessions to maintain their strategic position and economic well-being. Colonies were also indispensable for the French and British military effort because both powers depended on them for manpower to replenish the depleted ranks of their armies. As a result, much of the globe was dragged into a war which had begun in Europe.

It has been estimated that the per capita losses in the Ottoman Empire and Persia were among the highest of all nations affected by the war. While Germany and France lost, respectively, about 9 and 11 percent of their populations during the war, estimates for Ottoman losses run from 12 percent of the population to as

Vignette

Stranger than Fiction

Good storytellers are averse to using coincidences as a plot device. They seem a lazy way to advance a narrative that is bogged down, and audiences are almost always offended at being treated so shabbily. Historians do not share this aversion. So here is a story that would make both storytellers and their audiences wince:

World War I was a seminal event in the history of the modern Middle East, and the assassination of Archduke Franz Ferdinand was the spark that set it off. The reasons for the assassination are complex and explaining them would require a vignette in itself. Anyway, on 28 June 1914, the archduke and his wife paid a visit to Sarajevo to inspect army maneuvers being held outside the city. After a brief inspection, the archduke was scheduled to give a speech at the Sarajevo town hall. Little did he or his security detail realize that seven assassins were stationed at regular intervals along the archduke's route waiting for his motorcade to pass. When it did, the first two assassins, stationed together, did nothing. Reports were that they lost their nerve. The third assassin was more proactive. He threw a bomb directly at the archduke, but as luck would have it the bomb had a timing device and, apparently, time was not yet ripe for it to explode. Besides, his aim was not particularly good. The bomb hit the side of the archduke's car, bounced off, and exploded as the car behind passed. A number of spectators were injured, as were some of the occupants in the car. The motorcade sped away. The route's fourth assassin, realizing there was no point to his sticking around, abandoned his post to get a sandwich at a local sandwich shop.

After the speech, the archduke decided he would pay a visit to the injured who had been taken to a hospital. No one told the driver of the vehicle leading the motorcade about the change in plans, however. He thus began to take the scheduled route. One of his passengers realized the mistake and told the driver that the motorcade had to turn around in order to get on to the right street. He stopped his car to shift gears. The second car, carrying the archduke, also stopped—a few feet in front of the sandwich shop and the surprised assassin who had just left it. Whether their eyes met, whether the archduke recognized for a fleeting moment what was about to come, is not known. The assassin reached into his pocket, pulled out a pistol, and shot the archduke and his poor wife dead.

How history might have changed had the assassin craved a drink instead of a sandwich.

---

high as almost 25 percent—approximately five million out of a population of twenty-one million. These casualties occurred both on and off the battlefield. As a matter of fact, four out of every five Ottoman citizens who died were noncombatants. Included among them were one to 1.5 million Armenians in the Ottoman Empire who died as a result of starvation and ethnic cleansing. While many Armenians believe the Ottoman government planned genocide at the highest levels, Turkish governments still claim that the tremendous losses suffered by the Ottoman Armenian community were an unfortunate accident of war (according to the definition included in the United Nations Genocide Convention, what happened to Ottoman Armenians during World War I indisputably fits into the category of genocide). Although Persia was officially neutral in World War I, estimates put its per capita wartime losses in the same range as those incurred by the Ottoman Empire.

Many of the casualties suffered by the Ottoman Empire and Persia succumbed to famine. In Mount Lebanon, for example, famine killed upward of half the population. This tragedy still plays a central role in the Lebanese national narrative, which claims that the (Muslim) Ottoman government intentionally created the famine by requisitioning agricultural products and tools from the largely Christian population. While requisitioning (and an unfortunately timed plague of locusts) certainly aggravated the problem, it was in fact the French and British blockade of eastern Mediterranean ports that had created it. In Persia, tribal insurrections, the collapse of the political order, and the destruction of infrastructure so devastated agricultural production that it did not reach pre-war levels again until 1925.

World War I thus had immediate, tragic consequences for the populations of the region. But the war had other consequences as well. World War I was the single most important *political* event in the history of the modern Middle East. This is not to say that the war changed everything. The great nineteenth-century transformation did more to revolutionize the social and economic relations of the inhabitants of the Middle East than did World War I. So did events during another period of immense change—the period stretching from the 1930s to the 1970s. Nevertheless, World War I did bring about a new political order in the region, one that has lasted to this very day. Four aspects of this new political order are particularly significant.

First, World War I brought about the creation of the current state system in the region. At the beginning of the war, the Ottoman Empire ruled, in law if not in deed, Anatolia, the Levant, Mesopotamia, Egypt, parts of the Arabian peninsula, and a small sliver of North Africa. By the early 1920s, Turkey was an independent republic, the Asiatic Arab provinces of the empire had been divided into what would become separate states, Egypt had evolved from an Ottoman territory to a quasi-independent state, and much of the Arabian peninsula had been conquered by ᶜAbd al-ᶜAziz ibn al-Saᶜud, who would go on to found Saudi Arabia.

The ideological glue that bound together these states—and in some cases challenged them—was nationalism. After the war a variety of nationalist movements emerged in the territories previously controlled by the Ottoman Empire. Some of these movements were successful, others not. Nationalism itself was not new to the region. As the nineteenth-century Ottoman state extended its reach into the lives of its citizenry, many in the empire came to view themselves as part of expanded political communities, bound together by shared experiences and distinguishing traits. This is, after all, what nationalism is all about. But at the end of the war Ottoman nationalism—*osmanlilik*—was no longer an option. With the end of the Ottoman Empire, there no longer remained a political framework that could unite Arabs and Turks, the two largest ethno-linguistic groups housed within its boundaries. Nor was there a commonly accepted political framework to unite Arabs with one another. As a result, varieties of nationalism—Turkish nationalism, Arab nationalism, Syrian nationalism, Egyptian nationalism, and so on—spread throughout the region. Each nationalism claimed the exclusive right to command the loyalty and obedience of the citizens its proponents sought to govern.

One other nationalist movement achieved success as a result of the war: Zionism. Zionism might be broadly defined as Jewish nationalism. Zionists believe that Jews—a religious community that Zionists redefined as a national community—have the same right to self-determination as other peoples. More often than not, they have placed the site of that self-determination in Palestine. Although Zionism was a product of the nineteenth century, World War I brought the international Zionist movement its first real diplomatic success. In November 1917, the Zionist movement achieved recognition by a world power, Great Britain. This recognition accorded Zionism enough prestige and drawing power to ensure that it would not follow in the footsteps of hundreds of other nationalist movements that had appeared briefly, then faded into obscurity. During the period between the two world wars, Jewish immigration to Palestine soared. This led to the first large-scale intercommunal violence between Jewish settlers and the indigenous inhabitants of the region. Thus, World War I not only marks a milestone on the road to the establishment of the State of Israel, it marks the point at which the Israel-Palestine conflict became all but certain.

Finally, World War I brought about a political transformation in Persia. In the aftermath of wartime famine and political chaos, a military leader, Reza Khan, took control of Persia and established a political dynasty (if two rulers can be said to constitute a dynasty) that lasted until 1979. Reza Khan, who later adopted the title Reza Shah, and his son, Muhammad Reza Shah, centralized and strengthened the power of the state to an extent never previously accomplished in Persia. Their authoritarian but developmentalist strategy continues to influence economic, social, and political life in Iran to the present day.

CHAPTER 11

State-Building by Decree

The states that emerged in the Middle East in the wake of World War I were created in two ways. In the Levant and Mesopotamia, the site of present-day Syria, Lebanon, Israel/Palestine, Jordan, and Iraq, France and Britain constructed states. Guided by their own interests and preconceptions, the great powers partitioned what had once been the Ottoman Empire and created states where states had never before existed. The wishes of the inhabitants of those territories counted for little when it came to deciding their political future.

In contrast, Turkey, Iran, Saudi Arabia, and Egypt emerged as independent states as a result of anti-imperialist struggle (Turkey), *coup d'état* (Iran), revolution (Egypt), and conquest (Saudi Arabia). In each of these cases, the national myth recounting the deeds of a heroic leader or founding generation created a firmer foundation for nation-building than that enjoyed by the states created in the Levant and Mesopotamia.

To understand the origins of the states that emerged in the Levant and Mesopotamia, it is necessary to return to World War I. World War I drew the final curtain on the century of relative peace that had begun in Europe in the wake of the Napoleonic Wars. In addition to marking the end of the nineteenth-century European order, World War I marks a turning point in the relations between Europe and the Middle East.

During the second half of the nineteenth century, European powers acting in concert had taken responsibility for resolving the various crises brought on by the Eastern Question. True, European nations nibbled at the edges of the Ottoman Empire. The French picked away at North Africa, the British were ensconced in Egypt, Cyprus, and the Gulf, and the Italians occupied the territory that is contemporary Libya in 1911. Nevertheless, the concert of Europe provided a protective umbrella sheltering the Ottoman Empire from total dismantlement.

There is no telling what the future of the Ottoman Empire might have been had the concert of Europe remained in place. However, the unification of Germany

---

Vignette

Sweaters, Sleeves, and the Crimean War

During the period between the end of the Napoleonic Wars and the rise of Germany, the concert of European powers went to war only once to resolve a crisis originating in the Middle East: the Crimean War (1853–1856). The origins of the war were so murky that after its conclusion the government of one of the principal combatants, Great Britain, appointed a commission to determine what, in fact, it had been all about. In part the war began as a result of great power rivalry within the Ottoman Empire: The Orthodox Russians and the Catholic French quarreled over access to holy sites in Palestine. In part it began because of Russia's attempt to extend its patronage to all Orthodox Christians in the Balkans, even those who resided in the Ottoman Empire. When the Russians moved troops into Ottoman Moldavia and Wallachia (in present-day Romania), the Ottomans, British, French, and Piedmontese (!) launched a military campaign to drive them out. They chose the Crimean peninsula, of all places, as the site on which to challenge the Russians. After a truly abysmal showing by both sides, including the famous (and irresponsible) charge of the light brigade, the Russians backed down. In the wake of the war, the Ottomans were admitted into the concert of Europe. Henceforth, the European powers promised to act together to guarantee the independence and territorial integrity of the Ottoman Empire.

However important its diplomatic and military effects, the Crimean War also deserves notice because of its impact on men's fashions. If not for the war, there would be no raglan overcoats or sleeves, named for Fitzroy James Henry Lord Raglan, the British field marshal in charge of the Crimea campaign. Nor would there be cardigan sweaters, named for James Brudenell, the seventh earl of Cardigan, who led the infamous charge of the light brigade. And lest we forget, there is the balaklava, named for the site of the famous battle in which the light brigade charged and the "thin red line"—the 93rd Highlander Regiment—held its position against a Russian attack. Balaklavas are knit caps that drape over the wearer's face, leaving only the eyes and mouth exposed. They remain the headgear of choice for bank robbers and terrorists the world over.

---

in 1871 disrupted the European balance of power and crippled the ability of European states to act together on issues of common interest. By the beginning of the twentieth century, the concert of Europe no longer existed. Instead, on the eve of World War I European states divided themselves into two alliances. Britain, France, and Russia (and, after 1917, the United States) formed the core of the entente powers. Germany, Austria, and the Ottoman Empire formed the core of the Central Powers. Other states in Europe and elsewhere also signed on to one alliance or the other.

The Ottoman Empire joined the Central Powers for several reasons. Not only did Germany enjoy extensive political and economic influence in the empire, the empire was unlikely to join any alliance that included its archrival, Russia. In addition, the Austrians, anxious to control Ottoman ambitions in the Balkans, actively solicited the empire's participation in the war on their side. For their part, the entente powers did not try very hard to attract the Ottomans to their side. Because the entente powers assumed that the war would be short, they believed that including the Ottoman Empire in their alliance would not affect its outcome. They also believed that attracting Greece and Italy into their alliance was more important (both countries laid claims to Ottoman territory) and that the Ottomans would make up their minds about which alliance to join based on the progress of the war.

As soon as it became clear that the war would not be over quickly, each of the entente powers began to maneuver to be in a position to claim the spoils it desired in the Middle East in the event of victory. Russia had its eye on two prizes. The Russian government hoped to realize its long-standing dream of acquiring a warm water port by laying claim to the Turkish Straits. What made this dream all the more compelling was the fact that almost 40 percent of Russia's exports passed through the straits. Russia also had interests in the heartland of the Ottoman Empire, particularly Ottoman Palestine. Not only were sites holy to the Orthodox Church located there, but Orthodox Christians looked to Russia to protect their interests against Catholics, whose interests were backed by France. France, on the other hand, claimed to have "historic rights" in the region of the Ottoman Empire that lies in present-day Syria and Lebanon. France based this claim both on its role as protector of Lebanon's Maronite Christian population and on its economic interests in the region, such as investments in railroads and in silk production.

In contrast to the single-mindedness of the Russians and the French, the British were a bit flustered about the spoils of war they sought from the Ottomans. After all, for much of the nineteenth century Britain had been the staunchest defender of Ottoman integrity. The British government thus appointed a special committee to determine its war aims in the Middle East. The committee was made up of representatives from a variety of ministries, from the foreign office to the India and war offices. Each of these ministries had different preoccupations. As a result, the committee returned with an eclectic wish list. For the most part, this list focused on Britain's long-standing obsession with the protection of the sea routes to India and on ensuring postwar security for British investment and trade in the region.

Starting in 1915, the entente powers began negotiating secret treaties that pledged mutual support for the territorial claims made by themselves or their would-be allies. By negotiating these treaties, entente powers hoped to confirm those claims, attract to their alliance outlying states such as Italy and Greece, and, as the war went on, keep the alliance intact by promising active combatants a payoff at the close of hostilities. For example, the British assumed that continued Russian pressure on Germany was the key to entente victory in Europe. To prevent Russia from signing a separate peace with the Central Powers and withdrawing from the war, the British and French negotiated a deal with the Russians. According to what became known as the Constantinople Agreement, Britain and France recognized Russia's claims to the Turkish Straits and the city that overlooked them, Istanbul. In return for their generosity, France got recognition for its claims to Syria (a vague geographical unit never defined in the agreement), and Britain got recognition for its claims to territory in Persia.

What makes the Constantinople Agreement important is not what it promised. Russia never got the straits nor did it remain in the war until the bitter end. France and Britain enjoyed only temporary control of the territories promised them. What makes the agreement important is that it established the principle that entente powers had a right to compensation for fighting their enemies and that at least part of that compensation should come in the form of territory carved out of the Middle East. Other secret treaties and understandings soon followed: the Treaty of London, the Sykes-Picot Agreement, the Treaty of Saint-Jean de Maurienne. All of them applied the principle of compensation. Sometimes the treaties and understandings stipulated that compensation should take the form of direct European control over territories belonging to the Ottoman Empire. At other times, the entente powers masked their ambitions by promising each other the right to establish or maintain protectorates or to organize zones of indirect control. In those zones, one European state would enjoy economic and political rights not granted to other states, but would not rule the zone per se. That would be the function of local power brokers who would receive the support of the European state in charge. In yet another attempt to arrive at a formula that would satisfy all entente powers, the alliance at one point committed itself to establishing an "international zone" in Jerusalem. This was done mainly to relieve Russian anxieties by making sure that no single Christian group would be in a position to deny another access to the holy sites.

Britain not only initiated or signed on to secret agreements, it also made pledges to local or nationalist groupings to assure their support or, at least, quiescence. Two pledges are particularly important for understanding the story of state-building in the region. Most historians regard them as contradictory despite the efforts of diplomats to square the circle after the war.

In 1915, the British made contact with an Arabian warlord based in Mecca, Sharif Husayn. Husayn promised to delegate his son, Amir Faysal, to launch a rebellion against the Ottoman Empire. In exchange, the British promised Husayn gold and guns and, once the war ended, the right to establish an ambiguously defined Arab "state or states" in the predominantly Arab territories of the empire. The negotiations between Sharif Husayn and the British led to the famous Arab Revolt, guided by the even more famous British colonel T. E. Lawrence (Lawrence of Arabia). British military strategists championed the revolt because they thought it a useful way to harass the Ottomans and compel them to overextend their forces. They also believed the revolt would shore up the right flank of a British army invading Ottoman territories from Egypt. The leaders of the revolt, taking the British at their word, viewed it as a means to achieve Arab unity and independence from the Ottoman Empire. As we shall see later, the revolt was more successful in creating the legend of heroic Arab struggle and imperialist betrayal, in spreading the fame of T.E. Lawrence, and in advancing the careers of Peter O'Toole and Alec Guinness than it was in fostering Arab unity and independence.

While the negotiations that led to the Arab Revolt were held in private, the British government pledged support to another group openly, on the pages of *The Times* of London. According to the Balfour Declaration of November 1917, the British endorsed the Zionist goal of establishing a "national home" in Palestine for Jews around the world.

Historians disagree as to exactly why the British would make such a promise. Some assert that the British did so for strategic reasons. Because the Jewish settlers in Palestine would be far outnumbered by Muslim Arabs, they would remain dependent on the British and be more than willing to help the British preserve the security of the nearby Suez Canal. Others attribute the Balfour Declaration to a British overestimation of Jewish power in the United States and Russia. Britain wanted to maintain support in the United States for the entente side. It also wanted to keep Russia, which had just experienced a revolution, in the war. Thinking that Jews had a great deal of influence over the American president, Woodrow Wilson, and within the Bolshevik movement, the British figured a little pandering might go a long way. For his part, British prime minister David Lloyd George lists at least nine reasons for the Balfour Declaration in his memoirs. The most convincing is his assertion that "it was part of our propagandist strategy for mobilizing every opinion and force throughout the world which would weaken the enemy and improve the Allied chances." In other words, it couldn't hurt—and might even help. As we know, the British underestimated the effects of the Balfour Declaration. Their wartime promise had consequences far beyond those they anticipated at the time.

While the secret agreements and pledges set a number of diplomatic and political precedents, they were relatively ineffective in determining the postwar settlement. There were a number of reasons why this was the case. First, the agreements were both ambiguous and mutually contradictory. Take the issue of Palestine, for example. According to the French reading of one of the secret agreements, the Sykes-Picot Agreement, Syria was promised to France and Palestine was part of Syria. According to the Russian reading of the same agreement, Palestine was simply the territory surrounding Jerusalem, and Jerusalem was to be placed under international control. According to the Arab reading of the letters Sharif Husayn exchanged with the British government before the Arab Revolt, Palestine was to be part of the Arab "state or states." And then, of course, there was the Balfour Declaration.

Changed circumstances also muddied the waters of the postwar settlement. For example, during the war Britain had launched attacks on the Ottoman Empire from India and Egypt. At the close of the war British troops occupied Iraq and parts of the Levant. This gave them leverage in postwar negotiations with other victorious powers. At the same time, the Russian Revolution brought to power a government that, in theory at least, opposed the imperialist designs of the tsarist government. The new Bolshevik government of Russia not only renounced the claims made by its predecessor, it embarrassed the other entente powers by publishing the texts of the secret agreements signed by Russia.

Furthermore, the Bolsheviks were ideologically committed to atheism and thus had no desire to make an issue about Orthodox access to Christian holy sites. In other words, now there was no need to "internationalize" Jerusalem. Finally, a nationalist revolt broke out in Turkey. This prevented the Greeks, Italians, and French from dividing Anatolia as they had arranged in the secret treaties.

One last obstacle to implementing the secret agreements came from the United States. When the United States entered the war on the side of the entente powers, President Woodrow Wilson announced his intention to make his Fourteen Points the basis of a postwar peace. Included among those points were a number of relatively benign ones, such as freedom of navigation on the seas. There were, however, three items that made European diplomats wince. Wilson's first point called for "open covenants of peace, openly arrived at" and an end to secret diplomacy. After the war, nationalist leaders in the Middle East would claim that this point invalidated the secret agreements. Wilson's fifth point stated that, when it came to independence of colonies, "the interests of the populations concerned must have equal weight" with the colonial power. After the war, nationalist leaders in the Middle East would claim that this meant they should be consulted about their future. Finally, Wilson's twelfth point stated that "nationalities which are now under Turkish rule should be assured . . . an absolutely unmolested opportunity of autonomous development." After the war, nationalist leaders in the Middle East would read into this point their right to self-determination (a phrase, interestingly, coined by the leader of the Russian revolution, Vladimir Lenin, and only later picked up by Wilson). Increasingly frustrated British and French diplomats humored Wilson as best they could while they seethed in private. French president and foreign minister Georges Clemenceau reportedly scoffed at the Fourteen Points, remarking, "Even the good Lord contented himself with only ten commandments, and we should not try to improve on them." Nevertheless, Wilson had let the genie out of the bottle, and delegates to the peace conference ending the war were beset by Kurds, Arabs, Zionists, Armenians, and others, all demanding their place at the table.

Meeting in Paris, entente peace negotiators attempted to unravel the conflicting claims of their governments and lay the foundations for the postwar world. The negotiators agreed to establish a League of Nations to provide a permanent structure in which international disputes might be resolved peacefully. Although the original call for a league can be found in Woodrow Wilson's Fourteen Points, the United States did not join it once it had been created. Nor, initially, were Germany or the newly established Union of Soviet Socialist Republics members. This weakened the league from its inception. But while the league failed miserably in its main mission—its peacekeeping activities were unfortunately interrupted by the onset of World War II—its charter did sanction French and British designs for the Levant and Mesopotamia. Article 22 of the charter dealt directly with the region, establishing the so-called mandates system there:

> To those colonies and territories which as a consequence of the last war have
> ceased to be under the sovereignty of the states which formerly governed them

and which are inhabited by peoples not yet able to stand by themselves under the strenuous conditions of the modern world, there should be applied the principle that the well-being and development of such peoples form a sacred trust of civilization and that securities for the performance of that trust should be embodied in the covenant. The best method of giving practical effect to this principle should be entrusted to advanced nations who by reason of their resources, their experience, or their geographical position can best undertake this responsibility. . . . Certain communities formerly belonging to the Turkish empire have reached a stage of development where their existence as independent states can be provisionally recognized subject to the rendering of assistance by a mandatory [power] until such time as they are able to stand alone, the wishes of the communities must be a principal consideration in the selection of the mandatory.

Accordingly, after World War I, France got the mandate for the territory that now includes Syria and Lebanon while Britain got the mandate for the territory that now includes Israel, the Palestinian territories, Jordan, and Iraq. The phrase "territory that is now Syria, Lebanon, Israel, the Palestinian territories, Jordan, and Iraq" is used here deliberately. The states known as Syria, Lebanon, Israel, Jordan, and Iraq had never before existed, but were created under the auspices of France and Britain.

The mandates system was a compromise solution to a problem that divided the "Big Three" powers at the conference. As the largest manufacturer in the world, the United States wanted a level playing field in trade. In other words, the United States wanted free trade (point three of Wilson's fourteen points) and an end to the system of imperial trade preferences—a system in which colonial

French mandatory officials established a military academy in Damascus to train a "Syrian Legion." (*From: The Collection of the author.*)

powers had special trade privileges with their colonies. Britain and France, on the other hand, were perfectly happy with the colonial system as it stood. The mandates system broke the deadlock: Mandates were to be temporary "colonies" with equal access for all in trade.

But conciliation was not for everyone. Contrary to the Charter of the League of Nations, the inhabitants of the region were never seriously consulted about their future. For example, the elected parliament of Syria that met after the war, the Syrian General Congress, declared that it wanted Syria to be independent and unified. By unity, they meant that Syria should include the territories of present-day Syria, Lebanon, Israel/Palestine, and Jordan. If Syria had to have a mandatory power overseeing it, a majority of the representatives declared, it should be the United States. Their second choice was Great Britain. For the representatives to the congress, France was unacceptable as a mandatory power. Nevertheless, a geographically diminished Syria went to France as a mandate.

But there was more. Although they had to report their activities to a special committee of the League of Nations, the mandatory powers had absolute administrative control over their mandates. They could sever and join the territories under their control as they wished. Thus, the French took their geographically diminished Syria and rubbed salt into the wounds of those who had put their faith in the League's pledges. The French created what they thought would be a permanent Christian enclave on the coast by severing Lebanon from Syria. They included in Lebanon just enough territory to make it economically viable and strategically useful, but not enough to threaten Christian dominance—at least for the time being. They then divided and redivided the territory of present-day Syria into up to six ethnically and religiously distinct territorial ministates. While the French soon abandoned their ministate experiment, the local leaders they supported in each of them would remain a thorn in the side of Syrian governments for almost half a century.

Even though the British and the French could sever and join territories under their control as they wished, implementing the mandates system was not as easy as planning it. Although the two mandatory powers played the major role in the creation of states in the Middle East, there was a third actor involved as well—the Hashemite family of Sharif Husayn of Mecca. In the wake of the Arab Revolt, troops under the command of Amir Faysal had occupied Damascus. Immediately after the war, Faysal tried to assume administrative control over the surrounding region as well. The French, supported by the League of Nations, opposed Faysal's pretensions and sent an army to Damascus to depose him. The first and last king of Syria was king no more.

The British reacted somewhat passively to the French dismissal of their client. Fearing that only France stood between them and a resurgent Germany, the British had no desire to jeopardize their relations with France over some trivial problem in the Middle East. As Lloyd George put it, "The friendship of France is worth ten Syrias."

The French ouster of Faysal was only the beginning of a more complex story, however. Soon after the French took possession of inland Syria, another son of Sharif Husayn, Amir ᶜAbdallah, began marching north from his home in Mecca to avenge his brother's humiliation. The British now faced two problems: what to do with their wartime ally, Faysal, and what to do about ᶜAbdallah, who was threatening to make war on their more important wartime ally, France. The British persuaded ᶜAbdallah to remain in the town of Amman, which was then a small caravan stop on the route to Syria, while they called a conference to determine what to do about the worsening situation in the Middle East. At the Cairo Conference of 1921, the British came up with a solution. To divert ᶜAbdallah, the British divided their Palestine mandate into two parts and offered their new protégé the territory east of the Jordan River as a principality. The territory lying across the Jordan River was first called, appropriately enough, Trans-Jordan (across the Jordan, from a European vantage point). ᶜAbdallah made Amman his capital. Since Trans-Jordan was no longer part of the Palestine mandate, the British closed it to Zionist immigration. After independence in 1946, Trans-Jordan became the Hashemite Kingdom of Jordan. Descendants of ᶜAbdallah have ruled Jordan ever since, and the present king of Jordan is his great-grandson. The territory west of the Jordan River (Cis-Jordan, or "this side of the Jordan") retained the name Palestine. Although also a mandate, the British ruled Palestine like a crown colony until they withdrew in 1948. This territory comprises present-day Israel and the Palestinian territories.

While the British thus solved the problem of ᶜAbdallah, they still had the problem of Faysal to contend with. Once again, the British came up with an inventive solution. They granted Faysal the throne of Iraq, a realm they created by joining together the Ottoman provinces of Basra, Baghdad, and Mosul. The descendants of Faysal ruled Iraq until they were overthrown in 1958.

On paper, Iraq appeared to be a good idea. The northern territory of Mosul had oil, which would ensure the economic viability of the state and a ready supply of the valuable commodity for the mandatory power. Basra in the south provided the territory with an outlet to the Persian Gulf. The territory in between, irrigated by the Tigris and Euphrates rivers, includes rich farmland that the British planned to use as a granary for its Indian colony. Ironically, however, the very mandates system that had created Iraq also conspired against its full political and economic development. In this, Iraq was not exceptional. The mandates system also frustrated the full political and economic development of Lebanon, Syria, and Jordan.

In theory, the League of Nations had entrusted the territories of the Ottoman Empire to Britain and France so that the European states could prepare their charges for self-rule. Whatever the charter had said about "the sacred trust of civilization," however, Britain and France accepted the mandates so that they could retain control over those areas in which they felt they had vital interests. In their shuffling and reshuffling of their mandates' territories, the two mandatory powers rarely gave much thought to ensuring their mandates were both economically

---

Vignette

Drawing Boundaries

In the aftermath of World War I, French and British diplomats created states and the boundaries separating them where none had previously existed. Sometimes, their decisions seem to lack any rationale. If you look at a map of Jordan, for example, you will see a strange indentation in its eastern border with Saudi Arabia. There is no reasonable explanation for that indentation. No river runs through the area, no mountain range forms a natural division between the two states.

Jordan (or Trans-Jordan, as it was then called) was created at the Cairo Conference of 1921. Winston Churchill, who presided over the conference as the British colonial secretary, later bragged that at the conference he had "created Jordan with a stroke of the pen one Sunday afternoon." But why did it take the shape it did?

Churchill was a man who enjoyed a good meal, which, more often than not, meant heavy food topped off with brandy or whiskey. According to legend, Churchill began to draw the boundary dividing Jordan from Saudi Arabia after a particularly bounteous repast. Midway through drawing the boundary line, Churchill hiccupped and his pen deviated from the straightedge. Hence, according to the legend, the strange indentation in Jordan's border—and hence the reason why some Jordanians call the indentation "Churchill's hiccup" to this very day.

An apocryphal story, to be sure, but one that speaks to the artificial nature of the states created through the mandates system.

---

and politically viable. The invention of Jordan, for example, solved a political problem for the British but created an economic nightmare: a country with virtually no economic resources. Since its earliest days, Jordan's economic survival has depended on the kindness of strangers. Foreign subsidies have maintained Jordan since 1921, when the British began paying ᶜAbdallah a yearly stipend of five thousand pounds. Foreign subsidies increased steadily for the next half century, and by 1979 they provided over 50 percent of government revenue (by 2010 the figure slid to 45 percent).

Iraq presents us with a very different story, one that includes imperialist collusion in fostering sectarianism and instability. The territory that is now Iraq contained a variety of populations whose social organization ranged from that of pastoral nomads to cosmopolitan city dwellers. It also included groups which sought independence or autonomy. In May 1920, Sunnis and Shiᶜis began holding joint meetings in Baghdad demanding independence. The British civil commissioner countered with a proposal for limited self-rule. If he thought this would placate anti-colonial sentiment, he was mistaken: In June 1920, rebellion broke out in the mid-Euphrates valley, then spread south and eventually encircled Baghdad, uniting Sunnis and Shiᶜis in common cause. Kurds, pressing their own demand for sovereignty, launched a separate rebellion in the north. It took the British four months to put down the rebellions (although pockets held out until 1922), which they did in large measure by convincing Sunni tribesmen that a rebel victory would mean the end of Sunni domination which the Ottomans had ensured in the territory, and by experimenting with new tactics, such as "shock and awe" (to borrow a phrase from the Gulf War and the 2003 American invasion of Iraq) bombings of recalcitrant tribes by the Royal Air Force. In the end, about six thousand Iraqis died in the rebellion, along with five hundred British and colonial troops.

The rebellion convinced the British that the status quo was untenable. And the British were confident that its strategic interests in Iraq could be met most efficiently by appearing responsive to nationalist aspirations. The British thus placed Iraq on a fast track to independence, understanding full well that by leaving governance in the hands of the Sunni minority they were, in effect, guaranteeing the ruling elite's continued dependence on British friendship, if not the RAF's phosphorus and mustard gas bombs. Iraq, the mandated territory least prepared to face the "strenuous conditions of the modern world," was the first to receive independence, which it did in 1932 after Great Britain, finding its imperial ambitions frustrated there, effectively foreswore its obligation to the international community. One year later, Iraq's army participated in the first postwar massacre of a minority group (Christian Assyrians in northern Iraq) and four years later independent Iraq experienced its first military coup. The other mandates all had to wait until after World War II for their independence.

The mandates system created other problems as well. For example, it stacked the deck against economic development in the mandated territories. European investors were reluctant to invest in territories their governments were contractually bound to surrender. What little investment was made in the mandates was made in colonial-style infrastructure, such as transportation networks necessary to send locally produced raw materials to European factories and markets. And because the mandates were temporary and supposed to pay for themselves, neither Britain nor France was particularly keen on investing public funds.

Then there was the question of what the counterinsurgency strategy of the mandatory powers did to existing patterns of land tenure and relationships of labor. The mandatory powers were suspicious of urban notables who had enjoyed wealth and local power under the Ottomans. This is because urban notables were prone to identify with one nationalist movement or another. The mandatory powers thus sought to counterbalance them by creating a loyal base among tribal leaders and rural notables. In return for their loyalty, tribal leaders and rural notables gained access to property. This simple exchange—property for loyalty—sparked the greatest Middle Eastern land rush since the announcement of the Ottoman Land Code of 1858. It also resulted in the accumulation of vast agricultural estates by the new rural gentry, as well as the transformation of once independent pastoralists and farmers into tenant labor. As we shall see in Chapter 15, the extent of the holdings of this gentry, coupled with their newness, would make land reform a key issue in Arab domestic politics during the post–World War II period.

The thinly disguised colonialism that underlay the mandates system and led to the creation of modern Lebanon, Syria, Jordan, and Iraq affected the legitimacy of those states as well. State-building in the Levant and Mesopotamia was initiated by victorious European powers rather than by the inhabitants of the region. No Washington or Garibaldi forged nations through wars of national liberation. No Valley Forge became a mythic symbol of nation-building. No indigenous Bismarck or Napoleon stirred patriotism through conquest. States in the Levant and Mesopotamia were plotted on maps by diplomats and received their independence in stages, usually after painstaking treaty negotiations. The correspondence between patriotic sentiments and the national boundaries of newly independent states was, at best, sporadic, and many among the Arab population of the region saw the division of the Levant and Mesopotamia into separate nations as debilitating and unnatural. Many still do. This is one of the reasons for the emergence and persistence of pan-Arabism in the region, the sentiment that stresses the unity of all Arabs and, in its political form (which, admittedly, all but a few nostalgic octogenarians have long abandoned) calls for the obliteration of national boundaries separating them. This is also one of the reasons why many in the region—even those who should have and did know better—could cast Saddam Hussein in the role of an Arab Bismarck after his invasion of Kuwait in 1990.

There is no doubt that those genteel diplomats who met in Paris and elsewhere to draw up the boundaries of the states in the Levant and Mesopotamia were guided by a combination of whim, prejudice, avarice, and an overweening sense that by right they might determine the fate of those they knew so little about. Nevertheless, it would be a mistake to argue that they erred by ignoring "primordial attachments" of the peoples of the region, such as the attachments created by the bonds of tribe, ethnicity, or sectarian affiliation. This argument has frequently been trotted out since the Arab uprisings that started in 2010–2011 began to cast doubt on the durability of the states those diplomats conjured up. So-called primordial attachments *was* one of the factors those statesmen considered when drawing boundaries (in addition to inventing Lebanon as a Christian enclave, at one point the French created Alawite and Druze homelands in parts of Syria where those religious sects predominated). More often than not, however, what diplomats took to be primordial attachments lost out to other considerations, such as political expediency and the divide-and-rule benefits of mixing populations. As we have seen, tribal, ethnic, and sectarian affiliations come about as the result of choices people make under particular historical circumstances. They are neither permanent nor inflexible, and should be viewed as the product of history, not its driving force.

CHAPTER 12

State-Building by Revolution and Conquest

When the League of Nations established the mandates system in the Middle East, its member states had no intention of applying the system beyond the Levant and Mesopotamia. Nor did they have the capacity to do so. Outside that region, in Egypt, Saudi Arabia, Anatolia, and Persia, indigenous nationalist movements and nation-builders established states through revolution, conquest, *coup d'état*, and anti-imperialist struggle.

EGYPT

World War I had both political and economic consequences for Egypt. Although Britain had occupied it since 1882, Egypt had been legally part of the Ottoman Empire until World War I. In December 1914, after the outbreak of war, Britain declared Egypt a protectorate, ending Ottoman sovereignty once and for all.

British rule in Egypt had become increasingly unpopular over the course of its history, and by the end of World War I the British had managed to alienate virtually all segments of the Egyptian population. During the war, the British had established controls over the marketing of cotton, which infuriated the influential stratum of large landowners. Wartime inflation devastated the living standards of civil servants, the urban poor, and even the peasantry. Peasants also suffered from famine during the war. The complaints of Egyptians found voice among an educated group of intellectuals and activists who, at the close of the war, found release from the constraints of wartime repression.

All that was needed to ignite the tensions between much of the Egyptian population and their occupiers was a spark. That spark was touched off in November 1918, when a delegation of Egyptian politicians, testing the limits of Woodrow Wilson's twelfth point ("nationalities which are now under Turkish rule should be assured . . . an absolutely unmolested opportunity of autonomous development," in case you forgot), petitioned the British high commissioner in Cairo for permission to go to Paris to represent the Egyptian population at the peace conference. The leader of this group was Saᶜd Zaghlul. Although born into a family of mid-level peasants, Zaghlul had married well (his wife was a daughter of an Egyptian prime minister). He procured a number of important positions in the Egyptian government, including those of minister of education, minister of justice, and vice president of the legislative assembly. During the war, Zaghlul used the last position to organize nationalist committees throughout Egypt.

When the British arrested and deported Zaghlul and his colleagues for their presumption, the committees founded during the war sprang into action. Demonstrations and strikes broke out throughout Egypt in the spring of 1919. They spread from students and labor activists to artisans and civil servants and even the urban poor of Cairo. Peasants, fearing imminent starvation, attacked the rail lines by which scarce food supplies might be taken to distant cities. Alongside the peasants were many rural landowners, who not only had complaints of their own but who feared social upheaval if they stood on the sidelines. The revolt—called by Egyptian nationalist historians the 1919 Revolution—lasted two months before the British put it down by force.

In response to the uprising, the British government appointed a commission under Lord Milner to investigate its causes and to propose a solution. The Milner Commission concluded that Britain could not hope to keep direct control of Egypt and that British interests might best be maintained in Egypt if Britain gave Egypt conditional independence. Only then could the British hope to rein in the most vehement Egyptian nationalists. Thus, in 1922, the British granted Egypt conditional independence. The treaty they imposed on the Egyptians was a disappointment to Egyptian nationalists. The British asserted their right to control Egyptian defense and foreign policy, protect minorities and the Suez Canal, maintain their role (alongside the Egyptians) in the governance of the Sudan to the south, and safeguard the capitulations. Independence indeed. Making conditional independence into unconditional independence would be the focus of nationalist efforts for the next three decades, even after the British sought to placate Egyptian public opinion by negotiating a new treaty on the eve of World War II.

Independence was also hampered by the strange system of governance in Egypt that pit three powerbrokers against each other. First, there was the Wafd, the main nationalist party. Saᶜd Zaghlul had founded the Wafd not as a party but as the platform representing the aspirations of the Egyptian nation. This can be seen in the name itself, which means "delegation" in Arabic and refers to the delegation Zaghlul had put together to represent Egypt at the Paris negotiations. In the contentious environment of interwar Egypt, however, the Wafd was soon joined by a number of other parties also seeking to become the platform for Egyptian aspirations. Also arrayed against the Wafd were the king (still a descendant of Mehmet Ali) and the British ambassador. Although the Wafd was extremely popular, both the king and the British conspired against unfettered parliamentary rule. Ultimate power rested, of course, in the hands of the British. The British only allowed the Wafd to take power when it needed to exploit the party's popularity in times of crisis. The first time it did so was in 1936, when the

British, fearing the rise of the original "axis of evil," sought to negotiate a new, less provocative treaty with the Egyptians. The second time was in 1942 when, in the midst of World War II, German field marshal Erwin Rommel's troops threatened Egypt.

In the decades following World War I, the mainstream nationalist movement in Egypt did not advocate radical social change. Indeed, the mainstream nationalist movement in Egypt represented the interests of two groups in particular that feared unbridled democratic rule and social revolution: large landowners and members of the upwardly mobile intelligentsia. Neither group rejected Europe or European ideas, and their brand of nationalism demonstrated the role European conceptions of nation and state had in shaping their worldview. In 1914, one of Zaghlul's more articulate colleagues put the mission of the nationalist movement as follows:

> The wave of civilization has come to us with all its virtues and vices, and we must accept it without resisting it. All that we can do is to Egyptianize the good that it carries and narrow down the channels through which the evil can run. We must possess that civilization as it is, but not try to control it.

By narrowing their concerns to independence and by representing the interests of layers of the population that were anything but plentiful, the nationalist movement failed to encompass or even control the totality of the Egyptian public sphere. This left the door open to a host of other political and social movements that posed alternatives to the mainstream nationalist movement. A communist party, capitalizing on the success of the revolution in Russia and resurgent labor activism, opened its doors in the early 1920s. Then, toward the end of the decade, that apotheosis of modern Islamist organizations, the Egyptian Muslim Brotherhood, began recruiting its first members in the Suez Canal city of Isma'iliyya. The brotherhood was founded in 1928 by a charismatic school teacher, Hassan al-Banna, to promote personal piety, charitable acts, and a Muslim revival to counter what many Egyptians believed to be a Western cultural onslaught. While nationalism was not an essential part of its agenda, it was natural for its program to progress from hostility toward the intrusion of Western cultural values to anti-imperialism, and, finally, an affinity for nationalism. That affinity was strengthened by the fact that the Muslim Brotherhood claimed to represent the one true voice of Egypt, above the partisan fray. According to al-Banna,

> The love for one's country and place of residence is a feeling hallowed both by the commands of nature and the injunctions of Islam.... The desire to work for the restoration of the honour and independence of one's country is a feeling approved by the Qur'an and by the Muslim Brotherhood.... However, the love for party-strife and the bitter hatred of one's political opponents with all of its destructive consequences, is a false kind of nationalism. It does not benefit anybody, not even those who practise it.

On the other hand, the brotherhood articulated its message in a language that differed dramatically from that used by the mainstream nationalist movement, a language whose point of reference was Islam. The brotherhood thus spoke to layers of the population left unmoved by or alienated from the mainstream nationalist movement as well as those alienated from politics.

SAUDI ARABIA

As discussed in Chapter 8, in 1811 the Ottomans delegated an Egyptian army under the command of Mehmet Ali's son, Ibrahim, to dismantle the state founded by Muhammad ibn Sa^cud in 1744. When ibn Sa^cud had conquered territory in central Arabia, he was just an annoyance to the Ottomans. When his grandson had the audacity to capture the holy cities of Mecca and Medina, however, the Sa^cuds had clearly crossed the line. After all, part of the Ottoman sultan's title was "Protector of the Two Holy Cities" and what the Sa^cuds had done was just plain embarrassing. After recapturing the cities, the Egyptian army drove the retreating Saudi forces back to their stronghold in central Arabia, where they captured the remaining leader of the dynasty and shipped him back to Istanbul where he was beheaded.

The Sa^cuds established a second state in 1824 which stretched from central Arabia to the Persian Gulf. Although the state lasted almost ninety years, it was wracked by bickering among family members and ultimately fell to a rival tribe. The fact that it lasted so long was more a consequence of the insignificance of the territory it controlled (no oil yet) than to the vitality of the dynasty.

The third time, however, was the charm. In 1902, ^cAbd al-^cAziz ibn al-Sa^cud, a descendant of Muhammad ibn Sa^cud, retook control of Riyadh, the capital of the former Saudi states, and drove out competing tribes from the region with the help of the *ikhwan* (brothers). The *ikhwan* were fighters from an assortment of tribes whom Wahhabi missionaries, put off by "idolatrous" nomadic culture, won over to their teachings and settled in agricultural communities. By the time World War I broke out, the Saudi/*ikhwan* alliance proved a formidable force—so much so that they attracted the attention of the British. The British placed ibn al-Sa^cud's domain under a "veiled protectorate," which, unlike the French protectorates in North Africa, did not have international sanction. The British took this step for two reasons. First, although the British had allied themselves with the rival Hashemite family in western Arabia, they decided that making trouble for the Ottomans and their Arabian allies—which ibn al-Sa^cud was more than willing to do—was more important than mere loyalty. They therefore hedged their bets. In addition, the British wanted to check any designs ibn al-Sa^cud might have had on their Gulf protectorates. So they recognized the borders of his domain and agreed to defend its sovereign territory so long as he respected what was theirs. The veiled protectorate remained in effect until 1927.

While ibn al-Sa^cud kept his pledge to keep his hands off Britain's Gulf protectorates, he made no such pledge to the British about Hashemite domains. By 1925 he had conquered the Hijaz (kicking out Sharif Husayn) and several years later combined the Hijaz with the Najd to form Saudi Arabia. To this very day, every king of Saudi Arabia has been a son or grandson of ᶜAbd al-ᶜAziz ibn al-Saᶜud (they're about to run out), the doctrines of ᶜAbd al-Wahhab has been the official state ideology of Saudi Arabia, and Wahhabi ulama—many of whom have been descendants of ᶜAbd al-Wahhab and related by marriage to the royal family—have wielded tremendous power and, in return, have served to legitimate the dynasty. And since the government claims strict adherence to the Qur'an, it also claims that there is no need for any other constitution.

One side note of contemporary relevance: Once he had consolidated his state, ᶜAbd al-ᶜAziz ibn al-Saᶜud had no use for the *ikhwan*, whose raids into Iraq promised to bring down the wrath of the British Royal Air Force on Saudi Arabia. He therefore squelched them. But he took another step as well; He made sure that clerics who had once used the doctrines of ᶜAbd al-Wahhab to inspire a warrior ethos now preached another message—that Islam demands obedience to authority. In other words, according to the new dispensation clerics preached, Islam demands submission to a ruler so long as that ruler is Muslim. Even rule by a despot is better than *fitna* (strife) that disobedience to a ruler would bring. Thus, during the 2010–2011 Arab uprisings, the Saudis did everything possible to prevent Muslim Brotherhood governments from emerging wherever autocrats were removed. The brotherhoods—descendants of the original Egyptian Muslim Brotherhood—were not only political rivals, they were political rivals which claimed to derive their principles from the same source as the Saudis: the "true" interpretation of Islam. Even worse, however, is that the brotherhoods have encouraged Muslims to participate in politics as Muslims, something the Saudis would prefer to discourage both abroad (where brotherhood-led governments might upset regional stability and thus Saudi security) and on their home turf (where brotherhood activity might threaten dynastic rule).

TURKEY AND IRAN

In both Turkey and Iran, strongmen seeking to centralize authority and "modernize" their states took power in the wake of World War I. As a result, the post–World War I trajectory of the two countries was, in many ways, remarkably similar.

At the end of the war, the entente powers occupied Istanbul and held the Ottoman sultan virtual prisoner. In 1920, the government of the sultan signed the Treaty of Sèvres, which formally severed the connection between Turkish and non-Turkish regions of the Ottoman Empire. It also divided western Anatolia among Greece, Italy, and France. While all three states sent armies of occupation to affirm their claims, Greek ambitions in Anatolia were particularly expansive. Greek nationalists drew inspiration from what they called the *megali idea* (grand idea). They designed to unite all Greeks from the Mediterranean islands to the Black Sea coast into one state, thereby restoring the glory of the Byzantine Empire. They thus sought to snatch as much territory in Anatolia as possible. But Greek ambitions were also particularly obnoxious to many Turks who chafed at the idea that a former vassal state would now attempt to turn the tables on its former overlord. Throughout unoccupied Anatolia, popular "Committees for the Defense of Rights" sprang up to resist the occupiers. To restore order, the government in Istanbul sent General Mustafa Kemal east to suppress the committees.

Mustafa Kemal hailed from Salonika, formerly part of the Ottoman Empire but now the second largest city in Greece. Trained in various military academies, he fought for the Ottomans in Libya against the Italians and in the Balkan Wars against the Serbs, Bulgarians, and Greeks. He achieved his greatest fame as a military commander at the Battle of Gallipoli in 1915. The entente powers conceived the Gallipoli campaign as a quick stroke to knock the Ottoman Empire out of World War I. Their plan was to seize the peninsula south of Istanbul, then march on the Ottoman capital. Rather than a quick stroke, however, the battle degenerated into trench warfare that was catastrophic even by World War I standards. Between one-third and one-half of the British, Australian, New Zealand, French, and Ottoman combatants were killed, wounded, or succumbed to disease. Nevertheless, the Ottomans repulsed the invaders and Mustafa Kemal emerged from the battle a national hero.

Instead of suppressing the Committees for the Defense of Rights, Mustafa Kemal took charge of the rebellion. In a costly war that lasted two years, he forced foreign troops from Anatolia. In the wake of his victory, Mustafa Kemal adopted the name "Ataturk" (father of the Turks) and guided the establishment of a Turkish Republic that has ruled over an undivided Anatolia ever since.

As in the case of Turkey, a strongman emerged in Persia during the turmoil that followed World War I. At the beginning of the war, the Russians occupied northern Persia while the British occupied the south. When the Bolsheviks toppled the tsarist government, they withdrew Russian troops from Persia and the British occupied the entire country. After the war, the British attempted to impose a treaty on their hosts that would have made Persia into a virtual British protectorate. At the same time, the communist government in Russia backed separatist movements in the north.

The Anglo-Persian Treaty of 1919 was so unpopular that no Persian government could afford to ratify it. This created a dilemma for the British. British policy makers wanted to maintain their position in Persia to protect their oil interests and their Indian colony. They also wanted to prevent the expansion of Bolshevism to the south. But Britain could not afford to maintain an occupation force in Persia. Fearing a total breakdown of their Persian "buffer state," local British envoys encouraged the leader of the Cossack Brigade, Reza Khan, to take matters into his own hands.

Reza Khan came from a Turkish-speaking family in Mazandaran by the Caspian Sea. He had enlisted in the Cossack Brigade at the age of fifteen and rose through the ranks. Soon after British officers took over from the brigade's Russian officers in 1920, he became commander. Reza Khan marched on Tehran with three thousand men and forced the shah to appoint him defense minister. Within a few years he had outmaneuvered his political opponents. After purportedly toying with the idea of establishing a republic in Persia with himself as the first president, he had himself proclaimed shah in 1926. Reza Khan became Reza Shah, establishing a dynasty that ruled until 1979.

Since both Turkey and Iran (the name Reza Shah insisted foreigners call Persia after 1935) took their contemporary shape during the same period, it is not surprising that they developed along similar lines. Just as Ottoman leaders had borrowed from the British during the *tanzimat* period and the Germans later on, Mustafa Kemal and Reza Shah looked to contemporaneous models to provide them with a blueprint for state construction. Thus, in addition to adopting the standard policies any leader interested in holding on to power and building states from scratch would have to adopt, both cherry-picked from models then in vogue, including those established by the Bolsheviks in Russia and Benito Mussolini in Italy. Reza Shah also self-consciously modeled himself and his Iranian experiment on Mustafa Kemal and Turkey.

Like Mussolini, for example, each man placed himself at the center of a cult of personality. Both adorned cities with statues of themselves, had their images printed on postage stamps, and ensured their portraits were ubiquitous. In the case of Mustafa Kemal, the cult of personality lasted well beyond his death. When *Time* magazine asked readers worldwide to choose the most influential "Men of the [Twentieth] Century," it received over two hundred thousand votes for Mustafa Kemal, not only in the category of "Warriors and Statesmen," but in the categories of "Scientists and Healers" and "Entertainers and Artists." Presumably, most of these votes came from Turkey. Reza Shah was less fortunate: Because of his pro-German leanings during World War II, the British deposed him and put his son, Muhammad Reza Shah, on the throne in his place. The son replaced his father's statues and images with those of his own, only to see them removed or desecrated after the 1978–1979 Iranian revolution.

Both Mustafa Kemal and Reza Shah were unabashed Westernizers. Unlike, for example, the Islamic modernists who sought to find a compromise between Islam and Western ideas, Mustafa Kemal and Reza Shah sought to impose a model for modernity borrowed directly from the Western experience. They might have associated Westernization with modernization because it was easier to borrow from the West hook, line, and sinker than it was to sort out what was essential to borrow from what was not. They might have associated modernization with Westernization simply because they presumed Western modernity *was* modernity. They might have adopted the trappings of the West to gain stature among Europeans who also believed that their modernity was the only modernity. After all, European diplomats did not take their Japanese counterparts seriously until the latter substituted high hats and tailcoats for kimonos at international conferences. Or Mustafa Kemal and Reza Shah might have used the trappings of the West to distinguish themselves from their domestic opponents. Whatever the case, they looked at Western modernity and instead of seeing a source of inspiration, they saw a source from which to draw.

Mustafa Kemal, for example, had Turkey adopt the Western calendar in place of the Islamic one (Reza Shah replaced the Islamic calendar in Iran with the old Zoroastrian one), and he "Latinized" the Turkish alphabet, arguing that the new alphabet would be easier to read than the Ottoman script, which used Arabic letters. (Since over a billion people do quite well using Chinese characters, the argument rings hollow.) He even proposed legislation forbidding women from wearing the veil in public (contrary to myth, it never became law). Decrees about clothing were not for women only: Mustafa Kemal did away with the conical hat, the fez, that had been associated with high Ottoman modernity, in favor of Western-style headgear.

Although breaking down the fashion barrier between East and West was not far from the minds of either Mustafa Kemal or Reza Shah, who undertook similar initiatives, state-builders regularly legislated on matters of clothing during this period. They wanted to eliminate all clothing styles that alluded to regional, religious, or ethnic identities that might compete with the state for the loyalty of its citizens. They also wanted to advertise government policies (in this case, Westernization) by making citizens into walking billboards for them. And, perhaps most important, they regulated clothing because they could. By attacking something as personal as clothing, governments demonstrated their ability to cow their citizens. The reason why so many Turkish peasants to this very day wear flat caps like characters out of the comic strip "Andy Capp" can be attributed to Mustafa Kemal's policies.

Clothing wasn't the only way Mustafa Kemal and Reza Shah sought to imitate the West and simultaneously expand the reach of the state. They also supported the rights of women. Mustafa Kemal changed the civil code abolishing polygamy and granting women equal rights to men in divorce and inheritance. He had schools in Turkey opened to girls and young women all the way through the university level. Women gained the right to vote in municipal elections in 1930 and in national elections in 1934, eleven years before France allowed women to vote. He even promoted his adopted daughter as a role model: She was the first female fighter pilot in the world. The same year that Turkish women first voted in national elections, Reza Shah visited his Turkish counterpart, and that visit resulted in his own forays into women's rights. During his reign, the state mandated female education, outlawed discrimination against women in public facilities, and ended the segregation of men and women in places they might mingle, such as coffeehouses and cinemas. Iranian women did not have the right to vote (as they do now in the Islamic Republic), but then again, under Reza Shah voting did not mean much anyway.

In their crusades for women's rights, Mustafa Kemal and Reza Shah were hardly motivated by a desire to expand the range of civil liberties available to Turks and Iranians. That would have been too much out of character. Nor was it simply a matter of borrowing another Western idea, although one of the centerpieces of the West's derisive critique of "the East" was the way women were treated there. Like other authoritarian figures whose stance on the "woman question" appears progressive, both sought to expand the reach of the state into the home and to replace the "private patriarchy" of the husband/father-dominated family unit with a "public patriarchy" defined by the state. Granting women rights they had not previously enjoyed was a means of accomplishing this.

In addition to being Westernizers, both Mustafa Kemal and Reza Shah were secularizers. Both adopted the French model of secularism, according to which private beliefs are tolerated but religion and religious display have no place in the public sphere. In the early days of the new Turkish Republic, Mustafa Kemal abolished the caliphate, banned sufi orders, nationalized religious endowments, introduced a new legal code based on the Swiss code wherever Islamic codes had held sway, closed down Islamic courts, created a directorate to oversee religious affairs, and abolished the millet system, nationalizing its functions. And just as his attempts to regulate clothing made men and women walking billboards for his policy of Westernization, they did the same for his policy of secularization. For example, the fez had allowed men to put their foreheads on a carpeted floor during prayer—one of the positions required of practicing Muslims. On the other hand, the brim of the flat cap prevented Muslims who wore it from assuming that position.

Reza Shah faced greater problems in his attempts to secularize Iran than Mustafa Kemal faced in Turkey. This was because Iranian ulama were involved in a broader range of activities than their Turkish counterparts. They were also more closely interwoven with the rest of society. In Turkey, on the other hand, *tanzimat* and post-*tanzimat* policies had effectively done much of Mustafa Kemal's job for him. Nevertheless, the changes introduced by Reza Shah were sweeping. He required the ulama to be certified by the state and narrowed the domain covered by shariᶜa law, which they administered, to family matters only. For other matters, Reza Shah introduced the French civil code and the Italian penal code. But Reza Shah did not stop there. To keep any displays of religiosity out of the public sphere, the state banned public religious ceremonies and celebrations and the passion plays that lay at the heart of Shiᶜi religious practice and refused exit visas to pilgrims wishing to go to Mecca and Medina or to the Shiᶜi holy cities of Karbala and Najaf in Iraq. In the end, however, these policies, continued during the reign of his son, would backfire.

In addition to being Westernizers and secularizers, Mustafa Kemal and Reza Khan might also be viewed as heirs to the defensive developmentalists of the nineteenth century. Like their forebears, both attempted to expand the role of the state, centralize power, and spread a single, official ideology to bind citizens to each other and to the state. It was easier to accomplish this last task in Iran than Turkey. Because Iran had been a sovereign state before Reza Shah took over, the official nationalism spread by the "Society of Public Guidance"—the propaganda arm of the government which was modeled on similar institutions in Fascist Italy and Nazi Germany—could borrow from the writings of belletrists and activists of earlier eras, so long as those writings de-emphasized the role of Islam in shaping the Iranian nation. The society spread the state's official view of its past through radio broadcasts, journals, pamphlets, newspapers, and textbooks. Overall, its efforts seem to have paid off: The fact that most Iranians still believe, decades after the Islamic Revolution, that the tenth-century poem the *Shahnameh* is their *national* epic speaks to the effectiveness of Reza Shah's efforts. Demonstrating the connection between Turkic peoples from Central Asia and the Anatolian home of the Republic of Turkey was a bit trickier, but it could be done because there were few Hittites around to object to being made into "proto-Turks," nor were there many Sumerians, also "proto-Turks," to be found speaking their proto-Turkish "sun language" from which, pseudo-linguists decided, all the world's languages descended.

Since language played such a central role in both Iranian and Turkish nationalisms, it is no surprise that cleansing their respective languages of foreign words—removing Arabic and Turkish words from Persian, removing Arabic and Persian words from Turkish—would be a central plank in the construction of national ideologies in both countries. This project was more successful in Turkey than in Iran. In 1932—the year language "purification" began in earnest—60 to 65 percent of the vocabulary in written Turkish was borrowed. Currently, it is 20 to 25 percent. Except for Persianizing place names, however—changing Arabistan to Khuzistan, and the like—the project proved more trouble than it was worth in Iran, since about 40 percent of Persian words still come from Arabic and Turkish and Persian is the native language of only about 50 percent of Iranians anyway.

Both Mustafa Kemal and Reza Shah held power at a time when state intervention into economies had become the norm globally. However, states differed on how this intervention was to be done. Mustafa Kemal thus had a list of blueprints from which to draw. Initially, he settled on a program that mixed and matched various policies from elsewhere but which tailored them to a state which had suffered mightily during World War I, had lost all too many skilled Christian merchants and factory owners to genocide and forced relocation, and needed immediately to harness the entrepreneurial skills of the remaining population. Thus, it was determined that the state would support and direct the private sector when possible and intervene directly into the economy on its own when it had to. The onset of the Great Depression, however, forced Turkey's economists to rethink their development strategy. As a result, Mustafa Kemal increasingly followed the lead of the Soviet Union, which had avoided the worst the depression had to offer by cutting itself off from the sinking global ship and by making the state the engine of the economy. "Statism" in Turkey had a long life, lasting until about 1980. By that time, the global economic paradigm had shifted, and states, under pressure from international banking institutions and powers at the core of the world economy, began to withdraw from many of the functions they had taken on earlier.

Reza Shah's "New Order" (a name Mussolini used to describe his own policies) also advocated a strong role for the state in the economy to eliminate foreign control and to foster rapid development. Under the shah, the state canceled foreign concessions, established a national bank to take the place of the British-run "Imperial Bank," and took control of posts, telegraph, and customs from foreigners.

Mustafa Kemal shown demonstrating the new Turkish alphabet. *(From: Jacques Benoist-Méchin, La Turquie se dévoile, 1908–1938 (Paris: PML Editions, n.d.), p. 231.)*

The state also set high tariffs to protect the infant industries being established. To accumulate capital for investment, the state confiscated landholdings of many of the wealthiest landlords and ulama and instituted government monopolies over select industries. Most important, the state acquired revenues from oil. The shah himself negotiated new terms for the d'Arcy concession, first threatening to cancel the concession entirely, then granting the Anglo-Persian Oil Company (which became the Anglo-Iranian Oil Company two years later) a concession for another sixty years. Although the company increased its payments and obligations to the Iranian government, it was clear to all but the self-impressed shah that the British government had proved the more wily negotiator.

The capital accumulated from confiscations, monopolies, and oil enabled the shah to launch an ambitious program of what would later be called "import substitution industrialization." Reza Shah believed that Iran should produce as many domestically consumed goods as it could, rather than importing those goods from abroad. This would keep money circulating within Iran rather than pouring out. The policies of Reza Shah (and Mustafa Kemal) thus differed from those of nineteenth-century state-builders in a significant way. Because European imperialists disapproved, defensive developmentalists in the nineteenth-century Middle East could not do the sorts of things their successors could do to build industry. Instead, their only recourse to modernize was by selling cash crops or raw materials, by offering concessions, or by taking out loans. This only served to integrate their states further into the world economy. Times had changed, however.

The age of free trade was long gone. So was Europe's desire and capability to project direct power into Turkey and Iran. Reza Shah and Mustafa Kemal therefore tried to nurture their national economies by freeing them from the constraints of the world system. Unfortunately for them, it was a fool's errand. Nevertheless, import substitution industrialization would become the norm among states on the periphery of the world system after World War II.

State-building in the twentieth century was, more often than not, an ugly affair and was frequently accompanied by ethnic cleansing to "purify" populations of "foreign" elements and repression to ensure the obedience of those who remained. State-building in Turkey and Iran was no exception. For example, soon after the Turks expelled the Greek army from Anatolia, the governments of Turkey and Greece arranged a population transfer to rid themselves of minorities they viewed as untrustworthy. The Turkish government, working under guidelines which had, in fact, been set by the League of Nations, forced up to 1,300,000 Christian Turks out of the country. Many had lived for centuries in Anatolia, spoke Turkish as their native language, and only differed from their neighbors in terms of the religion (Orthodox Christianity) that they practiced. In return, about 380,000 Greek Muslims went to Turkey. Like the ethnic cleansing of Armenians that took place during World War I and the "dirty war" to suppress Kurdish separatism in the 1980s and 1990s, the transfer of "Greeks" to their "ancestral homeland" displays the dark side of nationalism in all its grisly detail.

There is a dark side to the history of Turkey's official ideology, Kemalism, as well. When Mustafa Kemal took charge of the Committees for the Defense of Rights, no one fighting by his side could have realized the breadth or depth of the changes he would oversee. In fact, many fought in the name of Islam. Others fought merely to eliminate a foreign presence from Anatolia. Thus, from its inception Kemalism met with opposition, and that opposition—and the state's response to that opposition—continues to color Turkish politics to this day.

Sometimes, opposition to Kemalism has broken down along ethnic lines. For example, Kurds have resisted the "Turkification" policies of the government. Although one former Turkish prime minister claimed that Kurds were merely "mountain Turks," Kurds continue to assert an ethnic and linguistic identity separate from Turks. To this day, some Kurds demand cultural autonomy while others go so far as to demand separation from Turkey. Other ethnic and religious minorities (such as the Alevi minority, which makes up about 20 percent of the Turkish population) have also experienced inequities because they, too, have not fit into the Kemalist mold.

Opposition to Kemalism has also come from those put off by its uncompromising secularism. As early as 1950, the Democratic Party, which had distanced itself from the official secularist line and wrapped itself in Islamic imagery, emerged the victor in Turkish national elections. The Democrats' victory sent a clear message of disaffection to the country's ruling elites, who did not take kindly to their displacement. The Democratic Party ruled until 1960, when it was overthrown in a military coup d'état.

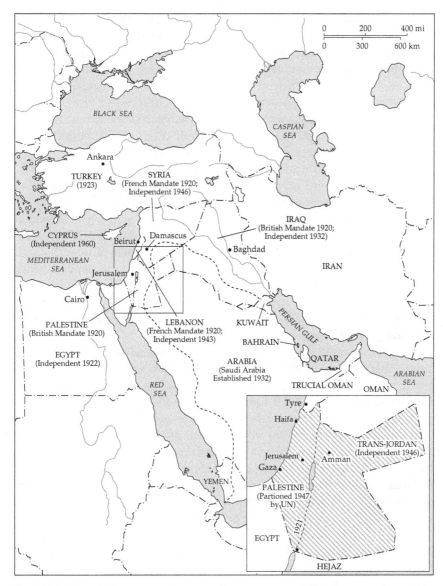

The Middle East, 1923

All of which brings up the thorny issue of military/civilian relations. Turkish democracy works until it doesn't. Whenever the Turkish military felt that stability or the principles of Kemalism were threatened, as it did in 1960, it stepped into the political process to "restore order" and "uphold the constitution." Mustafa Kemal may have set the precedent for this himself. In the wake of an internal rebellion in 1925, he assumed sweeping emergency powers for four years. In addition to the coup d'état of 1960, the Turkish military assumed emergency powers twice, in 1971, and 1980, and forced the replacement of the prime minister in 1997. Like Mustafa Kemal, it relinquished control, but only after "cleansing" the political system by disbanding political parties, jailing, and, in some cases, torturing those it deemed enemies of the state. In sum, any assessment of Turkish democracy has to balance a dynamic public sphere and parliamentary tradition with a history that includes repression and military intervention into politics.

The Iranian experience with repression matches the Turkish one. Throughout his sixteen-year reign, Reza Shah imposed strict censorship, controlled elections, and jailed and executed political opponents and labor activists. He built a well-equipped national army whose top priority was not to defend Iran from foreign aggression but, like most armies built in the Middle East since the end of World War I, was designed to quash internal dissent, prevent the emergence of mass movements such as had taken place during the Constitutional Revolution, and pacify tribes and separatists. When peasants and workers reacted to desperate economic conditions brought on by the Great Depression of the 1930s with rebellions and strikes, he used state terrorism to suppress them. In one instance he had 150 peasants executed and others interned or forced into exile as examples to others. Although the repressive policies of his son and heir were instrumental in sparking the Iranian Revolution of 1978–1979, when it came to brutality Reza Shah was no piker.

What, then, were the legacies left by Mustafa Kemal and Reza Shah? Certainly, after the Iranian Revolution the secularism promoted by the shah has gone by the board. And in 1980, the first cracks in the wall separating religion and politics began to appear in Turkey as well. In the wake of an economic and political crisis, a military junta took power and declared what was called the "Turkish-Islamic synthesis" the new state ideology. The synthesis, as the name implies, married a right-wing Turkish nationalism to what its advocates termed the "Islamic tradition." The junta hoped that the wide appeal of an ideology that included a call for both political unity and moral virtue would help stem the factionalism and violence in Turkish politics that had reached unprecedented proportions. More specifically, they believed the synthesis would link military officers with Islamic activists in the battle against the non-believers of the political left. But by promoting the Turkish-Islamic synthesis, the junta opened up a space in politics for Islamic political parties, such as the Justice and Development Party (AKP), which secured its first prime ministership in 2002.

For many Turks, the AKP-dominated government has led to what they call the "creeping Islamization" of Turkey. They point to a statement made by Prime Minister Recep Erdogan that Turkey must raise "a religious youth" and to a number of government initiatives that include imposing censorship on books and movies deemed "immoral," reintroducing Qur'anic education into primary schools, sponsoring mosque construction, and restricting the availability and consumption of alcoholic beverages. In addition, the Higher Education Board, dominated by members of the AKP, lifted the rule that prohibited women from wearing the veil on university campuses—an important symbolic gesture. Ironically, the ban had been imposed by the same military government that promoted the Turkish-Islamic synthesis because it viewed re-veiling as a political provocation in the immediate aftermath of the establishment of an Islamic republic in Iran. Sometimes, Turkish government policies have bordered on the bizarre: The government fined a television station for showing an episode of the Simpsons which purportedly insulted God, the Ministry of Education decreed that textbooks remove reproductions of Eugène Delacroix's painting "Liberty Leading the People" because Liberty is leading the charge bare breasted, and the Ankara subway system prohibited public displays of affection—provoking a "kiss-in" by outraged youth. The "creeping Islamization" Turkey has been experiencing under the AKP might broaden, but it has already met with widespread resistance from committed secularists, members of religious minorities, and those caught on the other side of the culture war. There is, however, little chance for the military once again to intervene to "set matters straight." In 2010, the AKP announced the discovery of a military conspiracy against their government, resulting in the imprisonment of more than three hundred high-ranking officers. For the first time in Turkish history, civilian rulers arrested the top brass and not the other way around.

On the other hand, much of the legacy left by Mustafa Kemal and Reza Shah remains intact. This is most obvious in Turkey, of course, whose very existence Mustafa Kemal midwifed. But it holds true for Iran as well, in spite of its revolutionary transformation. The mullahs (religious leaders) who run the country stand on a platform built by Reza Shah and would not be able to rule, for better or for worse, but for the structural and institutional infrastructure he brought to Iran. If they ever do something as "un-Islamic" as building a pantheon to the heroes of the Islamic Revolution, Reza Shah would certainly deserve a place in it.

CHAPTER 13

The Invention and Spread
of Nationalisms

In the spring of 1919, about six months after the end of World War I, political posters festooned the streets of Damascus. A pedestrian taking an evening stroll would thus not have been surprised to see a poster ending with the following sentences: "The Arab nation is indivisible. The Arabs make up a single nation that demands independence." Turning the corner, that same pedestrian might have encountered another poster, this time ending with the following slogan: "We demand complete independence for Syria within its natural boundaries." That pedestrian might be forgiven for wondering just who he was supposed to be. Was he a member of the Arab nation, the Syrian nation, both, or was there yet a fourth option? One year earlier it is doubtful that he would have had to ponder the question. The year before he had been, after all, an Ottoman.

In the aftermath of World War I, a variety of nationalist movements emerged and spread in the Middle East. Representatives of the Armenian, Arab, and Kurdish "nations" descended on Paris to lobby the peace conference, while Turkish, Egyptian, Syrian, and Lebanese ("Phoenician") nationalists made their voices heard in other ways. Each of these movements claimed to represent the political aspirations of populations that had previously been ruled by the Ottoman Empire. Each claimed that the Ottoman Empire had been little better than an imperial prison that had kept their nations in captivity. But as the nineteenth-century French philosopher Ernest Renan once put it, "Getting history wrong is part of being a nation." Despite the claims of nationalist movements, those movements did not represent age-old nations yearning to reestablish their freedom after four hundred years of bondage. Nationalist movements created those nations. Furthermore, it was the very Ottoman Empire the movements vilified that had laid the foundation for the explosion of nationalisms in the post–World War I Middle East.

To understand how this was the case, it is necessary to understand something of the nature of nationalism. Although every nationalist movement and creed asserts its uniqueness, all are, in fact, comparable. All share a common set of assumptions about the proper ordering of human society. All nationalists believe that humanity is naturally divided into smaller units, or nations. All nationalists believe that nations can be identified by certain characteristics that all its citizens hold in common. These characteristics include the linguistic, ethnic, religious, or historical traditions that make a nation distinctive. All nationalists believe that times might change but nations retain their essential characteristics. As we have seen, Persian nationalists believe that the Persian speakers who listened to the "national poet," Firdawsi, recite the "national epic," the *Shahnameh*, in the eleventh century are members of the selfsame nation as those who memorized Firdawsi in schools built by Reza Shah. They are linked across time by language, literary tradition, and history. All nationalists believe that a people has a special relationship to some particular piece of real estate in which their ancestors first emerged as a distinct group and flourished. Zionists "belong" in Palestine, Egyptians in Egypt, Persians in Persia. All nationalists believe that nations possess something called a "common interest" and that it is the role of the state to promote it. Indeed, all believe that the only form of government that can assure the common interest of the nation is self-government.

These, then, are the five essential assumptions of nationalism. In the modern world, these assumptions need no explanation or justification. They just *are*. And when populations believe that these assumptions are self-evident and part of the natural order, we can say that they live within a "culture of nationalism."

All nationalisms draw their assumptions from the culture of nationalism. All nationalisms take one or more linguistic, religious, or ethnic attributes of a given group of people and claim that the attributes they have highlighted make that group a nation and entitle it to political sovereignty in its ancestral homeland. Yet it is important to keep in mind that the culture of nationalism and the particular nationalisms that draw from it are different. The culture of nationalism has proven to be extraordinarily resilient wherever it has taken hold. In the modern world, everyone must belong to a nation. Specific nationalisms, on the other hand, come and go all the time. Thus, the Ottoman nationalism that Ottoman state-builders had floated during the nineteenth century (*osmanlilik*) could join Confederate nationalism in the dustbin of history in the twentieth. Because all nationalisms are rooted in a common set of assumptions, it is relatively easy for people to switch from one to another as circumstances demand. Over the course of the twentieth century, for example, loyal Ottoman citizens could become Arabs or Syrians or, over time, both, and some of these could later become Lebanese or Palestinians. Nationalists? Always. Ottoman or Arab or Palestinian nationalists? Maybe, sometimes.

True believers, of course, swear that their particular brand of nationalism deserves to succeed because it represents the authentic identity and aspirations of a given people. Most historians, on the other hand, wince at the idea of authentic identities and aspirations. For them, nationalisms succeed or fail not because they represent true or false identities and aspirations, but because of the often unpredictable circumstances in which they find themselves. After all, who is to say what the subsequent history of the Middle East might have been had the entente powers supported the establishment of a unified Arab state, or had Arab nationalism been anchored in a state that had the power to coerce and persuade its citizens?

The culture of nationalism differs from the various nationalisms that draw on its assumptions in another way as well. Because the culture of nationalism deals with assumptions about the organization of state and society, its advent in any given territory represents a truly revolutionary departure for the inhabitants of that territory. The culture of nationalism transforms subjects into citizens and citizens into cogs of a machine grinding away for something called "the common good" (or common wealth). Such transformations began to take place in the Ottoman Empire during the nineteenth century. The rise and fall of various nationalisms, on the other hand, is more superficial than revolutionary in nature. When compared to the extraordinary social and political changes that the Ottoman Empire had to effect for a culture of nationalism to emerge within its domains, the fact that Ottoman citizens would assert one or another nationalist creed down the road is of negligible importance.

Nationalism (and here I am referring to the category into which various nationalisms might be grouped) is a relatively new phenomenon in world history. We can trace it back only as far as the eighteenth century. Historians disagree about where nationalism first emerged. Theories range from the usual suspects, Britain and France, to the Netherlands, Germany, and even the Americas. It is probable that a culture of nationalism originated as a result of efforts made by rulers and statesmen to strengthen their states in the highly competitive European environment. They did this in two ways. First, they made the state and sovereign the focal point of their subjects' loyalty. After centuries of struggle, states finally supplanted their main rival, the Church, and eradicated or at least diminished the power of social groups (the aristocracy, tax farmers, etc.) that blocked the central government's direct access to its population. The second way rulers and statesmen strengthened their states was by mobilizing and harnessing the energies of their subjects in common endeavors and for that new invention, the "common interest." To do this, they conscripted townsmen and peasants alike into armies and labor gangs, standardized educational and legal institutions, and put in place policies designed to enhance their "national" economies, such as mercantilism. Over time, in those places where governments had imposed the new conception of state, populations internalized the notion that they were part of unified societies that had identities of their own and for whose benefit those populations had to direct their efforts.

Nationalism provided a narrative for those unified societies. It gave those societies an identity and a history. It also gave the state that presided over those societies legitimacy and purpose. Nationalism proved useful to state-builders as well, who used it to mobilize and harness the energies of their populations. As the modern state system spread throughout the globe, nationalism hitched a ride.

Nationalism could not emerge in the Ottoman Empire until a nurturing environment for it—a culture of nationalism—emerged. That came about after the modern economic and state systems absorbed the empire within their bounds. The reason for this was because the modern economic and state systems encouraged the spread of modern institutions of governance and market relations within every territory, principality, or empire with which those conjoined systems had contact. The Ottoman Empire, like the Habsburg, Russian, and Chinese empires, may have continued to call itself an empire. Nevertheless, over the course of the nineteenth and twentieth centuries it increasingly came to resemble a modern state. For example, the *tanzimat* decrees established the notion of citizenship as a legal principle. The announcement of this principle quickly struck roots among many in the empire. As early as the 1840s, peasants began asserting their newly acquired rights in local disputes. So did others, who also sought to use those rights to their advantage. Along with new rights, the Ottoman state demanded new obligations from its citizenry. It therefore increased its control and coercive capabilities over that citizenry. By taking responsibility for functions it had previously disregarded, by standardizing institutions, by attempting to set norms for public and even private behavior, the Ottoman state created the conditions in which new ties among its citizens might emerge.

Those ties also emerged as a result of the spread of market relations within the empire. Over the course of the nineteenth century, for example, peasants who had furnished most of their own needs and artisans who had produced for local markets found themselves bound up in larger economic networks. Sometimes those networks were regional. At other times, they were imperial or even international. The introduction of new transportation technologies such as railroads and steamships not only opened up new markets, it expanded the traffic in labor and goods between cities and countryside. That traffic flowed in both directions. Peasants, for example, might migrate seasonally to urban centers to supplement their incomes by engaging in wage labor. At the same time, increased urban economic control over the countryside broadened and deepened the spread of market relations in rural areas. The expanded interchange between city and countryside brought urban values and norms to outlying areas. It also enlarged the social, economic, and cultural space in which people lived their lives.

The spread of modern technologies and market relations, then, affected notions of social, economic, and cultural space. In some cases, the new notions of social, economic, and cultural space paved the way for regional loyalties that would later provide the basis for nationalist movements (and here, as earlier, we might define a nationalist movement as a stateless nationalism on the make). This can be seen in the case of Greater Syria. Over the course of the nineteenth century, trade and infrastructural development established Greater Syria as a distinct economic unit. By 1861, a British-built telegraph connected Aleppo, Beirut, and Damascus. By the 1880s a system of carriage roads connected the inland cities of Damascus and Homs with the coastal cities of Tripoli, Sidon, and Beirut. By the

1890s, rail service connected Beirut with Damascus and Damascus with the grain-producing region of the Hawran to the south. Commerce increasingly flowed along the lines of the new railroads and carriage roads. Urban-based merchants enriched by that commerce increasingly loaned money to and frequently repossessed the lands of peasants inhabiting the hinterlands of Syrian cities. Peasants increasingly swelled the population of nearby urban centers in search of jobs in industries fueled by that commerce. Elite families in Damascus, Jerusalem, and Aleppo increasingly sought marriage alliances with their peers in Sidon, Nablus, and Beirut in an effort to supplement commercial ties with family ties. All this contributed to the emergence of a Greater Syrian social and economic space.

At the same time that a regional social and economic space emerged in Greater Syria, the connections between Greater Syria and areas with which it was not so well integrated loosened. For example, over the course of the nineteenth century, Greater Syria and the territory that is now Iraq emerged as distinct economic units. By the beginning of the twentieth century, little remained of the overland trade that had connected the two regions in earlier centuries. After the opening of the Suez Canal in 1869, farmers of the upper Tigris valley began to ship grain via the Persian Gulf to Europe. This allowed them to abandon less profitable markets in geographic Syria. Not that it mattered all that much to the Syrian economy. With the opening of rail connections and ports, Syrian merchants could increase their profit margins as well by orienting to the Greater Syrian market or to the west.

The evolution of Greater Syria as a distinct unit capable of inspiring loyalty would rouse later generations of nationalists to champion the establishment of a Greater Syrian state. As we have seen, their plan ran afoul of the mandates system. Nevertheless, the legacy of the regional economic, social, and cultural ties that emerged in the empire in the nineteenth century affected even Arab nationalists. Most of the plans Arab nationalists floated to unite the eastern Arab world called for regional autonomy within a federated Arab state. And if economic integration affected Greater Syria in this manner, imagine how it affected the Ottoman province of Egypt, where the process of economic integration was much further advanced.

The economic, social, and cultural integration of a region does not necessarily mean that a nationalist movement will emerge there, of course. If that were the case, a California nationalism would have emerged years ago. For a nationalist movement to emerge, there must be nationalists to invent it, articulate its principles, and mobilize a population to realize its goals. Sometimes these nationalists work through states to produce what are called "official nationalisms." We have seen this in the case of the Ottoman Empire, and it would take place again among the various states that emerged in the aftermath of World War I. At other times, freelance nationalists have worked either in the absence of a state (as Palestinian nationalists have done) or in opposition to one (as Balkan nationalists did).

Groups of nationalists began to emerge in the Ottoman Empire during the nineteenth century for several reasons. Some bureaucrats and imperial functionaries consciously copied European techniques for state-building. The result was *osmanlilik*. They were soon joined by other nationalists who hailed from strata of the population created by defensive developmentalism. There was, for example, a Christian bourgeoisie in the port cities of the Ottoman Empire, created by the integration of the Ottoman Empire into the world economy. There were urban notables, enriched, in good measure, by the Ottoman Land Code of 1858 and empowered by the provincial and urban councils established during the *tanzimat*. They counted on Istanbul for positions of influence and were willing to toe the party line to get them. Finally, there were the professionals, intellectuals, and military officers, who had often attended imperial schools and had been educated according to standardized curricula (both products of the *tanzimat*). This is the same layer of society that had played such a key role in constitutional movements. These strata had been raised in an environment defined by the culture of nationalism. They were accustomed to the modern public sphere and an urban environment in which new techniques of mass politics could be deployed.

Often, individuals from these strata supported the nationalism of the Ottoman state. A number of them, however, were dissatisfied. For urban notables, there was only so much imperial patronage to go around. Some were sure to feel slighted. Many among the Christian bourgeoisie believed themselves excluded from a state that professed an Islamic *osmanlilik*. Other Christians felt bound by shared ties of religion, ethnicity, or both to one or another foreign nation or nationalist movement. And as we saw in Chapter 10, many professionals, intellectuals, and military officers failed to achieve the power and influence they felt they deserved. These were the layers that were at the forefront of oppositional nationalist movements.

The more the Ottoman state intruded into the lives of its citizens, and the more it attempted to establish norms of acceptable behavior and belief, the more the disgruntled members of these strata resisted. For example, some historians trace the origins of Arab nationalism to attempts made by the Young Turks to "turkify" the Ottoman Empire in the early twentieth century. Because the Young Turks sought to make Turkish the official language of the empire and eliminate non-Turks from positions of authority, these historians claim, some in the empire became conscious of themselves as members of a distinct Arab nation and demanded the right to rule themselves.

It is interesting to note that here as elsewhere a nationalist movement invented a nation. Before the nineteenth century, the word ʿarab did not have the same meaning among Arabic speakers it has today. Instead, the word was commonly used by town-dwellers as a term of contempt when referring to "savage" bedouin. Only in the nineteenth century did intellectuals begin using the term to refer to their linguistic and cultural community. Their nationalist descendants then appropriated the term and used it for their own purposes.

Lest any Turkish or Persian nationalist feel smug, both the idea of a "Turkish nation" and "Persian nation" has similarly shallow roots. During the nineteenth century, Ottoman and Persian intellectuals, trained in Europe or in elite institutions that borrowed their methods and curricula from those of Europe, began to apply assumptions about historical evolution and social cohesion to trace the genealogies of their respective societies. Using the tools of the newly established disciplines of archaeology and philology, they traced the lineages of their respective cultures and languages from pre-Islamic times forward. These intellectuals were not necessarily nationalists. More often than not, they weren't. Nevertheless, they provided a cultural, linguistic, and/or ethnic argument for the continuous existence of the Turkish and Persian nations that later nationalists, such as Ziya Gokalp and Sayyid Hasan Taqizadeh, could apply. When Mustafa Kemal and Reza Shah took power, they found the ideas of these nationalist ideologues useful for their nation-building projects and used the institutions of state to disseminate them. With what degree of cynicism they approached the ideas is anyone's guess.

Arab nationalism was, of course, just one of the nationalist movements that emerged in the Arab Middle East. It was not the first. That distinction belongs to the Egyptian nationalist movement. A nationalist movement emerged in Egypt before the other Arab provinces because of the peculiarities of Egyptian history. Under the mamluks and then Mehmet Ali and his descendants, Egypt had been virtually autonomous. This made it easier for the more politically motivated of its inhabitants to think of Egypt as a single unit that should be independent. At the same time, the effectiveness of Mehmet Ali's policies of defensive developmentalism, combined with the integration of Egypt into the world economy and British administrative practices, caused the breakdown of the social structures that had reinforced local identities: the autonomous village, the guild, the town quarter. As a result, inhabitants of the province could see themselves as part of a wider, yet clearly bounded, political community.

Egypt was also home to a large and concentrated stratum of intellectuals and political activists. Some of them were exiles from other Arab provinces who found shelter from Hamidian repression in British-controlled Egypt. Others were homegrown, the products of Western or Western-style institutions that defensive developmentalism had fostered. These intellectuals and political activists played the same role in fostering Egyptian nationalism as their counterparts would later play in fostering Arab nationalism. The only difference was that the target against which a nationalist movement in Egypt could mobilize was a foreign occupation. This, along with the aforementioned factors, contributed to the rise of a nationalist movement in Egypt that was distinctly Egyptian.

Beginning in 1907, a number of nationalist parties and associations began to materialize on the Egyptian scene. The first such party, the Nationalist Party, was organized by Mustafa Kamil (not to be mistaken for Mustafa Kemal of Turkey), a French-educated lawyer and newspaper publisher. Another party, the Umma Party, followed soon afterward. Although both parties wanted to bring the British occupation to an end, they divided along tactical lines. The Nationalist Party took a more combative stance than its rival, whose approach was anything but combative. Leaders of the Umma Party felt that Egyptians should cooperate with the British and hoped that the British would learn from this that Egyptians were

Nationalist demonstration in Aleppo, Syria, 1920. *(From: ᶜAbd al-ᶜAziz al-ᶜAzma, Mir'at al-Sham: Tarikh Dimashq wa ahliha (London: Riad El-Rayyes Books, 1987), p. 218.)*

ready to enter the "civilized" world as an independent nation. The British consul general called the Umma Party the "Girondists of Egypt," a reference to the "moderates" of the French Revolution who clashed with (and were decimated by) the more radical Jacobins of Robespierre fame.

Nationalist parties in the proper sense of the word did not emerge in the Levant and Mesopotamia until after World War I. That is not to say that no nationalists existed. There were a number of associations with branches in various cities of the Levant and Mesopotamia that advocated Arab or Syrian or Mesopotamian autonomy within and, eventually, even independence from the Ottoman Empire. But these associations were small and had limited influence. Because their members feared repression, and because they were more inclined to engage in conspiracies than mass organizing, these associations did not attract a large following. The largest of them, the Damascus-based al-Fatat, included only about seventy members before the war.

Arab, Syrian, and, to a lesser extent, Iraqi nationalist movements attracted a larger following in the aftermath of World War I. The Ottoman Empire had been destroyed and there was a political vacuum at the top that had to be filled. We have already seen how larger and more popular nationalist movements in Turkey and Egypt were able to take advantage of postwar realities. Nationalist movements in the Levant and Mesopotamia were less successful in realizing their goals. Arab nationalism had to compete with regional nationalisms, and both fell victim to the mandates system and its heir, the regional state system.

There is, however, no doubt that in most places in the Middle East, including the Levant and Mesopotamia, nationalist sentiments that matched states created in the aftermath of World War I grew stronger over time. There were two reasons for this. First, time's passage. Although most member states of the state system in the region received their complete independence after World War II, the process of formulating distinct national identities began even while those states were under colonial or mandatory rule. Ever since, states engaged their citizens in common practices and worked to develop their own internal markets and divisions of labor—necessary preconditions for the formation of distinct national identities. The states in the region also jealously guarded their borders, rewrote their histories, and, indeed, produced enough of their own histories to differentiate their national experience from that of their neighbors.

The second factor that strengthened national identities was the relative stability of the regional state system for half a century. With the exception of the unification of North and South Yemen in 1990, no attempt to adjust state borders by force or negotiation—including the 1958–1961 union between Egypt and Syria—bore fruit during the post-colonial era. In large measure, this was the result of big power intervention which protected states from their enemies, both foreign and domestic. Whenever some strongman rose to the surface threatening to upset the regional balance of power by playing the role of a Bismarck or Garibaldi, he was slapped down by one or another great power or coalition. This is exactly what happened to Saddam Hussein in 1991 when he attempted to integrate Kuwait into Iraq (although the Iraqi conquest of Kuwait was hardly in the same league as German unification or the Italian Risorgimento).

Events that unfolded after the outbreak of the Arab uprisings in 2010–2011 have complicated this picture somewhat. On the one hand, the uprisings and protests *were* transnational, but only in the sense that regime opponents in each state found inspiration in, and borrowed tactics and symbols from, other uprisings. Opposition movements sought the ouster of their own autocrats, the reform of their own systems, or both. When protesters across the Arab world chanted, "The people want the end of the regime," they meant the people of that particular nation wanted the end of their particular regime. On the other hand, when it comes to strengthening or diminishing nationalist sentiment in the various states of the Arab world, the effects of the uprisings and protests were dissimilar. As demonstrated by the popularity of patriotic rap and hip-hop music, the uprisings reaffirmed distinct Tunisian and Egyptian national identities. On the other hand, it is entirely possible that Yemen and Libya will fragment, with each fragment ordering itself in a manner appropriate for joining the world system of nation-states, much as South Sudan did when it broke away from Sudan in 2011. Then there are the cases of Syria and Iraq, where sectarian and ethnic identities are likely to trump national identity. As we have seen, sectarian movements resemble nationalist movements but differ on one critical point: As opposed to nationalists, sectarians do not seek sovereignty, only autonomy or rights within the national community. It is unlikely that the international community will allow the fragmentation of Syria or Iraq simply because it considers failed states better than shattered ones, particularly when their fragmentation is likely to have regional implications (a testament to the marginal importance of Yemen and Libya to the international order).

There is one further complication that bears mentioning: the formation of a "caliphate" by a group called the Islamic State (IS) in a territory that includes parts of Syria and Iraq. Previously, this chapter had differentiated between the staying power of a culture of nationalism and the transience of individual nationalisms. The caliphate claims to be an anti-nation. Indeed, IS, like al-Qaeda, views nationalism and the state system as a plot by the "Crusader-Zionist conspiracy" to keep the Muslim world divided and weak. It therefore rejects nationalism and favors uniting all Muslims on the basis of religion in a single entity that repudiates the assumptions that define the culture of nationalism. This would fly in the face of the assertion that wherever cultures of nationalism take root they become a permanent part of the local landscape were IS able to define exactly what it was for as well as it defines what it is against. In other words, IS, like al-Qaeda, did not announce the nature of its "anti-nation" simply because it doesn't know what exactly it's supposed to be. Like anarchist groups of the nineteenth, twentieth, and twenty-first centuries—most of which also have railed against the nation-state system—IS and al-Qaeda propose no realistic alternative because in a world of nation-states such alternatives are impossible to imagine. Indeed, as it consolidated its position and borders, IS increasingly took on the trappings of a nation-state, promising to issue license plates and passports, mint its own currency, and maintain the welfare systems that had been in place in the territory under its control. So far, it seems to have failed at most of this, but what choice did it have? After all, not only is IS situated within a world system that gives pride of place to the nation-state, it rules over populations whose only frame of reference is that particular political form. IS might offer a distinctive ideological rationale for the state it has carved out, but then again, what nationalism does not?

CHAPTER 14

The Israeli-Palestinian Conflict

So far, we have discussed three effects of World War I that make it the most important political event in the history of the modern Middle East: the destruction of the Ottoman Empire and the creation of the state system in the region; the political and social transformation of Persia under Reza Shah (and his son); and the emergence and spread of a variety of nationalisms that sought to define the political communities that would emerge in the wake of the cataclysm. Some of these nationalisms existed only briefly and attracted only a marginal following; others remain with us to this very day. As we have seen, one of the nationalisms that has lasted is Zionism. And while Zionism was not itself the product of World War I (its roots stretch back much further), the fact that during the war the Zionist movement received the endorsement, and later the support, of a major power was critical for its endurance. The establishment of the State of Israel in 1948 is one consequence of this; the Israeli-Palestinian conflict is another.

Although Zionist immigration to Palestine began even before the British announced the Balfour Declaration, the declaration was a coup for Zionist leaders, particularly because it soon took on the force of law. This was because the British incorporated it into the "draft instrument"—a cross between a constitution and a contract—they had to submit to the League of Nations before they could assume the role of mandatory power. The instrument not only set the terms for British administration of the Palestine mandate, it also outlined the procedures the British would use to "facilitate" Jewish immigration to Palestine. As should be obvious, Jewish immigration into Palestine, and the hostility that immigration aroused in the indigenous population, lie at the root of the Israeli-Palestinian conflict. While this might appear self-evident, however, it is important to keep it in mind because it shines a spotlight on the true nature of the conflict: Two peoples, Zionist immigrants and their descendants, on the one hand, and the indigenous inhabitants of the territory of the Palestine mandate, on the other, have spent close to 130 years disputing who will control all or parts of the territory that lies

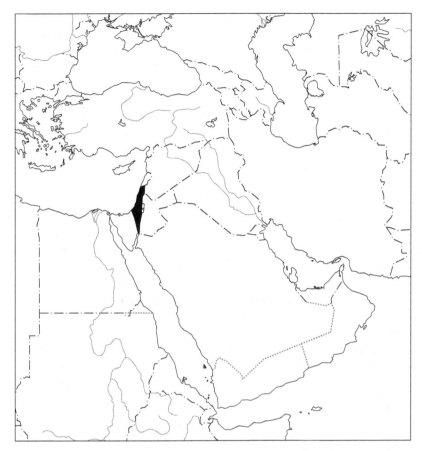

Palestine and the Middle East

between the Mediterranean Sea and the Jordan River on the west and east, and Lebanon and the Gulf of Aqaba in the north and south. Israel and its sovereign neighbors might make peace with each other, as two have already done, but until the principals resolve the conflict one way or another it will continue.

That the fundamentals of the conflict have remained unchanged, however, does not mean that the conflict has not evolved over time. It is possible to divide the conflict into three phases, each marked off from the next by a game-changing event or set of events. The first phase began in 1882 with the arrival of the first Zionist immigrants into Palestine. It lasted until 1948 with the establishment of the State of Israel and what Palestinians call the *nakba* (disaster), when 720,000 of them were forced into exile. The invasion of Palestine by Arab armies bent on destroying the newly declared State of Israel initiated the second phase. Because this seemed to shift the dynamic of the conflict from one between two peoples to one between sovereign states, the world's attention shifted to making peace between those states. In other words, during this phase the Palestinian question seemed to drop out of the equation entirely as the attention of the world focused on normalizing the relationship between Israel and its sovereign neighbors. While some historians have used the phrase "Arab-Israeli dispute" when referring to the entirety of the conflict, the phrase is only appropriate for this phase of the struggle. The heart of the conflict, after all, does not concern Israelis and generic "Arabs" or even their states, but rather Israelis and Palestinians, the indigenous population that was dispossessed and its descendants. The signing of the Oslo Accord in 1993, which laid the foundation for direct negotiations between the two principals, thus marks the beginning of the latest phase of the conflict.

1882–1948: THE INITIAL CONFRONTATION

The first phase of what would become the Israeli-Palestinian conflict took place during a period of global history marked by three characteristics. First, it was a period of late imperialism, a period in which many Europeans believed that they had a monopoly on "civilization" and that they had the right, if not the duty, to expand that civilization to benighted peoples around the globe and determine their future. Hence, the claim by Theodor Herzl, perhaps the most prominent advocate of Zionism in its early stages, that the establishment of a Jewish state in Palestine would "form a portion of the rampart of Europe against Asia, an outpost of civilisation as opposed to barbarism." Hence, the common use by early Zionists of the word "colonization," not as a term of opprobrium but of pride. And hence, the belief that a British mandate over Palestine would fulfill the "sacred trust of civilization." This period also marks the glory days of nationalist "awakenings" around the globe. Zionism emerged among the Jews of Europe early on during this period; Palestinian nationalism would emerge as a mass phenomenon about a half century later. Finally, this period marks a time of mass migration, when more people—over 150 million between 1850 and 1940—than had ever done so before left their homes in search of a better life or to escape persecution. Jewish emigration from Eastern Europe, particularly from the Russian Empire where most of the world's Jews lived, to Palestine and elsewhere might thus be seen as part of a global trend.

Jewish immigration to Palestine took place in waves, called in Hebrew *aliyot* (sing.: *aliya*, meaning "ascent"). Each *aliya* was distinguished by a number of factors: point of origin, destination in Palestine (cities or countryside, coastal or inland), the social and economic system by which the immigrants organized their communities, and ideology, if any. For example, the first wave of immigration, which began in 1882 and lasted until 1903, comprised Jews mainly from Romania and Russia who fled grinding poverty and periodic anti-Jewish riots (pogroms). The bulk of the immigrants settled in Jaffa, Jerusalem, and Haifa, although a few stalwarts tried their hand at farming. Since Jews had been prohibited from owning land in the Russian Empire, they had little hands-on experience with agriculture. Their "colonies" would have collapsed had the banker and philanthropist Baron Edmond de Rothschild not bailed them out. Rothschild attempted to consolidate

The Jewish settlement Nes Zionah, near Jaffa, was established in 1883. (*From: The Collection of Wolf-Dieter Lemke.*)

Jewish landholdings in order to establish plantations in Palestine similar to those established in Algeria. The effort failed, most Jewish agriculturalists left, and the plantation system was never again attempted in Palestine.

Four more *aliyot* took place between the first and the onset of World War II. The second and third *aliyot* (1904–1914, 1918–1923) and the fourth and fifth (1924–1929, 1929–1939) had more lasting results than the first. During the second and third *aliyot*, sixty-five thousand Jews emigrated to Palestine, mostly from the Russian Empire. These immigrants shaped many of the institutions and ideals that still exist in Israel. Influenced by both socialism and romantic, back-to-the-land ideas that were then popular in Germany's easternmost provinces, the new immigrants established agricultural settlements, including collective farms (*moshavim*, sing.: *moshav*) and communal farms (*kibbutzim*, sing.: *kibbutz*). They organized a labor federation (the Histadrut), which established schools and hospitals and which provided a variety of social and welfare services for the immigrant community. And they resurrected the biblical language of Hebrew for use as the national tongue.

Perhaps most important for the future of the Middle East was the labor policy adopted by the new immigrants. The Zionists of the second and third *aliyot* expressed their aspirations in two slogans: "conquest of land" and "conquest of labor." The first slogan refers to the need these Zionists felt to make their imprint on the land of Palestine by "taming the wilderness" through settlement activity. The second refers to the need these Zionists felt to remake the Jewish people by having Jews fill all jobs in the economy. Whereas the peculiar circumstances of Jews in Europe had restricted them to certain urban occupations, these

Zionists believed that to become a true nation Jews had to overcome their dependence on others and become autonomous in all spheres. The belief that the Jewish nation had to purge itself of the ill effects of centuries of exile is called "the negation of exile." It, too, played a central role in Zionist polemics.

Although the "conquest of labor" idea had its ideological roots in utopian socialism and romanticism, there were practical reasons for European Jewish settlers to shun Arab labor. Although many Zionists in Europe believed Palestine to be "a land without a people" and thus a perfect fit for "a people without a land," Arab labor was, in fact, plentiful, and Arabs were willing to work for lower wages than would European settlers. The expansion of the labor force to include low-wage workers would drive wages down and discourage the immigration of new settlers. As a result, influential Zionists felt that the success of their project depended on severing the economic links connecting the two communities. Thus, after the Zionists bought land, often from absentee landlords, they frequently displaced Palestinian farmers whose services were no longer required.

The fourth and fifth *aliyot* differed dramatically from their predecessors. Most of these immigrants were petit-bourgeois economic refugees fleeing rising anti-Semitism in Europe. They settled mainly in cities. Unlike their forebears in the second and third *aliyot*, these settlers had no time for what they considered socialist claptrap. And since their emigration occurred during a period of intense nationalism and militarism in Europe, they brought those beliefs with them as well. The ideology of the second and third *aliyot* became known as "Labor Zionism," the official ideology of the contemporary Labor Party of Israel. That of the fourth and fifth became known as "Revisionist Zionism" because they wanted to correct what they believed to have been the wrong turn taken by their immediate predecessors. Their political descendants can be found in the right-wing Likud Party.

As mentioned earlier, the migration of Jews from Europe, particularly the Russian Empire, took place during the period of the greatest migration of humans in history. From 1881 to 1914, more than 2.5 million Jews—about 40 percent of the entire Jewish population—migrated from the Russian Empire. Between 1.5 and 2 million ended up in the United States. From 1882 to 1923, however, only 115,000 went to Palestine, demonstrating the lackluster support for Zionist goals among Jews there. And most Jews who ended up in Palestine, discouraged by the conditions they found, didn't stay very long. Beginning in the early 1920s, however, as the United States began imposing stricter and stricter immigration restrictions that prevented Jews from emigrating there, emigration to Palestine rose dramatically. As a result, between 1924 and 1939—a period of only fifteen years—close to three times as many Jews emigrated to Palestine as had done so over the course of the previous forty years.

The indigenous inhabitants of Palestine resisted Zionist settlement policies from the beginning. This resistance took a variety of forms, from land occupations to violence against settlers and destruction of property. But while the indigenous inhabitants of Palestine resisted Zionist settlement early on, this resistance was mainly defensive, devoid of political goals, and rather haphazard. No Palestinian national movement existed until after World War I. Even then it had to compete with other nationalist movements for support. Before World War I, most educated Palestinians viewed themselves as Ottoman subjects and later as Ottoman citizens. As we saw in Chapter 13, the fact that educated Palestinians would express their political aspirations in the form of nationalism was inevitable. That they would advocate Palestinian nationalism was not. After World War I, when an Ottoman identity was no longer a viable option, some Palestinians were attracted to Arab nationalism. Others viewed themselves as Syrians.

In addition to the competition a Palestinian national movement faced from rival national movements, there were other factors that hindered its consolidation. The Palestinian community was hardly as well organized or as unified as the Zionist community. As citizens of the Ottoman Empire, there had been no need. Whereas the Zionist community embraced the mandates system and organized itself accordingly, political elites in the Arab community in Palestine accepted neither the Balfour Declaration nor the British mandate. They thus did not organize themselves in a way that could take advantage of the mandate. Further hindering the organization of a unified Palestinian national movement was the problem of internal fissures in the Arab community—fissures that were exacerbated by British policies. Political elites had competed with each other for positions and prestige under the Ottomans and the British were not reluctant to use that competition for their own ends as well. The British also continued the Ottoman policy of allowing each religious community to organize its own affairs. Because the Arab community of Palestine included both Muslims and Christians, each community maintained parallel but separate institutions for such functions as social welfare and personal, family, and inheritance law.

Over the course of the mandate period, both the Arab nationalist and the Syrian nationalist options became less and less viable. The mandates system not only divided the Arab world into a variety of states, but severed Palestine from Syria. Because the Palestinian Arab community could not reasonably expect to unite with Syrians, the lure of Syrian nationalism eventually faded away. Over time, the history and institutional development of Palestine and Syria diverged. But there was another reason why a separate Palestinian identity began to emerge during the mandate period. The inhabitants of Palestine faced a problem that no other inhabitants of the region faced: Zionist settlement. While British and French administrative control in their mandates left long-term traces, they did not alienate the main resource—land—from those dependent on it, establish a rival and competing economy, or establish rival and competing political structures as the Zionists did in Palestine. And, according to the terms of the mandates, the British and French were destined to leave. Zionist settlers had no such intention. Nationalisms throughout the region developed in response to local circumstances. The circumstances in Palestine were unique.

The fact that Palestinian nationalism developed later than Zionism and, in fact, developed in response to Zionist immigration does not mean that Palestinian nationalism is any less legitimate than Zionism. All nationalisms arise in opposition to some internal or external nemesis. All are defined by what they oppose. Zionism itself originally arose in reaction to anti-Semitic and nationalist movements in Europe. It would be perverse to judge Zionism as somehow less valid than European anti-Semitism or those nationalisms. Furthermore, Zionism itself was also defined by its opposition to the indigenous inhabitants of the region. Both the "conquest of land" and the "conquest of labor" slogans that became central to Zionist thinking originated as a result of the confrontation of Zionism with its Palestinian "other."

As Zionist immigration and land purchases increased during the late 1920s and 1930s, so did tensions between the two communities. By 1931, Zionist land purchases had led to the ejection of approximately twenty thousand peasant families from their lands. Close to 30 percent of Palestinian farmers were landless and another 75 to 80 percent did not have enough land for subsistence. Thus, in 1936 Palestine exploded in violence.

What Palestinians call the Great Revolt was, after the 1948 War, the most traumatic event in modern history for Palestinians. To put down the revolt, the British launched a brutal counterinsurgency campaign, employing tactics all too familiar to Palestinians today: collective punishment of villages, "targeted killings" (assassinations), mass arrests, deportations, and the dynamiting of homes of suspected guerrillas and their sympathizers. The revolt, and the British reaction to it, ravaged the natural leadership of the Palestinian community and opened

Palestinian houses demolished by the British during the Great Revolt. *(From: Fondation Arabe pour l'image, Beirut.)*

up new cleavages in that community. Many wealthy Palestinians fled rather than face what they considered to be the extortionate demands of rival Palestinian gangs, while the British imprisoned many of the community's leaders or forced them into exile. Palestinian society never recovered. The roots of the *nakba* of 1948 can be found in the Great Revolt.

The Great Revolt compelled the British to find some diplomatic solution to the Palestine imbroglio. In 1937, they proposed dividing Palestine into two separate territories, one "Jewish" and one "Arab." In 1939, they backed away from partition and issued a White Paper that had just the right ingredients to offend leaders of both communities. The White Paper of 1939 advocated restricting (but not ending) Jewish immigration and proposed closer supervision of (but not the end of) land sales. It also promised independence for Palestine within ten years in the unlikely event that the two communities learned to work together. Both communities felt betrayed by the White Paper. Both communities rejected it.

Although the White Paper remained official British policy during World War II, Palestine was relatively quiet during the war. Much of the Zionist community balked at the idea of sabotaging the British war effort against the Nazis, and the Arab community of Palestine was still recovering from the trauma of the Great Revolt. Furthermore, since Palestine hosted the largest British base in the region after the one in the Suez Canal Zone, the war was an economic boon to Palestine. But the lull was not to last. As the ten-year deadline stipulated by the White Paper loomed on the horizon, the struggle between the two communities—and between the two communities and the British—resumed. By 1947, at a time when India was about to achieve independence and the cold war was in its initial stages, the British had to station one hundred thousand soldiers in Palestine to keep the peace. Their soldiers and diplomats targeted by Zionist splinter groups and their economy in shambles, the British decided that enough was enough and dumped the Palestine issue in the lap of the newly established United Nations. The United Nations was, after all, the successor organization to the League of Nations, which had granted Britain the mandate to begin with. In November 1947 the General Assembly of the United Nations voted to terminate the mandate and partition Palestine, dividing it into a "Jewish State" and an "Arab State."

In the wake of the United Nations' vote to partition Palestine, a civil war broke out between the two communities, followed by the intervention of surrounding Arab nations on behalf of the Palestinians. The Arab states were suspicious of each others' political agendas, and their armies, designed mainly to keep the peace at home and not fight foreign wars, performed miserably. In the end, the Jewish forces prevailed. The war for Palestine led to the creation of the State of Israel whose de facto borders corresponded to the ceasefire lines. Although the state quickly received international recognition, no peace treaties were signed between Israel and its neighbors—only armistice agreements. For the next forty-five years, the attention of the world focused on getting Israel and its neighbors to sign such treaties.

1948–1993: THE ARAB-ISRAELI CONFLICT

Two global phenomena shaped the second phase of the Israeli-Palestinian conflict. The first was the cold war. The fact that both the United States and the Soviet Union viewed conflicts in the Middle East through the lens of their global, existential struggle added fuel to the Arab-Israeli and the Israeli-Palestinian fires and inhibited a resolution to the overall conflict. One example of this—the role played by the Soviet Union in precipitating the 1967 War—is discussed below. A second example took place after the 1973 War, when the United States deliberately broke up direct talks between the Israelis and Egyptians in order to ensure a third player—the United States—would be permanently entwined in any peace process and that the Soviet Union would be locked out of it. And there are countless other examples as well.

The second phenomenon that shaped this phase of the conflict was decolonization. Decolonization will be discussed in more detail in Part IV of this book. Suffice it to say, in the immediate aftermath of World War II a number of national liberation movements emerged in the colonized world and battled for the right of the peoples they claimed to represent to self-determination. This was the environment in which the Palestine Liberation Organization (PLO) emerged. The PLO was very much of its time, reinventing or borrowing the tactics, strategies, goals, and organizational structures of other national liberation movements. While its goal of establishing a sovereign Palestinian state remained elusive, it did achieve another sort of victory: At a time when most of the world either ignored the Palestinian question or wished it would go away, the PLO kept it alive.

While recent events have made us all too familiar with the failings of the PLO, this in itself was no mean achievement. The 1948 War devastated Palestinian society, driving a vast majority of Palestinians who lived in what became Israel into exile. Although the reasons for the *nakba* have been a subject of debate for over sixty years, most scholars now agree that a combination of factors led to it. On the one hand, many of those Palestinians who fled quite sensibly chose to escape from a war zone. On the other hand, there were calculated expulsions. In some places Zionists deliberately frightened Palestinians into leaving by committing acts of terror. In the village of Dayr Yassin alone, between 110 and 240 men, women, and children were butchered, and the bodies of many were stuffed in the village well. Acts such as that one were hardly kept secret. After all, as Lenin once put it, the purpose of terrorism is to terrorize.

Most Palestinian refugees ended up in the West Bank (which was occupied by Jordan until 1967), the Gaza Strip (occupied by the Egyptians until the same year), and neighboring Arab countries. Those who had an education or money tried to rebuild their lives as best they could on their own. Others who were not so lucky ended up in camps supported by the United Nations Relief and Works Agency (UNRWA), where they and their descendants have lived to this very day. Those Palestinians who remained in Israel were subject to martial law until 1966.

Israel/Palestine, 1921, 1948

Palestinian Israelis—often called "Israeli-Arabs"—make up about 20 percent of the current population of the country.

   Israel, too, underwent dramatic demographic change after the 1948 War as a result of two factors. The first was the flight of Palestinians. Israel only repatriated a handful of Palestinians—a gesture it made to win the goodwill of the international community. Although welcoming Jewish immigrants—in 1950, the Israeli parliament, the *knesset*, passed the Law of Return guaranteeing Jews from around the world citizenship—Israel could hardly retain its Jewish character if it granted the right of citizenship to large numbers of non-Jews, such as Palestinians. Hence, the second factor that shifted the demographic balance: the influx of Jews, many of whom came from the Arab world, which doubled the population of Israel in its first four years of existence.

The problem of repatriation and restitution for Palestinians was complicated by the fact that the Israeli government confiscated abandoned Palestinian property and redistributed it to Jewish immigrants from Europe. Some Palestinians attempted to reclaim their property by crossing the armistice lines to harvest crops or carry away moveable property to their new homes. Others crossed the lines to commit acts of sabotage or violence. The Israeli government did not differentiate between the two groups. To deal with the problem of "infiltration," it launched reprisal raids against the states from which the infiltration occurred, thus shifting the burden of stopping infiltration to Israel's neighbors. Obviously, it did little to endear Israel to them. In 1953, an Israeli raid into Jordan resulted in sixty-six civilian casualties. In 1955, an Israeli raid into the Gaza Strip, led by future Israeli prime minister Ariel Sharon, left thirty-eight Egyptian soldiers dead and about forty wounded and touched off a series of events that would lead to war between Israel and Egypt in 1956 and 1967. Little wonder, then, that the international community concentrated on promoting some form of reconciliation between Israel and its neighbors to tamp down the Middle East tinderbox.

Although the Arab states that surrounded Israel never granted it recognition and even imposed an economic boycott on the new state, and although the dismal showing of the Arab armies in the 1948 war contributed to the rash of *coups d'état* that brought populist governments into power in the region, the conflict between Israel and its neighbors remained stalemated for twenty years. That stalemate ended in 1967. In May 1967, the Soviets informed the president of Egypt, Gamal ʿAbd al-Nasser, that the Israelis were massing troops on the Syrian border. Israel and Syria had been engaged in hostilities triggered by conflicting claims to Jordan River water, so war was certainly a possibility. The report, however, was false. The Soviets hoped that a report of potential Israeli aggression would compel the surrounding states to coalesce into an anti-Israel, pro-Soviet alliance. Nasser realized the report was false, but was engaged in his own struggle for supremacy in the Arab world and acted otherwise. Nasser ordered the entrance of the Red Sea closed to Israeli shipping. Because this effectively cut off Israel's southern outlet to the sea, and because most of the world considered that part of the Red Sea an international waterway, the Israelis regarded the Egyptian action as an act of war. On 5 June 1967, Israel launched an attack against its neighbors.

The 1967 war lasted a mere six days and resulted in a resounding defeat for the Arab armies. The Israeli army captured all of Jerusalem (which had been divided between Israel and Jordan since 1948), the West Bank, the Sinai peninsula, the Gaza Strip, and part of Syria (the Golan Heights). The war broke the stalemate. Before the war, the main concern of both Israel and the Arab states was the continued existence of the State of Israel. After the war, the main focus for the Arab states was the return of their conquered lands. In exchange, the Israelis wanted recognition and peace treaties. This formula—land for peace—embodied in United

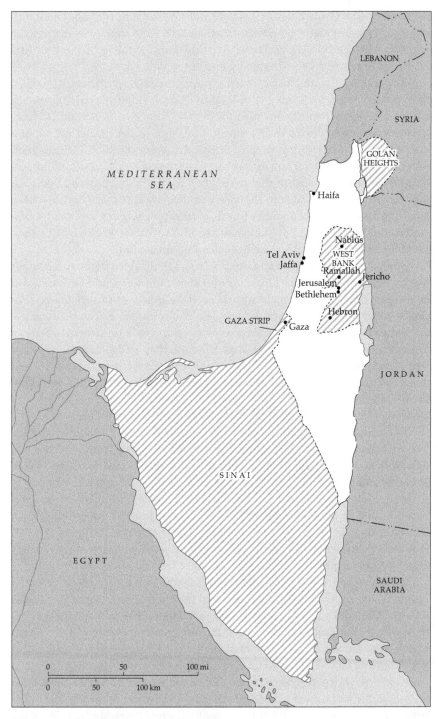

Israel and the Occupied Territories after 1967

Nations Security Council Resolutions 242 and 338—became the basis for all subsequent peace negotiations between Israel and the Arab states. For example, as stipulated by the 1978 Camp David Accords, Israel withdrew from the Sinai Peninsula in return for recognition by, and peace with, Egypt.

The exchange of land for peace is a simple formula. Nevertheless, it has been hard to accomplish for a number of reasons. First, it is (purposely) ambiguous. United Nations Resolution 242 calls for the withdrawal of Israeli forces "from territories occupied during the recent conflict"—not, as the Israelis like to point out, "from *all* the territories occupied during the recent conflict." The resolution also calls for the "termination of all claims or states of belligerency and respect for and acknowledgement of the sovereignty, territorial integrity, and political independence of every state in the area and their right to live in peace within secure and recognized boundaries free from threats or acts of force"—not, as the Arab states like to point out, diplomatic relations with Israel or peace treaties. Why not declare a state of non-belligerence and call it a day?

Then there was the postwar strategy adopted by the Arab states. At a summit meeting held in Khartoum, Sudan, Arab leaders rallied around a policy known as "the three no's": no negotiations with Israel, no peace with Israel, no recognition of Israel. Although this seems the height of intransigence, it marked a subtle tactical shift. The Arab states agreed to unify efforts to "eliminate the effects of aggression"—not eliminate Israel. And although they pledged not to negotiate with Israel, they did not pledge not to negotiate. The Arab heads of state instead looked to the superpowers—the United States and the Soviet Union—to resolve the dispute. And since the Soviet Union had broken diplomatic relations with Israel, they counted on the United States to bring the Israelis around.

This tactic was dangerous for the Arab states because it assumed that the United States so wanted a settlement that it would put pressure on Israel to reach one. This assumption was overly optimistic. After the 1967 war, the United States was all too willing to sit back and wait for the Arab states to come to it. After all, the Arab states wanted their land back and all they had to do to get it back was to sign peace treaties with Israel. To re-engage the Americans, Egypt and Syria once again launched a war against Israel in October 1973. The October War resulted in eleven to sixteen thousand more Arab and Israeli casualties, was used by Arab members of OPEC as an excuse to hike oil prices, and brought the United States and the Soviet Union to the brink of nuclear war. It certainly caught American attention. At a time when the United States had bigger fish to fry—the United States was still involved in Vietnam, had just opened up relations with China, and had to figure out the intricacies of détente with the Soviet Union—the American secretary of state, Henry Kissinger, was spending his time shuttling between Damascus, Cairo, and Tel Aviv working out minutiae of Israeli and Arab troop redeployments. But there was an upside for the United States: For the first time the United States assumed the role of the sole and indispensable middleman and broker in the conflict, a role it would maintain for the next forty years.

The Israelis also contributed to complicating the "land for peace" equation. Immediately after the 1967 war, the Israeli government declared Jerusalem to be Israel's eternal, indivisible capital. Settlers began moving in and the municipal boundaries were extended far into the West Bank. The Israelis also built settlements in the West Bank (called by the Israeli government "Judea and Samaria," after its biblical name), the Golan Heights, and the Gaza Strip. The first settlements were built along the Jordanian border, ostensibly for security reasons. Then came religious settlers, political die-hards, and those interested in low-cost housing subsidized by the Israeli government. At the same time, the Israelis integrated their electrical grid, water system, and even their labor market with those of the Palestinian territories, making separation all the more complex and creating a dependent economy in the territories.

The final problem with the "land for peace" solution is that it reduced the conflict to one between states. The PLO begged to differ. The PLO was founded in 1964 at the instigation of Gamal ʿAbd al-Nasser, who wanted to maintain control of the Palestinian movement. Various guerrilla groups—such as Fatah, founded by Yasir Arafat in 1959—and a host of others, had other ideas. For them, the 1967 War demonstrated that Palestinians could not rely on Arab states to bring about their liberation. They had to do it themselves. The PLO elected Arafat chairman in 1968, and Fatah, along with other guerrilla groups, has continued to dominate it ever since.

Over the course of the 1970s, the PLO not only kept the Palestinian issue alive, it brought it center stage. Thus, it might be said that the PLO played the same role for Palestinian nationalism that the Balfour Declaration played for Zionism. The PLO asserted Palestinian claims through both diplomacy and spectacular acts of terrorism. "Armed struggle" was a central pillar of PLO doctrine as it was for many national liberation movements in the Third World. While terrorism meant Israel and the United States would refuse to recognize and negotiate with it, the Arab states and the United Nations General Assembly recognized the PLO as the "the sole legitimate representative of the Palestinian people" in 1974.

Nevertheless, "land for peace" remained the only game in town from 1967 to 1993 and served as the basis for innumerable attempts on the part of intermediaries to resolve the conflict. As recently as 2002, it provided the foundation for the "Arab Peace Initiative," proposed by Saudi Arabia. According to the initiative, Israel would withdraw from all the remaining occupied territories in exchange for peace treaties with all Arab states. As the old saying goes, insanity might be defined as doing the same thing over and over and expecting different results. Although the "land for peace" formula *was* successfully applied twice—the Israel-Egypt peace treaty of 1979 and the Israel-Jordan peace treaty of 1994—the lesson to be learned from those two treaties is that the initiative has to come from those who were motivated to sign them and not from outside players. In the first case, the president of Egypt, Anwar al-Sadat, believed he could win legitimacy and the adoration of Egyptians he so craved if Israel returned the Sinai peninsula to Egypt. Israel did—one year after al-Sadat was assassinated. The Israel-Jordan treaty came one year after Israel began negotiating with the Palestinians in an attempt to resolve *their* issues. In other words, if the Israelis and Palestinians were to reach a settlement, what was the point of Jordan—or any other Arab state for that matter—remaining in a state of war with Israel? Which brings us to the current phase of the conflict.

1993–PRESENT: BACK TO FUNDAMENTALS

The end of the cold war in 1989 or 1991 (depending on what markers one chooses to use) inspired utopian fantasies for the future. As described in more detail in Chapter 17, some spoke of a "New World Order," a period stretching into the distant future of peace, international cooperation, and prosperity brought on by a fully globalized world economy. As we shall see below, this particular fantasy, along with the end of the cold war and other factors, contributed to a meeting of Israeli and Palestinian minds in Oslo, Norway, the signing of the Oslo Accord in 1993, direct negotiations between Israelis and Palestinians, and the anticipation that those negotiations might, over time, lead to a permanent settlement. The accord was revolutionary in nature: After fifty years of the world viewing the conflict as an Arab-Israeli problem, Israelis and Palestinians affirmed that, in fact, the conflict was theirs and theirs alone. But just as the New World Order proved elusive, so has a final settlement between the two principals in the Israeli-Palestinian conflict. Although the period since 1993 has been marked by the establishment of a Palestinian governing authority and a partial Israeli withdrawal from Palestinian territory, it has also been marked by countless rounds of failed negotiations, periods of extreme violence, and, at one point or another, each side walking away from the negotiating table and attempting to resolve the conflict on its own terms unilaterally.

The Oslo Accord and the subsequent Oslo II Agreement consist of an exchange of letters and more concrete proposals to establish Palestinian rule in the territories. In the exchange of letters, the PLO recognized Israel and Israel recognized, for the first time, a Palestinian nation represented by the PLO. The exchange of letters was significant for both the Palestinians and Israelis. For many Palestinians, mutual recognition meant that the establishment of an independent Palestinian state in the West Bank and Gaza Strip was all but inevitable (they were wrong). All that had to be worked out were the parameters of statehood. For the Israelis, the fact that the Palestinians accorded them recognition meant that close to 80 percent of the territory of the Palestine mandate—the territory they had won in the 1948 war—was forever removed from the bargaining table. While other aspects of the Oslo process have been suspended or failed, this exchange of letters changed the nature of the dispute forever.

Oslo was born of desperation. Palestinians signed on to the accord for a number of reasons. First, the PLO had to regain the initiative or risk losing the support of the Palestinian population. Life under Israeli occupation was difficult and the conditions in the Palestinian territories were deplorable. Tightfisted Israeli public investment policies—or disinvestment policies, as some observers called them—wreaked havoc on infrastructure. At the same time, the Israelis had buried the Palestinian population beneath a mound of regulations that were not only irksome, but that intruded into all aspects of life in the territories, from land use to employment to travel. When Gaza and the West Bank exploded in rebellion (*intifada*—Arabic for shaking off) in 1987, there was little the PLO could do from its headquarters in Tunisia, where it sought refuge after being expelled from Jordan in 1970 and Lebanon in 1983, except cheer it on from afar. To make matters worse, during the *intifada* a rival to the PLO emerged—Hamas, an Islamist movement that was based in the territories and had gained popularity through its network of schools, service organizations, and charitable works. And with the collapse of the Soviet Union, the PLO could not count on unconditional East Bloc support. The organization desperately needed a political breakthrough to maintain its leadership of the Palestinian national movement.

Many Israelis also felt that the situation they were in was untenable. The *intifada* not only demonstrated that the Palestine question was not about to fade away, it transformed the occupation from a fact of Israeli life into a financially and morally debilitating problem. Israeli soldiers who had been trained to fight wars with Arab states now spent their tours of duty among a hostile population, under orders to break the arms of rock-throwing children. During the first seven months of the *intifada* alone, about six hundred Israeli soldiers refused to serve in the territories. And with the collapse of the Soviet Union, many Israelis looked forward to a future in which they could reap the benefits of globalization, particularly if they could open up Arab markets by resolving the single most important issue underlying their neighbors' hostility. Longing for a "normal" existence, some even spoke of a "post-Zionist" future. If Israelis were to forgo the ideological obligations imposed by Zionism, they claimed, and accept the fact that Israel was just another small state in a world filled with small states, they could begin to live "normal" lives like the citizens of those other states.

But it was not to be. After an initial round of Israeli troop redeployments, the establishment of a Palestinian Authority (PA) to take charge of areas no longer under direct Israeli occupation, and elections for a Palestinian parliament and president (a position held first by Arafat, then by Mahmoud Abbas after Arafat's death), the Oslo process sputtered along until it fell into a vegetative state. The reasons for this are multiple. First, the Oslo process followed a formula known as "step-by-step diplomacy." The idea behind step-by-step diplomacy is that both sides would tackle small issues first to build confidence in both the process and each other. Once that confidence is built, they could tackle the more difficult issues, such as Jerusalem and the Palestinian right of return. Unfortunately, confidence was never built, in large measure because of spoilers on both sides. In Israel, those spoilers have included the extreme right and the settler movement, both of which want to keep control over all the territories and both of which have had the ability to make or break ruling coalitions. Between 1993 and 2012, the number of settlers living in the West Bank more than tripled to about 350,000, not including about 200,000 in East Jerusalem. Palestinian leaders assert settlement construction is the biggest obstacle to reaching a final resolution (in a way, settlement construction *is* a unilateral means of reaching a final resolution). On the Palestinian side, there is Hamas, which never agreed to the terms of Oslo or recognized Israel, along with other groups which have felt no compunction about using violence to halt the process. For example, in 2000, Palestinians launched a second, bloodier *intifada*. This time the symbol of rebellion was no longer children throwing stones but suicide bombers murdering Israelis.

There have been other obstacles to reaching an agreement as well. In 2006 Hamas won a majority of seats in the Palestinian parliament. Since the Palestinian president was still a member of Fatah, the result was a split government. But that split widened after Hamas, fearing repression at the hands of Fatah security forces, broke with the PA and seized control of Gaza, where its strength was greatest. Now there were two independently run Palestinian territories and no organization that could claim to speak for all Palestinians. Although negotiations between Israel and the PA in the West Bank continued, everyone realized it would be virtually impossible for the PA acting alone to seal the deal.

But sealing a deal was not consistently on the minds of either Israelis or Palestinians either. At different times both walked away from the bargaining table, the Israelis to impose a settlement unilaterally, the Palestinians to do an end run around stalled negotiations. The Israeli plans included the construction of a separation barrier that in some places stretched far into the West Bank. Although ostensibly built to prevent the infiltration of suicide bombers into Israel, for Palestinians and their supporters the fence represented an Israeli attempt to draw its borders—and the borders of a Palestinian entity—unilaterally. The Israeli withdrawal from impoverished and overpopulated Gaza seemed to confirm their worst suspicions. Only after subsequent rocket attacks launched from Gaza on Israel in 2006 (then again in 2007, 2008–2009, 2012, and 2014) did Israelis come to the realization that they could not attain the security they craved by hunkering down behind a wall—although this realization hardly whet the appetite of Israeli governments for reaching a negotiated settlement either. For its part, the PA also temporarily abandoned negotiations, taking its case for statehood directly to the United Nations where the General Assembly granted Palestine recognition as a "non-voting member state" of the organization in 2012. It also reached a shaky reconciliation with Hamas and joined with it in a unity government—a move which made a negotiated settlement all the more difficult since those who could possibly sponsor negotiations shun Hamas as a terrorist organization. After one final effort at brokering a negotiated settlement in 2014, even the Americans seemed to lose interest.

All of this calls into question the very possibility of resolving the conflict, or at least achieving a two-state solution. (The idea of working toward a one-state solution which would bring Israelis and Palestinians together in a single democratic state has also been floated, mostly by outsiders, but remains immensely unpopular among the principals.) And there is reason for skepticism: The

Israeli-Palestinian conflict is the longest running nationalist conflict still in play. Three factors have contributed to the conflict's longevity. First, the creation of Israel took place in the mid-twentieth century, as opposed to the mid-nineteenth century or earlier. In previous centuries it was possible for settlers simply to eradicate indigenous peoples when they proved troublesome, without a sense of wrongdoing or anything more than finger-wagging by the international community. Second, more than four decades of the Israeli-Palestinian conflict—from 1948 to 1991—took place during the cold war. As we have seen, the superpowers viewed the conflict as just one more front in a global battle, and both the Soviet Union and the United States attempted to manipulate it to gain tactical advantage in that battle. Finally, the conflict has gone on so long and has been so difficult to resolve not only because it has been shaped by the antagonists, but because it has shaped them as well.

Like all nationalisms, both Zionism and Palestinian nationalism defined themselves in relation to what they opposed. Early Zionist settlers saw their mission as establishing an outpost of civilization within a land inhabited by primitives. The Zionist settler—with rifle in one hand and plow in the other—became their heroic ideal and the center of a national cult. Palestinian nationalism reflects its "other" in like manner. After all, had it not been for Zionism, Palestinian nationalism might never have existed or would have existed in a very different form. But beliefs are only part of the problem. The conflict has also encouraged the emergence of the distinct institutions, social organization, and patterns of behavior within each community that have kept the conflict alive. Since its inception, Israel has depended on foreign aid and private contributions to maintain itself as a "national security state." The Israeli state has used Israeli law to legitimate settlement activity and the appropriation of Palestinian property, and the government has constructed special institutions to oversee the same. For its part, by raising armed struggle and heroic guerrilla fighters to the status of a cult, the PLO injected violence into the very DNA of Palestinian political culture. At the same time, it shirked responsibility for mobilizing the population it represents and building the institutions necessary for a future state.

This does not mean that the conflict will remain unresolved. What it means is that if a final resolution to the conflict is in the cards, it will take place under circumstances that are unforeseeable today. After all, who could have predicted in 1948 that thirty years in the future a president of Egypt would so much need to bolster his credentials at home that he would fly to Jerusalem and negotiate with the enemy to do so? Or, for that matter, who in 1977 could have predicted that in just about a decade and a half, events ranging from the onset of a Palestinian uprising to the end of the cold war (!) would converge to induce Israelis and Palestinians to sit down together? In the end, it is entirely possible that the wounds that afflict the two principals to the conflict, as well as the demands that are held as non-negotiable today, may yet recede in importance tomorrow as shifts in international and regional conditions extend the realm of the possible.

DOCUMENTS

An Arab Soldier in the Ottoman Army

Ihsan Hasan al-Turjman (1893–1917), was a conscripted soldier in the Ottoman army during World War I. His diary, edited by Salim Tamari and published as *Year of the Locust: A Soldier's Diary and the Erasure of Palestine's Ottoman Past*, provides a unique view of the life and dreams of an ordinary Arab during wartime.

An Unintended Pleasure

[Wednesday afternoon]

This must be one of the happiest days in my life. I can hardly believe that this is not a dream. For I came across my beloved and (I hope) my future partner *[sharikat hayati]*. She was standing in front of her house chatting with one of the neighbors, with her veil lifted. When she saw me, she slowly lowered her veil but kept chatting with her friend. Beneath the veil I saw a shining moon and a beauty that is without parallel. I wish I were a poet so that I could compose a stanza for this occasion. How happy I will be to marry her. I have met many women in my life—European and American, Muslims, Christians, and Jews—but never encountered a lady with such graces. Glory be to your creator. Until today I loved her only in my mind's eye. I would recall her image from my younger days, when I knew her as a child. But now I realize that her beauty far exceeds the image I have had of her all these years. I stood there paralyzed, staring at her visage and the light that emanated from her. It was already early evening when I saw her, and the dusk light had set in, but that was enough for me. I used to pass by her house daily, hoping to catch a glimpse of her. And when I did see her, she was always veiled—and even then I was overwhelmed by her sight.

My main fear is that someone will come and take her away from me. Whenever I think of this possibility, I go mad with worry. Of all the maidens in the world, I want her as my lady. Let love be our guide. I used to be in love with [Sakakini], and no one else. But now my affection for him and his family has increased for they have arranged for me to meet her, may the Lord reward them for this. Adieu, my beloved, until we are joined together in a few years.

Locust Swarms Reach Baq'a

May 20, 1915

Locust swarms are spreading everywhere, and the insects are laying their eggs. Crops have been laid waste across the country, but the situation is particularly severe around Jaffa and its environs. People arriving from the city report that citizens are compelled to go out in the fields and destroy the locusts. Those who refuse, or are unable to do so, are fined one Ottoman lira for each six days [of abstaining from collecting the insects]. I was told by my mother that her brother saw the locust swarms in Baq'a. May God protect us.

Typhus Is Spreading in Jerusalem

Monday, May 24, 1915

I was shocked to hear today about the death of Ahmad Effendi Nashashibi, the son of Haj Rashid Effendi and the brother of Ragheb Bey, the current deputy from Jerusalem. He died from typhus in the prime of his youth. He was buried this afternoon. Diseases are spreading like wildfire among the population, especially among Muslims—for they do not take the proper precautions, may God forgive us. I was told from one of the health inspectors in town that four typhus cases were reported in one day alone in Bab Hutta. When I heard the news, I was struck with great dread, not only for the people but also for myself. First, because I live and breathe all day among soldiers, in a place that is full of bugs and lice; and second, because of the lack of good hygiene in the workplace. Even though our home is one of the cleanest places, the roads and the entry to our neighborhood are among the filthiest places. I love life and enjoy its offerings. Please God, I am still very young, do not take me away.

I Am Ottoman by Name Only, the World Is My Country
Friday, September 10, 1915

[Cemal Pasha] issued an order, communicated by phone to the Commissariat Wednesday evening at 5:30 P.M. It became known to him that many of those employed in the department of censorship, as well as the local police force and gendarmes, had been recruited from the local population. He therefore ordered that no members in the armed forces be allowed to serve in their [home] regions. Those serving will now be recorded in a special registry and transferred to the Beersheba Commissariat, where they will be dispatched away from their districts. Exception will be made for those in the fighting battalions [tawabcer]. Officers who violate this order will be subject to court-martial. This order was circulated within all sections of the Eighth Army here, to the offices of the Fourth and Eighth Armies in Damascus, and to all the military commissariats under Cemal Pasha's jurisdiction. The order requests the names of all soldiers in Jerusalem and its rural districts. The deadline for execution is the first of September (Ottoman calendar).

This circular led to a general panic in our area. Officers and soldiers began to seek all sorts of medical excuses to remain in Jerusalem.

The head of our Commissariat [Rusen Bey] became very upset, since he did not want to lose his local staff, to whom he has become very attached, and because he knew that public works [a'malkhana] will be paralyzed in his region, since the majority of personnel come from the Jerusalem area. I heard the news within fifteen minutes of its arrival. Many of us were hoping that it would not be carried out. I was at a loss about what to do. I have too much dignity to plead exemption for myself, for I prefer to go to the front than to beg for mercy.

However, I cannot imagine myself fighting in the desert front. And why should I go? To fight for my country? *I am Ottoman by name only, for my country is the whole of humanity.* Even if I am told that by going to fight, we will conquer Egypt, I will refuse to go. What does this barbaric state want from us? To liberate Egypt on our backs? Our leaders promised us and other fellow Arabs that we would be partners in this government and that they seek to advance the interests and conditions of the Arab nation. But what have we actually seen from these promises? Had they treated us as equals, I would not hesitate to give my blood and my life—but as things stand, I hold a drop of my blood to be more precious than the entire Turkish state.

If I go to the front, what will happen to my father and mother, and my siblings? When my parents heard of this circular, they started worrying about my fate even before any actual steps were taken. For they were already in great distress about the conditions at the war front and the miserable lot of our compatriots fighting there.

Ihsan's Dreams

Jerusalem, Wednesday, September 22, 1915

Today I began taking private lessons in French. At the end of the war, I intend to attend college in Beirut. There I hope to perfect my French, reading, and writing. Then I will seek my family's approval to study agriculture in Switzerland. Then I will come back, buy a piece of land to cultivate, and live with my beloved away from the crowds. Farming is the best profession, for if we look at all other crafts, we can find nothing nobler. My problem is that I have no command of French, and my family probably will not approve my travel to Europe.

Attack on Egypt Postponed

Thursday, October 25, 1915

An agency telegram was received today announcing a sultanic decree promoting Fourth Army Commander Ahmad Cemal Pasha to the rank of *fareeq* [vice admiral], as a reward for his services and military victories. Which victories is not clear. Certainly not the Egyptian campaign.

Rumors abound that Cemal Pasha is to be recalled to Istanbul and that the Supreme Command in Turkey has decided against a [second] Egyptian campaign this summer for the lack of military preparedness.

Diseases are taking their terrible toll in Aleppo and Homs. Sixty to seventy deaths a day, mostly Armenians.

Are We about to Have a Bread Rebellion?

Monday, December 17, 1915

I haven't seen darker days in my life. Flour and bread have basically disappeared since last Saturday. Many people have not eaten bread for days now. As I was going to the Commissariat this morning, I saw a throng of men, women, and boys fighting each other to buy flour near Damascus Gate. When I passed this place again in midday, their numbers had multiplied. Most of the newcomers were peasants. I became very depressed and said to myself, "Pity the poor"—and then I said, "No, pity all of us, for we are all poor nowadays."

Two days ago we ran out of flour at home, and we had nothing to eat. My father gave my brother Aref a few pennies to buy us bread. He looked everywhere, but there was no bread to be bought anywhere. One of our cousins sent us a bag of semolina *[smeed]* when he heard of our distress. Yesterday my grandmother's sister Um Ibrahim also sent us three pounds of flour. Without this help we would have gone hungry.

I never thought we would lack flour in our country, when we are the source of wheat. And I never in my life imagined that we would run out of flour at home. Who is responsible but this wretched government? It tried to establish a pricing regime *(fi'a)* for wheat and flour—which was a good idea—but it should have established means for the delivery of flour before establishing the rations. What will happen when [the merchants] refuse to sell? The rich in Jerusalem, as in other cities, have taken provisions and hoarded a year's supply in their cellars. But what can the poor do? If the government had any dignity, it would have saved wheat in its hangars for public distribution at a fixed price, or even have made it available from military supplies.

If these conditions persist, the people will rebel and bring down this government—and then it will be too late for the leaders to atone for their sins. We have so far tolerated living without rice, sugar, and kerosene. But how can we live without bread? Beginning with the new month [Ottoman calendar], the price conversions have been fixed as follows:

New Currency	Old Currency
gurush	gurush
120 per English pound	136.10 per English pound
108 per Ottoman lira	125.10 per Ottoman lira
95 per French pound	109 per French pound
20 per majidi	23 per majidi
One qirsh is worth	
3 matleeks, and 2.5 paras	xxxxxxxx

Turjman, Ihsan Salih. *Year of the Locust: A Soldier's Diary and the Erasure of Palestine's Ottoman Past*, edited by Salim Tamari. Berkeley, CA: University of California Press, 2011.

Resolution of the Syrian General Congress at Damascus, 2 July 1919

In the aftermath of World War I, the Syrian General Congress met and agreed upon a program for the future of a Syrian nation. In violation of Article 22 of the Covenant of the League of Nations, the following resolution of the congress was ignored by the entente governments.

We the undersigned members of the Syrian General Congress, meeting in Damascus on Wednesday, July 2nd, 1919, made up of representatives from the three Zones, viz., the Southern, Eastern, and Western, provided with credentials and authorizations by the inhabitants of our various districts, Moslems, Christians, and Jews, have agreed upon the following statement of the desires of the people of the country who have elected us to present them to the American Section of the International Commission; the fifth article was passed by a very large majority; all the other articles were accepted unanimously.

1. We ask absolutely complete political independence for Syria within these boundaries: The Taurus System on the North; Rafah and a line running from Al Jauf to the south of the Syrian and the Hejazian line to Akaba on the south; the Euphrates and Khabur Rivers and a line extending east of Abu Kamal to the east of Al Jauf on the east; and the Mediterranean on the west.
2. We ask that the Government of this Syrian country should be a democratic civil constitutional Monarchy on broad decentralization principles, safeguarding the rights of minorities, and that the King be the Emir Feisal, who carried on a glorious struggle in the cause of our liberation and merited our full confidence and entire reliance.
3. Considering the fact that the Arabs inhabiting the Syrian area are not naturally less gifted than other more advanced races and that they are by no means less developed than the Bulgarians, Serbians, Greeks, and Roumanians at the beginning of their independence, we protest against Article 22 of the Covenant of the League of Nations, placing us among the nations in their middle stage of development which stand in need of a mandatory power.
4. In the event of the rejection by the Peace Conference of this just protest for certain considerations that we may not understand, we, relying on the declarations of President Wilson that his object in waging war was to put an end to the ambition of conquest and colonization, can only regard the mandate mentioned in the Covenant of the League of Nations as equivalent to the

rendering of economical and technical assistance that does not prejudice our complete independence. And desiring that our country should not fall a prey to colonization and believing that the American Nation is farthest from any thought of colonization and has no political ambition in our country, we will seek the technical and economical assistance from the United States of America, provided that such assistance does not exceed 20 years.

5. In the event of America not finding herself in a position to accept our desire for assistance, we will seek this assistance from Great Britain, also provided that such assistance does not infringe the complete independence and unity of our country and that the duration of such assistance does not exceed that mentioned in the previous article.

6. We do not acknowledge any right claimed by the French Government in any part whatever of our Syrian country and refuse that she should assist us or have a hand in our country under any circumstances and in any place.

7. We oppose the pretentions of the Zionists to create a Jewish commonwealth in the southern part of Syria, known as Palestine, and oppose Zionist migration to any part of our country; for we do not acknowledge their title but consider them a grave peril to our people from the national, economical, and political points of view. Our Jewish compatriots shall enjoy our common rights and assume the common responsibilities.

8. We ask that there should be no separation of the southern part of Syria known as Palestine, nor of the littoral western zone, which includes Lebanon, from the Syrian country. We desire that the unity of the country should be guaranteed against partition under whatever circumstances.

9. We ask complete independence for emancipated Mesopotamia and that there should be no economical barriers between the two countries.

10. The fundamental principles laid down by President Wilson in condemnation of secret treaties impel us to protest most emphatically against any treaty that stipulates the partition of our Syrian country and against any private engagement aiming at the establishment of Zionism in the southern part of Syria; therefore we ask the complete annulment of these conventions and agreements.

The noble principles enunciated by President Wilson strengthen our confidence that our desires emanating from the depths of our hearts, shall be the decisive factor in determining our future; and that President Wilson and the free American people will be our supporters for the realization of our hopes, thereby proving their sincerity and noble sympathy with the aspiration of the weaker nations in general and our Arab people in particular.

We also have the fullest confidence that the Peace Conference will realize that we would not have risen against the Turks, with whom we had participated in all civil, political, and representative privileges, but for their violation of our national rights, and so will grant us our desires in full in order that our political rights may not be less after the war than they were before, since we have shed so much blood in the cause of our liberty and independence.

We request to be allowed to send a delegation to represent us at the Peace Conference to defend our rights and secure the realization of our aspirations.

J. C. Hurewitz, *The Middle East and North Africa in World Politics: A Documentary Record, vol. 2: British–French Supremacy, 1914–1945* (New Haven, Conn.: Yale University Press, 1979), pp. 180–82.

Theodor Herzl: A Solution of the Jewish Question

> Theodor Herzl (1860–1904) was one of the founders of the Zionist move-
> ment. In an 1896 article written for the London weekly *The Jewish Chronicle*,
> he outlines his argument for the establishment of a Jewish homeland and
> discusses alternative sites for the location of such a homeland.

The Jewish Question still exists. It would be foolish to deny it. It exists wherever Jews live in perceptible numbers. Where it does not yet exist, it will be brought by Jews in the course of their migrations. We naturally move to those places where we are not persecuted, and there our presence soon produces persecution. This is true in every country, and will remain true even in those most highly civilised— France itself is no exception—till the Jewish Question finds a solution on a politi- cal basis. I believe that I understand antisemitism, which is in reality a highly complex movement. I consider it from a Jewish standpoint, yet without fear or hatred. I believe that I can see what elements there are in it of vulgar sport, of common trade, of jealousy, of inherited prejudice, of religious intolerance, and also of legitimate self-defence. . . .

We are one people—One People. We have honestly striven everywhere to merge ourselves in the social life of surrounding communities, and to preserve only the faith of our fathers. It has not been permitted to us. In vain are we loyal patriots, in some places our loyalty running to extremes; in vain do we make the same sacrifices of life and property as our fellow-citizens; in vain do we strive to increase the fame of our native land in science and art, or her wealth by trade and commerce. In countries where we have lived for centuries we are still cried down as strangers; and often by those whose ancestors were not yet domiciled in the land where Jews had already made experience of suffering. Yet, in spite of all, we are loyal subjects, loyal as the Huguenots, who were forced to emigrate. If we could only be left in peace. . . .

We are one people—our enemies have made us one without our consent, as repeatedly happens in history. Distress binds us together, and thus united, we suddenly discover our strength. Yes, we are strong enough to form a state, and a model state. We possess all human and material resources necessary for the pur- pose. . . . The whole matter is in its essence perfectly simple, as it must necessarily be, if it is to come within the comprehension of all.

Let the sovereignty be granted us over a portion of the globe large enough to satisfy the requirements of the nation—the rest we shall manage for ourselves. Of course, I fully expect that each word of this sentence, and each letter of each word, will be torn to tatters by scoffers and doubters. I advise them to do the thing cautiously, if they are themselves sensitive to ridicule. The creation of a new state has in it nothing ridiculous or impossible. We have, in our day, witnessed the pro- cess in connection with nations which were not in the bulk of the middle class, but poor, less educated, and therefore weaker than ourselves. The governments of all countries, scourged by antisemitism, will serve their own interests, in assist- ing us to obtain the sovereignty we want. These governments will be all the more willing to meet us half-way, seeing that the movement I suggest is not likely to bring about any economic crisis. Such crisis, as must follow everywhere as a natu- ral consequence of Jew-baiting, will rather be prevented by the carrying out of my plan. For I propose an inner migration of Christians into the parts slowly and systematically evacuated by Jews. If we are not merely suffered to do what I ask, but are actually helped, we shall be able to effect a transfer of property from Jews to Christians in a manner so peaceable and on so extensive a scale as has never been known in the annals of history. . . .

Shall we choose [the] Argentine [Republic] or Palestine? We will take what is given us and what is selected by Jewish public opinion. Argentina is one of the most fertile countries in the world, extends over a vast area, and has a sparse population. The Argentine Republic would derive considerable profit from the cession of a portion of its territory to us. The present infiltration of Jews has certainly produced some friction, and it would be necessary to enlighten the Republic on the intrinsic difference of our new movement.

Palestine is our ever-memorable historic home. The very name of Palestine would attract our people with a force of extraordinary potency. Supposing His Majesty the Sultan were to give us Palestine, we could in return pledge ourselves to regulate the whole finances of Turkey. There we should also form a portion of the rampart of Europe against Asia, an outpost of civilisation as opposed to barbarism. We should remain a neutral state in intimate connection with the whole of Europe, which would guarantee our continued existence. The sanctuaries of Christendom would be safeguarded by assigning to them an extra-territorial status, such as is well known to the law of nations. We should form a guard of honour about these sanctuaries, answering for the fulfillment of this duty with our existence. This guard of honour would be the great symbol of the solution of the Jewish Question after nearly nineteen centuries of Jewish suffering. . . .

Paul Mendes-Flohr and Jehuda Reinharz, *The Jew in the Modern World: A Documentary History* (New York: Oxford University Press, 1995), pp. 534–36.

The Balfour Declaration, 2 November 1917

The following is the text of the Balfour Declaration in its entirety.

I have much pleasure in conveying to you, on behalf of his Majesty's Government, the following declaration of sympathy with Jewish Zionist aspirations which has been submitted to and approved by the Cabinet:—

His Majesty's Government view with favour the establishment in Palestine of a national home for the Jewish people, and will use their best endeavours to facilitate the achievement of this object, it being clearly understood that nothing shall be done which may prejudice the civil and religious rights of existing non-Jewish communities in Palestine, or the rights and political status enjoyed by Jews in any other country.

I should be grateful if you would bring this declaration to the knowledge of the Zionist Federation.

J. C. Hurewitz, *The Middle East and North Africa in World Politics: A Documentary Record, vol. 2: British–French Supremacy, 1914–1945* (New Haven, Conn.: Yale University Press, 1979), pp. 180–82.

Mahmud Darwish: Eleven Planets in the Last Andalusian Sky

Mahmud Darwish is considered by many Palestinians to be their national poet. Born in a village destroyed during the 1948 war, Darwish spent most of his life in exile. The experience of exile provides a touchstone for many of his poems—as it does for the poems of other Palestinian poets. The poem that follows is titled "Eleven Planets in the Last Andalusian Sky." According to the Qur'an, the patriarch Joseph saw "eleven planets" in a prophetic vision. "The last Andalusian sky" is an allusion to the expulsion of the Moors (Muslims) from Spain.

> On the last evening
> we tear our days down from the trelisses
> tally the ribs we carry away with us
> and the ribs we leave behind.
>
> On the last evening
> we bid farewell to nothing,
> we've no time to finish,
> everything's left as it is,
> places change dreams the way they
> change casts of characters.
>
> Suddenly we can no longer be lighthearted,
> this place is about to play host to nothing.
>
> On the last evening
> we contemplate mountains surrounding the clouds,
> invasion and counter-invasion,
> the ancient era handing our door keys over to a new age.
> Enter, O invaders, come, enter our houses,
> drink the sweet wine of our Andalusian songs!
> We are night at midnight,
> no horseman galloping toward us
> from the safety of that last call to prayer
>   to deliver the dawn.
> Our tea is hot and green—so drink!
> Our pistachios are ripe and fresh—so eat!
> The beds are green with new cedarwood
>   —give in to your drowsiness!
> After such a long siege, sleep on the
>   soft down of our dreams!
> Fresh sheets, scents at the door, and many mirrors.
> Enter our mirrors so we can vacate the premises completely!
>
> Later we'll look up what was recorded in our history
>   about yours in faraway lands.
>
> Then we'll ask ourselves,
> "Was Andalusia
> here or there? On earth
> or only in poems?"

Mahmud Darwish, *Adam of the Two Edens: Selected Poems*, ed. Munir Akash and Daniel Moore (Syracuse, N.Y.: Syracuse University Press, 2001), pp. 147–70.

SUGGESTED READINGS

Aghaie, Kamran Scott, and Marashi, Afshin, eds. *Rethinking Iranian Nationalism and Modernity*. Austin: University of Texas Press, 2014. A wide-ranging collection of essays that situates Iranian nationalism and related movements within the broader field of nationalist studies and cultural history.

Aksakal, Mustafa. *The Ottoman Road to War in 1914: The Ottoman Empire and the First World War*. Cambridge, England: Cambridge University Press, 2010. A new approach to the Ottoman decision to enter World War I on the side of the Central Powers that examines diplomacy through the lens of Ottoman elite culture.

Arsan, Andrew, and Schayegh, Cyrus, eds. *The Routledge History Handbook of the Middle East Mandates*. London: Routledge, 2015. Collection of essays covering multiple facets of the mandates, the League of Nations, and the response of Middle Eastern populations to the mandates system.

Chehabi, Houchang E. "Staging the Emperor's New Clothes: Dress Codes and Nation-Building Under Reza Shah." *Iranian Studies* 26 (Summer/Fall 1993): 209–21. Explains the origins and experiences of Reza Shah's policies with respect to clothing.

Commins, David Dean. *The Wahhabi Mission and Saudi Arabia*. London: I. B. Tauris, 2009. Revisionist account of the past, present, and future of Wahhabism and its connection to the Saudi state.

Doumani, Beshara. *Rediscovering Palestine: Merchants and Peasants in Jabal Nablus, 1700–1900*. Berkeley: University of California Press, 1995. Path-breaking social, economic, and cultural history of central Palestine over two centuries.

Fromkin, David. *A Peace to End All Peace: Creating the Modern Middle East*. New York: Henry Holt, 1989. Very readable account of great power bargaining and conflict over the Middle East in the wake of World War I.

Gelvin, James L. *Divided Loyalties: Nationalism and Mass Politics in Syria at the Close of Empire*. Berkeley: University of California Press, 1998. Close examination of the development of both popular and elite nationalism in the Levant in the aftermath of World War I.

Gelvin, James L. *The Israel-Palestine Conflict: One Hundred Years of War*. 3rd ed. Cambridge, England: Cambridge University Press, 2013. More an analytical essay than a narrative history of the conflict, this book provides an interpretive account of competing nationalisms from the nineteenth century through the present.

Gelvin, James L. "Modernity *and* Its Discontents: On the Durability of Nationalism in the Arab Middle East." *Nations and Nationalism* 5, no. 1 (January 1999): 71–89. Investigation of the origins and persistence of nationalism in the Middle East.

Halliday, Fred. "The Nationalism Debate and the Middle East." In *Middle Eastern Lectures*, edited by Martin Kramer, 3. Syracuse, N.Y.: Syracuse University Press, 1999. Presents a cogent theoretical model for understanding nationalism in the region and then applies it.

Hertzberg, Arthur, ed. *The Zionist Idea: A Historical Analysis and Reader*. New York: Atheneum, 1981. Excerpts from a broad range of Zionist authors, with an excellent introduction on the intellectual history of Zionism.

Hurewitz, J. C. "The Entente's Secret Agreements in World War I: Loyalty to an Obsolescing Ethos." In *Palestine in the Late Ottoman Period*, edited by David Kushner, 341–48. Jerusalem: Yad Izhak Ben-Zvi, 1986. Situates the agreements made by the entente powers during World War I within the context of the breakdown of the European concert of powers.

Jankowski, James, and Gershoni, Israel, eds. *Rethinking Nationalism in the Arab Middle East*. New York: Columbia University Press, 1997. Excellent collection of essays on all aspects of nationalism in the Arab Middle East, including the historiography of nationalism.

Khoury, Philip S. *Syria and the French Mandate: The Politics of Arab Nationalism, 1920–1945*. Princeton, N.J.: Princeton University Press, 1987. The definitive study of the effects of French mandatory policies on the rise of nationalism in Syria.

Smith, Charles D. *Palestine and the Arab-Israeli Conflict: A History with Documents*. Boston: Bedford/St. Martin's, 2001. Probably the best comprehensive history of the conflict over Palestine.

Turjman, Ihsan Salih. *Year of the Locust: A Soldier's Diary and the Erasure of Palestine's Ottoman Past*, edited by Salim Tamari. Berkeley: University of California Press, 2011. The World War I period as seen through the eyes of an Arab soldier from Palestine.

PART IV

The Contemporary Era

If a Middle Eastern Rip van Winkle had fallen asleep in the decade following World War I and then awoke seventy or eighty years later, there would be much that he would recognize. The state system that had been in embryo at the beginning of his nap was, by the time of his awakening, fully realized. While various nationalisms had emerged or withered during his sleep, the populations of the region still looked to the principles of nationalism to organize their political communities—much as they had done when van Winkle's eyes were just getting heavy. While he was asleep, the confrontation between Zionist settlers and the indigenous inhabitants of the region had changed to a confrontation involving Israel, its neighbors, and a seasoned Palestinian national movement. Yet the conflict remained a lasting and seemingly intractable problem. The influence of Britain and France had waned, but great power meddling in the region continued under the aegis of the United States. And, although an Islamic republic had replaced the Iranian monarchy, Iran's boundaries remained much as they had been in the aftermath of World War I. Certainly, the post-revolutionary Iranian state did not surrender any of the powers it had accumulated under Reza Shah and his heir.

In many ways, World War I and its aftermath had a profound influence on the subsequent history of the Middle East. That influence should not be overestimated, of course. History is cumulative, and so-called revolutionary events are as much the product of change as they are the source of it. No nationalist movements or state system could have arisen in the Middle East had not the great nineteenth-century transformation prepared the ground for them. Furthermore, the war hardly affected the nature of economic and social relations in the region at all. That would come later. Nevertheless, World War I remains a useful benchmark, so long as we remember its usefulness has limitations.

One should also be wary of glossing over the equally profound changes that took place in the region subsequent to World War I. But how should the historian approach those changes? Historians writing today are so close to the events of the past three-quarters of a century that they are unable to gain the perspective distance provides. To put it another way, few historians would deny the significance of the French Revolution, although there are many disagreements about exactly what its significance was. On the other hand, how can historians be expected to judge the significance of the Iranian Revolution of 1978–1979, much less the contemporary Arab uprisings? As in the case of journalists, the best that historians writing about the past three-quarters of a century can offer is a first draft of history.

This should not discourage historians from attempting to make sense of the most recent period, however. Thus far, this book has argued that the only way to understand Middle Eastern history is to place that history within its global context. It has also argued that the establishment of a modern world economy and the modern state system distinguish the modern period from previous epochs. If we continue to think globally and use the world economic and state systems as our guideposts, it might be argued that the history of the contemporary period can be subdivided into two parts. The first had its roots in the 1929–1945 interval and ended in the early 1970s. The second period began in the 1970s and has lasted to the present day.

The first period started with the onset of the Great Depression and World War II. Both events changed the nature of social, economic, and political relationships in the region. The Great Depression spawned the need for states to intervene into their economies somehow to set them right. Many political leaders took to heart the theories of the British economist John Maynard Keynes, who outlined procedures to achieve what he believed the two aims of proper economic policy should be: full employment and stable prices. Governments throughout the world also had to deal with the economic dislocations brought on by the depression to alleviate the suffering of their populations and, in some cases, prevent popular rebellion. Hence the invention of welfare states in all its varied forms. This was the period, for example, when the United States put in place such New Deal programs as Social Security to combat widespread poverty among senior citizens. Over time, many of these programs and those that followed became known as "entitlements," a telling word that indicates that Americans believe them to be a right of citizenship. Policies adopted by states throughout the world during World War II also brought about a changed relationship between governments and their citizens. Governments had to direct the activities of their populations to ensure large-scale, uninterrupted production for the war effort. The launch of "war economies" throughout the world further broadened and deepened the commitment of states to full employment, government regulation of labor relations, and government regulation of business. All the while, governments had to maintain the devotion of their citizens who would not only bear the brunt of production, but of the fighting as well.

The new responsibilities governments took on and asked their citizens to assume brought about a transformation of what political scientists call the "ruling bargain," a metaphor they use when referring to the mutual rights and obligations states and their citizens demand from each other. As in many places throughout the developing world, the ruling bargain that emerged in the Middle East in the wake of the Great Depression and World War II might be summed up in a simple formula, "benefits for compliance."

This ruling bargain struck roots in the region as a result of five factors. The first was the heritage of defensive developmentalism and imperialism in the region. As we have seen in previous chapters, both processes created structures and institutions designed to expand the reach of the state and more effectively mobilize and harness the social power of populations. True, individual programs initiated by Middle Eastern states or their colonial overlords may not have been successful. And, true, their application was certainly uneven in the region. Overall, however, defensive developmentalism and imperialism effected a fundamental shift in attitudes about statecraft, social practice, and the responsibilities of governments toward their citizenry among both political elites and populations upon which later generations of statesmen and politicians might build.

Then there was the post–World War I experience. Chapter 12 discussed how Turkey and Iran, for example, borrowed from models available at the time, from fascism to communism, when institutionalizing their economies and political orders. In those areas of the Middle East under League of Nations mandates, mandatory powers brought welfare state policies, economic planning, and developmental assistance incubated in the laboratories of Western Europe. They did not do so out of benevolence. The mandatory powers feared nationalist rebellion and peasant and labor unrest that would put the entire enterprise at risk. In Egypt, governments and political parties advocated for rudimentary policies associated with the new ruling bargain to gain support in a highly competitive political environment.

The third factor that secured the new ruling bargain in the region was the nurturing environment created by the postwar international economic system, the Bretton Woods system, named after the resort in New Hampshire where representatives from 44 nations met in 1944 (ironically, the leading American economist at the Bretton Woods Conference—which produced the structures that would stabilize and expand the international capitalist system for close to three decades—was Harry Dexter White, a Treasury official and the Soviet Union's highest ranking spy ever to penetrate the American government). The system will be discussed in greater detail later in this introduction, but two aspects are important here. First, the system established a global economic structure marked by what political scientist John Gerard Ruggie has called "embedded liberalism": While economic decision-making on issues like trade and tariffs was to be handled by general agreement among states, individual states were free to intervene in their domestic economies as they saw fit. Some states might choose to take a relatively hands-off approach to their domestic economies; others might choose to be more interventionist to ensure full employment, industrial expansion, and so forth. Second, those who planned the system created two institutions, the International Monetary Fund (IMF) and the World Bank. The purpose of the

IMF was to ensure the overall stability of the system. The purpose of the World Bank was to promote development by funding large-scale infrastructural projects. The World Bank was active in the Middle East as it was elsewhere. Between 1957 and 1974 the bank lent Iran alone $1.2 billion for various projects, and the cancellation of a World Bank loan to Egypt for the construction of the Aswan High Dam in 1956 triggered a chain of events that led to the Suez War that same year. The most important consequence of the establishment of the World Bank, however, was the fact that its very existence ensured that "development" would be enshrined as an international norm.

At the center of the postwar international economic system was the United States, the preeminent economic power in the world. Its policies also encouraged the spread of the new ruling bargain globally. The motivations for American policy were ideological, economic, and, because Americans viewed privation as an entry ticket for Soviet influence in the developing world, political. For fifty years, American foreign policy centered on containing the Soviet Union and preventing the expansion of its influence in the rest of the world. American policy makers believed that states in which there was a large number of poor people and large-scale inequality were states in which communism might strike roots. The United States therefore promoted economic recovery for the war-ravaged economies of Western Europe and Japan and economic development elsewhere.

To promote development, the United States adopted a multifaceted approach derived, in good measure, from its own Depression-era and wartime experiences. Thus, the United States encouraged and supplied the expertise for planning boards throughout the Middle East and elsewhere. American policy makers championed the empowerment of the developmentally oriented "new middle class." In some cases—the number is still debated—the United States encouraged the "vanguard" of that middle class, "modernizing" military officers, to force the hand of history by taking power. American policy makers backed the construction of large-scale public works projects which were modeled on such Depression-era projects as the Tennessee Valley Authority and the Hoover Dam. They believed these projects would provide the foundation for national economic development. Finally, American policy makers urged governments in the Middle East and elsewhere to undertake land reform. They did so not only to take the wind out of the sails of communist-inspired revolutionary movements, but to invigorate national economies. Newly enriched peasants, policy makers believed, would stimulate demand for domestically produced goods.

The final factor that allowed the new ruling bargain to strike roots in the Middle East was decolonization. Decolonization refers both to a period (roughly the 1950s–1970s) and to the process by which formal empire ended in most of the world, resulting in the "post-colonial state." Before World War II only five states in the Middle East—Turkey, Iran, Saudi Arabia, Oman, and Iraq—enjoyed complete independence. Algeria was part of France, while Tunisia and Morocco were French protectorates (parts of Morocco were under Spanish protection as well) and Lebanon and Syria French mandates. Jordan and Israel/Palestine were

British mandates, and Britain had protectorates scattered throughout the Persian Gulf, a colony in Aden, and, after 1922, a convoluted relationship with a semi-independent Egypt. Finally, Libya was still part of Italy. Both formal and informal dependencies had no independent control over their economies and, for the most part, imperial powers viewed them as cash cows to enrich the imperial center. By 1971, however, every contemporary state in the region (with the exception of Palestine) was independent (although there were twice as many Yemens as there would be after 1990). This meant that states could take control (as far as possible, considering the power of the international system) of their national economies and direct them for the benefit of their populations.

The gospel of development found receptive ears throughout the periphery of the world economy. It thus inspired common imperatives and approaches to that end for nations located there. It was on the periphery of the world economy that a remarkable generation of leaders—a generation that included Marshal Tito of Yugoslavia, Achmed Sukarno of Indonesia, Jawaharlal Nehru of India, Ahmed Sékou Touré of Guinea, Patrice Lumumba of the Congo, Kwame Nkrumah of Ghana, and Gamal ʿAbd al-Nasser of Egypt, among others—took advantage of the system of embedded liberalism to introduce political/economic policies designed to support the new ruling bargain. Most commonly, these policies included state-led economic development, centralized economic planning, and import substitution industrialization (once again, import substitution industrialization refers to producing whatever manufactured goods a country could itself rather than importing them, thus reserving scarce foreign currencies held by governments to purchase more sophisticated imported goods). To pay for it all, individual states attempted to assert their sovereign control over their nations' most valuable resources, which were often in the hands of foreigners. Sometimes they were able to (as when Nasser seized ownership of—nationalized—the Suez Canal in 1956) and sometimes they weren't (as when the Iranians attempted to do the same with petroleum in 1951). Collectively, these policies are known as economic nationalism. The leadership of some states—post-1952 Egypt, post-independence Algeria, Iraq and Syria at various times—linked economic nationalism to the new ruling bargain through a populist discourse that extolled anticolonialism and the virtues of the "revolutionary masses." The leadership of others—Saudi Arabia, Jordan—did not.

If the immediate postwar period was one marked by optimistic visions of a ruling bargain supported by economic nationalism in what became known as the "Third World," by the end of the 1960s that optimism had soured. As early as 1960, statistics indicated the Third World's declining share of both world trade and world income. Over the course of the decade the economic gap between industrialized and industrializing states had become a chasm. Furthermore, few states on the periphery had changed their position in the world economic system. A number of prominent economists from the Third World blamed the Bretton Woods system and the economic order it sanctioned for this. After all, they reasoned, the developing world could never catch up to the developed world if it had to exchange cheap raw materials for the expensive manufactured goods necessary for development. And making catch-up even more difficult was the fact that the ownership and pricing of raw materials were still predominantly in the hands of foreigners. Third World leaders thus demanded compensation, the right for individual states to set tariffs and the like, and new rules regulating the ownership, pricing, and exchange of the commodities they exported. Just as important, they demanded a seat at the table: Rather than relegating decision-making about international economic policy to the world's most prosperous states—particularly the United States, which ignored their interests—they claimed the right to participate in deliberations as well. By 1973, seventy-seven Third World nations—from "radicals" like Algeria and Iraq to "moderates" like Lebanon and Jordan—had taken up the call for the replacement of the Bretton Woods system with a New International Economic Order that would overhaul the structure of the global economic system to make it more responsive to Third World needs.

The Third World based its demand for a New International Economic Order on a notion of "collective rights" (also called "peoples' rights" and "solidarity rights") that had become part of the international vocabulary since Vladimir Lenin and Woodrow Wilson voiced support for the right of self-determination of peoples. Over time states added a number of other rights, such as economic rights and the right to development, which expanded on the right of self-determination. Those who believed in the notion of collective rights believed that collectivities such as nations possessed rights of their own and that it was the duty of individuals within those collectivities to direct their activities to achieve them. It was also the duty of the international community to honor those rights. This notion differs from contemporary human rights rhetoric, which emphasizes the civil, political, and personal rights intrinsic to individuals (the term "personal rights" refers to the inviolability of people's bodies). Although the Covenant of the League of Nations makes no reference to an unfettered right to self-determination, the logic behind such a right was firmly embedded in the DNA of the organization. It also provided the rationale for decolonization.

The demand for a New International Economic Order would have constituted little more than a minor irritant to industrialized nations in general and the United States in particular had it not been for two events that took place in the early 1970s. The first was the collapse of the Bretton Woods system. From 1945 through the late 1960s, the United States had been the unrivaled economic power in the world. The American dollar was strong and the United States government guaranteed that dollars could be traded by other governments for gold at an official, fixed rate. The dollar provided the foundation for international exchange. All other Western countries pegged their currencies to the dollar. By the early 1970s, however, the United States was no longer the unrivaled economic power it had been in 1945. Germany and Japan challenged America's position of preeminence and began to accumulate dollars at a rate that alarmed financial experts. By 1971, the value of American imports outran the value of its exports for the first time in the post–World War II period. As a result, the dollars held outside the United States began to exceed the gold reserves in Fort Knox that backed those dollars. Faced with a potential run on its gold reserves, the United States government severed the relationship between the dollar and gold and allowed the dollar to "float." In point of fact, it sank. With its dollar anchor gone, the international economy lurched from one monetary crisis to another. All the while, world leaders squabbled about how to reform or reorder the international system.

The second event that made the developed world sit up and pay attention to the demands of the developing world was the oil shock of 1973–1974. "Oil shock" is the name given to the 380 percent increase in the price of oil that took place over a three-month period. The price increase came about after oil producers seized control over pricing from the oil companies that had previously set the "posted price." The oil shock marked an unprecedented assertion on the part of a group of Third World countries of sovereign rights, market power, and unity of purpose. It also frightened many American policy makers who saw a shift in the balance of power between the industrialized world and the Third World—a shift that they believed represented a threat to the very existence of the United States. What was to prevent Third World nations, working alone, in groups, or *en masse*, from using their power to provoke competitive scrambles for raw materials and markets among industrialized nations? What was to prevent them from upsetting stock and bond markets, or singling out the United States for discrimination? What was to prevent the exporters of copper, tin, rubber, bauxite, coffee, and even timber from taking their cue from oil producers by organizing their own associations to coordinate the production, pricing, and distribution of their commodities?

Since oil enters into the production of all commodities (try getting vegetables to market without trucks), the "oil shock" led to "stagflation"—the rare coincidence of stagnant economies at a time of inflation—throughout the developed world, particularly the United States. Unemployment and higher prices also threatened to upset the ruling bargain there. While the Europeans sought compromise with the Third World and the Japanese tried to negotiate bilateral deals with its members, the United States took a combative stance. In the words of the American representative to the United Nations, Daniel Patrick Moynihan, it was time for the United States to "go into opposition."

That opposition took two forms: economic and political. In terms of the former, American policy makers countered the economic nationalism of Third World states by pushing a policy that would become known as "neoliberalism." Neoliberalism was just the opposite of economic nationalism: According to this new paradigm, politics and economics were like oil and water—they should not mix. As a matter of fact, the more governments interfered with the free market through employment guarantees, the establishment of publicly owned enterprises, and the like, the more they would distort the natural order of things. Instead, markets should be allowed to govern themselves with only minimal government interference. The United States thus took aim at the developmentalist state and the ruling bargain it supported. Over time, the United States was able to flex its political and economic muscles to bring other industrialized nations on board.

It was primarily the global economic crisis of 1979–1982 that enabled the United States to run the table on the Third World. The 1973 oil price hikes created a strange problem for newly enriched oil producers: what to do with the enormous wealth those hikes generated. Over the course of the next ten years, much of that wealth—$96 billion worth—found its way to branches of American banks in Europe, which loaned that money to developing nations. Those nations needed the money to cover the higher cost of manufactured goods imported from developed nations. Oil was, after all, a crucial ingredient in the production of those goods, and the higher price manufacturers had to pay for oil was passed on to their customers. But there was one problem with this arrangement: For developed nations to pay for more expensive oil, more and more dollars had to be printed. The more dollars that were printed, the less those dollars were worth. Cheap money might have been great for borrowers because it meant low interest rates. It was not good for American businesses and consumers, who had to pay more for the goods they needed. Therefore, in 1979, the Federal Reserve Bank of the United States, which sets interest rates, upped those rates to make borrowing more difficult and to reverse the outflow of dollars. The era of easy credit was over. The action of the Federal Reserve pulled the rug out from overextended borrowers, precipitating the Third World debt crisis of the 1980s.

To deal with the debt crisis, the most economically powerful nations restructured the Bretton Woods institutions. They also enacted a series of policy initiatives that not only quashed the call for a New International Economic Order, but removed the support system for the ruling bargain that had become widespread in the postwar period. Economic nationalism was out; the Washington Consensus was in. Under the terms of the Washington Consensus (a term that, again, reflected the origin of the new policies), a newly reinvigorated IMF guaranteed emergency credit to overextended Third World borrowers. In exchange, borrowers had to agree to accept a set of neoliberal "conditionalities" imposed by the IMF. Included among those conditionalities were the liberalization of trade, the removal of barriers to foreign investment, the reduction in government expenditures, and the privatization of state enterprises—all in the name of economic efficiency.

Neoliberal policies got their tentative start in the Arab world in December 1976, when Egypt negotiated a $450 million credit line with the IMF, which also gave Egypt the wherewithal to postpone $12 billion in foreign debt. In return, Egypt cut $123 million in commodity supports and $64 million from direct subsidies. The result was what one might imagine: two days of bloody rioting in which eighty to one hundred protesters died and twelve hundred were arrested. Similar "IMF riots" broke out in Morocco (1983), Tunisia (1984), Lebanon (1987), Algeria (1988), and Jordan (1989, 1996) after the IMF attempted to impose conditions on loans and loan guarantees.

Spontaneous IMF riots were not the only means by which populations in the region vented their anger at states that attempted to walk away from the "benefits" side of the "benefits for compliance" ruling bargain. Nor were economic issues the only spark that ignited popular anger. While authoritarian regimes confronted illiberal Islamist movements during the 1980s–1990s, they also increasingly confronted social movements that targeted the structures and institutions of the authoritarian state itself. To understand how this came to be and why those struggles took the form they did, it is necessary to return to the story of America's battle with the Third World and the New International Economic Order in the 1970s.

The United States accompanied its economic juggernaut with a political one. Just as the United States met the Third World demand for a New International Economic Order with neoliberalism imposed through the IMF, it took on the ideological underpinning for that demand—the notion of collective rights—by substituting its own notion of rights—individual human rights—and placing it on the international agenda. Besides challenging the rationale for the New International Economic order, this benefitted the United States in two ways. First, individual human rights were a logical foundation for neoliberalism. An open economic market depends upon autonomous citizens free to gather information, make decisions, and freely enter into voluntary associations with one another whether on the floor of a stock exchange or in a town meeting. In other words, equating human rights with individual rights minimized the Third World state's capacity to intervene into and regiment the lives of its citizens, thereby undercutting the foundation of that state both economically and politically. Second, by promoting the idea of individual human rights, the United States put Third World states, where individual human rights were rarely observed, on the defensive in international assemblies. Algerians might introduce the Palestinian question or apartheid—the two questions that epitomized the Third World commitment to collective rights—at every opportunity in international fora, but, to cite Moynihan once again, every time they did so the United States should bring up the question of whether Ahmed Ben Bella (Algeria's first president who was overthrown in a coup d'état) was "still presumably rotting in an Algerian prison cell."

The United States pushed for its definition of human rights in international conferences and at the United Nations, with varying levels of sincerity. Its first foray in this arena was the Helsinki Accords of 1975, a treaty signed by states in North America and Europe that confirmed the inviolability of national boundaries in Europe. The United States insisted the treaty also contain a section that committed signatories to upholding freedom of conscience, thought, and belief, thereby giving human rights legal endorsement (and placating anti-communist critics of the treaty at home who complained that by signing the treaty the United States had sold out Eastern Europe to the Soviet Union). The United States also selectively placed economic sanctions on regimes, sometimes those on the right (Somoza-led Nicaragua during the Carter administration), sometimes those on the left (Sandinista-led Nicaragua during the Reagan administration) which it targeted as notable human rights abusers.

It was, of course, easy for the United States to condemn the inability of Soviet Jews to emigrate, the suppression of Polish trade unions, and the imprisonment of Eastern bloc and Cuban dissidents. On the other hand, it was not so easy for the United States to apply pressure on its allies in the Middle East since so much— oil, Israel, shipping lanes, and the like—was at stake. As a matter of fact, during the 1980s–1990s states throughout the region expanded their repressive apparatus. Some leaders claimed that the danger to the state posed by Islamist groups forced them to impose emergency laws and make liberal use of torture and extrajudicial detentions. Some feared a backlash that was sure to come as a result of the state's reneging on the ruling bargain. Others did so simply because they could: With treasuries engorged by money from oil sales with which they might buy the latest security and military equipment, why be shy? All the while, the United States tended to turn a blind eye toward every fraudulent election, mock trial, and broken promise of reform. It even allowed the foxes to guard the henhouses by urging governments to establish official human rights councils to measure their governments' compliance with international standards. By 2008, such councils existed in nine Arab states and the Palestinian territories.

Placing human rights in the text of the Helsinki Accords had an unforeseen result. In various places in the Eastern bloc, non-governmental organizations (NGOs), such as Charter 77 in the former Czechoslovakia and the Moscow Helsinki Watch Group in the former Soviet Union, sprang up to monitor their states' compliance with their international obligations. A similar phenomenon occurred in the Arab world where official human rights councils catalyzed the emergence of non-governmental bodies that kept tabs on human rights abuses and made the discourse on rights part of a shared political vocabulary. The first such group, the Tunisian League for Human Rights, was founded in 1976—two years before the founding of Human Rights Watch. Since that time, human rights organizations have mushroomed throughout the region.

Lest it be thought that agitation for human rights and democratic governance was limited to a small, Westernized elite, the numerous protests and uprisings that have swept through the Arab world since the 1980s provide evidence to the contrary. Many of these protests and uprisings were inter-sectarian and many included a broad coalition of Islamists, liberals, trade unionists, and leftists. The first such uprising in the region, which ironically combined demands for human rights with a healthy dose of anti-Americanism/anti-imperialism, took place in Iran in 1978–1979. It was followed by a host of others in the Arab world, which included those demanding minority rights in Algeria and Syria, multiparty elections in Egypt, one-man-one-vote in Bahrain, and women's suffrage in Kuwait. These protests and uprisings culminated in those that took place beginning in December 2010. In most cases, they failed to bring about the results envisioned by many of their participants. The Iranian Revolution provides a glaring example of this, as do most of the 2010–2011 Arab uprisings to date. Nevertheless, as the twenty-first century progresses, it has become increasingly difficult to view the Middle East as a region impervious to global norms of human and democratic rights, or to discuss with the assurance political scientists displayed until December 2010 the durability of authoritarianism in the region.

This section explores the history of the contemporary period by highlighting three themes: the rise and decline of the authoritarian state in the Middle East, the twin pillars of support for that system—American foreign policy and the exploitation of oil—and, finally, popular resistance to the authoritarian state in its various forms.

CHAPTER 15

The Autocratic State

Every year, *The Economist Intelligence Unit*, a subsidiary of *The Economist* newspaper, publishes a "Democracy Index." The index ranks the democratic practices and cultures of every state in the world according to five criteria: electoral process and pluralism, functioning of government, political participation, political culture, and civil liberties. In 2010—the year before the outbreak of most of the Arab uprisings—not one state in the Middle East made it into the category of "full democracy." Only one state—Israel—made it into the category of "flawed democracy," coming in at a ranking of #37 among all the countries of the world. In flawed democracies there are free and fair elections and respect for basic civil liberties. However, there are significant weaknesses in other democratic practices, including problems in governance. The next highest ranked state in the region was Lebanon (#86), followed by Turkey (#89), Palestine (#93), and Iraq (#111). *The Economist* called these states "hybrid democracies." Elections in all four had substantial irregularities and there was widespread corruption and a weak civil society. All twenty of the remaining countries in the Middle East and North Africa fit into the category "authoritarian regimes." The lowest ranked was Saudi Arabia, which came in at #160 on a scale in which the lowest ranking overall was 167. (If Saudi Arabia ever adopts a national motto, one possibility might be "Thank you, Central African Republic," which was one step down on the list.) Overall, the Middle East and North Africa region had the lowest composite score of any region in the world with the exception of sub-Saharan Africa.

From the different rankings on *The Economist* list, it is evident that the level of autocracy is not uniform across the region. Autocratic regimes come in various shapes and sizes. Although Kuwait (#114) and Jordan (#117), for example, are monarchies like Saudi Arabia, both have parliaments which can, at times, be raucous. Saudi Arabia does not. Nevertheless, in all three, kings maintain ultimate control: They can dismiss prime ministers, appoint cabinets, and in Kuwait and Jordan electoral districts are heavily gerrymandered. Before its uprising Egypt had a form of government one political scientist has called "semiauthoritarian."

In other words, the government allowed the opposition (the main component of which during the pre-uprising period was the Egyptian Muslim Brotherhood) some ability to organize and compete in elections but no opportunity of winning. Egypt, like practically every other state in the region, was called by a United Nations report a "black hole state," meaning that the executive branch—that is, the office of president or king—was so powerful that it "converts the surrounding environment into a setting in which nothing moves and from which nothing escapes." On the other hand, Libya, under its "brotherly leader" Muammar Qaddafi, claimed to have no government at all. Instead, it was a *jamahirriya*, a word made up by Qaddafi to mean "rule by the masses." Qaddafi claimed Libya was a direct democracy in which everyone participated in governance without the mediation of representatives. Since such a system could not possibly work, Libya had, in fact, two governments: a "people's government" on paper and a real government, made up of Qaddafi, his kin, and those he favored, which actually ran things. Libya narrowly beat out Saudi Arabia on *The Economist* index, tying Iran at #158.

The hybrid democracies also differed in form as well as ranking, although they did share one characteristic in common: They all dropped in the rankings in the years subsequent to 2010. The Lebanese system might be termed a "sectarian oligarchy," in which voters can choose their leaders from a list of the same old political bosses whose posts are determined by sectarian affiliation. For example, one of the two top contenders for the presidency—a position reserved for a Maronite Christian—in 2014 was the only Lebanese commander actually convicted of the murders he carried out during the Lebanese civil war of 1975–1991. That same year, Lebanon was forced to postpone parliamentary elections, fearing descent into violence should Hizbullah, the Shiʿi movement-cum-militia-cum-political party, win too many or too few seats. In other hybrids, 2014 was the year political leaders went in the opposite direction, throwing caution to the wind. Recep Erdogan, barred from seeking another term as prime minister of Turkey, decided to emulate Vladimir Putin and ran instead for president. He obviously hoped to transform the largely ceremonial post into one from which he could play puppet master. And in Iraq, Prime Minister Nouri al-Maliki, whose misrule had sparked widespread disaffection, stubbornly clung to his post despite the fact that his remaining in power could only fuel support for an invading force in which the Islamic State played a dominant role. The Islamic State's goal is to undo the state system entirely and replace it with a universal caliphate.

How did this dismal state of affairs come to pass?

A number of factors contributed to the emergence of strong states ruled by authoritarian governments in the Middle East. First, authoritarian structures were inscribed into the DNA of most states in the region early on. To understand the prevalence of authoritarianism, we might divide the states of the region into three categories. First, there are those which emerged in the interwar period—Iran, Turkey, and Saudi Arabia. In all three, militaries played a key role in establishing the states, and military leaders emerged as their initial rulers. Autocrats in Iran and Saudi Arabia both benefited from foreign (British) support and, in the case of the latter, protection. Furthermore, during the interwar period autocratic models of state-building and governance were ascendant globally. The second category of state includes those which maintained the structures put in place during the period of colonial domination. These include not only most of the remaining monarchies (Morocco, Jordan, Bahrain, Qatar, Kuwait, and the UAE), but Lebanon as well (Oman's relationship with Britain was more informal). The British and French viewed monarchs as reliable collaborators so long as they governed with a firm hand. Like Lebanon, the path to independence taken by monarchies was mainly peaceful (in the Gulf it was the British, not the various monarchs, who insisted states cut the cord), and so their transition from colonial to post-colonial states was marked more by continuity than rupture. The final category of state consists of the post-colonial republics which took shape with the overthrow of the colonial order after independence: Tunisia (the only state in this category where a civilian wrested control of the government, overthrowing a monarch), Algeria, Libya, Egypt, Syria, Iraq, and Yemen. Again, timing was everything: With the exception of Yemen—created through a shotgun marriage of two formerly independent Yemens in 1990—all emerged at the height of decolonization, when coups d'état undertaken by colonels hell-bent on destroying the remnants of the old order were the tactic du jour. We shall revisit this group again later in this chapter.

The great powers also played a key role in ensuring autocratic governance in the region. Over the course of the twentieth century, the great powers not only established states but intervened directly into their internal affairs and protected them from internal and external threats. The great powers have also used their leverage in both the political and economic spheres to dictate policy to governments and have granted them financial assistance. Underwriting democracy was not a high priority for those powers.

Governments in the region could also count on other financial resources to bolster their power. For example, almost all Middle Eastern states have been enriched by oil, either directly or indirectly. Those states not fortunate enough to have oil lying under their territory have received financial assistance from those that are. Because governments, not individuals or private corporations, control revenues derived directly or indirectly from oil, governments—not individuals or private corporations—have achieved unrivaled economic power throughout the region. With unrivaled economic power came unrivaled political power.

A fourth factor contributed to the emergence and endurance of strong, authoritarian governments in the region as well. Over the course of the past two centuries, both elites and non-elites in the Middle East increasingly came to equate economic development with social justice and nation-building. They have also come to view government as the primary engine for economic development. The widely held belief that a leading function of government is to guide economic development and ensure social justice enabled governments in the region to concentrate an inordinate amount of power in their hands.

What might be termed a "developmentalist ethos" emerged in the Middle East during the nineteenth century. It spread among the populations of the region in much the same way as did the ideology of nationalism. Both found an avid following in an environment in which state capabilities had begun to expand dramatically. In those regions where states were most effective in imposing new institutions and structures and in mobilizing and harnessing the energies of their populations in the name of the "common interest," a change occurred. The populations affected by state initiatives began to internalize the principles by which the state justified its actions and adopt them as their own. In effect, it was the defensive developmentalist activities of rulers and bureaucrats that generated a shared developmentalist ethos among the inhabitants of the territories they governed.

Nationalists interested in the practical details of state-building were, of course, among the most vocal advocates of developmentalism. Zia Gokalp, the so-called father of Turkish nationalism, thus wrote in the early twentieth century,

> In the future Turks must possess the same economic well-being that they once enjoyed in the past, and the wealth which is earned must belong to everyone. . . . The large sums that will result from collecting surplus values in the name of society will serve as capital for the factories and farms to be established for the benefit of society. Earnings of these public enterprises will be used to establish special refuges and schools for paupers, orphans, widows, invalids, cripples, the blind and the deaf, as well as public gardens, museums, theatres and libraries; to build housing for workers and peasants; and to construct a nation-wide electric power network.

But overt nationalists like Gokalp were not the only ones to believe in these ideals. For example, in 1899 the Islamic modernist and grand mufti (chief religious figure) of Egypt, Muhammad ʿAbduh, issued a religious ruling that included the following sentences:

> Establishing industries is a delegated duty. The nation must have a group within it to establish industries necessary for survival. . . . If the industries are not available, whoever is in charge of the affairs of the nation must establish them so that they might provide for the needs of the people.

Shortly after ʿAbduh's ruling, self-described orthodox ulama in Damascus joined the chorus, warning the Young Turk government, "Whoever does not work to advance the economy strays from Islam."

Thus, by the early twentieth century, the developmentalist ethos had become widespread in those areas of the Middle East that had been most affected by defensive developmentalism during the previous century. When, in the wake of World War I, new governments began expanding their power over territories that had once been beyond the reach of imperial authority, the territorial stretch of the developmentalist ethos expanded along with it. The developmentalist ethos achieved its greatest influence in the region during the period between the 1950s and the 1970s, when state-led economic development was the international norm, when the postwar economic system created a supportive environment for developmentalism, and when a series of military *coups d'état* established new regimes in Egypt, Syria, and Iraq. These new regimes based their legitimacy on their ability to bring about economic development and social justice. They also established a new set of standards for state behavior that continue to influence both governments and populations throughout the region.

Few observers looking at Egypt, Syria, and Iraq in the immediate aftermath of World War I would have imagined that within a few decades those states would be regional trendsetters. Egypt won its sovereignty under conditions largely defined by an outside power. The latter two states were directly created by outside powers. The structure of the governments of all three reflected the imperialist legacy.

During the period between the two world wars, both the British and the French relied on local notables and sympathetic rulers to maintain their influence in the region. They found notables and rulers reliable proxies for a number of reasons. The economic interests of most notables matched those of Britain and France. After all, most notables derived their wealth from landownership. The lands they owned produced agricultural commodities such as cotton and silk, which sustained British and French mills. Furthermore, the populations of the mandated territories and Egypt would have chafed at direct control from Paris or London. The British and French banked on the assumption that those populations would tolerate indirect control by their compatriots. Besides, indirect control was also cheaper. This was a primary concern for powers that had endured such large losses of men and matériel during World War I. Finally, relying on notables and sovereigns made British and French control easier. Competition among notables and between notables and sovereigns for power and influence impeded the emergence of unified nationalist movements that might have dislodged the imperialist powers. We have already seen how this worked in Egypt, where the palace, often with the connivance of the British ambassador, prevented the Wafd from dictating the course of Egyptian politics. For all these reasons, the states left by the British and the French in the Levant, Mesopotamia, and Egypt were initially weak, unrepresentative, and divided.

There had been, of course, no tradition of kingship in Egypt or Iraq before World War I. Egypt did not become a monarchy until 1922. In Iraq, the establishment of a royal house coincided with the invention of the state itself. But just as kings were a new phenomenon in Egypt and Iraq, so was the class of landowning notables upon whom the British and French also relied. Some of these notables could trace the roots of their wealth only as far back as the nineteenth century, when high prices for cash crops and the Ottoman Land Code of 1858 made real estate an attractive arena for investment. The roots of others were even shallower. In Syria and Iraq, the French and British granted tracts of land to rural and tribal leaders when those states were mandates. They did this in order to buy their loyalty and counterbalance the power of urban notables. The holdings of both urban and rural notables were not negligible. By the mid-twentieth century, 1 percent of the population of Syria owned about 50 percent of the land. In Egypt, about 1 percent of the population held about 72 percent of the land. The newness of many of these holdings and the disparities in wealth in societies that were still predominantly rural would make land reform a hot-button issue in the period following World War II.

All this has not prevented historians and others from looking back on the period stretching from the 1920s through the mid-1930s—and in some cases even later—with a great deal of nostalgia. This period, they point out, was one of cosmopolitanism in culture and the "liberal experiment" or the "liberal age" in politics. There is much to commend this view. As late as the 1940s, 40 percent of the population of Alexandria, Egypt, was "foreign." It consisted mainly of Greeks, Italians, Syrians, Maltese, and Jews. Until the early 1950s, the largest single group in the multiethnic, multireligious capital of Iraq, Baghdad, was Jews. Today, the population of Alexandria is overwhelmingly made up of descendants of native-born Egyptians, and less than a handful of Jews remain in Baghdad. In the realm of politics, those who call some slice of the interwar period the "liberal age" describe it as such because during this period parliaments were convened,

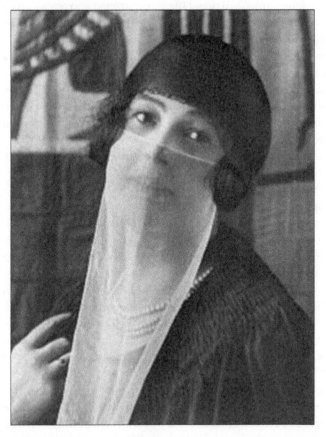

Upper Class Egyptian Woman, 1920s. (From: The Collection of the author.)

political parties formed, constitutions promulgated, secular rights institutional-ized, and newspapers published. And as described in Chapter 8, Egyptian femi-nism even celebrated a legendary founding moment during this period.

But celebrating the moment of unveiling also points to a fundamental weak-ness in the "liberal age" argument. Veiling was practiced predominantly among upper-class women. Whether they donned or doffed veils was of little concern to most Egyptian women. Looking at the period as a golden age draws attention away from the social cleavages that permeated Arab Middle Eastern societies and made the "liberal age" liberal for only a few. In cosmopolitan Alexandria, for ex-ample, the foreign community enjoyed privileges unavailable to most Egyptians. As a matter of fact, it was common practice for native Egyptians to be segregated in or excluded from tramways, clubs, and cafés and to fill the least rewarding niches of the economy. While it is also true that during this period states in the Arab East often took on the formal trappings of democratic life, more often than not these trappings masked underlying practices and social divisions that were undemocratic. Although there were parliaments, the franchise was limited and assemblies were unrepresentative. Although political organizations and trade unions were founded, associational life was restricted and often curtailed by im-perialist powers or local autocrats. Although newspapers were published, they were subject to censorship.

The overriding fact of political life from the 1920s through the 1940s was that there was little that governments or nationalist parties in Egypt, Syria, and Iraq could or would do to change this state of affairs. Governments were weak and unstable and governed at the sufferance of the imperialist powers that main-tained a presence throughout the region. Nationalist movements reflected the interests of the elites who dominated them. They concentrated their efforts on gaining or confirming national independence and paid only limited attention to social and economic concerns.

Nevertheless, during the period between 1918 and the end of World War II, the developmentalist ethos not only continued to find adherents, but became a key element in the politics of the three states. Merchants, homegrown industrial-ists, and even landowners played an important role in this. Working through the governments they dominated, these groups planned rudimentary programs for economic development, if for no other reason than it would be beneficial to all involved. For example, all supported the construction of basic infrastructure like roads, which would enable governments to maintain control over the country-side, industrialists to obtain labor and raw materials for their factories, and landowners to ship goods to market. Likewise, all supported a rudimentary ex-pansion of educational facilities, centralized economic planning, and incentives for private enterprise.

Groups of industrialists and bankers that emerged first in Egypt in the early 1920s, then in Syria and Iraq, played a particularly important role in energizing the principle of developmentalism. They made developmentalism a key compo-nent of nationalism by spreading the gospel of economic nationalism. Not only did they encourage Egyptians, for example, to "buy Egyptian"; they attempted to infuse nationalist movements with enthusiasm for economic and social reform. True independence, they claimed, was not limited to political independence. True independence meant economic independence as well. Economic independence could only be achieved through economic development and establishing a social system that would allow all to participate in nation-building.

The message of the economic nationalists was spread by new types of mass political parties and associations. As poverty in the countryside increased during the Great Depression, and as cities began to lure peasants with the promise of employment or educational opportunities, the population of urban centers exploded. In 1917, for example, the population of Cairo and Alexandria together was one and a quarter million; by 1947, it was over three million. As urban populations increased, so did the number of those available for political mobilization. A host of political parties and associations emerged, splintered, and re-formed during this period, from assorted communist parties and Muslim brotherhoods to the Syrian Social Nationalist Party, the League of National Action (in Syria), the National Democratic Party (in Iraq), and the Wafdist Vanguard and Young Egypt. These parties and associations differed from earlier nationalist parties in three ways: They were tightly structured, they possessed a middle-class leadership and middle-class and lower middle-class following, and they championed doctrines that went beyond mere calls for political independence. They sought to address the bread-and-butter concerns of their new constituents. The founder of the Syrian Social Nationalist Party put it this way:

> The aim of the Syrian Social Nationalist Party is the achievement of unity which will enable the Syrian nation to excel in the struggle for existence. This national unity cannot be obtained within an unsound economic system just as it cannot be realized within an unwholesome social order. That is why the achievement of social and economic justice is of extreme importance to the success and triumph of the Syrian Social Nationalist Party.

Ironically, the activities of the Great Powers encouraged the spread of new political movements and their developmentalist doctrines as well. Britain, France, and, during World War II, the United States introduced into the region new administrative practices that they had devised to meet the challenges of the Great Depression or World War II. These practices expanded the capabilities of governments, made populations accustomed to close governmental supervision of economic affairs, raised popular expectations, and opened up fresh possibilities for developmentalist currents. For example, during the Depression, French mandatory authorities in Syria introduced measures designed to stabilize the economy and maintain order. These measures were based on the welfare-state policies introduced by the Popular Front government that governed France from 1936 to 1938. But once price supports, wage guidelines, labor codes, poor relief, commodity subsidies, and the like were put in place, urban Syrians increasingly viewed them as an obligation of government, not a gift from government.

The activities of the Middle East Supply Centre (MESC) reinforced the developmentalist ethos even further. The MESC was designed by the Allies in World War II to collect data on consumer needs in the region so that they might allocate cargo space on freighters more efficiently. Over the course of the war, the MESC expanded its role. By the time the program was terminated, the MESC was regulating imports, guiding and supporting industrial investment, distributing essential commodities, and supervising production in Egypt and the Levant. The MESC fostered a 40 percent increase in manufacturing output in Egypt. Investment in Syrian industry quadrupled during the war years. The activities of the MESC not only set a standard for state-led economic development but provided the developmental blueprint for postwar governments to follow.

The developmentalist policies promoted by elites and popular political associations, along with the intrusive activities of foreign powers, redefined the criteria for political legitimation in Egypt, Syria, and Iraq. More often than not, the "old guard" politicians who dominated parliamentary politics had to respond to new demands. But more often than not they responded in word rather than in deed. All this was to change over the course of the next two decades. Beginning in 1949, cliques of military officers launched *coups d'état* against civilian politicians in all three countries and then against already empowered military regimes in Syria and Iraq.

While the first military coup in the post–World War II period took place in Syria, it was the Free Officers coup in Egypt in 1952 that would set the standard and provide a model for other states in the region. The Free Officers movement was established in the late 1940s by a group of mostly younger officers. Soon after the coup, its guiding member, Gamal ʿAbd al-Nasser, became Egypt's president. Nasser had been born in 1918 in a village near Alexandria. He was the son of a postal clerk and had risen in the Egyptian military to the rank of colonel. He had fought in the 1948 Palestine war, during which he was seriously wounded. For him, like many in his cohort, the war was a turning point. It represented the corruption, ineptitude, and treason of the old regime. The Free Officers claimed to have launched their coup to put an end to that corruption, ineptitude, and treason. They did not, at first, offer a grand ideological vision. Instead, they promised to work with the private sector and the least objectionable political parties, and to restore democracy once they had ironed things out. For this reason, the Free Officers referred to themselves and their coup merely as a "movement." Only later did they retrospectively overstate their sense of purpose by replacing the word "movement" with "revolution."

This is not to say, however, that the Free Officers or other military cliques who seized power between 1949 and 1958 were ideologically barren. As urban dwellers, graduates of military academies, and the products of lower middle- or middle-class upbringing at a time when those classes formed the nucleus of new political currents, military officers were steeped in the political controversies of the day. They also had been raised in an environment that provided them with a set of assumptions about modernity and progress. Once in power, even the unimaginative Husni al-Zaᶜim, who seized power in Syria in 1949, was instinctively drawn to the sort of policies that came to be associated with all military-led revolts in the region. Colonel al-Zaᶜim, who ruled for only three months, reportedly proclaimed, "Give me five years and I will make Syria as prosperous and enlightened as Switzerland" shortly before he was deposed.

Nevertheless, military conspirators throughout the region only began promoting comprehensive programs to restructure their economies and societies after the Suez War of 1956. The war was a debacle, an ill-conceived invasion of Egypt by British, French, and Israeli forces that is still called the Tripartite Aggression by Egyptians. The three states launched their invasion to topple Nasser's government because the Egyptian leader had proved himself to be a thorn in the side of all three. He had nationalized the Suez Canal, was supporting Algerian insurgents against French rule, obstructed Israeli sea lanes, and had just concluded an arms deal with Czechoslovakia that threatened to upset the regional balance of power. The British, French, and Israelis felt he clearly had to go.

The invasion did not topple Nasser's government. To the contrary, international pressure forced the invading states to withdraw their forces before they could achieve their aim. As a result of the failure of Britain, France, and Israel to realize their goal, the war actually raised Nasser's political stock both at home and throughout the region. Overall, the invasion had three results for the eastern Arab world and Egypt. First, it convinced Nasser that the Free Officers had not yet eliminated the twin threats of domestic reaction and foreign imperialism. From that moment on, the regime would no longer seek accommodation with the forces of reaction and imperialism, but would take control of its own destiny. It would do that by seizing the property of reactionaries and imperialists and using it to finance rapid economic and social development.

The Suez War also created a political atmosphere in Iraq that made the overthrow of the monarchy by a military coup almost a foregone conclusion. That coup took place in 1958. It was soon followed by others, which introduced to Iraq policies first sampled in Egypt. Finally, Nasser's anti-imperialist stance incited political groupings in Syria to demand unification with Egypt. Foremost of these groupings was the Baᶜth (Resurrection) Party. Founded in 1949, the party found support among romantic intellectuals who waxed eloquent about Arab unity as well as among hard-core organizers. This latter group had received its political education during the Depression of the 1930s. It thus brought to the party populist demands for economic and social reform. Baᶜthist regimes, a bit less ideological but no less fervent about holding onto power, have controlled the Syrian government since 1963 and retained control of Iraq until 2003. The unification of Egypt and Syria took place in 1958 with the establishment of the United Arab Republic. It lasted for three years. During that time, the Egyptians exported their model for development directly to Syria.

Wherever military officers and their "civilianized" successors took control (first in Egypt, Syria, and Iraq, then in Yemen, Libya, and Sudan), their first goal was to weaken or break the power of previously existing elites. They did this in

Gamal ʿAbd al-Nassar greeted by supporters in Port Said after the Suez War. (*From: Fondation Arabe pour l'image, Beirut.*)

several ways. In some cases—Egypt, Iraq, and Libya—they deposed a monarch, confiscated his property, and dissolved the venue for distributing royal patronage, the court. Coup leaders also dismissed parliaments that had provided landowning notables with a base for their political operations and disbanded political parties they felt were more part of the problem than part of the solution.

Alongside these political measures, the coup leaders destroyed the power of the old elites by striking at their economic power. One of the ways they did this was through land reform.

As noted in the Introduction to Part IV, land reform was hardly a revolutionary idea. It was advocated by not only the American government, but the British government and the World Bank as well. Like the Americans, the British and the World Bank believed that land reform in the region would alleviate rural poverty and build a class of rural consumers who would buy goods produced domestically as a result of import substitution industrialization. There also appeared to be a crying need for land reform. On the eve of the 1963 revolution in Syria, for example, 60 percent of peasants were landless. In Iraq, the figure was 80 percent. But whatever the need, the revolutionary regimes found land reform to be a convenient way to weaken their rivals. At the same time, the new regimes viewed land reform as a means to gain the support of the rural masses and extend their control over them.

The Egyptian program of land reform was typical of the sort of program other states would come to adopt. The Egyptian government placed ceilings on the amount of land that individuals or families could own. Those ceilings were initially set at two hundred feddans, then reduced to one hundred, and finally to fifty. By 1971, nearly one million feddans had been distributed to about 350,000 peasant families. Peasants who received land had to join cooperatives set up by the state to organize and improve production, control the sale and pricing of agricultural goods, and provide credit. In effect, the cooperatives were created to enable the government to take over activities like money lending and marketing that had previously been in the hands of landholding elites. At their height, there were five thousand cooperatives with three million members. Similar cooperatives and even communes were established in Syria and Iraq.

The weakening or elimination of entrenched political elites paved the way for new political elites to rise to power. Military coups empowered representatives of the so-called new middle class (professionals, administrators, managers), and of provincial and rural society. In Egypt, eight of the twelve members of the governing Revolutionary Command Council established after the Free Officers coup had rural roots. Nasser himself came from a provincial, middle-class background. In a like manner, thirteen of the fifteen members of the Revolutionary Command Council that ruled Iraq from 1968 to 1977 came from small peasant or petit-bourgeois backgrounds. Throughout the region, employees of the expanded bureaucracy came from similar provincial and lower middle-class backgrounds. As a result of this expansion of political and bureaucratic power to those who had previously been excluded, governments responded to the needs and ideals of strata that had never before been the object of government concern. These strata became the main beneficiaries of expanding services, such as healthcare, education, rent stabilization, and food subsidies provided by governments.

To pay for these services, military governments took over entire sectors of the economy. They did this for other reasons as well: to end their nations' dependence on international markets and the industrialized West, to break the back of industrialists and others who had, more often than not, proven themselves hostile to the new rulers, and to tighten their control over their populations. The state mobilized resources and directed them through expanded state planning and investment.

Some of the mobilized resources directed by the state were obtained through the nationalization of foreign or private holdings. Through nationalizations, the regimes not only gained control over the properties and businesses they seized, but acquired revenue to invest as they chose. Furthermore, nationalizations enabled the regimes to diminish the influence of foreigners, political enemies, and "resident-aliens" over the economies of their countries. In the case of Egypt, this last category included many of the Greeks, Italians, Syrians, and Jews whose families had lived in Egypt for decades, if not centuries. The Egyptian government not only seized control of the Suez Canal and most British and French investments in the country, it took charge of the hundred million Egyptian pounds locked in the vaults of the largest bank in Egypt. By the mid-1960s, the Egyptian government found itself owning and running banks, insurance companies, textile mills, sugar-refining and food-processing facilities, air and sea transport, public utilities, urban mass transit, cinemas, theaters, department stores, agricultural credit institutions, fertilizer plants, and construction companies. After more than thirty years of economic liberalization, the Egyptian government still monopolizes power production, transport, heavy industry, and insurance, and has significant stakes in other services and industries.

If measured by profit, state control over so much of the economy has been highly inefficient. But the success of nationalizations and the ensuing program of "state socialism" or "state capitalism" (depending on your point of view) cannot be measured in terms of efficiency alone. By administering so many productive and commercial establishments, states have been able to allocate resources for their own ends and to gain control over strategic industries. Furthermore, states significantly reduced the ranks of the unemployed—even if they had to hire many of the unemployed themselves. For example, in 1961 the Egyptian government passed the "Public Employment Guarantee Scheme" which, like the name says, guaranteed every university graduate a job in the public sector. The scheme was amended three years later to include all graduates of secondary technical schools. The result was as one might expect: The Egyptian bureaucracy, never a pretty sight, swelled from 350,000 in 1952 to 1.2 million in 1970. Although the government repealed the bill in 1990 after International Monetary Fund prodding, the bureaucracy continued to grow. As of 2008, the government employed approximately 5 million Egyptians. With such numbers, those who work for the government are, more often than not, underemployed and paid ridiculously low salaries. Those who can, supplement their incomes by spending their off-hours working in the private sector, where salaries are more lucrative but hiring more competitive.

Controlling economic resources enabled states to expand their role in society and to rearrange society so that they might control it better. Through centrally planned economies and unopposed state power, governments used economic incentives to gain the compliance of their citizens and reward those sectors of society the governments claimed to represent. The benefits states delivered were extensive. States undertook road and school construction, rural electrification, and healthcare and literacy campaigns. States expanded educational opportunities by reducing or eliminating school fees. Enrollment at Damascus University, for example, doubled between 1963 and 1968, with half the students coming from rural backgrounds. States have also kept food and other household commodities affordable by providing subsidies for many of them: wheat, flour, cooking oil, rice, sugar, tea, petroleum, and gas. As of 2009–2010, spending on subsidies, along with social benefits such as healthcare and education, represented close to 42 percent of Egyptian government expenditures. Subsidies on household commodities alone accounted for about 23 percent. By 2012–2013, that percentage had risen to about one-third of all expenditures.

In addition to rewarding their supporters and punishing their opponents economically, the governments of Egypt, Syria, and Iraq attempted to manipulate society by recognizing certain groups as legitimate and withholding recognition from others. The former groups were given the right to participate in the councils of government (if that phrase can be applied to party congresses and rubber stamp parliaments) and to bicker with other recognized groups over the division of spoils from the state. For example, during the 1960s the Egyptian government recognized five groupings as the building blocks of the new society: peasants, workers, intellectuals and professionals, national ("good") capitalists, and the army. Handpicked representatives of these groups were called upon to ratify the 1962 Charter for National Action and to keep their constituents informed of government decisions.

Interestingly, while this system diminished the rights enjoyed by some groups in Nasserist Egypt and Baʿthist Syria and Iraq, it had the opposite effect on the rights enjoyed by others. For example, the system substantially curtailed the rights of workers. In all three countries the state destroyed the organizational independence of trade unions. First, the state purged liberals, leftists, and Islamists from union leadership. Then, the state integrated unions into broader labor confederations. These confederations held the exclusive right to represent their members to the government. Other groups that had organized themselves before the onset of the revolutionary period, such as the press and professional and trade associations, likewise lost their independence.

But while the revolutionary states curtailed the rights of organized labor, they expanded the rights of women. The Egyptian government, for example, recognized women as a distinct category of society whose needs were deemed worthy of special consideration. The Egyptian constitutions of 1956 and 1962 guaranteed equal opportunities to all Egyptians regardless of gender. The Egyptian state granted women the right to vote (as had the Syrian state after its first military coup), and guaranteed women paid maternity leave and the right to child care if employed at a large facility. The Baʿthist regimes of Syria and Iraq legislated similar measures in the 1970s. Like the Egyptian government during the same period, they also expanded women's rights in marriage and protected women's rights of inheritance. Notwithstanding their stated commitment to social justice, the regimes stepped into this social minefield and promoted "state feminism" for two other reasons. First, they aspired to appease middle-class sentiment and to displace feminist organizations that had been active in the region since the 1920s. These organizations might have participated in liberal challenges to their rule. In addition, the regimes sought to further their control over the private lives of their citizens in much the same way as had Mustafa Kemal Ataturk and Reza Shah before them.

The revolutionary regimes thus pioneered approaches to politics, economics, and social policy that provided a model from which other Middle Eastern states drew. Even states in the region that had not experienced military takeovers adopted many of the administrative, economic, and social measures Nasser had imposed in Egypt or the Baʿthists had imposed in Syria and Iraq. More often than not, they did this to win the hearts and minds of their populations who were literally listening to the siren song of Gamal ʿAbd al-Nasser on Radio Cairo. Imagine being King Hussein of Jordan and hearing Radio Cairo call on Jordanians to "take the dwarf [King Hussein, whom the British and the Americans called "our PLK"—plucky little king] and hang him from the gates of the British embassy." Besides, leaders throughout the region understood that the end product of the political, economic, and social policies introduced by Nasser and the Baʿth was a highly centralized state that brooked no challenge. This, alone, was enough to make those policies alluring.

In spite of the fact that almost all states in the region came to adopt programs similar to those adopted in Egypt, Syria, and Iraq, however, not all of them took their developmentalist cues directly from their revolutionary neighbors. There were other influences at work as well. There were the none-too-subtle nudges from a United States worried about the survival of friendly governments. There was the influence of a legion of cookie-cutter development experts who imparted much the same advice everywhere. There was the encouragement and incentives offered by international institutions lost in the developmentalist moment. And there was the fact that once a state decided to go down the path of consolidation and development, there was only a limited number of off-the-shelf policy options from which it could choose. In 1963–1964, for example, the Baʿth Party took control of governments in both Syria and Iraq. The party then presided over the most radical attempts to restructure the economics and politics of those countries ever undertaken. Governments of both states nationalized banks, insurance companies, and commercial and industrial establishments. A key element of their program was the expansion of land reform. At the same time, the shah of Iran announced his own plan for development known as the White Revolution. Like the Baʿthists, the shah committed his government to wide-ranging social and economic reforms, including a land reform program. The shah felt that land reform would placate American policy makers who continued to believe that land reform imposed from the top would prevent a social upheaval from below. The shah also sought to take the wind out of the sails of his liberal and leftist opponents who were influenced by Cuban, Chinese, and homegrown revolutionaries. Besides, land reform would break the power of rural landlords, link the peasantry directly to the central government, and thus strengthen the shah's power. The program restricted the number of villages that landowners could own and redistributed land to those peasants who could prove they had sharecropping rights. Landowners were compensated with shares in state-owned industries that the White Revolution also expanded. Unfortunately for the shah, many were left unsatisfied. Historians often cite the unpopularity or failure of the White Revolution when cataloguing the reasons behind the Iranian Revolution of 1978–1979.

Because most states in the region copied or reproduced on their own the economic and political strategies pioneered by the revolutionary republics, their political, economic, and social systems hold a lot in common. From republican Egypt to monarchic Saudi Arabia to Islamist Iran, governments still play a major role in the economic sphere. In most states a small, close-knit ruling group stood above the fray, dispensing goodies to favored clients. This bound populations to their governments and made those populations complicit in a political system that otherwise excluded them. In most states, what passed for political debate entailed little more than disputes over the allocation of resources. In most states, the government effectively pitted social groups against each other for shares in the economic bounty. This policy all too often encouraged the fragmentation of society along kinship, ethnic, regional, and/or religious lines.

Then there is the problem of repression. Because the revolutionary regimes claimed to represent the "will of the nation," they repressed their opponents and classified whole layers of society as "enemies of the people." Well before the Arab uprisings of 2010–2011, governments throughout the region did not shy away from using force when they have felt threatened or when it suited their purposes. Within a month of taking power, the Free Officers of Egypt brutally suppressed a strike that had broken out at a textile factory. They arrested 545 workers and staged a show trial, after which two workers were hanged to demonstrate the commitment of the Free Officers to maintaining order. Far worse was yet to come. Nasser filled his jails with political dissidents, from leftists to Islamists. His successor, Anwar al-Sadat, once told a foreign reporter who asked a question he didn't like, "In other times I would have shot you, but it is democracy I am really suffering from [!] as much as I am suffering from the opposition." When the Syrian government faced an Islamist rebellion in the city of Hama, it shelled the city and killed from ten to twenty thousand of its residents. During the notorious Anfal campaign waged by the Iraqi government against its own Kurdish citizens in 1988, government troops killed between 50,000 and 150,000 Kurdish fighters and noncombatants.

The heyday of the so-called revolutionary model in the Arab East was short-lived. The economies of Egypt, Syria, and Iraq had been buoyed from their inception through the 1970s by a combination of nationalizations, foreign assistance, and oil revenues. By the early 1980s, the governments of all three were compelled to change course. Centralized economic planning had proved to be just as inefficient in the Arab Middle East as it had in other parts of the world. States had run out of properties to nationalize and, after a rapid climb, oil prices once again bottomed out. To make matters even worse for all three states, the world economy had entered into a crisis period. And with the triumph of the United States over its Third World adversary, neoliberal economic policies became the order of the day.

The introduction of neoliberal economic policies into the Middle East did not take place overnight, nor were they adopted wholesale. States were wary of backtracking on the ruling bargain they had hammered out with their populations, feared popular revolt, and balked at abandoning the political/economic apparatus that had kept regimes secure and populations politically immobilized. Neoliberalism also undercut the raison d'être of the revolutionary states, whose rhetoric of anti-imperialism and populism increasingly rang hollow. Nevertheless, poor economic performance and the lack of an alternative economic model

---

Vignette

A Joke

According to the father of psychoanalysis, Sigmund Freud, jokes provide the means by which one part of the brain outwits the "psychic censors" of another part of the brain, thereby transforming pain into pleasure. Because psychic censors have not been the only censors present in the Arab Middle East, jokes there perform another function as well: They allow Middle Easterners to vent their grievances in a medium that flies under the radar of the state.

Here is a story I first heard in Syria in the early 1990s. It was then repeated to me in Jordan and Egypt. For the latter versions, just substitute the words "Jordanian" or "Egyptian" for the word "Syrian":

> One day, the world's best intelligence agencies decided to stage a contest to see which was, indeed, the best. Invited to the contest were America's CIA, Russia's KGB, Israel's Mossad, and Syria's *mukhabarat* (secret intelligence agency). To determine which was the best agency, a rabbit was to be released into a forest. The first intelligence agency to bring the rabbit out of the forest would be deemed the finest in the world.
>
> And so a rabbit was released and given a brief head start. Shortly thereafter, teams from the various intelligence agencies went in after it. After about an hour, the American team emerged with the rabbit. The contest was over. Two hours later the KGB team emerged (rabbitless, of course), followed by the Israeli team.
>
> One day passed, then two, yet the Syrian team still did not emerge from the forest. After a week, the other teams decided to send in a search party. The search party scoured the forest, searching for the missing Syrians. Finally, the search party came to a clearing. In the middle of the clearing was a tree on which a donkey had been strapped. The Syrian team was surrounding the tree, while one of the Syrian agents was beating the donkey with a stick shouting, "Admit it—you're a rabbit."

(North Korea or Cuba, anyone?) forced the hands of political leaders throughout the region. Caught between the rock of international lenders demanding compliance with the new norm and the hard place of populations who resisted any renegotiation of the ruling bargain, states adopted a piecemeal approach to reform that combined a jury-rigged market economy with an inefficient command economy. This is reflected in the contradiction inherent in the name the Syrian government gave its "revised" economic system of 2005: a "social market economy."

The result everywhere was the worst of both possible worlds. States held on to the most profitable sources of income, such as oil production, along with the least profitable, which they could not sell off even at fire sale prices. Privatization did not lead to capitalism, but rather to crony capitalism as regime insiders took advantage of their access to the halls of power to make insider deals. They then pared down bloated enterprises or sold them off piecemeal, expanding unemployment and curtailing guaranteed pensions. And as in other parts of the globe (including the United States) where neoliberal policies were put in place, income disparities grew. Little wonder, then, that corruption and economic privation, along with unfettered autocracy, would emerge as principal grievances expressed by those who took to the streets in 2010–2011, or that the first impulse of the autocrats who faced uprisings was to promise their populations jobs, increased subsidies, and other goodies that would have, in effect, turned back the clock to a period before "economic reform."

If the developmentalist ethos, which rested heavily on government intervention to guide the economic life of the nation, gave inordinate power to states and was one of the cornerstones upon which autocracy in the Middle East rested, why didn't economic liberalization undercut that autocracy and lead to political liberalization? During the 1990s, a number of political scientists connected political liberalization to the economic liberalization of neoliberalism. Neoliberalism, they argued, would engender a citizenry which would come to view itself as made up of rational, autonomous, freedom-seeking actors, endowed with legal rights. All this would compel them to demand democratic rights. After the outbreak of the 2010–2011 uprisings, some revived the argument, once again connecting neoliberalism to demands for human rights and democracy in the region. Besides the fact that neoliberalism really took off in the region in the early 2000s, making its connection to a change in "subjectivities" (consciousness) among protesters only a decade later unlikely, even then it was hardly thorough and did not permeate society to the extent it would have had to in order to effect such a shift.

So what happened? First of all, while it would be wrong to think neoliberalism in the region was a complete mirage, its roots remained shallow. At the time of the Egyptian uprising, the Egyptian army controlled anywhere from 5 to 40 percent of the economy and 50 percent of manufacturing. After all, if it was not going to go to war against Israel, it had to do something to keep it busy. In addition, some have argued that states in the region are so powerful that they do not have to "bargain" with their populations about expanding democratic rights. Finally, states were able effectively to "decouple" economic and political liberalization. In the 1974 "October Paper" that laid out the blueprint for the first wave of Egyptian "economic reform," for example, Anwar al-Sadat warned that the social progress realized since the Free Officers revolution could only be protected if the government maintained a firm control over the political process. After the announcement of the "October Paper," Egyptian governments parried halfhearted foreign pressure and domestic threats by adopting the formal trappings of pluralist democracy. All the while, they attempted to ensure regime survival by repressing potential opponents, manipulating the electoral system, attempting to buy off the population with continued subsidies, and playing off the divisions created in society by the regime itself against one another. Once again, Egypt proved to be a regional trendsetter.

CHAPTER 16

Oil

During the 1950s and 1960s, promises of economic and social development became the linchpins of government policy throughout the Middle East, just as they did in other areas on the periphery of the modern world system at the same time. Middle Eastern states supported the expansion of their activities with revenues they acquired from a variety of sources. Governments acquired revenues from the nationalization of properties of foreigners and "enemies of the state." They acquired revenues from foreign aid. And they acquired revenues, directly or indirectly, from the exploitation of oil.

Oil production has affected state formation and sustained autocratic governments in the Middle East in a number of ways. First, those states blessed with oil revenue used it to manipulate public attitudes and behaviors and to maintain the "benefits" part of the "benefits for compliance" ruling bargain, thus possibly buying off dissent. It enabled oil-producing states to assist less fortunate states so that those states might attempt to buy off their populations as well. It did this by providing direct grants to those states and by providing the surplus labor living in those states with jobs. It also did this by enabling oil-producing states to come to the aid of their less fortunate neighbors to fight external aggression (the Saudis supported the Yemeni monarchists against Yemeni republicans backed by Egyptian troops in the 1960s) and domestic insurrection (as when Saudi Arabia and the UAE sent troops and police into Bahrain during Bahrain's 2011 uprising). And it gave the West, particularly the United States, an incentive to support some of the most hideous regimes on the planet in the name of promoting stability. Myanmar got sanctions; Saudi Arabia got F-15 Eagles.

Economists call the type of revenue generated from oil and similar sources "rent." They define rent as income acquired by states from sources other than taxation. Some economists call states that are dependent on rent for a certain proportion of their income "rentier states." Other economists call them "allocation states" because the states distribute the rent they receive to favored clients and projects. In no other area of the world have so many states been so reliant on income derived from rent as in the Middle East. Every state in the region depends on income from rent to a greater or lesser extent. Saudi Arabia, Kuwait, and Iraq might be placed in the "greater extent" category. As of 2013, oil exports accounted for 90 percent of Saudi Arabia's revenue and 83 percent of Kuwait's (other major oil exporters had more success diversifying their economies, mainly into the financial sector). The same year, oil exports accounted for 99 percent of Iraq's revenue. That was down from 2003, the year of the American invasion, when oil exports accounted for 100 percent of its revenue. Even those countries not usually associated with oil production, such as Egypt and Syria, have an inordinate dependence on rent. In 2010, the year before the uprisings in Egypt and Syria, rent provided 40 percent of Egypt's revenue and 50 percent of Syria's. In the case of the former, oil provided $11 billion to the national treasury, but there were other sources of rent as well. These included U.S. aid (about $1.6 billion) and Suez Canal tolls (about $5 billion). Syria has had to be more creative, combining lackluster revenues from oil sales with protection money paid by other states in the region seeking peace and quiet from their often troublesome neighbor or bribes to continue to make trouble. For the sake of comparison, it is worth noting that in 2010, China derived 5.4 percent of its income from rent.

At the present time, oil constitutes the largest source of rent in the region. Nevertheless, oil was not an important commodity for the Middle East until the twentieth century. In fact, oil was not a particularly important commodity anywhere until the last decades of the nineteenth century. What economic historians

"And up through the ground came a bubblin' crude": oil seeping to the surface in Iraq, 1909. *(From: The Gertrude Bell Collection, University of Newcastle.)*

call the "first industrial revolution" began during the last decades of the eighteenth century. The "dark satanic mills" most of us identify with the first industrial revolution were fueled first by water power, then by coal. During most of the nineteenth century, coal generated heat for homes and fueled the great navies of the world. People even derived the kerosene used in lamps from coal. The importance of coal to modern life began to decrease during the second half of the nineteenth century with the onset of the "second industrial revolution." If textile mills and the primitive factory system have come to symbolize the first industrial revolution, the internal combustion engine, oil-burning naval ships, and the petrochemical industry might be used to symbolize the second. The second industrial revolution thus established petroleum-based economies.

Even after the uses for oil expanded in the late nineteenth century, however, there were other sources closer to Europe and North America than the Middle East. In 1900, Russia was the world's largest producer of oil—just as it sometimes is today. About 50 percent of the world's supply of oil came from Russia. Among the other sources for oil at that time were the United States, Mexico, and Romania. Oil was not even discovered in Saudi Arabia until 1931. Production there did not begin for another seven years.

Most historians trace the history of the exploitation of oil in the Middle East from the d'Arcy concession of 1901, discussed in Chapter 5. The d'Arcy concession underscored the importance of sharing risk when it came to the oil business. Because the business requires a huge outlay of capital to begin operations, d'Arcy ran out of money before he was able to draw a profit. He was thus forced to sell the rights he had been granted to the British government, which established the Anglo-Persian Oil Company. This lesson was not lost on investors when the Ottoman government granted a similar concession several years later. The Turkish Petroleum Company (later the Iraq Petroleum Company), which received the right to exploit all the oil in territory in present day Iraq, was a joint effort bringing together the Anglo-Persian Oil Company, Royal Dutch Shell (which, as its name suggests, traces its history to a trading company that dealt in abalone shells for cameo jewelry), and various German interests. The Anglo-Persian Oil Company owned 50 percent of the shares of the venture, while the others held 25 percent each. This sort of arrangement is known as a consortium (pl.: consortia). A consortium is a group of companies that band together to undertake a project that would be beyond the means of any single company. For the first few decades after the d'Arcy concession, all concessions were granted to consortia.

The concessions granted in the first thirty years of the twentieth century resembled one another in other ways as well. Like the d'Arcy concession, all subsequent concessions were of long duration, usually from sixty to seventy-five years (the d'Arcy concession was granted for sixty years). They covered huge areas, such as most of Persia or all of Kuwait. The consortia had the right to pursue all operations connected with the industry, including exploration, production, refining, transport, and marketing. In return for the concession, a consortium paid the state that granted it royalties and fees. Only later, in the 1950s, did the consortia begin to pay the governments of oil-producing states a share of their profits. Finally, the consortia, not the governments of the oil-producing countries, had a free hand in determining the quantity and price of the output. Thus, beginning in the twentieth century and continuing for more than half a century, the West was able to exploit the oil resources of the Middle East with little interference from, and few benefits for, the states from which that oil was extracted.

The so-called oil revolution that culminated in the 1970s was nothing more than a step-by-step whittling down of these privileges by the countries under whose territory oil lay. For example, in 1961 the Iraqi government asserted its right to drill for oil in areas of Iraq not being exploited by the Iraq Petroleum Company. The oil-producing countries won the right to haggle with the major oil companies about prices only in 1971, and it took until 1973 for them to win the right to set prices unilaterally. They also had to wait until the early to mid-1970s—the high point of economic nationalism and Third World assertion—to take full control over the consortia operating in their countries. Algeria and Iraq led the way, nationalizing their oil industries in 1971 and 1972, respectively. Libya, too, began its nationalization campaign in 1971. In 1973, Iran negotiated what was, in effect, a takeover of the Anglo-Iranian Oil Company. With an ironic tip of the linguistic hat to the d'Arcy concession, the agreement read that Iran was to assume responsibility for "the administration and control of all activities pertaining to the oil industry in the area of agreement, including exploration, development, investment, production, refining, and transportation of crude, gas, and oil products."

Persian Gulf countries, beginning with Kuwait and Dubai, joined the bandwagon in 1975. Rather than using the term "nationalization," which would have set off red flags in the minds of Western diplomats, they called their takeovers "100 percent participation" in the consortia working in their territories. Most did not attempt to acquire 100 percent participation overnight. For example, in 1973 the government of Saudi Arabia acquired 25 percent of the shares of ARAMCO (Arabian-American Oil Company), the consortium that controlled the oil business in the kingdom. A year later, it acquired 60 percent. It was not until 1980 that it acquired 100 percent participation. One hundred percent participation is, in effect, nationalization.

Oil-producing states were able to assume greater control over their most important resource in part because they acted in concert. Cooperative action among producers began at the instigation of Venezuela after World War II. In 1947, the Venezuelan government demanded that oil companies drilling in Venezuela pay for the privilege by splitting their profits with the government 50–50. To make sure the oil companies did not simply substitute more profitable Middle Eastern oil for theirs, the Venezuelans sent emissaries to the Middle East to spread the word about 50–50 profit sharing there. It proved popular, not in the least because it promised to increase the revenue of producing countries dramatically. In 1960, Venezuelan emissaries returned to the region with the idea for an association to represent the common interests of producers. Historians disagree about the reasons for this sudden interest in institution building. Many believe it was triggered by the deep cuts in the price of oil made by the oil companies in response to excess supply. The companies did not consult the producers about the price cuts, as was the norm at the time. Under the 50–50 formula, price cuts meant revenue cuts for the producing country. Outraged by this turn of events, the Venezuelan government initiated talks with four other affected governments—Kuwait, Saudi Arabia, Iran, and Iraq. The result was the Organization of Petroleum Exporting Countries (OPEC), founded to ensure "the unification of the petroleum policies of member countries and the determination of the best means for safeguarding their interests."

OPEC came into its own during the late 1960s and early 1970s as Third World states, which came to dominate international fora such as the United Nations General Assembly, put the economic dimension to the right of self-determination on the international agenda. In 1974, the United Nations adopted the "Charter of Economic Rights and Duties of States," which, among other claims, asserted the right for each state to have complete control over its resources, to regulate and supervise the activities of transnational corporations operating within its borders, to nationalize and expropriate foreign property, and to associate in cartels of primary commodity producers. By that time, the OPEC horse had already left the barn. During the decade leading up to the adoption of the charter, OPEC producers had already forced the major oil companies to accept price increase after price increase. They made the companies accept their right to collective bargaining and their participation in consortia operating in their territory. They introduced a pricing system that would automatically adjust for inflation. And they were able to do all this because of increased competition for their product in uncertain economic times.

When the 1973 October War broke out between Israel, on one side, and Egypt and Syria, on the other, what turned out to be the last round of negotiations about prices between OPEC and the major oil companies had just collapsed. OPEC seized the moment. For the first time in history, OPEC set the price of oil without any input from the companies. Then OPEC members made sure that price stuck. Proclaiming their solidarity with the two Arab belligerents, Arab members of OPEC temporarily decreased production. This limited supplies and thereby raised prices. The price of oil jumped 380 percent and wealth flowed back into the region from the industrialized, petroleum-importing world.

The final transformation of OPEC took place in 1982 when the organization became a cartel. Economists define cartels as groups of businesses, or, in this case, states, that coordinate policies to limit competition. This enables them to ensure a high price for their product. By 1982, the price of oil had leveled off, despite the spectacular price rise of 1973 and another price spurt in the wake of the Iranian Revolution of 1978–1979. To keep prices high, the OPEC countries decided to assign themselves shares of the international market.

OPEC ministers meet regularly to decide how much oil each producer should pump. The meetings are commonly contentious, a perennial clash between "price hawks" and "price doves." Saudi Arabia is in the latter category (one of the reasons why American statesmen refer to a kingdom in which women need the permission of their male "guardians" to travel, get an education, or undergo medical treatment as "moderate"). Saudi Arabia will never become an industrial powerhouse and will never overcome its dependence on revenues from oil. Saudi Arabian ministers have traditionally fought to keep prices down to prevent new sources of oil from becoming economical. After the price hike of 1973, for example, the exploitation of North Sea and Alaskan oil fields became profitable. The Saudis also fear that high oil prices would encourage the West to turn to alternative sources of energy, such as nuclear or solar power.

Iran, on the other hand, has a large population and an industrial infrastructure that Saudi Arabia can only envy. Since the 1950s, it has sought to end its dependence on oil revenues by becoming an industrial power. As a matter of fact, the last shah of Iran, obviously overestimating the vitality of the Soviet economy, boasted that he would make Iran the world's fifth great military and economic power. Iranian ministers therefore argue for higher prices so that they might reap immediate profits to invest in their industrial economy of the future. This quest is not without its ironic dimension. One of the reasons Iran has been pursuing its nuclear program has been to fulfill that dream. Unfortunately for Iran, the West distrusts Iran's nuclear ambitions and slapped sanctions on that country, curtailing the sale of oil, until it puts limits on its program. The result was that Iran's revenue from oil (and natural gas) fell 47 percent in 2011–2012, the first year of the sanctions, then another 11 percent the following year.

In the end, the various oil ministers representing their countries in OPEC councils usually hammer out a deal setting out each country's production quotas. Then they return home and present the determination of that round of negotiations to their governments, which then cheat. In 2011, for example, Saudi Arabia produced 2 million barrels/day over quota.

In spite of attempts at price fixing, the complaint by Western politicians and consumers that they are being held hostage by a greedy cartel is a little like Claude Rains in *Casablanca* discovering there is gambling going on in Humphrey Bogart's nightclub. Before 1973, a cartel of Western oil companies known as the "seven sisters"—Exxon (Standard Oil of New Jersey), Mobil (Standard Oil of New York), Chevron (Standard Oil of California), Gulf, Texaco, and British Petroleum (Anglo-Iranian Oil Company)—controlled all aspects of the oil industry. Because of the importance of oil for national economies, the cartel could count on the support of Western governments in their negotiations or confrontations with their hosts. Thus, in 1951, when the Iranian government had the temerity to nationalize the holdings of the Anglo-Iranian Oil Company, the British and American governments imposed sanctions on Iran, arranged for an international boycott of Iranian oil, and organized a coup d'état that brought the Iranian government down. The oil revolution merely replaced one cartel with another—and a not particularly effective one at that. As of 2013, OPEC's market share of oil production was only about 40 percent of global production, and as new technologies, such as "fracking" (which extracts oil and natural gas from shale) and new sources, such as Alberta, Canada's "tar sands" deposits (sand and clay drenched in oil) come on line, that share is bound to decline even further. In 2013 Russia produced more oil than Saudi Arabia, which produced 30 percent of OPEC oil, and it was estimated that a year later the United States would overcome both as the world's largest producer. The incentive to prevent fracking from becoming economically viable was, perhaps, one of the reasons Saudi Arabia's pumps worked overtime.

Nevertheless, the decade of the 1970s seemed to mark the beginning of a new era for both the Middle East and the rest of the world. Fernand Braudel, the great French historian, speculated at that time that the oil revolution might be epoch-making because it would reverse the flow of wealth from the East to the West that had been ongoing for two centuries. From the Middle Ages through the eighteenth century, he wrote, wealth flowed from west to east as the value of goods Europeans bought from the East—spices, silks, etc.—exceeded the value of goods bought by the peoples of the East from Europeans. Beginning in the eighteenth century and continuing through the first three-quarters of the twentieth, the value of goods the peoples of the East bought from the West—mostly finished products—exceeded the value of goods the peoples of the West bought from the East. It was entirely feasible, Braudel surmised, that the oil revolution would herald the beginning of an epoch in which the flow of riches would be reversed once again.

Four decades later, it is clear that the effects of the oil revolution have not been as epoch-making as, for example, the European discovery of the Americas or the onset of the industrial revolution. Middle Eastern oil producers and Western oil consumers are not two adversaries locked in combat. They are more akin to codependents locked in an uneasy embrace. The Middle Eastern oil producers must sell their oil. The West must buy it. Hence, in spite of the continued animosity between the United States and Iraq in the aftermath of the 1991 Gulf War, and in spite of the fact that the United States continued to enforce sanctions on the regime in Baghdad, the United States was the biggest consumer of the oil that the Iraqi government was permitted to sell. Large sums of money from the West did go to the Middle East, but much of it returned to the West as investments or was deposited in Western banks, where it was "recycled." In other words, no dramatic change took place in the relative positions of the West and the Middle East as a result of the oil revolution. In fact, oil has had much the same effect on the twentieth-century Middle East as had cotton on nineteenth-century Egypt. Both reinforced a pattern of trade that has been favorable to the West.

This is not to say that the oil revolution brought no changes to the region. Rather, it is to say that the changes brought about by the oil revolution have mainly affected economic, political, and social life within the Middle East itself. For example, as discussed in Chapter 15, access to rent has sustained governments in the region and has given them an unprecedented ability to control and direct their states. What this has meant for the region is, however, controversial. Some political scientists argue that an overdependence upon rent is actually the Achilles heel of Middle Eastern governments. They assert that governments in the region have been dangerously dependent on the international market or on the goodwill of foreign governments. If those sources of revenues dry up—if, for example, the price of oil plummets or foreign governments cut off aid—states have no safety net to make up the shortfall. Because citizens of rent-dependent states are bound to their governments in the same way that clients are bound to patrons, they maintain, once the subsidies or jobs or welfare benefits dry up, the bond connecting them may very well break. It was for this very reason that soon after the outbreak of the Arab uprisings of 2010–2011, the Saudi Arabian government offered Saudi citizens a particularly generous bonus package to keep them quiet. Citizens received walking-around money worth $130 billion in the form of sixty thousand new government jobs, a raise in the public sector minimum wage, bonuses for state employees, half a million new housing units, and personal debt relief.

On the other hand, the effectiveness of such expenditures is hardly guaranteed: On the eve of the most turbulent protests that broke out in a monarchy in 2011—the uprising in Bahrain—the king announced an unprecedented lump-sum payment of $2,650 to every Bahraini family. The protests not only continued; they escalated. Historians in the past "discovered" the roots of the French Revolution in the rise of bread prices, thereby reducing the Parisians who stormed the Bastille to laboratory rats who respond impulsively to stimuli rather than treating them as humans who can weigh options and make choices. It would

Wealth from oil revenues financed this housing project in Baghdad. (*From: Fondation Arabe pour l'image, Beirut.*)

be unfortunate to make the same mistake about the inhabitants of the contemporary Middle East.

In addition to affecting individual states in the Middle East, there is a regional dimension to the oil revolution as well. In the wake of the revolution, the lines dividing rich from poor states in the region became more tightly drawn. The former states export oil. The latter states export labor to the oil-producing nations. In 1968, for example, no more than ten thousand Egyptians worked abroad. Within ten years that number increased to over half a million. Between 1973 and 1985, one-third of all rural Egyptian men worked at some time during their lives in the Gulf. During the same period, 40 percent of the Jordanian workforce was abroad.

As a result of this export of labor, the labor-exporting states have become increasingly dependent on remittances—money sent home by expatriate laborers employed abroad—to ease their financial burdens. Remittances are a peculiar form of rent. They go to individuals and families, not to governments. For this reason, some political scientists argue that remittances actually weaken the governments of labor-exporting states by lessening the dependence of the citizenry on them for economic favors. Again, this view is not undisputed. Skeptics maintain that the export of labor has an entirely different effect. For example, it may act as a safety valve in states where population growth and the spread of education have far outpaced economic opportunities. Furthermore, remittances add to states' coffers. They increase the revenue from import duties: Returning guest workers and their families provide non-oil-producing states with a steady income from their purchases of Toyota pickups, Sony television sets, and Chinese knockoff jeans. They also provide states with foreign exchange.

Like the uneven distribution of oil, the export of labor has had regional political effects as well. Since remittances have become an important source of supplementary income for the states that export labor, the threat that labor importers will expel guest workers can be a potent tool in their hands to exact concessions from their labor-exporting neighbors. Sometimes, labor-importing nations have moved beyond merely making threats. On the eve of the 1991 Gulf War, Iraq expelled one million Egyptian workers. Egypt was a member of the Gulf War coalition. After the war, Kuwait expelled upward of seventy thousand Palestinians whom they accused of acting as a fifth column for the Iraqis. Not to be outdone by their smaller neighbor, Saudi Arabia expelled one million Yemeni guest workers the same year to protest Yemen's support for Iraq. Labor migration has thus further strengthened the hand of labor importers in the regional balance of power.

Labor migration has also affected social life throughout the region. For example, the employment of male workers in the Persian Gulf has led to what one Egyptian sociologist has called the "feminization of the Egyptian family" and a shift in women's roles there. In the absence of men, lower- and middle-class Egyptian women have become temporary heads of households, play a greater role in domestic decision making, and have built broad, community-based networks outside the home and family upon which they have come to depend. But if labor migration has created new forms of community bonds in Egypt, it has had an opposite effect in many states that import labor. There, labor migration has created cleavages between citizens who are entitled to government benefits and non-citizens who are not. As of 2013, noncitizens (from within and without the region) made up about 30 percent of the inhabitants of Saudi Arabia, about 70 percent of the inhabitants of Kuwait, about 75 percent of the inhabitants of the United Arab Emirates, and about 85 percent of the inhabitants of Qatar. While the Pakistanis and Bangladeshis who live in the impoverished Kuwaiti towns of Fuhayhil, Jahrah, Hawalli, or Kaifan, for example, provide unskilled labor for the oil-rich principality, they are shunned by the privileged minority of native-born citizens.

The social cleavages created by the presence of large numbers of guest workers in oil-rich states have done little to diminish the strength and stability of those states. Indeed, there is evidence that the guest worker phenomenon has had the opposite effect. Take the case of Qatar, a state of close to 2 million inhabitants— that is, 278,000 citizens, entitled to all the benefits that go with citizenship, and close to 1.75 million (mostly South Asian) guest workers. Guest workers have little stake in (and therefore little concern with) the political process of the states in which they work. Furthermore, they can always be replaced and their involvement in politics would lead to their deportation. It might be coincidence, but Qatar was one of only five Arab states that did not experience protests or an uprising in 2010–2011 (the UAE, with 1.6 million citizens and 6.4 million guest workers, was another).

The divide separating guest workers from citizens is not the only cleavage opened up by the oil revolution. Another has emerged as the oil-producing countries of the Gulf have had to balance the aspirations of their more Westernized citizens with the social norms of societies that had been little more than frontier territories before the contemporary period. The split between "traditionalists" and "Westernizers" often takes place within a context of a struggle pitting former elites against royal households. Tribal leaders, merchants, landowners, and ulama, claiming to represent the "traditional" values of society, often resist the policies and practices of the Westernizers. Those policies and practices, not coincidentally, would further reduce their already diminished power. On the other hand, many of the so-called Westernizing policies and practices in the smaller Gulf states are imposed from the top by kings and shaykhs. Not coincidentally, those policies and practices would increase the popularity of the central government among the more cosmopolitan elements of the population and strengthen its power.

Oil has had two further effects on the Middle East that merit mention here. First, as a result of its income from oil, the Gulf region, considered a social and cultural backwater by many in the more populous and cosmopolitan regions of the Middle East, assumed a new and important role in the inter-Arab balance of power. For example, after the 1967 Arab-Israeli War, Saudi Arabia, Kuwait, and

Libya (at that time a conservative monarchy) began paying subsidies to the so-called frontline states bordering on Israel to enable them to restock their arsenals. Because the payments were made in quarterly installments, the oil states maintained constant leverage over the foreign policies of Egypt, Jordan, and Syria.

More recently, both Qatar and Saudi Arabia have played an outsized role in the 2010–2011 uprisings. The Qatar-based news service, *al-Jazeera*, spread the news of the Tunisian and Egyptian uprisings well beyond those countries, ensuring copycat "Days of Rage" in a number of places. Qatar also sent troops to fight in Libya and, along with the UAE, deployed its air force there. Qatar has deployed its oil wealth directly as well: As of 2014, Qatar was the largest benefactor of the Syrian opposition and financed the Muslim Brotherhood government of Egypt to the tune of $8 billion before the Egyptian military staged a coup d'état against it. Saudi Arabia was just as active. It was instrumental in brokering the deal that forced the president of Yemen from power and, along with the UAE, sent forces into Bahrain to put down that uprising. It even put out feelers to integrate Morocco and Jordan into the Saudi-dominated Gulf Cooperation Council, which would have given the council regional breadth. And like Qatar, Saudi Arabia has financed the Syrian opposition and, along with Kuwait and the UAE, donated upward of $20 billion in 2013–2014 to keep the military government in Egypt afloat.

It is in Syria and Egypt where we see the possibility that the enhanced role of oil rich states in the inter-Arab balance of power might diminish as a result of contradictory policies adopted by those states, particularly Saudi Arabia and Qatar. In Syria, each country backs different proxies; in Egypt, each country has supported rival claimants to power. The Saudi/Qatari rivalry exists because regimes in each country have adopted different survival strategies in an environment in flux. Saudi Arabia is a status quo power whose sheer size and enormous wealth has enabled it to dominate the Gulf region. And with the elimination of Egypt and Iraq as major players in inter-Arab politics (at least for the time being), it has made a bid to play the dominate role in the Arab world in its entirety. Saudi Arabia does not like change and certainly does not like the sort of change brought about by the Arab uprisings. It thus took it upon itself to become the central command of counter-revolution. As part of that strategy, it has worked to destroy the transnational Muslim Brotherhood movement, which mobilizes Muslims for political participation—which, as we have seen, the Saudis wish to discourage, particularly at home. Qatar, on the other hand, has adopted the opposite strategy: Viewing the unrest throughout the Arab world as a fact of life rather than as a temporary aberration, it has sought to ride the wave of protest by supporting Muslim Brotherhood movements which have proven popular wherever they have set up franchises. It therefore decided to throw its support behind them, hoping to reap the benefits of their support in the future. Whatever else it might prove, the Saudi/Qatari rivalry demonstrates that those who assume that a Sunni/Shiʿi rivalry is the critical conflict in the region are just plain wrong. In both Saudi Arabia and Qatar the Wahhabi strain of Sunni Islam is the religion of state.

Finally, oil has made the region strategically important to outside powers, particularly the United States. Think of it this way: The United States has a historic connection to the West African country of Liberia. Liberia was founded by freed American slaves in 1822 and over the course of the nineteenth and twentieth centuries Liberia resembled an American colony, in deed if not in word. Between 1989 and 1996, Liberia experienced a bloody civil war in which a quarter of a million of its citizens died (another civil war broke out in 1999). On the other hand, the United States has no historic connection to Kuwait, which was a British protectorate until its independence in 1961. According to Amnesty International, during the Iraqi occupation of Kuwait (1990–1991), far fewer Kuwaitis—several hundred—were killed than the numbers of Liberians who perished in that country's civil wars. Yet the United States put together an international coalition and sent five hundred thousand of its own troops to liberate Kuwait. The American response to events in Liberia was tepid at best. Even after the secretary general of the United Nations personally appealed to the American administration to send peacekeeping troops to Liberia in 2003, the United States sent only a token force of two hundred marines. Kuwait is one of the world's largest producers of oil (ranked thirteenth in the world as of 2013) and is located in the midst of one of the biggest pools of oil on the planet. Even the Liberian government classifies Liberia's oil reserves as "moderate."

It would be simplistic to say the United States waged the 1991 Gulf War—or launched the 2003 invasion of Iraq—just for oil. It would also be simplistic to deny the importance of oil in the calculations of policy makers. Those calculations are a complex story, as are the interests they juggle and the policies they shape. It is for this reason they are the subject of the next chapter.

CHAPTER 17

The United States
and the Middle East

During the latter part of the cold war, an eminent historian described American-Soviet competition in the Middle East as "new wine in old bottles." What he meant by this was that the cold war struggle for influence in the region might be seen as an extension of the Eastern Question of the nineteenth century. Once again, great powers outside the Middle East intervened in the region to gain strategic advantage over their rivals. Only the cast of players and their immediate goals changed. Instead of the main actors being Great Britain, imperial Russia, and France, the main actors in the cold war drama were the United States and the Soviet Union. Instead of great powers defining their interests in terms of protecting their route to India or seeking warm water ports, the great powers defined them in terms of a struggle between rival ideological systems locked in a titanic contest for the future of the world. Each viewed their competition in the Middle East as just one more front in that contest.

As we have seen, historians debate the exact date of the end of the cold war (1989? 1991?), and the road to the much heralded "New World Order" proved to be quite a bit bumpier than many had expected. Nevertheless, the world in which we currently live is a world defined by the defeat of the Soviet Union in the cold war by the United States and its allies. It is also a world in which the United States has held a dominant position in international affairs. For these reasons, this chapter is written from the standpoint of the sole remaining superpower, the United States.

Even before the end of the cold war, the United States proved itself to be the dominant superpower in the Middle East. As Anwar al-Sadat put it when he switched Egypt from the Soviet to the American camp in the early 1970s, the United States held "99% of the cards in the region." The United States owed its dominance to a number of factors: the alliance system it built and maintained throughout the cold war, its unique ability to advance a negotiated settlement between Israel and its neighbors based on the land-for-peace formula, and its willingness to set aside its values when dealing with Middle East autocrats so long as they looked after

American interests. Interestingly, the United States continued to approach the region in the same way even after the end of the cold war.

American engagement with the Middle East is a recent phenomenon. Before World War II, the Middle East held little interest for the United States government. This is not to say that private citizens and nongovernmental groups ignored the region. Ever since the first governor of the Massachusetts colony, John Winthrop, called on colonizers to make their new home a "city on the hill," this image has resonated with Americans. Accordingly, over the course of American history, many Americans have felt a special affinity for that original city on the hill, located in the "Holy Land." American missionaries and travelers went to the region to save souls and survey sites from the Bible. They also founded schools and hospitals. In 1866, American missionaries established the Syrian Protestant College, now known as the American University in Beirut. Its motto was, and continues to be, "That they might have life and have it in abundance." In other words, American missionaries assumed the burden of bringing civilization and progress to the site of Christianity's birth—a site that, after the rise of Islam and centuries of "Turkish" rule, they believed had fallen on hard times.

The American government did undertake the occasional and desultory diplomatic and even military foray into the region before the cold war. Thomas Jefferson sent a naval squadron to "the shores of Tripoli" (in present-day Libya) after a local potentate declared war on America. The trouble began when the frugal president balked at paying the protection money his predecessors had paid to prevent the potentate's pirate ships from attacking American merchant vessels. Jefferson's successor, James Madison, followed suit, only this time sending a

"A little piece of home": American University in Beirut, 1920. (*From: The Collection of the author.*)

Vignette

From Basra, Iraq to Mecca, California

Before there were Hershey Bars (invented 1900), Americans satisfied their sweet tooth with dates imported from eastern Arabia and Basra. As a matter of fact, over the course of the nineteenth century, America became the world's most lucrative market for the sticky fruit. One particular variety of date, called *fardh*, was an immediate hit with merchants and consumers alike. Merchants liked it because it could withstand the rigors of the one-hundred-day voyage from the Persian Gulf to America. Consumers liked it because it ripened in August, earlier than dates from cooler climes. The arrival of dates in New York thus coincided with the onset of the winter holiday season. And just as the Macy's Thanksgiving Day Parade now signals the beginning of our holiday season, the arrival of dates came to signal the same then.

Over the course of the century, sail gave way to steam, and with the opening of the Suez Canal, the one-hundred-day voyage gave way to a voyage that lasted sixty. This meant that later-ripening "golden dates" from Basra were now available to complement Thanksgiving Day meals. Then, something was added to make America's date-craving even sweeter: a competition. In 1899, shipping companies began competing with each other in an annual "date race" to see whose ship would arrive in New York first. American newspapers followed the progress of the ships steaming from Basra. At stake was not only bragging rights and a prize, but higher prices in a date-deprived market. In combination, the excitement of the date race, increased urbanization, an expanding consumer culture, and the domestication and commercialization of the fall/winter holidays resulted in a sevenfold increase in American date imports from 1885 to 1925.

---

squadron to Algiers. Rather than warships, Abraham Lincoln sent a brace of pistols as a gift to ʿAbd al-Qadir al-Jazaʾiri, the former Algerian resistance leader who, while in exile in Damascus, had intervened to protect Christians during the 1860 sectarian riots there. Lincoln also signed a treaty of commerce and navigation with the Ottoman Empire at a time when much of the world was unsure that there would be a United States for much longer. When a Moroccan bandit, Ahmad al-Rasuli, kidnapped an American businessman, Ion Pericardis, Theodore Roosevelt won public acclaim by storming, "Pericardis alive or Rasuli dead." While Roosevelt was strutting around with his "big stick," the Moroccan government quietly paid Rasuli the ransom he demanded. And during and immediately after World War I, U.S. presidents and Congress weighed in on the Armenian massacres and Zionism (they deplored the former, supported the latter). Overall, however, when it came to foreign policy, the interest of the U.S. government lay outside the region. The Middle East—that is, the Ottoman Empire—was, after all, part of the concert of Europe throughout much of the nineteenth century. The United States thus let Europeans deal with Middle Eastern problems.

Even when the U.S. government stepped in to protect American oil interests in the Gulf from the "rapacity" of British and French oilmen during the interwar period, it was with the idea that others—the French and particularly

There was a disturbing feature to the global trade in dates, however. Date farming is labor-intensive. Date palms need irrigation and pollination, for example. The first was done with primitive technology. The second was done by hand. Adding into the mix harvesting and packing, the date industry required a large workforce. It is ironic that the expansion of date exports, fueled by a modern world economy, encouraged the expansion of one of the oldest systems of labor: slavery. The labor of enslaved Africans was integral to satisfying America's sweet tooth.

Global trade sowed the seeds (so to speak) of the date trade's expansion and it sowed the seeds of its demise. In 1902, representatives from the United States Department of Agriculture began sending seedlings and offshoots of date palms home from the Persian Gulf. The USDA determined that the Salton Basin of California (where the Mecca of the title is located) held the most promise for their planting, and a little over a decade later a visitor estimated that the basin contained about 200,000 date palms. By the 1920s, American date production had taken off, throwing the Persian Gulf date economy into a tailspin.

And there was more to come. There was a second commodity that linked the nineteenth-century Persian Gulf to the world economy: pearls. Pearl diving, done in large measure by slaves, was a centuries-old tradition in coastal communities. In 1896, a Japanese noodle-shop owner named Kokichi Mikimoto perfected a method of creating artificial pearls. Between 1908 and 1911, his "cultured pearls" hit international markets. The Persian Gulf pearl industry collapsed alongside the date industry. Neither recovered.

(From the work of Matthew S. Hopper)

the British—had the primary imperial responsibility for the area. Only after World War II did American policy makers work to replace the old imperialist powers in the region. It was not until after 1956, in the wake of the Suez War, that the United States accomplished this, finally replacing France and Britain as the primary Western power in the region.

Surprisingly, American policy with regard to the Middle East remained fairly stable throughout most of the second half of the twentieth century. This can be seen by comparing a policy statement made at the beginning of the cold war with one made toward its end. In July 1954, the National Security Council sent to President Dwight D. Eisenhower a report entitled "United States Objectives and Policies with Respect to the Near East." Under the section titled "Objectives," the report lists the following:

a. Availability to the United States and its allies of the resources, the strategic position, and the passage rights of the area and the denial of such resources and strategic positions to the Soviet bloc.

b. Stable, viable, friendly governments in the area, capable of withstanding communist-inspired subversion from within and willing to resist communist aggression.

   c. Settlement of major issues between the Arab states and Israel as a foundation for establishing peace and order in the area.
   d. Reversal of the anti-American trends of Arab opinion.
   e. Prevention of the extension of Soviet influence in the area.
   f. Wider recognition in the free world of the legitimate aspiration of the countries in the area to be recognized as, and have the status of, sovereign states; and wider recognition by such countries of their responsibility toward the area and toward the free world generally.

In April 1981, Peter Constable, deputy assistant secretary of state for Near East and South Asian affairs in the administration of Ronald Reagan, testified before Congress "to provide an integrated picture of our policies toward the Middle East and Persian Gulf region." He listed the fundamental American objectives in the region as promoting the security of friends, assuring the security and availability of resources, and protecting vital transportation and communications routes. Constable then identified three "threats and challenges." First and foremost was Soviet expansion, both direct and indirect. Constable's testimony took place two years after the Soviet invasion of Afghanistan. The second threat to American interests was regional disputes and conflicts that jeopardized regional stability and provided fertile opportunities for external (Soviet) exploitation. Although a number of conflicts—the Lebanese Civil War, Iran vs. Iraq, Ethiopia vs. Somalia, and so on—posed a danger in American eyes, Constable focused much of his remarks on the Arab-Israeli conflict. Constable stated that "deep divisions and unresolved issues . . . will continue to affect United States interests, relationships, and objectives until they can be composed on broadly accepted terms." Finally, Constable pointed to the destabilizing effects of political change, social development, and economic growth. In the age of Third World assertiveness and turbulence in Iran, it appeared that "change," "development," and "growth" did not bring stability, as policy makers had predicted they would at the onset of the cold war. They brought false hope, instability, and risk to America.

Between 1954 and 1981, and continuing through the end of the cold war, policy planners issued other pronouncements delineating American goals in the region. Although there were a few changes in the margins, most repeated pretty much the same policy objectives as the National Security Council and Peter Constable. Overall, then, we can identify six such objectives that guided American policy toward the region for over forty years.

First and foremost among American goals in the region was the containment of the Soviet Union. That is to say, the primary objective of the United States in the Middle East, as in all other areas of the cold war world, was to prevent the expansion of Soviet influence into the region. The United States had every reason to worry. The Soviet Union was located in the geographic heartland of the Eurasian continent and there was no reason to believe that its geopolitical ambitions were different from those of its predecessor, imperial Russia. As a matter of fact, the first cold war confrontation between the United States and the Soviet

Union took place in the Middle East. In 1946, the Soviet Union refused to remove its troops from northern Iran, which it had occupied during World War II. It eventually withdrew them, but only under pressure. The heartland of the Middle East became a battleground between the two superpowers as Soviet strategy shifted in the late fifties. Under Nikita Khrushchev, who led the Soviet Union in one capacity or another from 1953 to 1964, Soviet strategists sought to spread Soviet influence by leapfrogging over surrounding states into the wider world. By doing so, Soviet strategists believed they could break containment, take advantage of anti-imperialist sentiments and the Third Worldist clamor for social and economic justice, and outflank the United States without directly confronting its nuclear-armed nemesis. Thus, from 1955 onward, the Soviet Union sought out allies in the heartland of the Middle East, including the three revolutionary republics: Egypt, Syria, and Iraq.

The second goal of the United States in the Middle East was to assure Western access to oil. There are two reasons for this: economic and strategic. Access to oil for domestic consumption was, of course, a major concern for American policy planners for many years. At the beginning of the cold war, however, the United States did not depend on the Middle East for its oil. As a matter of fact, in the 1950s the international oil market was so glutted that President Eisenhower imposed import quotas to protect oil companies from falling prices. It was only in 1969 that the United States began importing crude oil from the region for domestic consumption. By the time of the oil crisis of 1973, the United States was importing more than a third of its oil from the Middle East. Subsequently, imports from the Middle East have been deliberately reduced: As of 2013, only 25 percent of imported oil came from the Middle East (i.e., the Persian Gulf and North Africa)—about 9 percent of America's total energy supply. Canada remains America's largest source for imported oil.

But if oil for domestic consumption was not an immediate concern for the United States at the onset of the cold war, oil as a strategic commodity was. After World War II, the United States sustained European and Japanese economic recovery with cheap Middle Eastern oil. The United States viewed economic recovery in those regions as essential to prevent social revolutions—communist revolutions. American policy makers have viewed oil as a strategic commodity ever since. As of 2013, Europe still imported about 39 percent of its oil from the Middle East; Japan imported about 83 percent.

The third goal of American policy in the Middle East was to ensure the peaceful resolution of conflicts and to maintain a balance of power in the region. The U.S. government feared that interstate conflicts—most of all the Arab-Israeli conflict—would polarize the region. This would encourage some states to turn to the Soviet Union (always the second-best option for Middle Eastern states during the cold war) and might destabilize the governments of America's friends. The best way to ensure stability in the region was to establish some sort of regional balance of power. During the Truman administration, the United States and its allies agreed to coordinate arms sales to Israel and surrounding Arab states to make sure neither side would have a clear advantage. After that policy broke down (no one bothered consulting the Soviets), most American policy makers sought to assure peace by keeping Israel at least as strong as the sum total of its potential adversaries. American policy makers also sought to establish a balance of power in the Gulf. As a result, the United States "tilted" toward Iraq during the Iran-Iraq War and, three years after the war ended, led a coalition against Iraq in the Gulf War.

To ensure regional stability, the United States promoted stable, if autocratic, pro-Western states in the region. In addition, policy makers believed that if the states of the region were strong, and if they fulfilled the aspirations of their populations, they and their populations would resist Soviet blandishments. At first, American policy makers defined popular aspirations in terms of anti-imperialism, nationalism, and economic development. Thus, in the immediate aftermath of World War II, the United States encouraged decolonization wherever the Soviets couldn't take advantage in the region but hedged where they might. Thus, when the British announced their "East of Suez" policy (that is, their withdrawal from all bases east of the Suez Canal Zone by 1971) and their plan to grant independence to their weak Gulf protectorates, the United States offered to assume the burden of paying for Britain's colonial infrastructure if only the British remained (they left). What made the United States skittish was the establishment of the pro-Soviet People's Democratic Republic of Yemen four years earlier and the outbreak of a Marxist rebellion in Oman. For the most part, however, the United States saw which way the tides of history were flowing. And it did not hurt that decolonization upset the system of "imperial preferences," whereby colonial powers had privileged access to colonial markets, and opened up those markets to American business.

In order to ensure the newly independent states would follow the proper path to "modernization," state department officials, policy planners, and Central Intelligence Agency spooks often supported the "modernizing" military officers who took power in military coups d'état. Military men were uniquely qualified to lead, they felt, because they knew how to work as a cohesive group, were more technologically savvy and better trained than most others in the region, and were already in the coercion business, in accordance with their job description—meaning they could get results when dismantling the "feudal" and "corrupt" "traditional order." The annals of contemporary Middle Eastern history are thus filled with stories—some probably fabricated—of ambassadors giving winks and nods to colonels and CIA agents distributing suitcases of money to local politicians and military officers who understood what was required of them. According to a number of accounts, the United States was responsible for the first post–World War II coup d'état in the Arab world which overthrew an elected government in Syria in 1949. Soon thereafter (again according to unverified accounts), American officials began meeting with a group of officers in Egypt, including Gamal ʿAbd al-Nasser, to let them know the United States would not be averse to their taking power. And to ensure Nasser stayed bought, they attempted to bribe him with $6 million (he took the bribe, which he disdainfully used to build the Cairo Tower to mock the Americans, but he did not stay bought).

Since stability and anti-communism were high on the American agenda, however, the United States (and its allies) also intervened to support monarchs threatened by real or imagined communist subversion. The British intervened in Oman and Jordan in the 1950s to put down anti-government movements, but the story with the most resonance was the Anglo-American-backed coup d'état that brought down a democratically elected government in Iran. Muhammad Mossadegh became prime minister of Iran in 1951 soon after the Iranian *majlis* (parliament) had voted to nationalize the British-held Anglo-Iranian Oil Company, an act he strongly supported. He also pledged to restrict the power of the shah (Muhammad Reza Pahlavi, the son of Reza Shah) and affirm Iran's neutrality in the cold war. The nationalization infuriated the British; that nationalization, Mossadegh's neutralism in the cold war (a policy he called "negative equilibrium"), and rumors of possible communist influence over Mossadegh disquieted the Americans. The shah's attempt to dismiss Mossadegh backfired, and huge anti-shah demonstrations forced the shah to flee. Nevertheless, the United States and Britain spread around enough largesse to buy their own crowds, along with the right politicians, religious leaders, and generals. The army seized control, arrested Mossadegh, and restored the shah. For American participation in the coup d'état, American oil companies won the right to 40 percent of Iranian oil. The American and British countercoup entered Iranian historical memory and provided proof positive of a legacy of Western—particularly American—perfidy during the 1978–1979 Iranian Revolution.

To further strengthen states and prevent social revolution, the United States also supported the economic development in the region, acting both as a contributor of foreign assistance and as an advocate in international economic institutions such as the World Bank. As was the trend during the 1950s, development experts often encouraged the construction of colossal projects which they believed would provide the magic bullet for economic development. From 1953 to 1955, for example, the Eisenhower administration sent Eric Johnston, the former head of the Motion Picture Association, to the Middle East to negotiate a comprehensive plan for dividing the waters of the Jordan River among Israel, Lebanon, Jordan, and Syria. Johnston's efforts failed, as did all American peace-through-economic-development schemes proposed during the 1950s and 1960s. (A Jordanian government official actually told the American ambassador there, "We've been impoverished for a thousand years. Rather than making peace with Israel, we'll be impoverished for another thousand.")

Although the United States replaced Britain and France as the dominant outside power in the Middle East in the wake of the Suez War, it soon found its ambitions in the region threatened by the very anti-imperialism and nationalism it had sought to channel. The United States had supported Nasser and the Free Officers in Egypt in 1952, but by 1958 Secretary of State John Foster Dulles was referring to Nasser as "nothing but a tinhorn Hitler." In the wake of the 1958 coup d'état in Iraq that toppled a pro-Western monarchy, the United States placed itself in opposition to Nasser and the pan-Arab nationalism Nasser personified. About a decade and a half later, when the United States perceived "excessive" economic nationalism to be a direct threat to its national security, it did the same with state-guided economic development. By the close of the cold war, the United States, once again in conjunction with the international financial institutions it dominated, was preaching the message that economic growth and political stability could only be achieved in the Middle East if states would liberalize their economies and give vent to private initiative. "Neoliberalism" had replaced "modernization" as the mantra of economists.

The fifth goal of American policy during the cold war was the preservation of the independence and territorial integrity of the State of Israel. The American-Israeli alliance did not begin immediately. The decision made by President Truman to recognize Israel in 1948 was by no means a sure thing. Policy planners feared that the partition of Palestine would lead to a bloodbath that would divert American troops and attention away from Europe. They also feared that U.S. recognition of Israel would jeopardize American relations with the Arab world and thus jeopardize European and Japanese economic recovery. When President Truman announced at a closed-door meeting with policy makers that he planned to endorse partition, Secretary of State George Marshall stated, "Mr. President, if you proceed with that position, in the next election I will vote against you." Eight years later, Eisenhower was so outraged by Israel's participation alongside Britain and France in the Suez War that he threatened economic retaliation if Israel did not withdraw from Egyptian territory. It was not until John F. Kennedy that an American president used the word "ally" when referring to Israel.

Nevertheless, the United States has consistently reaffirmed its commitment to Israeli sovereignty and security. Numerous factors contributed to the American-Israeli alliance, from ideological to strategic to domestic. In terms of ideology, the Israelis have presented their case well in the United States, portraying Israel as the sole democracy and repository of American values in the region. In terms of strategy, U.S. policy makers oftentimes viewed Israel as a proxy in the fight against Soviet influence in the region. In terms of domestic politics, presidents and congressmen have attempted to garner Jewish—and, more recently, Christian evangelical—votes by portraying themselves as supporters of Israel. None of this means, however, that the American-Israeli relationship has been trouble-free, or that the United States has agreed with Israel across the board on such issues as borders, Israeli settlement policies in the occupied territories, approaches to ending the Arab-Israeli conflict, or the status of Jerusalem.

The final objective of American policy during the cold war was the protection of sea lanes, lines of communications, and the like, connecting the United States and Europe with Asia. The Middle East is, after all, the *middle* East. Its geographic position alone makes it a prize worth fighting for by any power with global pretensions.

In the most abstract sense, then, American objectives in the Middle East—containing the Soviet Union, maintaining access to oil, achieving a peaceful resolution of conflicts and a balance of power among states of the region, safeguarding Israel, and capitalizing on the strategic location of the region—remained consistent over the course of the forty-year cold war. Why, then, does it appear to have been otherwise?

There are several reasons why U.S. policy appears to have been inconsistent. First of all, although American administrations faithfully advocated the same six policy objectives for forty years, the approaches the American government used to achieve them varied over time. For example, over the course of the cold war there were two main strategies of containment: peripheral containment and strong-point containment. The idea behind peripheral containment was to ring the Soviet Union with an unbroken string of pro-American states linked together through a system of alliances. This seemed the appropriate response to Soviet expansion across its borders during the early cold war period.

While the most famous and most successful of these alliances was the North Atlantic Treaty Organization (NATO), there were others. In 1955, for example, the British organized the "Baghdad Pact," made up of Britain, Turkey, Iraq, Pakistan, and Iran. The pact was a failure. Because Egypt and Iraq were locked in a rivalry for leadership of the Arab world throughout much of the cold war, Egypt opposed it. The Egyptians signed an arms deal with the Soviet-bloc state of Czechoslovakia in 1955, thus rendering the alliance irrelevant. After military officers deposed the Iraqi monarchy in 1958, Iraq withdrew from the alliance anyway. All that was left was an empty shell called the Central Treaty Organization (CENTO), made up of the remaining states. In all, the Baghdad Pact and CENTO proved as effective in preventing the spread of Soviet influence in the Middle East as SEATO (Southeast Asia Treaty Organization) did in Southeast Asia.

With the failure of peripheral containment in regions outside Europe, American policy makers adopted the strategy of strong-point containment. Strong-point containment called for the judicious strengthening of a few "fortress" allies in various regions. It was hoped that this would prevent the Soviets from projecting their power abroad through proxy states bound to the Soviet Union by treaty. The United States chose its fortress states on the basis of the strength of their economies or militaries or governments. Thus, during the 1970s the United States came to depend on Israel in the western Middle East to prevent the Soviets from using their Syrian ally to spread their influence. In the eastern Middle East, the United States depended on the Iranian government (and, to a lesser extent, Saudi Arabia) to prevent the Soviets from using Iraq in the same way. While successful in the short term, strong-point containment in the Middle East ultimately contributed to disastrous consequences for the United States in the region: the Iranian Revolution of 1978–1979 and the Israeli invasion of Lebanon in 1982.

The containment of the Soviet Union was one policy goal that might be achieved in multiple ways. The preservation of the independence and territorial integrity of the State of Israel was another. During the cold war, some policy makers believed that this goal could be achieved by regarding Israel as a "strategic asset," a phrase coined during the Reagan administration. Another approach was expressed in the title of an article written in 1977 by that embodiment of the pipe-smoking American foreign policy establishment, George Ball. The article was entitled "How to Save Israel in Spite of Herself." According to Ball, Israel's long-term security depends on a settlement of the Arab-Israeli dispute and good relations with its neighbors. Israeli intransigence not only prolongs the atmosphere of hostility, but undermines the governments of moderate neighbors, such as Jordan, which have nothing to show for their moderation. Therefore, if the United States truly has Israel's best interests at heart, it should adopt a more "evenhanded approach" and drag Israel, kicking and screaming if need be, to the bargaining table to negotiate a fair peace. Needless to say, successive Israeli governments and their supporters in the United States have had problems with Ball's approach.

A second reason why U.S. cold war policy in the region seems inconsistent is that policy planners often attempted to achieve one objective at the expense of others. In 1969, on his way home from a trip to Asia, President Richard Nixon stopped on the island of Guam and held a press conference at which he alluded to what would become known as the Nixon Doctrine. The United States was, at that time, embroiled in Vietnam and was looking for ways to avoid similar entanglements in the future. According to the Nixon Doctrine, the United States would give support to regional surrogates engaged in the fight against international communism without itself deploying forces. The idea was to put teeth in the words of Nixon's predecessor, Lyndon Baines Johnson, who announced (falsely as it turned out), "We are not about to send American boys nine or ten thousand miles away from home to do what Asian boys ought to be doing for themselves." Soon thereafter, OPEC decided to raise oil prices. While this sent shivers down the spines of many policy makers (at least those who had spines) and touched off America's mano a mano struggle with the Third World, others saw an upside to the price rise. Price increases would allow America's regional surrogates (particularly Iran) to use their newly acquired wealth to buy the American weapons that, in turn, would enable them to block Soviet and Iraqi ambitions in the Gulf. In this case, containment trumped oil.

U.S. policy also seems to have been inconsistent because of what might be termed "the law of unintended consequences." When formulating and implementing Middle East policy, the United States does not operate in a vacuum. For every move the United States made in the Middle East, the Soviets and local actors could be expected to make a countermove—very often an unexpected countermove—thereby forcing the United States to reevaluate its tactical or strategic approach.

Moves that the United States made not only affected individual states; they frequently had effects—often unintended—on the regional balance of power. Although Jimmy Carter was widely applauded for his role in mediating the Camp

David Accords between Israel and Egypt, the accords had consequences none of the negotiators could have anticipated. After Egypt signed a peace treaty with Israel, it was expelled from the Arab League. This left Iraq as the dominant force in the inter-Arab balance of power. Many political scientists argue that Iraq invaded Iran in 1980 to consolidate its hegemonic position in the Gulf. Many also trace the Israeli invasion of Lebanon in 1982 to Camp David. With its southern border with Egypt secure, the Israelis felt free to go after the PLO, which was based in Lebanon, and destroy the organization which was hampering Israeli attempts to pacify the West Bank once and for all. It is doubtful that the Israeli government would have committed itself to this adventure had it not believed that Egypt would abide by the peace treaty it signed. Add to the mix the assassination of Anwar al-Sadat, which came about as a direct or indirect result of Camp David (depending on whom you ask), and the handshake on the White House lawn loses much of its luster.

Finally, U.S. policy during the cold war appears to have been inconsistent because even a superpower does not have a boundless capacity to impose its will on the world, and failures prompted the reassessment of policies. As successive American administrations learned from attempts to move Israelis and Arabs to the bargaining table, to impose unpopular economic policies in Egypt, or to build a viable state in Lebanon, the American ability to direct events or reconstruct states in its own image is, at best, limited.

Consistent or not, was American policy in the region successful during the cold war? Before the events of 11 September 2001, former National Security Council member William Quandt wrote a number of articles arguing that it was. Quandt compared the costs of U.S. policy in the region with the benefits the United States derived from that policy. According to his tally, U.S. policy in the Middle East was far more successful than United States policy in many other parts of the world. During the forty-year cold war, approximately five hundred Americans lost their lives in service to their country in the Middle East. Almost half that number were American servicemen killed in a single incident in Beirut in 1983. Compare that figure with the number of Americans killed in ten years (1965–1975) in Southeast Asia—over fifty thousand. And America was far more successful in achieving its objectives in the Middle East than in Southeast Asia. Of its six policy objectives, the United States clearly accomplished five (containment, oil, stable states, Israel, sea lanes and communications) and split on one (the United States was not able to end regional conflicts, particularly the Arab-Israeli dispute, but for the most part was able to maintain a regional balance of power). All this, for a mere expenditure of an estimated $150 to $200 billion over forty years. (This figure apparently includes the $6 million bribe allegedly paid by the U.S. government to Gamal ʿAbd al-Nasser.) In terms of current value, it is less than half the amount spent by the United States to wage the futile Vietnam War. Holding the expenditures in blood and treasure against the results the United States gained from those expenditures, it might be said that Americans got "more bang for the buck" (to borrow a phrase from the Eisenhower administration) from their involvement in the Middle East during the cold war than from probably any other region in the world.

Quandt does qualify his triumphalism a bit. He does not ignore the fact that American policy in the region had its share of disasters and near-disasters during the cold war. In the first category we might include the inability of the United States to foresee or deal effectively with the Iranian Revolution. In the latter category, we might include the narrowly averted nuclear confrontation with the Soviet Union that occurred at the tail end of the 1973 Arab-Israeli War. Quandt is also conscious of the fact that his cost/benefit analysis weighs success in American terms and takes no account of the effects of American policy on the region itself. The United States has achieved its goals by supporting truly appalling regimes, for example, and U.S. policy has inflicted its own share of horrors on the population of the region as well. American weapons have been used against civilian populations in Lebanon in 1982 and in the Palestinian territories to this very day. The United States cynically abandoned Palestinians and Lebanese to their fate in 1983, the Kurds to theirs in 1975 and 1988, and the Shi'is of southern Iraq to theirs in 1991. The United States pressured regimes in the region to adopt economic policies that have, more often than not, brought hardship rather than benefit to the populations of the Middle East. These effects might be more easily brushed away as unfortunate side effects of an otherwise successful U.S. policy were it not for their human cost, the legacy they left for the region and the world, and the disjuncture between American claims of benevolence and a reality obvious to those affected by that "benevolence."

FINDING A NEW BEGINNING

When Barack Obama became president in 2009, the prevailing view among his foreign policy staff was that the United States had expended far too much time and effort on Middle East issues during the administration of his predecessor, George W. Bush, and far too little time and effort on Asia which, they believed, would be the epicenter of global competition in the twenty-first century. The Obama administration therefore decided to "pivot" its attention from the Middle East to Asia. Unfortunately for policy planners, developments in the former region—from winding-down wars in Afghanistan and Iraq and the campaign against al-Qaeda and its allies to the ongoing Israel-Palestine conflict and the Arab uprisings and their aftereffects—made the pivot impossible. If anything, American policy makers expended as much attention on the region during the Obama administration as they had during the previous administration. Obama even launched another war in the region against the Islamic State.

While the pivot was not practicable, Obama's instincts were at least reasonable. As we have seen, the Middle East became a focal point of American foreign policy during the cold war and that policy was, for the most part, shaped by that conflict. With the end of the cold war, the overarching goal of American foreign policy—containing the Soviet Union and curbing its influence—was no longer necessary, and American policy toward the region had to shift in tandem. The question was how.

In the immediate aftermath of the collapse of the Soviet Union, some foreign policy analysts argued for a continuation of the policies that had brought the United States victory in the cold war and "success" in the region. Those policies fell under the broad rubric of what political scientists call "realism." Realists believe in two fundamental principles. First, states are not driven by ideals; they are driven by self-interest. Hence, American support for authoritarian regimes in the Middle East during the cold war even while presidents and secretaries of state preached democracy and human rights elsewhere. Second, realists believe that the international system can only attain stability when competing states achieve a balance of power among themselves, and that it is the duty of wise policy makers to pursue such a balance. Hence, the policy of containment during the cold war: The goal of containment was to keep the Soviet Union and its influence in check, not to destroy it or roll it back in Eastern Europe. To be sure, the United States competed with the Soviet Union for influence, but that competition took place on the periphery of the Soviet empire.

Soon after the end of the cold war, President George H.W. Bush announced the emergence of a New World Order. Although his successor, Bill Clinton, focused mainly on domestic issues, when it came to foreign policy he was, for the most part, on the same page as his predecessor. The New World Order stood on three pillars. First, realism. For example, when Iraq invaded Kuwait in 1990, the United States went to war to liberate the kingdom because, it was argued, regional stability, the international order, and vital American interests were at stake. But once it had accomplished that goal, the United States did not attempt to democratize Iraq, nor did it offer assistance to anti-government rebels who sought to oust Iraqi president Saddam Hussein. The second pillar upon which the New World Order stood was multilateralism. Whenever possible, the United States would work with other governments to achieve mutual foreign policy goals, sharing costs and responsibilities. This, too, was a continuation of the cold war policy that led the United States and its European allies to join in a united front against Moscow by creating NATO. Thus, in 1991 the United States, backed by a United Nations resolution, put together a coalition of thirty-two countries to dislodge Iraq from its unfortunate neighbor. Finally, policy makers adopted "globalization" as the official buzzword of the New World Order. With the rout of the Third World in the 1980s and the fall of the "iron curtain" at the end of the decade, neoliberalism—the concept underlying a world economy in which capital, goods, and labor would be interconnected in a truly global network of trade—would reign supreme.

Continuing cold war policies was one option that the United States might choose after the collapse of the Soviet Union. There was, however, another. Why not take advantage of America's uncontested hegemony to reconstruct the world according to an American blueprint? The more ideologically motivated of these anti-realists came to be known as neoconservatives. Neoconservatives might be

considered the descendants of those who put neoliberalism and the global pursuit of individual human rights—for whatever reasons—on the international
agenda in the 1970s or, going even further back, Woodrow Wilson who entered
World War I to "make the world safe for democracy." They were an eclectic group:
There were conservative Democrats who pushed for a stronger defense and took
up causes—freedom for Soviet dissidents and the right of Jews to emigrate from
the Soviet Union—that highlighted the totalitarian nature of America's adversary. There were former Marxist-Jewish intellectuals who felt the sting of the
Left's abandonment of Israel as well as its infatuation with hot-button domestic
programs like affirmative action. There were intellectuals inspired by University of Chicago–based philosopher Leo Strauss, whose philosophy challenged
moral relativism and championed a special role for intellectual elites in making
public policy.

While neoconservatism is, at best, an imprecise category, most neoconservatives hold to four principles. First, they believe that American interests are linked
to the spread of American values, such as democracy, human rights, and free
enterprise. Second, they believe that America's friends are those nations that
adhere to those values and its enemies are those that oppose them and that it is
legitimate to use force in the pursuit of policy goals. Third, like their counterparts
in the 1970s who watched with scorn as the Third World pressed its case in the
United Nations General Assembly and other venues, they believe that the United
States cannot trust international institutions, international law, or international
agreements to protect American interests. As a matter of fact, since the United
States was the uncontested superpower in the world, why should it have to?
Finally, they believe that the United States was and had to remain the sole dominant power in the world. This meant that the United States was free to do what it
wanted, where it wanted, when it wanted, regardless of whatever roadblocks
other members of the international community might put in its way. Some even
began to talk of a "benevolent American empire."

Neoconservatives had been a marginal group during the 1990s, standing off
to the sidelines bemoaning the "wimpiness" of President George H.W. Bush and
looking back on the Reagan years, with its "Mr. Gorbachev, tear down this wall,"
with nostalgia. After the al-Qaeda attacks on the United States on 9/11, however,
the neoconservatives and their enablers in the administration of George W. Bush
came to the fore. Almost immediately after the attacks, the Bush administration
announced a Global War on Terrorism. The United States invaded Afghanistan
to depose a government which sheltered al-Qaeda and its leader, Osama bin
Laden, and to track bin Laden and his associates down. Within a year of the attacks, the National Security Council issued a new set of foreign policy guidelines
that reflected the neoconservative agenda. According to the guidelines, the
United States had a right to take preemptive and unilateral action when necessary
to protect American interests. This was the so-called Bush doctrine, used to justify America's invasion and occupation of Iraq which, the administration falsely
argued, possessed weapons of mass destruction. The guidelines also stipulated

that the United States was to remain unchallengeably dominant in international affairs, and, finally, that the United States should actively promote pro-American democracies throughout the world. Hence, in 2003, Bush announced his "Freedom Agenda" to accomplish just that so that the United States might "drain the swamp where terrorism breeds."

Applying these three policy goals across the board was not unproblematic. If one wants success in the Global War on Terrorism, for example, one cannot be too choosy about one's allies. Hence, the Bush administration abandoned the "Freedom Agenda" whenever it felt it counterproductive. For example, Egypt's peace treaty with Israel was unpopular among the Egyptian population, so the United States overlooked Egyptian president Husni Mubarak's rigged elections and repressive apparatus that kept a lid on things. Likewise, Libya's psychopathic leader Muammar Qaddafi renounced weapons of mass destruction, so he couldn't be such a bad guy after all.

America's neoconservative moment ended even before Bush's terms ran out. Military adventures in Afghanistan and Iraq proved costly in terms of lives and treasure, open-ended, increasingly difficult even for government officials to justify, and unproductive or even counterproductive in terms of goals. Arguably, rather than enhancing American power and prestige, the two campaigns did enormous damage to both. Americans had had it, particularly after the global financial meltdown of 2008, and, to put a positive spin on it, the lackluster results of the two wars.

When the Obama administration came into office, it was not only determined to pivot to Asia, it was determined to scale back U.S. adventures abroad. As a result, it returned for the most part to the realism of the cold war era. Instead of asserting the right to take preemptive and unilateral action when necessary, which spawned the attack on Iraq, the United States downgraded the Global War on Terrorism to "overseas contingency operations," replacing "boots on the ground" with targeted drone strikes against individuals identified as terrorists. Instead of asserting unchallengeable American dominance in international affairs, the Obama administration restored the policy of seeking multilateral alliances. Hence, the United States joined with other NATO members in waging an air campaign in Libya (in the process popularizing the phrase "leading from behind") and adopted the same strategy in its war against the Islamic State in Syria and Iraq. The United States was also a principal organizer of the "Friends of Syria" group, which consisted of more than one hundred nations and was established to bypass the United Nations where Russia might veto any resolution it felt was too harsh on its Syrian ally. And instead of actively promoting pro-American democracies throughout the world, the Obama administration operated as if the world were a messy place that defied even the best intentions. It not only approached the Arab uprisings with extreme caution, it helped ensure the victory of only one opposition movement in spite of decades of preaching about human rights and democracy. The exception was Libya, which the administration immediately abandoned to its own devices.

The Obama administration also refused to assert a one-size-fits-all doctrine in the Middle East as the Bush administration had attempted to with its Freedom Agenda or the "you're either with us or with the terrorists" pronouncements. It believed such declarations had tied the hands of American policy makers during the previous administration and made them bend themselves out of shape in an attempt to justify any actions that deviated from the doctrine. Hence, the approach taken by Obama was based on a country-by-country assessment of policy needs and American capabilities.

Critics of Obama's approach to the Middle East have argued that it made the United States appear indecisive and weak, which is why America's adversaries, like Iran, seemed emboldened while America's allies, such as Saudi Arabia and Turkey, needed to assert independent policies in regional politics in ways unimaginable until recently. But is American power in the region on the wane? To be sure, most Americans are loath to undertake new military adventures in the region. That is why President Obama, in his speech to the American people proclaiming his intention to "degrade and destroy" the Islamic State, made sure to assure his audience that there would be "no [American] boots on the ground." And the American people are not alone in their skepticism about the benefits of American intervention in the region. "In my opinion," former secretary of defense Robert M. Gates (quoting General Douglas MacArthur) told cadets at West Point in 2011, "any future defense secretary who advises the president to again send a big American land army into Asia or into the Middle East or Africa should have his head examined." But war making is not the only criterion by which power might be measured. Power is also the ability to influence by non-lethal means. So as far as the United States being a waning power in the Middle East is concerned, here are two things worth considering: First, during the uprisings of 2010–2011 protesters throughout the Arab world went out on the streets demanding human and democratic rights, two values the United States had been promoting—sometimes cynically, sometimes sincerely—in every international venue for close to four decades. And no matter how much pain it might cause, the only formula for economic recovery in the Middle East and the rest of the world currently on the table is neoliberalism, which might as well come with the label "made in America."

CHAPTER 18

Resistance

On 5 January 2008, protests broke out in the town of Redeyef in western Tunisia. The economy of the town depended upon the mining of phosphate, a chemical included in a wide variety of compounds, from fertilizers to fire retardants. The protests began over a hiring dispute at the publically owned Gafsa Phosphate Company, the largest employer in this impoverished region of Tunisia. Employment practices were particularly important because unemployment in this area ran as high as 39 percent, which is why the Tunisian Union of Unemployed (college) Graduates had been so successful organizing there. As a matter of fact, the act that kicked off the protests was a hunger strike in front of the local headquarters of the government-affiliated official trade union federation by four unemployed graduates. Protests spread to other mining towns in the region, and thousands of high school students, temporary workers, unemployed miners, and women whose husbands had been killed or maimed in mining accidents joined the original protesters. Tunisian president Zine al-ᶜAbidin bin ᶜAli, who would be overthrown in the first of the Arab uprisings almost exactly three years later, soon realized he was facing a full-scale rebellion by protesters whose demands had become increasingly political. After six months of protests that combined a variety of non-violent and violent tactics, including demonstrations, sit-ins, the blockage of railroad tracks, and attacks on police, the government managed to put down the unrest using the full arsenal of repressive measures available to states.

On 27 May 1995, a group of Turkish women calling themselves the "Saturday Mothers" began a vigil on one of the busiest streets in Istanbul. They modeled themselves on *Las Madres de Plaza de Mayo*, a group of Argentine mothers who held weekly demonstrations in the heart of Buenos Aires beginning in 1977. Those demonstrations were intended to shame the government into accounting for their children who had been "disappeared" during the Argentine government's Dirty War against its own citizens. The Saturday Mothers of Istanbul sought to publicize their grief and hold the Turkish government accountable for the torture and disappearance of their children following the 1980 military coup d'état in Turkey. Their loved ones included leftists and those disappeared during the brutal counterinsurgency campaign the generals waged against the Kurdish independence movement during the 1990s. Meeting every Saturday at noon, the mothers combined silent vigil with street theater: They held pictures of their missing loved ones and recounted the stories of the lives of their children and the circumstances of their disappearances. They, too, were met with state violence, which included beatings, tear gas, and arrest. They suspended their demonstrations in 1999, only to return ten years later.

In the wake of the Iranian presidential elections of 2009 which the incumbent "won" with more than 60 percent of the vote and which supporters of his opponents charged he had stolen (in seventy cities the number of votes exceeded the number of eligible voters), protests broke out throughout Iran. Within two days, crowds estimated at anywhere between one and three million participated in a mass rally in Tehran, and tens of thousands more took to the streets in other cities as well. Caught off guard by the popular anger, Supreme Guide Ayatollah Ali Khamenei ordered a partial recount, then verified the original election result. As the slogan chanted by crowds changed from "Where's My Vote?" to "Death to the Dictator," the regime cracked down hard, deploying paramilitary thugs to beat up protesters, making mass arrests, and torturing those whom it had imprisoned. Although the regime won the initial round of the "Green Revolution," its victory was far from complete. On 14 February 2011, a "Day of Rage" in solidarity with the Tunisian and Egyptian uprisings in which thousands participated turned into anti-government demonstrations. Government opponents returned to the streets a week later to commemorate the deaths of two demonstrators who had been killed in Tehran on what truly turned out to be a day of rage. In 2013, Hassan Rouhani, widely seen as someone who could act as a bridge between the ruling clerics and the Green Movement, became the Islamic republic's seventh president in an election believed, this time, to have been fair.

The events in Tunisia, Turkey, and Iran demonstrate the breadth of issues contested by populations in the post-colonial Middle East. They also demonstrate that neither religion, tribalism, unique history, nor any other factor commonly attributed to the region has prevented it from experiencing the same social and political movements found elsewhere in the world.

With the exception of Marxist-type movements, which seek to rebuild society wholesale, there have been two possible foundations for social and political movements in the post-colonial Middle East, as elsewhere: nativism and demands for the restoration or expansion of rights. Nativists believe that the only means to bring about the regeneration of a particular community is by that community's embrace of its authentic, defining traditions. Inasmuch as the Young Ottomans of the nineteenth century believed that the only way to preserve the empire from the depredations of the West was by reasserting the Islamic principles upon which it had been built, they might be considered to have had a strong nativist streak. So might the "orthodox" ulama who wrote for the journal al-Haqa'iq in Damascus in the early twentieth century. The only thing that makes nativism in the Islamic world different from nativism elsewhere is that Islam can be mobilized to play a role in defining authenticity there.

The second basis for social and political movements in the post-colonial Middle East is the claim for rights, be they for social and economic justice or for collective or individual rights. The three episodes with which this chapter began depict social and political movements organized to assert claims for such rights, although in all three cases instead of sticking with their original demands for the redress of specific grievances, protesters went on to challenge the authority of the state itself.

Some social and political movements have been exclusively nativist or rights-based. Wahhabism, salafism (in its contemporary incarnation), and, as we shall see, al-Qaeda and its various franchises derive their belief systems entirely from nativism. On the other hand, contemporary labor activism and consumer boycotts usually speak the language of economic justice without appeals to tradition. So did the IMF riots that spread throughout the region in the 1980s. Most post-colonial social and political movements, however, have combined nativism with an appeal to rights. The few remaining stateless nationalities in the region—the Palestinians, the Kurds, the Sahrawis in southern Morocco, for example—certainly do, as do all nationalists, who claim a right to self-determination based on a distinct linguistic, ethnic, religious, or historical tradition. Likewise other groups. For example, in 1980 the Berber community of Algeria—an ethno-linguistic minority which makes up anywhere between 18 and 30 percent of Algerians (the number depends on whether one stresses the ethno- or linguistic part of their identity and whom you ask)—mounted demonstrations and demanded the government in Algiers recognize their collective right to maintain their Berber identity and their language, Tamazight. In other words, the so-called Berber Spring—the first in a series of mass movements in the Arab world to use a rights-based discourse—claimed the right for Algerian Berbers to maintain their traditions.

The Iranian Revolution of 1978–1979 also combined nativism with demands for social justice and individual rights. Shah Muhammad Reza Pahlavi had used Iran's vast oil wealth to engage in social engineering, consolidate his own power, and expand the state's intrusion into the lives of its citizenry as well as the state's repressive power. The shah's policies sparked widespread disaffection. He alienated rural landowners by implementing a draconian land reform program (the "White Revolution") that upset the social and economic order in the countryside and placed much of Iran's agricultural sector in the hands of multinational agribusiness companies (peasants weren't too keen on being forced to join cooperatives and transformed into rural proletarians either). He alienated urban shopkeepers (bazaaris) by bulldozing their places of business under the guise of urban redevelopment, making government surveillance of their activities all the easier. He further victimized them through anti-profiteering campaigns which resulted in the exile of more than twenty-three thousand of them. He alienated ulama, many of whom were also landlords, by expanding public education at the expense of religious education, by signing a treaty granting legal immunity to large numbers of American diplomatic and military personnel in Iran—a move they interpreted as submitting Iran to foreign domination—and by enfranchising women. He alienated intellectuals, human rights advocates, labor activists, and members of the middle class in multiple ways. He imposed strict censorship. He restricted political participation and banned independent political parties. He was at the center of a network of corruption that enriched him and his family to the tune of anywhere between $5 billion and $20 billion. He built a security apparatus (SAVAK) of upwards of sixty thousand agents to spy on and terrorize the population. And he jailed and tortured political dissidents. In 1976, Amnesty International reported that "no country in the world has a worse record in human rights than Iran."

By the early 1960s, the shah's policies had begun to spark resistance. Armed groups, modeling themselves on the Algerian and Palestinian liberation movements, undertook a guerilla war against the state. Some in those groups borrowed their ideas from such celebrity revolutionaries as Che Guevara of Cuba and Ho Chi Minh of Vietnam. Others borrowed their ideas from an Iranian writer and political activist, Ali Shariati, who promoted a doctrine that combined elements of Islamic modernism and Marxist analysis. Shariati's ideas influenced a wide spectrum of Iranians, from university students to ulama. Little wonder. His denunciation of those who slavishly imitate the West, his advocacy of cultural authenticity, his division of individual societies and whole nations into the categories of oppressor and oppressed, and his belief that the principal function of the state is to promote equal economic, political, and social rights combined the language of nativism with that of social justice and contained many of the elements of other Third World ideologies popular at the time.

As influential as he was, Shariati was not the Iranian Revolution's foremost theoretician. That honor goes to Ayatollah Ruhollah Khomeini (ayatollah is a title granted to prominent teaching *mujtahids*). Khomeini had first come to public attention in 1964 when he called on the shah to resign for signing the treaty with the Americans ("They had reduced the Iranian people to a level lower than an American dog," he thundered). As punishment, the shah forced him into exile, initially in Iraq, then France. It was during his exile in Iraq that Khomeini first proposed establishing Iran as a theocracy run, ultimately, by ulama. During his sojourn in France, he maintained contact with his followers via cassette tapes which were widely distributed. When the revolutionary tide—what might be considered the first "people power" revolution in the Middle East—forced the shah into exile, Khomeini returned to Iran to ecstatic crowds, his stature assured.

Khomeini's ideas for the governance of Iran are embodied in the Iranian constitution, adopted in 1979. According to the document, all laws of the Islamic republic are to be based on "Islamic principles." It is up to the ulama to ensure these principles are respected. At the top of the political pyramid stands the *vali-e faqih*, commonly translated as "supreme leader"—a nice Orwellian touch. The supreme leader, as the constitution puts it, is to be a "just and pious *faqih* [a legal expert qualified to rule on matters pertaining to Islamic law] who is

Khomeini sends the shah packing. Poster from the Iranian Revolution, 1978–1979.
(*From: Barry M. Rosen, ed.,* Iran Since the Revolution: Internal Dynamics, Regional Conflicts,
and the Superpowers (*Boulder, Colo.: Social Science Monographs, 1985), p. 43.*)

acquainted with the circumstances of his age; courageous, resourceful, and possessed of administrative ability; and recognized and accepted as leader by the
majority of the people." The first supreme leader was Ayatollah Khomeini,
who dubbed this type of government a *velayat-e faqih*—that is, a government
of the *faqih*. An assembly of clerics—the Assembly of Leadership Experts, to be
precise—elected his successor, Sayyed Ali Khamenei, upon his death in 1989, as
the constitution authorizes. Neither of the two supreme leaders chose to view the
position as that of a mere figurehead. Thus, the leading cleric in Iran has not only
overseen but intervened in the legislative and executive branches of government.
The supreme court of the Islamic republic, the Supreme Judicial Council, is also
to be composed of ulama, as is the Council of Guardians, whose job it is to ensure
that laws passed by the *majlis* are compatible with Islam.

   Khomeini's blueprint for the future of Iran was not the only one that was
circulating at the time, and while ulama played a critical role in honing the message of the revolution, the revolution succeeded because of the widespread support it attracted. For example, a strike by oil field workers played an essential role
in turning the tide in favor of the revolutionaries because it limited the access of
the government to revenue. This frustrated the government's ability to suppress
the revolution. Students, leftist guerrillas, members of the Tudeh (Communist)
party, even women's groups all mobilized to get rid of the shah, putting issues of

---

Vignette

The Making of a Revolutionary Symbol

In successful revolutions, a broad coalition of groups unites around common slogans and common symbols. Hence, the "bread, peace, land" of the Russian Revolution of 1917 and the tricolor of the French. The participants in the Iranian Revolution united around a single demand—the shah had to go. They also adopted symbols from Shiʿi lore.

The central event in the Shiʿi calendar is the commemoration of the killing of Husayn, the third imam and grandson of Muhammad, at the Battle of Karbala in A.D. 680. Husayn was killed on his way to the city of Kufa, in present-day Iraq, where the population had proclaimed him the rightful caliph. When the governor of Kufa sent out an army to meet Husayn's challenge, most of Husayn's army melted away, leaving only about seventy men, women, and children to do battle. The results were as one might expect. As recorded in a ninth-century chronicle, a soldier in the governor's army described the battle in the following manner:

> We attacked them as the sun rose and surrounded them on every side. Eventually, our swords took their toll of the heads of the people; they began to flee without having any refuge; they sought refuge from us on the hills and in the hollows as doves seek refuge from a hawk. By God! . . . It was only a time for the slaughtering of animals, or for a man to take his siesta before we had come upon the last of them. There were their naked bodies, their blood-stained clothes, their faces thrown in the dust. The sun burst down on them; the wind scattered dust over them; their visitors in this deserted place were eagles and vultures.

Every year, in the month of Muharram, Shiʿis recall the Battle of Karbala in ritual and pageant. As penance for the abandonment of their imam in his hour of

---

economic and social justice and human rights on the revolutionary table. Nevertheless, the ulama emerged on top for a number of reasons. Besides the fact that they enjoyed close ties to the urban masses, particularly the bazaaris who also played a prominent role in the revolution (even under the shah, ulama, and not the state, had exclusive power to notarize commercial contracts), they were able to speak a language that had broad appeal. The ulama were able to counterpose their own brand of "cultural authenticity," as represented by the symbols of Shiʿi Islam, to the secular nationalism of the shah's regime or the communism of the Tudeh party, both of which, they argued, were inauthentic because they had been imported from the West.

And here is the true irony of the Iranian Revolution. As much as Khomeini and his followers might argue that they sought to purify Iranian society by returning it to its roots, the Iranian revolutionary model of government *is*, in many ways, borrowed from the West. Where in the Qurʾan or hadith is there mention of an Islamic *republic*? Where is there mention of elections, parliaments, or constitutions? The Islamic Republic of Iran has all three. Indeed, the constitution seems to waffle on the idea of popular sovereignty. While the constitution

need, Shiᶜi men march in processions, whipping themselves and chanting, "Oh Husayn, we were not there."

Commemorations of acts of cowardice do not, of course, contribute to revolutionary fervor. Enter Ayatollah Khomeini, who, on the eve of the Iranian Revolution, offered his followers a different reading of the Battle of Karbala. Khomeini counseled his followers not to fixate on the community's abandonment of their imam. Rather, he advised, Iranians should take heart from the courage displayed by Husayn and his handful of followers who stood up to tyranny in the face of overwhelming odds. According to Khomeini:

> I tell you plainly that a dark, dangerous future lies ahead and that it is your duty to resist and to serve Islam and the Muslim peoples. Protest against the pressure exerted upon our oppressed people every day. Purge yourselves of your apathy and selfishness; stop seeking excuses and inventing pretexts for evading your responsibility. You have more forces at your disposal than the Lord of Martyrs (upon whom be peace) did, who resisted and struggled with his limited forces until he was killed. If (God forbid) he had been a weak, apathetic, and selfish person, he could have come up with some excuse for himself and remained silent. His enemies would have been only too happy for him to remain silent so that they could attain their vile goals, and they were afraid of his rebelling. But he dispatched [a messenger] to procure the people's allegiance to him so that he might overthrow that corrupt government and set up an Islamic government. If he had sat in some corner in Medina and had nothing to do with anyone, everyone would have respected him and come to kiss his hand. And if you sit silently by, you too will be respected, but it will be the kind of respect that is given a dead saint. A dead saint is respected by everyone, but a living saint or Imam has his head cut off.

proclaims sovereignty belongs to God, it also stipulates that God "has placed man in charge of his social destiny." Nor has the Islamic republic rejected the ideology of nationalism. The president of the Islamic republic must be Iranian, and Khomeini himself spoke of the "Iranian fatherland." Rather than Islamizing the nation, then, it might be argued that the revolution nationalized religion. Such is the power of the nation state system which sets the rules of the game.

Soon after the Iranian Revolution, nativist movements that equated the regeneration of their communities with a return to Islamic governance or Islamic mores emerged throughout the region. These Islamist movements were not new to the region. As we have seen, Hassan al-Banna had founded the Egyptian Muslim Brotherhood in 1928 as a tool for Islamic regeneration, and a number of other groups emerged thereafter, some committed solely to missionary or charitable works and some with more political ambitions. But during the 1980s and 1990s, the number of Islamist associations, parties, and even governments seeking to order their societies according to what they considered to be Islamic principles, be they Sunni or Shiᶜi, swelled.

Vignette

Islamism—or Fundamentalism?

This book uses the terms "Islamic movements" and "Islamist" to refer to those groups that use Islamic symbols and rhetoric and advocate the return to Islamic law and "Islamic values." These terms are not the only ones that have been applied to those groups. Indeed, finding an agreed-upon term in English for them has not been easy for scholars and commentators. It is not simply a question of taking the Arabic term and translating it into English—there is, after all, no agreed-upon Arabic term for them either.

One term that has commonly been applied to these groups is "fundamentalist," as in Islamic fundamentalist or Muslim fundamentalist. Many scholars of the Middle East have found this term inappropriate because it so obviously borrows from the Western—particularly American—experience. The word "fundamentalism" emerged in the United States at the end of the nineteenth century to describe a school of theology that advocated a return to the fundamentals of Christianity. While this school was particularly strong among American Protestants, it affected American Catholics as well.

The desire to return to Christian fundamentals arose in response to two movements in American Christianity: modernism and the social gospel movement. Protestant and Catholic modernists, like Islamic modernists, sought to make religion compatible with the findings of modern science, social theory, and social practice. Those who preached the doctrine of the social gospel sought to apply Christian principles to solve social problems—the sort of problems (poverty, crime) sparked by the industrialization and urbanization of America. Many American Christians thought that the advocates of modernism and the social gospel doctrine had lost touch with their theological roots. In particular, they felt that any attempt to use Christianity to create a "heaven on earth" ignored two foundational precepts of Christianity: original sin, which made the effort sacrilegious, and the imminent return of Christ, which made the effort superfluous.

Beginning in 1878, those associated with the attempt to return to Christian orthodoxy began holding meetings in upstate New York, an annual event called the Niagara Falls Bible Conference. At the same time, conservative Protestant

---

There has been some disagreement among Islamists and Islamist groups as to what those principles are and how to apply them. Some Islamist activists, such as those who dominated the Taliban government of Afghanistan overthrown by the Americans after 9/11 or the Islamic State in Iraq and Syria, believe that those principles provide them with a strict roadmap to be followed without deviation. Hence, their single-mindedness when it comes to issues like dress codes for men and women (beards for the former, veils for the latter) and prescribed punishments. The Islamic State goes so far as to proclaim itself the sole arbiter of that which is true Islam. It therefore assumes the right to declare Muslims who do not meet their standards to be non-Muslims (a process called *takfir* in Arabic), expelling them from the community and rendering them suitable for killing as apostates. Other activists, such as those who dominate Tunisia's Ennahda, which

theologians associated with the Princeton Theological Seminary began to weigh in on the issue. Believing in the literal truth of the Bible, these theologians founded a school of theology called the "Princeton School" or the "Princeton Theology." A marriage of these two groups took place in 1895 when the organizers of the Niagara Falls Bible Conference drew up a list of five principles in which, they maintained, all real Christians had to believe: the literal truth of the original Bible, the virgin birth and deity of Christ, the redemption of mankind through Christ's death, the bodily resurrection of Christ, and the imminent return of Christ. To make these principles widely known, two brothers, Milton and Lyman Steward, published a twelve-tract series called "The Fundamentals." Because they were wealthy—the brothers were founders of the Union Oil Company—they were able to print and distribute over three million copies of their tracts. By the early 1920s, those who held to the principles of "The Fundamentals" began to be labeled "fundamentalists" by their modernist adversaries.

If Christian fundamentalists advocated a return to the original sources of Christianity, why can't the term fundamentalism be used to describe Muslims who also advocate a return to the original sources? Many Middle Eastern scholars believe that the circumstances surrounding the emergence and growth of the two movements are so different that calling them both "fundamentalism" does more to obscure than enlighten. They assert that applying a term originally coined to denote a Western phenomenon demonstrates cultural arrogance— once again, it appears, the West has provided a model, whereas the Middle East has only a cheap knockoff. They also point out that the social composition of the American movement is different from that of the Middle Eastern movement: Whereas contemporary Islamist movements have a particularly strong following among better-educated urban dwellers, Protestant fundamentalism is a doctrine of choice among lesser-educated Americans living in rural areas. Interestingly, this was not always the case. American fundamentalism began as a predominantly urban movement and found strong support in such cities as Philadelphia, Minneapolis, and Los Angeles. In the beginning, the movement also attracted the well educated, as one would expect with a movement that was expounded by theologians at the Princeton Theological Seminary.

came to power in the aftermath of the 2010–2011 uprising there, treat those principles more gingerly, either because it is politically expedient to do so or because they honestly believe that Islam is compatible with Enlightenment values. Hence, their declared belief in the democratic process and their willingness to compromise with secularists on a constitution that does not even mention Islamic law and grants equal rights to women unconditionally. And as we shall see, a number of these groups, including Ennahda, have worked in coalitions with like-minded secular activists, combining nativism with a rights-based discourse in a manner reminiscent of the Islamic modernists of the nineteenth century.

Over the years, social scientists have given a number of reasons for the proliferation of Islamist groups in the decades following the Iranian Revolution. Some have argued that the success of that revolution indicated to many in the region that Islam provided greater potential for social cohesion and successful political action than secular nationalisms—particularly after the dismal showing of those Arab states that advanced one or another form of secular nationalism in the 1967 War against Israel. Others have pointed out that the so-called Islamic resurgence that took place in the Middle East coincided with the oil price revolution and the infusion of huge amounts of money into the Gulf region. The governments of Gulf countries, along with newly enriched foundations sponsored by them and their citizens, used their wealth for mosque construction throughout the Muslim world, which provided the spaces in which Islamist groups might take shape. They also set up Islamic charities which influenced popular attitudes and practices, and educational institutions which inculcated a conservative brand of Islam prevalent in the Gulf. Still others have noted that governments of some countries in which Islamist movements have appeared also contributed to the phenomenon, either intentionally or unintentionally. In terms of the former, governments have, at times, assisted their formation and spread, or at least looked the other way while Islamist groups incubated. Anwar al-Sadat, for example, released from prison members of the Muslim Brotherhood whom Gamal ʿAbd al-Nasser had jailed in order to counter Nasserists and others who conspired against him. And the extent to which Israel abetted the formation of the Palestinian Islamist group Hamas—either by ignoring its growth or actively supporting it so that it might act as a counterweight to the PLO—is still hotly contested. In terms of the latter, governments inadvertently provided spaces in which individual Islamists might meet, debate, and strategize. Some of the biggest names among Islamists—Sayyid Qutb of the Egyptian Muslim Brotherhood and Ayman al-Zawahiri of al-Qaeda—used their time in prison to do all three.

While all these explanations are plausible, none are demonstrable. There is no way to account for intellectual fashion or why at a certain moment in history an idea becomes an idea whose time has come. And we shouldn't ignore other types of movements that formed in the post-colonial Middle East. As we shall see later, while most of the world was fixated on Islamist movements in the region, movements whose objective was to establish a social order in which human and democratic rights would be respected also engaged in struggles with autocracies, as did those whose primary concerns were for social and economic justice.

Not all Islamist movements that flourished in the 1980s and 1990s took it upon themselves to target homegrown autocrats and their regimes. While both Hizbullah and Hamas have successfully engaged in partisan politics in quasi-democratic systems and have even used violence against their domestic opponents, both had emerged in response to Israeli occupations of their homelands—Lebanon (1982–2000) and the Palestinian territories (1967–). They made resistance to Israel, a foreign enemy, their guiding principle. The Justice and Development Party of Turkey built a sophisticated political machine which, when the time was ripe, won elections and formed governments. Over time, it became "the man" against which a left/liberal opposition (and opposing Islamists) railed. Most salafi groups (at least before the Arab uprisings of 2010–2011), treated politics and politicians with derision. They believed there was no point to governing populations whose Islam had become so watered down that they are neither ready nor worthy of living in an Islamic state. Thus, they viewed their task as spreading the word (*dawa*) and engaging in social service and charity work. Then there is the anomalous al-Qaeda, which, as we have seen, views the nation-state system as a trick perpetrated by the Crusader-Zionist conspiracy to divide Muslims from one another. Their fight is therefore not with local autocrats and their regimes, but with those autocrats' puppet masters, the far enemy. Nevertheless, during the 1980s and 1990s a significant number of Islamist groups saw themselves engaged in struggles—sometimes violent, sometimes not—against the regimes under which they lived.

Let's start with those groups involved in violent struggles. During the twenty-year period that followed the Iranian Revolution, governments throughout the Arab world engaged their violent Islamist opponents in wars of extermination. Some of these groups are remembered for spectacular acts of violence: The Egyptian Islamic Jihad assassinated Egypt's president, Anwar al-Sadat, in 1981. The Armed Islamic Group (GIA) of Algeria waged a campaign against the government during the 1990s that resulted in the deaths of tens of thousands. Egypt's Islamic Group perpetrated a massacre at the popular tourist destination of Luxor, killing more than sixty, in an attempt to cripple that vital sector of the Egyptian economy and thus bring down the Egyptian government. Other groups have largely disappeared from memory.

Infamous or forgotten, however, groups such as the aforementioned shared a number of characteristics. First, as was the trend at the time among groups that aspired to revolution, they tended to be small, or at least organized in small units. The GIA, for example, consisted of autonomous militias whose size varied from twenty or fewer members to three hundred or so. The groups operated clandestinely, attempting to fly beneath the radar of the state's ever-expanding security apparatus. The groups assumed that success could only come through acts of violence. These acts were intended, variously, to eliminate leaders and regimes that were "un-Islamic," force those regimes to engage in acts of repression that would unmask their brutality to the population at large (a tactic first employed by the Marxist Tupamaro guerrillas of Uruguay), cripple regimes by undermining tourism and financial institutions, and rouse the population through heroic acts of resistance. The groups were Leninist; that is, like Vladimir Lenin, they believed that change would come through the activities of a small number of devoted members and not through mass mobilization. Finally, except for calls for the replacement of the regimes against which they fought with ones committed to "Islamic governance" and rule by *shariʿa*, they were programmatically vague. Ideology aside, then, the groups against which Arab governments warred during the 1980s and 1990s more closely resembled Germany's Baader Meinhof Gang or America's Weather Underground than they did the various parties that took part in elections in the aftermath of the Arab uprisings of 2010–2011.

The aforementioned groups were not the only ones against which Arab governments campaigned during this period. Governments targeted, to a greater or lesser extent, even those groups that had pledged to work within the system. Among those targeted to a greater extent were Ennahda in Tunisia and the Islamic Salvation Front (FIS) in Algeria. Both groups emerged during the late 1980s, when the full effects of failed economic and social policies led to popular rebellion. This compelled the Tunisian and Algerian governments to flirt temporarily with more open political systems. When both groups demonstrated their popularity in free elections for parliament—candidates affiliated with FIS, for example, won close to 50 percent of the vote in 1991—the Tunisian and Algerian governments dissolved them and began jailing their members. Rachid Ghannouchi, leader of Ennahda, fled to London, from where he called for an uprising. Similarly, with the dissolution of FIS, a number of its members founded armed groups which declared war on the state. The lesson learned from the brief periods of "liberalization"—that the Tunisian and Algerian regimes would never surrender their privileges peacefully—encouraged the emergence of violent organizations in both cases.

In Egypt, the Mubarak regime's campaign against the Egyptian Muslim Brotherhood was less dramatic but no less effective. After years of repression, the general guide of the brotherhood had renounced violence altogether in 1972, a pledge he renewed in 1987. Banned but tolerated and prohibited from forming its own party, the brotherhood formed alliances with officially sanctioned parties, running candidates under their banner or as independents. In the parliamentary elections of 1987—held one year after the same sort of popular insurrection that rocked Tunisia and Algeria broke out in Egypt—opposition candidates won sixty seats—an unprecedented number—in spite of manipulation and irregularities. Then came the reaction in the 1990s—what one political scientist has called the "political deliberalization of Egypt." The regime rolled back the electoral gains made by the brotherhood and undertook other repressive measures against it. Again, a lesson was learned: The 1972 brotherhood renunciation of violence had precipitated an organizational split and the formation of the Islamic Group and Egyptian Islamic Jihad. The deliberalization of Egypt seemingly validated their position that violence was the only effective means to bring about political change.

During the 1980s and 1990s, states undertook far-reaching measures to combat their real and perceived enemies. The Egyptian and Algerian governments cited Islamist violence as the reason to declare states of emergency in 1981 and 1992, respectively, and the Syrian government cited it as one of the reasons to maintain the state of emergency it had imposed in 1963. In all three cases, governments used states of emergency to empanel extraordinary courts and military tribunals and to suspend constitutionally guaranteed rights, such as habeas corpus. This enabled those governments to arrest suspected militants *en masse* (between 1992 and 1997, for example, the Egyptian government arrested 47,000). By the early twenty-first century states throughout the Middle East regularly tortured the prisoners they held. Sometimes these prisoners were interned under authorization of "state security courts," which operated without judicial oversight; at other times prisoners were interned without even the façade of a trial.

To ensure the smooth functioning of their repressive apparatus, states relied on a pervasive security network which, as time went on, only grew more and more bloated. During the period of insurgency, the Algerian government availed itself of fifty thousand police to keep order. Even as the insurgency wound down, the government kept expanding the numbers of police until they reached, by the second decade of the twenty-first century, 170,000. In Egypt, Yemen, Bahrain, and Syria governments expanded their security apparatus to such an extent that they had to outsource the job to local hoodlums: "*baltagaya*" ("hatchet men") in the case of Egypt, Yemen, and Bahrain; and "*shabiha*" (a word derived from the Arabic for "ghosts") in the case of Syria, who hailed from the same sect and region as the inner circle of Syria's ruling elite. These thugs not only acted as the eyes and ears of the state, they created a threatening atmosphere to cow populations. On the eve of the 2011 uprising in Egypt, it was estimated that the security apparatus engaged approximately one million Egyptians, from interior ministry bureaucrats to agents in the field to common snitches. And alongside the security apparatus throughout the region were special military units deployed when regimes felt particularly threatened by widespread insurgency.

Overall, the Arab governments' campaign against violent Islamist groups during the 1980s and 1990s might be judged a success for two reasons: It wiped out their violent opposition and it demonstrated that the tactics adopted by those groups were unproductive. There is another side to the story, however: It might also be argued that the Arab governments' campaign against violent Islamist groups during the 1980s and 1990s was an unmitigated disaster for those governments. There are two reasons this might be said. First, by demonstrating the inefficacy of violence, the governments' campaign created a political opening in which mass-based, non-violent Islamist organizations—such as those which performed so well in the 2011–2012 elections held in Morocco, Tunisia, and Egypt—might flourish. This is one of the reasons for the spread of people power-style movements throughout the region which, unlike their Leninist forebears, engaged huge numbers in protests that were not easily marginalized or suppressed. Second, the very tactics governments used to destroy violent Islamist groups—imposing emergency laws, expanding repression and the repressive apparatus, and the like—would inspire rights-based protest movements that culminated in the uprisings of 2010–2011.

That which abetted and, indeed, encouraged, the emergence of rights-based protest movements was the diffusion of international norms of human rights and democratic governance throughout the world. As discussed in the introduction to Part IV, trends in the Middle East reflected broader trends, and while they did not affect governments' policies much, if at all, they established regional precedents. Evidence for this diffusion of international norms of human rights and democratic governance in the region might be found in a wave of protests and uprisings that began with the Berber Spring and continued throughout the region for the next thirty years. Like the uprisings of 2010–2011, these protests demanded social justice, democratic reform, and an end to human rights abuses. Among their number were the following:

- The so-called Black October riots in Algeria (also dubbed, dismissively, the "Couscous Riots"), which began as a bread riot in Algiers and quickly took a political turn as protesters targeted regime corruption, torture and other forms of repression, and the lack of democratic institutions and rights. Protests spread throughout the country, propelled by a strike wave among students and workers and newly established civil society groups. The ruling FLN took the protests so seriously that it offered a new constitution which guaranteed freedom of expression and association and which made no mention of the FLN at all. The FLN also issued a new electoral law that set the stage for the first truly free elections in the Arab world in which more than forty parties competed (although, as mentioned above, the Islamic Salvation Front's success in the first round of voting led the government to nullify the results, with disastrous consequences).

- The Bahraini intifada of 1994–1999, which began with a petition movement demanding an end to emergency rule, the restoration of rights suspended by that emergency rule, the release of political prisoners, pardons for political exiles, and the expansion of the franchise to women. Petitioners also demanded a restoration of the 1973 constitution, which provided for a parliament in which two-thirds of the members were elected. Approximately one-tenth of the nation's citizens signed the petitions. After the government arrested a prominent religious scholar, the population staged mass demonstrations. When the government responded with violence, widespread rebellion broke out. The rebellion only subsided when a new king ascended to the throne and held a referendum on a National Action Charter. The charter guaranteed basic freedoms, universal suffrage, and the rule of law. (In the end, the new king showed his true colors by abandoning the promises made in the charter and issuing a new constitution in 2002 which suspended the democratic rights promised by the charter.)

- The brief "Damascus Spring" of 2000, a period of intense political ferment that began after the death of Syria's president of thirty years, Hafez al-Assad, and the accession of his son, Bashar al-Assad, to the presidency. The Damascus Spring began in informal salons whose participants expanded the movement first through one petition, the "Statement of the Ninety-nine," then through a second, the "Statement of a Thousand." The statements demanded, among other things, the end of the emergency law, the release of political prisoners, multiparty elections, and freedom of speech, assembly, and expression. Even after the Damascus Spring turned into the Damascus Winter, aftershocks of the mobilization continued.

Among those aftershocks was the Damascus Declaration Movement of 2005, which (initially) united the secular and religious opposition in a common demand for democratic rights.

- Two "color revolutions" in Kuwait. The first, the "Blue Revolution," lasted from 2002 to 2005. It derived its name from the blue signs carried by demonstrators protesting in front of parliament and won for Kuwaiti women the right to vote. Considering the issue involved, it received support from an unlikely source: Islamist groups. In 2006, Kuwait had an "Orange Revolution," named for the color of the tee shirts worn by the mostly young demonstrators. They took to the streets after a group of parliamentarians walked out of parliament frustrated by the government's unwillingness to back measures intended to curtail rampant vote buying by candidates in parliamentary elections. The protesters and parliamentarians eventually got their reform, but not an end to vote buying.

- The formation of Kifaya (*Enough!*) in Egypt in 2004, shortly before the Egyptian government held a referendum to confirm a fifth term for Mubarak. Kifaya, was an amalgam of political currents ranging from nationalist to communist to Islamist that united around demands for electoral reform. It was the first group ever to call for Mubarak's resignation. Not only would Kifaya make demands echoed by activists in 2011, it pioneered tactics such as non-violent protest and the use of social media exploited during the uprising as well. This should not be surprising: Although Kifaya had faded years before the uprising, one of the founders of the April 6 Youth Movement, which played a principal role in organizing the January 2011 Tahrir Square protests, came from Kifaya's youth movement.

- Popular agitation that led to the establishment of the Equity and Reconciliation Commission in Morocco, also in 2004. King Muhammad VI charged the commission to investigate human rights abuses during the brutal "Years of Lead," a three-decades-long period of repression and extra-judicial executions that took place while his father reigned. During the Years of Lead, the regime killed and disappeared hundreds of its opponents. Once the commission had completed its work, the king apologized to Moroccans on behalf of the throne. (A similar demand for justice was made in Bahrain, where the National Committee for Martyrs and Torture Victims circulated a petition signed by 33,000 demanding the repeal of a law that denied the right of victims of human rights violations to bring suit against their persecutors.)

- The Cedar Revolution of 2005 (known locally as the "independence intifada"), which broke out after the assassination of Lebanese prime minister Rafik Hariri, probably by members of pro-Syria Hizbullah (Hariri was too independent for Syria's taste). The revolution consisted of a month-long series of demonstrations held in central Beirut which brought out multisectarian crowds which, at one point, reached 1.2 million people—more than a quarter of the entire population of Lebanon. Protesters demanded

332 THE MODERN MIDDLE EAST

the removal from Lebanon of Syrian forces that had been occupying the country since 1976, the dissolution of the pro-Syrian government, free parliamentary elections, and the formation of an independent commission to investigate the assassination. The last Syrian troops left Lebanon two months later, the government fell, and a new anti-Syrian government took its place.

And the list goes on.

Rights-based popular agitation in the region was not limited to demands for individual human rights. The imposition of neoliberal economic policies throughout the region also made demands for economic and social justice compelling and provoked popular resistance (such as the IMF riots of the 1980s) and a wave of worker activism of which the Gafsa strike was only one example. There were many others, including a surge of Egyptian labor activism from 2004 to 2010, during which time two million Egyptian workers and their families participated in more than three thousand strikes, sit-ins, and walkouts. The growing militancy of Egyptian labor set the stage for the strike wave that spread throughout the country beginning on 8 February 2011. It was this strike wave that likely convinced the military—a major stakeholder in the Egyptian economy—to depose Mubarak three days later.

The history of mass agitation for human and democratic rights that swept the region for thirty years raises the question of why no one saw the eruption of 2010–2011 coming. The answer is probably twofold. First, most observers were focused on the wars being waged between Arab regimes and their Islamist opponents. They thus viewed each protest for free elections, freedom of assembly, the end of emergency rule, etc., as an anomaly, driven by local issues, and not part of a pattern or wave. Second, it was commonplace to lump all Islamists together into an anti-democratic camp; to write off Islamists who participated in electoral activity, whether in professional organizations or parliamentary elections, as opportunists; to highlight the differences between the nativist discourse of Islamists and the rights-based discourse of the liberal and leftist opposition; and to dismiss that opposition as being hopelessly out of touch with their deeply religious societies and as being minuscule in size. While it is true that over the course of the past thirty years a significant number of Islamists doubled down on their nativism to the exclusion of all else and scorned the rhetoric of human rights as *bida^c* (unlawful innovation), a significant number of particularly younger Islamists responded to the possibilities for building coalitions with their more secular counterparts around a shared set of values against a common enemy (a further demonstration that nativism and the demand for rights are not incompatible). After all, Islamist groups that chose to participate in politics had to operate in a political environment increasingly affected by demands for human and democratic rights and social and political justice. Thus, the proliferation of secularist-Islamist coalitions which played a significant role in a number of protests and rebellions for human and democratic rights during the past thirty years, such as those highlighted above—the dress rehearsals, as it were, for the uprisings of 2010–2011.

Since February 2011, it has become commonplace to refer to the protests and uprisings that broke out in the Arab world in 2010–2011 as the "Arab Spring." The term is unfortunate for a number of reasons. First, it is calendrically incorrect: Not one of the uprisings broke out in the spring (although the Syrian uprising, which erupted two days before the vernal equinox, came closest). Second, spring is associated with joy and renewal. The term Arab Spring raised expectations so high that they were bound to be dashed. And so it happened, as Tahrir Square became the killing fields of Syria and the universal sugar rush turned into a sugar crash. Perhaps the most compelling reason to abandon the term once and for all, however, is that it makes it appear that the struggle in the Arab world—and the broader Middle East—against authoritarianism and for human and democratic rights and social and economic justice took place within the span of a single season guided by a single group of actors. As we have seen, this is far from the case.

CHAPTER 19

The Arab Uprisings

As we saw in the previous chapter, the Arab uprisings that broke out in the wake of Muhammad Bouazizi's self-immolation should not be seen as discrete events but rather as a continuation of protests and uprisings that broke out throughout the region over the course of the previous thirty years. Like their predecessors, the Arab uprisings of 2010–2011 (and some which broke out thereafter) spoke the language of human and democratic rights and social and economic justice.

Bouazizi's act struck a chord among Tunisians, and protests quickly spread from Bouazizi's hometown of Sidi Bouzid across the country. Tunisian protesters brought a number of issues to the table: unemployment, food inflation, corruption, poor living conditions, lack of freedoms, and lack of government responsiveness. The Tunisian General Labor Union, the sometime lapdog of the regime, saw which way the wind was blowing and threw its support behind the protests. At first, Tunisian president Zine al-ʿAbidin bin ʿAli, who had ruled for a quarter century, tried to pacify the protesters. In a pattern that would be repeated time after time in the Arab world, he promised three hundred thousand new jobs, new parliamentary elections, and a "national dialogue." This did little to mollify the protesters. By 14 January 2011—less than a month after Bouazizi's self-immolation—military and political leaders decided to take matters into their own hands. With the army surrounding the presidential palace bin ʿAli resigned and appointed his prime minister to head a caretaker government. Continued protests forced the appointment of another prime minister, not as closely identified with the old regime, shortly thereafter. The uprising in Tunisia was the first ever in the Arab world to bring down an autocrat.

About a week and a half after bin ʿAli resigned, young people, many of whom belonged to the "April 6 Youth Movement," began their occupation of Tahrir Square in Cairo. (While Tahrir Square was but one site of many in Egypt where protests were held that day, it emerged as the symbolic center of the Egyptian uprising.) The April 6 Youth Movement got its name from a date in 2008 when young people, using Facebook, called for a general strike to support striking workers at a state-run textile factory. The general strike failed, giving lie to the miraculous powers frequently ascribed to Facebook and other social media. That was 2008. This time around they were more successful. The security forces and goons-for-hire failed to dislodge the protesters from the square, and the army announced it would not fire on them. Strikes and anti-government protests spread throughout Egypt. On 11 February 2011, the army took matters into its own hands: It deposed President Husni Mubarak and established a new government under the Supreme Council of the Armed Forces. This phase of the Egyptian uprising—what might be called the first street phase of the Egyptian uprising—was over in a mere eighteen days.

Soon after the Tunisian and Egyptian uprisings seemingly demonstrated what could be done, populations elsewhere began to smell blood in the water. Nevertheless, it would be wrong to view subsequent protests and uprisings through the lens of the first two. It is true, for example, that after Egypt, a similar-style protest movement emerged in Yemen. Nevertheless, it had very un-Tunisian, un-Egyptian results: A stalemate between opponents of the government—a category that included social networking youths, labor, opposition members of parliament, and tribal leaders—and the regime ensued until foreign powers intervened diplomatically, ensuring the old guard would remain in place, only without the provocative presence of the former president. After protests modeled on those of Egypt broke out in Bahrain, the government struck back violently, and using the excuse that Iranian subversion was behind the protests, invited in troops and police from neighboring Saudi Arabia and the United Arab Emirates to help "restore order," initiating a period of fierce repression. In Saudi Arabia and Morocco, kings who had presented themselves as "reformers" faced their own protest movements which demanded expanded representation, an end to corruption, and constitutional checks on monarchic power—but, significantly, not the end of the regime, as protesters in Tunisia and Egypt had demanded. The governments were able to placate their populations—in the former kingdom with promises of a $130 billion benefits package to its citizens, in the latter with superficial reforms.

Uprisings in both Libya and Syria were long, violent affairs. In Libya, a "Day of Rage" was held after the arrest of a prominent human rights lawyer. He represented families of the twelve hundred "disappeared" political prisoners who had been murdered in cold blood in one single incident in 1996. Libya soon descended into a six-month civil war which only ended after a fierce NATO air campaign. For the second time, outside intervention determined the course of an uprising. And after months of predictions that "it couldn't happen in Syria," it did. In March 2011, Syrian security services arrested ten schoolchildren age fifteen and younger in the provincial city of Daraa. Their crime? Borrowing a slogan from the Egyptian uprising, they wrote as graffiti "down with the *nizam* [regime]" on walls. When their parents went out on the streets to protest, the security services fired, killing several. The next day, twenty-thousand residents of Daraa took to the streets. The Syrian bloodbath had begun.

Vignette

Who Was Abdesslem Trimech?

The event which touched off the Tunisian uprising—and, indirectly, all the other uprisings that began in 2010–2011—was the suicide of a produce vendor, Muhammad Bouazizi. His death took on all the trappings of martyrdom and became such a powerful symbol that Tunisian president Zine al-ᶜAbidin bin ᶜAli felt compelled to visit Bouazizi while he lay dying in a hospital. A widely disseminated photograph taken of the president at the dying man's bedside was meant to show Tunisians the compassionate side of the brutal bin ᶜAli. Since it took him two weeks to visit Bouazizi, however, it only served to remind them of bin ᶜAli's true nature. Exactly a year after Bouazizi set himself on fire, residents of Sidi Bouzid, Bouazizi's hometown and the place he performed his desperate act, unveiled a concrete statue in the form of a pushcart in his honor. The new Tunisian president did not repeat bin ᶜAli's mistake—he was present at the moment of the unveiling.

Bouazizi's suicide was not the first self-immolation that year in Tunisia. On 3 March 2010, for example, a street vendor named Abdesslem Trimech anticipated Bouazizi's act almost to a tee. Trimech set himself on fire in front of the office of the general secretary of Monastir, a town on the Tunisian coast. Earlier in the day, Trimech had gone to the municipal building to protest the revocation of his vending license. Rebuffed, he, too, went to the market and bought a flammable liquid with which he doused himself. Then he lit his lighter. Trimech was in his early thirties, the father of two children. Like Bouazizi, he lingered for a while, while angry residents of Monastir clashed with the police. Tens of thousands attended his funeral (one report puts the number at 50,000 in a town of 80,000), which turned into an angry anti-government demonstration. The proceedings were videotaped and posted on social media outlets. But for all the similarities between the stories of the two suicides, there was one huge difference: The day after Trimech's funeral, life in the town returned to normal and few outside Monastir cared much if anything about the incident. Trimech's act failed to inspire the same reaction among Tunisians as Bouazizi's would.

These were the main sites of protest. There were others, less publicized. So what has been going on?

Aside from the nearly ubiquitous title, "Arab Spring," a common word that is used to describe what has been taking place in the Arab world since Bouazizi's death is "wave." There are pluses and minuses to viewing the various uprisings as part of a wave. On the plus side, there is no denying that later Arab uprisings borrowed techniques of mobilization and symbols from earlier ones. Town squares that became the sites of protest throughout the Arab world were renamed "Tahrir" square after the main site of protest in Cairo, and many uprisings began with a scheduled "Day of Rage," also borrowed from the Egyptian model. In addition, slogans first chanted on the streets of Tunisia and Egypt, such as "The People Want the End of the Regime," and "*Irhal*! [Go!]," shouted at Tunisian and

But that is not the end of a story which, as Lewis Carroll might have put it, gets "curiouser and curiouser." It seems that between Trimech's suicide and Bouazizi's, seven Tunisians committed acts of self-immolation. One of them, Chams Eddine Heni, a thirty-one-year-old from Metlaoui in west/central Tunisia, did so less than a month before Bouazizi. He had quarreled with his father over money he needed in order to obtain travel documents to Italy so he might escape the grinding poverty of his hometown. So the question remains: Why the differing reactions to events that were fundamentally similar?

Some observers have cited the fact that Sidi Bouzid is significantly poorer than Monastir—but then again so is Metlaoui. Others claim that local leaders, like trade union representatives and leaders of professional associations, did not link Trimech's death to broader political and economic issues—although the slogans shouted by the crowds after his self-immolation and at his funeral, along with the attacks on symbols of authority, seem to challenge any need for them to have done so. Still others argue that there was one significant difference between Bouazizi's suicide and the others: His was not merely videotaped on cell phones; *al-Jazeera* ("old media") picked up those videos and rebroadcast them on its satellite channel endlessly throughout Tunisia and the Arabic-speaking world. This increased the awareness—if not the significance—of that event.

While appealing in its simplicity, this explanation, too, fails to convince. By tying the Tunisian uprising to television coverage, this explanation is what historians call "mechanistic": Between stimulus and response, it leaves no room for human choice. Tunisians not only chose to put Bouazizi's tragic death in a political framework, they chose to do something about it. And that something was to demand the "fall of the regime," as the ubiquitous slogan of the Arab uprisings put it.

In the end, will we ever know why Trimech's and Heni's deaths did not trigger a Tunisian uprising while Bouazizi's death did? Of course not, because that is the wrong question to ask. Uprisings such as the one Tunisia experienced in 2010 are exceptional, not commonplace, occurrences in world history. Their nonoccurrence needs no explanation. The real mystery is why Tunisians and the rest of the Arab world reacted to the death of Bouazizi as they did. And that, too, we shall probably never know.

Egyptian presidents Zine al-ᶜAbidin bin ᶜAli and Husni Mubarak, went viral. Then there is the highly touted use of social networking sites for the purpose of mobilization, not to mention the common demands for human and democratic rights and social justice.

There are, however, two main objections to the use of the wave metaphor. Most significantly, the metaphor makes it seem that the spread of the uprisings and protests from state to state was inevitable, like a wave washing over a beach. Its use thus obscures the fact that the uprisings and protests spread as a result of tens of thousands of individual decisions made by courageous participants who chose on a daily basis to face the full repressive power of the state. The wave metaphor also obscures the fact that the goals and styles of the uprisings and protests have varied widely from country to country. The goal of some has been the complete overthrow of the regime, while the goal of others has been the reform of the regime. In some places, initial protests came about after meticulous preparation; in others, the spark was spontaneous. And there have been times when uprisings have been predominantly peaceful, and other times when they took a violent turn.

It is possible to salvage the wave metaphor if we remain aware that what has been taking place in the Arab world has both transnational elements and national elements. The transnational elements are found mainly in terms of inputs: As we have seen, over the course of the past half century, all Arab states came to share similar characteristics, and over the course of the past two decades, all Arab states have faced similar shocks that made them vulnerable to popular anger. The national elements are found in the distinctive paths taken by the uprisings: Variations in state institutions and capabilities, the cohesiveness of the military, the ability of the opposition to maintain a broad and unified coalition, and foreign intervention—or lack thereof—have all influenced the trajectory of each uprising.

Overall, there are four transnational factors that made all states in the Arab world vulnerable to popular anger. The first should by now be familiar: neoliberalism. Neoliberal policies shredded the post–World War II benefits-for-compliance ruling bargain that had connected Arab governments with their populations and increased the vulnerability of those populations. It did this by fraying the social safety net, reducing middle class welfare benefits, widening the gap between rich and poor, and introducing a class of crony capitalists who are widely resented.

The second factor that made regimes in the Arab world vulnerable is demography. Approximately 60 percent of the population of the Arab world is under the age of thirty. Even more telling is the percentage of youths between the ages of fifteen and twenty-nine, the period during which most enter the job market and compete on the marriage market. Youths between the ages of fifteen and twenty-nine make up 29 percent of the population of Tunisia, 30 percent of the population of Egypt, 32 percent of the population of Algeria, and 34 percent of the population of Libya. They also make up the bulk of the unemployed (for example, in Egypt they make up 90 percent of the unemployed).

Demography is not, of course, destiny, and frustrations about job or life prospects do not necessarily translate themselves into rebellion. And youth has hardly been the only segment of Arab populations that has mobilized during the uprisings: In Tunisia and Egypt, labor played a major role; in Libya and Syria, parents protesting the way the state had dealt with their children sparked them. Nevertheless, by 2010 there was a cohort of youth throughout the Arab world with a significant set of grievances. Under the proper circumstances, this cohort was available to be mobilized for oppositional politics.

The third factor that made regimes in the Arab world vulnerable was the disruption of the international food supply chain. The Arab Middle East is more dependent on aggregate food imports than any other region in the world. Egypt alone is the world's largest wheat importer. Beginning in mid-2010, the world price of wheat more than doubled, spiking in January 2011. Economists attribute this to a number of factors, from speculation to drought to more acreage in the United States and Europe devoted to growing corn for biofuel.

But in addition to its dependence on food imports, there are two reasons why sky-rocketing food prices are a particular burden in the Arab world. First, the portion of household spending that goes to pay for food in the Arab world ranges as high as 63 percent in Morocco. Compare that to the average percentage of household spending that goes to pay for food in the United States: 7 percent—a figure that includes eating as entertainment; that is, dining outside the home. The second reason the damage caused by sky-rocketing food prices in the Arab world is particularly punishing is neoliberalism. Pressure from the United States and the International Monetary Fund constrained governments from intervening in markets to fix prices and has forced governments to abandon across-the-board subsidies on food.

The final factor making regimes vulnerable is their brittleness. The years between the onset of the economic crisis of 2008 and the first uprising, in Tunisia, were not good ones for governments throughout the world. Governments found themselves caught between bankers and economists recommending austerity on the one hand, and populations fearing the end of the welfare state they had come to know on the other. Populations voted out ruling parties in the United Kingdom, Greece, Ireland, Portugal, Spain, Iceland, Slovakia, Canada, the Netherlands, France, and Italy, among other countries. In the United States, elections first threw out a Republican president, then a Democratic congress. And throughout Europe protesters and rioters took to the streets to prevent governments from cutting workers' pay and unemployment benefits, increasing the retirement age and cutting pensions, and eliminating bonuses to families having children. Yet through it all, not one government was overthrown, nor were political institutions uprooted. Blame fell on politicians and parties and the policies they pushed.

Now turn to the Arab world, where political institutions are weak and the lines separating the ruler, the ruling party, and ruling institutions (from the party congresses and "parliaments" to the military and intelligence services) are often blurred, if they exist at all. In most cases, popular representatives cannot be turned out of office because there are no popular representatives. In those few cases where there are, their power is limited. This is why populations throughout the region have taken to the streets as their first option. This also explains why the most common slogan during the uprisings was "Down with the *nizam* (regime, system, order)," and not "Down with the *hukuma* (government)."

These four factors, then, made all regimes throughout the Arab world vulnerable to the sort of protests and uprisings witnessed since December 2010. They did not, of course, cause the uprisings. To attribute the uprisings to these factors or to any others overlooks a key variable—the human element—that determines whether an uprising will or will not occur. That being said, however, the remarkable fact remains that since December 2010 uprisings or protests of one sort or another broke out in all but possibly five of the twenty-two member states of the

Arab League (depending on one's definition of protests or uprisings, those five are the Comoros, Lebanon, Somalia, Qatar, and the UAE). Once uprisings began to break out in the region, they took a number of forms. In the main, the uprisings that have broken out so far might be placed into five clusters.

The first cluster consists of Tunisia and Egypt, where militaries stepped in to depose autocrats—Husni Mubarak who had ruled for thirty years in the case of Egypt, Zine al-ʿAbidine bin ʿAli who had ruled for twenty-three in Tunisia—who faced widespread disaffection. The militaries thus cut the revolutionary process short which, in turn, prevented a thorough housecleaning in both states.

As we have seen, Tunisia and Egypt are unique in the Arab world: Beginning in the nineteenth century, both experienced two centuries of continuous state-building. As a result, in both there were long-lived, functioning institutions autonomous from the executive branch of the government. The military is one of those institutions, but there are others as well, including the judiciary and security services. Together, these institutions make up what political scientists call the "deep state." When faced with an unprecedented crisis, the institutions of the deep state closed ranks to protect themselves.

The struggle between the deep state and the forces promoting change in both places defined the course of the two uprisings. When moderate Islamist organizations—Ennahda in Tunisia, the Muslim Brotherhood in Egypt—won popular mandates to form governments, the deep state joined forces with other remnants of the old regime and more secular-oriented groups within the population in defiance. In Egypt, the brotherhood saw itself locked in a battle to the death with its adversaries, who felt likewise. It therefore refused to share power with them, and even pushed through a constitution it drafted when it appeared that the judiciary was about to dissolve the constitution-drafting assembly on procedural grounds. As the crisis escalated—and as the Egyptian economy went into a free fall—hundreds of thousands of Egyptians took to the streets. Once again, the military stepped in, dissolved the brotherhood, had a constitution drafted that enhanced the power of the deep state, and established a regime far more repressive than Mubarak's (according to the Egyptian Centre for Economic and Social Rights, between July 2013, when the military retook power, and November/December 2013 the military killed 2,665 of their fellow citizens, wounded 16,000, and arrested 13,145).

Things in Tunisia did not end up as badly. Unlike the Egyptian Muslim Brotherhood, Ennahda did not overplay its hand. As a matter of fact, from the beginning Ennahda reached out to opposition parties and brought them into the government. And when faced with the same crises and oppositional forces faced by the Egyptian Muslim Brotherhood, Ennahda, as well as its opponents, stepped away from the precipice. Ennahda not only dissolved the government it dominated and called for new elections (which it lost), it signed on to the most liberal constitution in the Arab world. If any of the uprisings is to have a happy ending, the Tunisian uprising is the most likely candidate.

The second cluster of states undergoing uprisings includes Yemen and Libya, where regimes fragmented, pitting the officers and soldiers, cabinet ministers, politicians, and diplomats who stood with the regime against those who joined the opposition. (Tribes and tribal confederations, upon which the regimes depended to compensate for institutional underdevelopment, also divided into opposing camps.) The fragmentation of regimes in the two states is not surprising: In contrast to Tunisia and Egypt, both Yemen and Libya are poster children for what political scientists call "weak states." In weak states, governments and the bureaucracies upon which they depend are unable to assert their authority over the entirety of the territory they rule. Nor are they able to extend their reach beneath the surface of society. It is partly for this reason that populations in weak states lack strong national identities. Such is the situation in both Yemen and Libya.

To a certain extent, the weakness of the Yemeni and Libyan states came about as a result of geography. Neither country has terrain which makes it easy to govern—Yemen because of the roughness of its terrain, Libya because of the expansiveness of its. To a certain extent, the weakness of the Yemeni and Libyan states is a result of their history (or lack thereof). Both states are relatively recent creations, artificially constructed from disparate elements. Yemen had been divided between an independent North Yemen and South Yemen until 1990. Contrasting social structures found in each Yemen reflect the legacies of formal imperialism in the south and the absence of formal imperialism in the north. The United Nations created an independent federated Libya in 1952 from the remnants of three former Italian colonies that had been kept separate until 1934. Even then, regional differences remained. Finally, the weakness of the Yemeni and Libyan states was a product of the ruling styles of their leaders: Both President ʿAli ʿAbdullah Saleh of Yemen and Muammar Qaddafi of Libya purposely avoided establishing strong institutions in favor of a personalistic style of rule so they would not have to defer to them.

Because regimes in both states fragmented, there was no unified military to step in to end the uprisings, as had happened in Tunisia and Egypt. As a result, uprisings in both states were both violent and prolonged and ended only when foreign powers stepped in. In the case of Yemen, the Gulf Cooperation Council (an association of Gulf States dominated by Saudi Arabia), the United States, and the United Nations intervened to foster a "national dialogue." In the case of Libya, NATO airpower broke the stalemate between the regime and the opposition, tipping the balance in favor of the latter. Ultimately, neither intervention might be considered a success, mainly because the removal of autocrats left political chaos in its wake while the international community turned its attention elsewhere. This was because the only common ground linking regime opponents with each other in both countries was their hostility toward the regime. With the removal of ʿAli ʿAbdullah Saleh of Yemen and Muammar Qaddafi of Libya, opposition elements began to compete with one another and with remnants of the old regime for power.

"The People Want the End of the Regime." Sana, Yemen, March 2011. (*From: Corbis Images.*)

In the case of Yemen, the opposition consisted of two camps: political elites who, as "outs," merely wanted a piece of the action, and a coalition of social media–savvy youths and labor activists, among others, who wanted real change. The latter coalition refused to participate in the national dialogue which had been stacked in favor of the old elites, some of whom had belonged to the regime, some of whom acted as its loyal opposition. So did those who wanted independence for South Yemen. No national consensus was reached and with secessionists in the south gaining ground, there is a real possibility that Yemen will cease to exist as a single entity. And since Yemen is a geographic outlier and of negligible importance to the inter-Arab balance of power, there is less incentive for the international community to intervene to prevent such a breakup, as it has attempted to do in Syria and Iraq.

As for Libya, locally based militias—some Islamist, some not—vied for control over resources, territory, and political power in the immediate aftermath of the uprising. Over time, Islamist militias, on the one hand, and non-Islamist militias and regime holdovers, on the other, coalesced into two opposing camps. As in the cases of Tunisia and Egypt, then, the main fault line in Libyan politics in the aftermath of the uprising became one separating Islamists from their anti-Islamist opponents. Unlike the cases of Tunisia and Egypt, however, outside powers have fueled Libya's civil war, with Qatar and Turkey supplying the Islamists with weaponry and Egypt and the UAE spearheading military intervention on behalf of their secular opponents.

A third cluster of states includes Syria and Bahrain, where regimes maintained their cohesion against the uprisings. One might even say that in Syria and Bahrain regimes had no choice but to maintain their cohesion against uprisings.

Thus, once uprisings broke out in these states, there was little likelihood that one part of the ruling institution would turn on another, as happened in Tunisia or Egypt, or that the ruling institution would splinter, as happened in Libya and Yemen.

In Syria and Bahrain rulers effectively "coup-proofed" their regimes by, among other things, exploiting ties of sect and kinship to build a close-knit, interdependent ruling group. In Syria this group consisted of President Bashar al-Assad, his extended family, and members of the minority Alawite community (Alawites are an offshoot of Shiʿi Islam and make up about 11 percent of the population). Thus, Bashar al-Assad appointed his cousin head of the presidential guard, his brother commander of the Republican Guard and Fourth Armored Division, and his brother-in-law deputy chief of staff. None of them could have turned on the regime; if the regime goes, they would go, too. As a matter of fact, few persons of note have defected from the regime and, of those who have—one brigadier general, a prime minister (which in Syria is a post of little importance), and an ambassador to Iraq—not one was Alawite.

The core of the regime in Bahrain consists of members of the ruling Khalifa family who hold critical cabinet portfolios, from the office of prime minister and deputy prime minister to ministers of defense, foreign affairs, finance, and national security. The commander of the army and commander of the royal guard are also family. As in Syria, members of a minority community—Sunni Muslims, who make up and estimated 30–40 percent of the population—form the main pillar and primary constituency of the regime. The regime has counted on the Sunni community to circle its wagons in the regime's defense, although the uprising started out as non-sectarian in nature, as had Syria's. But as happened in Syria, repression by a regime identified with a minority community, along with the regime's deliberate provocation of inter-sectarian violence to ensure their communities would stick with the regime until the bitter end, sectarianized the uprisings and intensified the level of violence.

Foreign intervention has played a critical role in determining the course of the uprisings in both Bahrain and Syria. The one thousand Saudi soldiers and five hundred Emirati policemen who crossed the causeway connecting Bahrain with the mainland took up positions throughout the capital, Manama. This freed up the Bahraini military and security services (led by members of the ruling family and made up of Sunnis from Pakistan, Jordan, and elsewhere) to crush the opposition. The regime then embarked on a campaign of repression that was harsh even by Gulf standards. Regime opponents have faced mass arrests and torture in prison, all demonstrations have been banned, insulting the king can result in a prison sentence of up to seven years, and security forces armed with riot gear have cordoned off rebellious Shiʿi villages, terrorizing residents with nighttime raids. The government also made it illegal to possess a Guy Fawkes mask, the accessory of choice of anarchists and members of Occupy movements the world over. All the while, the regime hid behind the façade of a series of national dialogues whose outcomes the regime fixed.

While foreign intervention helped curtail the Bahraini uprising, it had the opposite effect in Syria. Both supporters of the regime—Iran, Russia, and Hizbullah—and supporters of the opposition—the West, Saudi Arabia, Qatar, Turkey, and others—have funneled arms and money to their proxies, while Hizbullah fighters and, perhaps, Iranian soldiers, joined the fray. This has not only served to escalate the violence but has created the environment in which the Islamic State of Iraq and Syria—later just the "Islamic State"—might incubate before it set out to create its caliphate from portions of the two states. To date, the foreign backers of the government have been more effective in their efforts than the foreign backers of the opposition for two reasons. First, the latter supports a number of groups acting at cross-purposes—ranging from the inept "moderate" forces supported by the West to salafis supported by the Qataris and Saudis. Second, the opposition's supporters act at cross-purposes: The West, fearing a sectarian bloodbath and the strength of Islamist groups within the opposition, has been ambivalent, at best, about facilitating a clear-cut opposition victory. On the other hand, the Saudis and Qataris have supported groups that seek to rule post-uprising Syria according to a strict interpretation of Islamic law. All told, by 2014 Syria hosted approximately 120,000 opposition fighters who had joined upwards of one thousand opposition groups, many of which took control over villages and towns and the surrounding countryside. As the United Nations and Arab League special envoy to Syria, Lakhdar Brahimi, put it, in the end the uprising will quite possibly lead to the "Somalization" of Syria. That is, like Somalia, Syria will remain a state on paper only, while real power will be divided among the government and rival gangs which control their own fiefdoms.

The fourth cluster of states consists of four of the seven remaining monarchies—Morocco, Saudi Arabia, Kuwait, Oman—in which uprisings occurred. Here the word uprising is a misnomer: With the exception of the uprising in Bahrain (and Jordan), *protests* in the Arab monarchies share two important characteristics that set them apart from *uprisings* in the Arab republics: They have, for the most part, been more limited in scope, and they have demanded reform of the *nizam*, not its overthrow.

It is not altogether clear why this discrepancy has been the case—or, for that matter, whether it will continue to be so. Some political scientists have maintained that the reason why the demand in monarchies has been for reform and not revolution is that monarchs have an ability presidents—even presidents for life—do not have: They can retain executive power while ceding legislative power to an elected assembly and prime minister. As a result, the assembly and prime minister, not the monarch, become the focal point of popular anger when things go wrong. Unfortunately, this explanation rings hollow. While it might hold true for Kuwait, which has a parliament which can be, at times, quite raucous, Saudi Arabia does not even have a parliament and the king *is* the prime minister. Others argue that oil wealth enables monarchs to buy off their opposition or prevent an opposition from arising in the first place. This might explain the Gulf monarchies, but neither Morocco nor Jordan have oil while Bahrain—which has had a long history of rebellion and had a full-fledged uprising in 2011—is hydrocarbon rich.

It is entirely possible in the future it might be necessary to reassess whether a monarchic category even exists. Bahrain was not the only monarchy in which opposition leaders called for the removal of the king. The same occurred in Jordan during demonstrations in November 2012, and although those demonstrations soon ran out of steam, there is no way to determine how deep the sentiment runs or whether it might reemerge in the future. And while the world was focused on the anemic demonstrations of social-networking youths in Saudi Arabia's capital, violent protests, which met with violent suppression, broke out in the predominantly Shi'i Eastern Province of the country. Taking these latter protests into account challenges the notion that protests in the monarchies were uniformly limited in scope. Ultimately, the small number of monarchies included in this category (four out of eight in the region) makes any conclusions about a monarchic exception problematic.

The fifth and final cluster includes two places where uprisings occurred but have been overlooked: Iraq and Palestine. The fact that both states are "hybrid democracies" influenced the demands and targets of protesters: Populations went out on the streets demanding accountability from elected governments that had proved corrupt and dysfunctional. Iraq experienced two waves of protest. The first began with calls for a Day of Rage on 25 February 2011. From Mosul in the north to Basra in the south, tens of thousands of Iraqis went out on the streets protesting shortages of electricity and water, high unemployment, and the government corruption and gridlock that they held responsible for their plight. Fifteen Iraqis died on February 25. The protests were quelled when the prime minister pledged to hold government ministers responsible—and when security forces deployed in full force. The second wave of protests began in the winter of 2014 in the Sunni areas of the country. Protesters demanded the end of discriminatory policies against their community perpetrated by the Shi'i government of Nouri al-Maliki. The government met those protests with extreme violence, including the use of barrel bombs (barrels packed with TNT dropped from aircraft) which encouraged tribal leaders to establish a "tribal army" to protect their community. It also encouraged much of that community to sit on their hands or openly support the Islamic State when it began its conquests.

The Palestinian uprising took place in several stages. In January 2011, a group calling itself "Gaza Youth Breaks Out" issued its first manifesto which stated, "There is a revolution growing inside of us, an immense dissatisfaction and frustration that will destroy us unless we find a way of canalizing this energy into something that can challenge the status quo and give us some kind of hope." That energy was "canalized" through the March 15 Youth Movement, a loose association of social media–savvy young people similar to Egypt's April 6 Youth Movement that had sparked the uprising there. Like the April 6 Youth Movement, the March 15 Youth Movement began its protests with a "Day of Rage" in which tens of thousands of Palestinians took part. Rather than demanding the ouster of the regime as their Egyptian compatriots had done, however, movement leaders demanded reconciliation between Fatah and Hamas. The final stage in the Palestinian uprising took place in the West Bank in September 2012 after the government raised prices on food and fuel. Spurred on by the same sort of labor activism that had proved decisive in the Egyptian uprising, protesters soon escalated their demands from the economic to the political: They called for the dismissal of the prime minister of the Palestinian Authority (and, in some cases, the resignation of its president, Mahmoud Abbas), the dismantling of the Authority, renunciation of the Oslo Accord and its associated economic protocols, and the establishment of a Palestinian state within the 1967 borders with East Jerusalem as its capital. The protest deeply shook the Palestinian leadership. It not only led to the firing of the Palestinian Authority prime minister, it encouraged Abbas to seize the initiative and assuage public opinion by taking the case for Palestinian statehood to the General Assembly of the United Nations.

Overall, the scorecard for the uprisings that began in 2010–2011 is depressing. In Egypt and all the monarchies the forces of reaction snuffed out the demands for change. Libya and Yemen face fragmentation, Syria's bloodbath shows no sign of abating, and Iraqis now face more serious challenges than shortages of electricity and potable water. Even the fate of Tunisia's "success story" is not a sure thing. As with all the other oil-less states in the region that have experienced uprisings, the fate of the Tunisian uprising will likely be determined by the Tunisian government's ability to do something about the wretched state of the Tunisian economy. And in a world in which neoliberalism reigns supreme, governments of all those states will find themselves squeezed between the demands of the IMF and the demands of their populations, if it hasn't happened to them already.

On the other hand, there are two grounds for optimism, if not in the short term, then in the long term. First, looking at the uprisings that began in 2010–2011 as part of a thirty-year process and not as an isolated event enables us to put the four-month period in which most of the protests and uprisings broke out in a wider perspective. Who's to say how long this decades-old process will continue and where it will eventually take the Arab world? Second, while the previous chapter argued against using the phrase "Arab Spring" because it decontextualizes what happened beginning in 2010–2011, it might be helpful to remember the first time historians used the spring metaphor. They used it in reference to the revolutions of 1848—the "Springtime of Nations"—when it seemed revolutions based on liberal ideals and nationalism would engulf all of Europe. While historical analogies are always deficient, perhaps the events of 1848 might provide us with insight as to how to understand the Arab uprisings. Although none of the revolutions in that bleak year succeeded, their outbreak signaled in retrospect that the field of political struggle in Europe forever after would include alternatives to the autocratic order—even if the realization of those alternatives might take a century and a half or so. Succeed or fail, the same lesson might be learned from the current spate of Arab uprisings.

CONCLUSION

The End of an Era?

At the end of the twentieth century, historians began to look back and assess what had taken place and what the meaning of it all was. One of the questions they raised concerned the problem of periodicization, that is, where to put the historical boundaries of the twentieth century.

Chronologically, of course, the twentieth century began in 1900 (or 1901, if you are a stickler for details), just as the nineteenth century had begun in 1800 (or, again, 1801). But most historians do not plot history simply by referring to a calendar. In the case of the nineteenth century, for example, many historians use a periodicization that places the beginning of the century in 1789—the year of the French Revolution—and the end of the century in 1914—the year World War I broke out. Historians call this the "long nineteenth century." According to their accounts, the long nineteenth century was distinguished by a number of characteristics. During the long nineteenth century the modern world economic system reached the far corners of the globe as workers and farmers on every continent came to participate in a worldwide division of labor. The nation-state replaced the empire as the prototypical political unit and spread throughout the world. Certain dogmas, such as a belief in progress, standards of civilization, popular sovereignty, and nationalism, gained almost universal currency as a result of European global dominance, also a hallmark of the long nineteenth century. Finally, new social classes—the bourgeoisie and the working class—appeared on the world stage for the first time as a result of the twin processes of urbanization and industrialization.

If all or some of these phenomena have come to mark the long nineteenth century, what phenomena mark the century that followed? Some historians have placed a "short twentieth century" alongside the long nineteenth century. The great British historian Eric Hobsbawm, for example, began his twentieth century with World War I and ended it in 1991. His timing of the twentieth century coincides with the establishment of the first great "socialist experiment" in Russia, which divided the world into rival socialist and capitalist camps. According to

Hobsbawm, the rise of Soviet communism not only created a socialist state, it affected the entire world. To save capitalism, he argued, nonsocialist states had to undertake reforms. These reforms led to the emergence of the welfare state in the West and to the rescue of liberal capitalism. Hobsbawm ended his periodicization of the twentieth century with the demise of the Soviet Union, the end of the cold war, and the emergence of the United States as the world's only superpower.

As we have seen, the welfare state idea did leave a lasting impression on the states and citizens of the Middle East. In other ways, however, this periodicization ill suits the Middle East or other regions outside Europe. It is likely that states in the Middle East would have gone down the road of state-directed development and would have assumed many of the attributes of welfare states no matter what was going on in Europe. As a matter of fact, some historians and political scientists, following in the footsteps of economist Alexander Gerschenkron, have proposed a model of "late development" for nations that emerged in the wake of the industrial revolution. According to Gerschenkron and his followers, nations as diverse as nineteenth-century Germany and twentieth-century India commonly found market forces an insufficient basis for industrial development. Instead, there had to be some central mechanism—a state or a group of industrial elites— that took charge of industrial development and that won over various classes to its endeavors by extending promises to them. None of this can be attributed to the rise of the socialist bloc. And while the superpower rivalry between the United States and the Soviet Union did leave an imprint on the region and did aggravate regional conflicts, it hardly provides the hallmarks of an epoch. Instead, as we have seen, American-Soviet competition in the region was more akin to "new wine in old bottles."

Like Hobsbawm, other historians and political scientists have tried their hand at defining the twentieth century. Some have opined that Hobsbawm's notion of the short twentieth century should be replaced by a long twentieth century. Historian Charles S. Maier, for example, has proposed a twentieth century that stretches from 1850 to 1970. His twentieth century coincides with the rise and fall of the territorial state. How this periodicization would deal with the problem of defining the boundaries of the nineteenth century is not clear. Nor is it clear whether the highly touted weakening of the territorial state in the wake of an increasingly globalized world economy is anything more than a shortsighted infatuation on the part of social scientists.

These bold attempts to figure out the central theme of twentieth-century history illustrate the principal problem historians confront when they attempt to divide history into bite-size pieces. For historical periods to have any meaning, historians assign to them certain attributes that distinguish them from earlier and later periods. This means that historians must make choices and stress certain events or phenomena at the expense of others. We all know that the Renaissance was a period of great artistic achievement in Europe, but just how much did social or economic life during this period differ from daily life in the Medieval period that preceded it or in the Reformation period that followed it?

The division of history into periods is thus both helpful and deceptive. On the one hand, it enables historians to highlight elements of change. On the other, it compels historians to privilege some types of change over others and to lose sight of historical continuities.

Take, for example, the common practice of using World War I as the dividing line between two historical eras. Part III of this book argued that World War I was perhaps the most important political event in the history of the modern Middle East for four reasons: the creation of the state system; the onset of the Israeli-Palestinian imbroglio; the spread of a variety of nationalist sentiments throughout the region, many of which were embodied in states; and the consolidation of Iran as a modern nation-state under the guidance of Reza Shah. These are certainly important developments, but there are two things that are worthy of note. First of all, the roots of all these post–World War I developments might be traced to developments in the second half of the nineteenth century. It would have been impossible for nationalist movements to spread in the region had the Ottomans not already introduced modern institutions and structures of governance into the region, the Zionists who came to Palestine put themselves squarely within the tradition of European colonialism and the imperative to spread "civilization," and recent scholarship has demonstrated that many of the innovations attributed to the Reza Shah period—nationalism and defensive developmentalism, for example—also had their roots in late nineteenth-century Qajar rule. In addition, while World War I may have been the most important political event in the history of the modern Middle East, the war did not substantially change the social and economic history of the region. As we have seen, the region remained locked in a colonial relationship with the industrialized world, and the social and economic structures that had defined Middle Eastern society during the nineteenth century remained pretty much intact until they were disrupted in the 1930s and 1940s and reconstituted in the 1950s and 1960s.

So if World War I did not mark the beginning of a new twentieth-century dispensation, what did? Perhaps nothing. Turning Maier on his head, it is possible to argue that there was no twentieth century in the Middle East. This does not mean that the Middle East is backward in some way. Rather, it might be argued that after the twin Middle Eastern revolutions of the nineteenth century—the integration of the region into the modern world economy and into the international state system—nothing took place in the Middle East that would have comparable revolutionary effects on the region. And it is for this very reason that historians have not been able to come up with a yardstick for historical periodization that has any true meaning for the Middle East.

There is, however, something dissatisfying about this way of viewing the past. It is static and lacks nuance and detail. It reduces history to, in the words of the nineteenth-century philosopher G.W.F. Hegel, "a night in which all the cows are black." The Middle East at the end of 2011 *was* a different place than the Middle East at the end of 2009, and the so-called human rights revolution of the 1970s *did* have a profound impact on the region which is still playing itself out. What is perhaps necessary, then, is rather than just focusing on benchmark events—the integration of the region into the twin systems that mark the modern period—to look instead at history through two different chronological frameworks. The first highlights the revolutionary, long-term, and irreversible changes brought about by the integration of the Middle East into the world economy and the world system of nation-states—what might be called "epochal time." The other—what might be called "historical time"—highlights changes that took place within that broader chronological framework, such as those of a political nature.

If we shift our focus to historical time, there is no doubt that we are currently in the midst of perhaps the most contentious period in the history of the Middle East since World War I, and certainly since 1958—the date when the Arab world was in the throes of its Nasserist and Pan-Arab moments and when revolutionary transformations of multiple states in the region seemed imminent (and, indeed, took place in Iraq). Between 2009 and 2014, seventeen of twenty states in the Middle East/North Africa region experienced civil disorder, mass protests, uprisings, or a combination of the three. There were, of course, the Arab uprisings, but Turkey, Iran, and Israel also faced large-scale protest movements. Government high-handedness (manifested through its attempt to bulldoze a popular park in Istanbul) and creeping Islamization of all aspects of life sparked them in the first case; electoral fraud in the second; and a lack of affordable housing and the deterioration of services in the third. In perhaps five states (Bahrain, Iraq, Syria, and perhaps Jordan and Iran) these upheavals were regime threatening; in three (Tunisia, Egypt, and Yemen) they forced the removal of autocrats, and one (Libya) brought down an entire regime. Throughout the region politics took a violent turn, although several states—Syria, Libya, Yemen, and Iraq—stand out in particular in this regard. And division seemed to threaten one state (Yemen) while three (Libya, Syria, Iraq) were likely to enter the "failed state" category, existing as states on paper with little or no government control over much of their territory.

In the past, historical changes have provided the wherewithal for epochal changes. We have seen, for example, how events, discoveries, and inventions that took place in the fifteenth and sixteenth centuries enabled the Commercial Revolution, which, in turn, set the stage for the contemporary world economy. In light of the aforementioned developments in the Middle East, then, can we be sure that the region is not on the cusp of an epochal shift? Can it be that we are in the midst of a game-changing moment that threatens (or promises, depending on your point of view) to put an end to the epoch-making transformation of the region that began in the nineteenth century and that will ultimately affect every aspect of life in the region?

Let's start with the relationship of the region with the world economy. At the end of the cold war, the word "globalization" was just entering popular consciousness, and the much-debated question was whether globalization was a "good thing" or a "bad thing." The debate is over because the point is now moot. The triumph of neoliberalism—the benchmark factor that distinguishes this period in the history of the world economy from earlier ones—and the fact that your Levi's are more likely to be made in Mexico or Cambodia than in the United States are part of everyday experience. But does this new period of globalization portend a shift in the position of the Middle East in the world economy? After all, as neoliberals like to argue, a rising tide raises all boats.

For all the talk that this or that country in the region is on the verge of becoming the "Switzerland of the Middle East," the position of the Middle East in the world economy is even worse now than it had been before "globalization" became a buzzword. The Middle East remains locked in its peripheral position in the world economy, and with the possible exceptions of Turkey and Israel, the states of the region are likely to remain so in the foreseeable future. As a matter of fact, the Middle East is the least globalized region on the planet, save sub-Saharan Africa. With the exception of oil, gas, and unemployed youths, exports from the Middle East have remained flat in recent decades, while the remainder of the developing world has more than doubled its share of the international market since 1980. Close to 60 percent of the region's exports go to Europe, indicating two problems. First, the only comparative advantage the region has over other regions is its proximity to Europe. Second, the region is isolated from the global economy in general and from emerging markets such as China in particular.

All that globalization has brought to the Middle East has been pressure for all countries in the region to adopt neoliberal economic policies—what else is there?—which has raised levels of unemployment, shredded the ruling bargain between states and their citizens, and widened the income gap within each country. According to a World Bank report, "The substantial progress in reducing poverty in earlier decades came to a halt in the latter half of the 1980s. . . . An additional 11 million people were added to the ranks of the poor between 1987 and 2001 because the region's population continued to grow but its economies didn't." The trend the report highlighted continued into the next decade. And poor economic performance—attributable to isolation from the world economy, corruption, and half-hearted attempts at economic "reform" that combine the worst aspects of state-dominated economies with the worst aspects of a market economy—makes it hard to imagine just how any of the Arab uprisings, were they to succeed, will improve the lot of their populations and bring about social stability.

Globalization enthusiasts believed that the trend toward economic integration would break down national boundaries and transform, weaken, or perhaps lead to the demise of nation-states and the nation-state system. In their starry-eyed vision, economics would reign supreme over politics. This, obviously, has not happened, and skeptics have noted that nationalism and the nation-state system have proved to be remarkably resilient. Not that it matters much for a region which missed the bus on globalization anyway. Nevertheless, pundits point to other trends that threaten the nation-state and the current arrangement of nation-states in the Middle East. The three most common trends cited are the sectarianization of politics, which has led many inhabitants in the region to privilege religious affiliation over national affiliation; challenges to the post–World

War I state system in the region; and the challenge posed by alternative conceptions about the organization of political communities which seem to put the nation-state idea on the defensive. Let's look at these in turn.

As we have seen, sectarianism becomes a factor in politics whenever some political entrepreneur finds it a useful tool to achieve political goals. That entrepreneur might be a government, a foreign power, or an individual or group. In the contemporary Middle East, all three have played a role.

It is possible to pinpoint a number of causes for the recent sectarianization of politics in the Middle East. First, regimes throughout the region have become identified with one or another religious community, sometimes a minority community (as in those regimes that have been "coup-proofed" such as Syria and Bahrain), sometimes the majority community (as in Turkey, Yemen, and post-Saddam Iraq). The identification of a regime with a particular community and its discriminatory acts against citizens who are not members of that community compel those citizens to see themselves in sectarian terms. Then there are the spillover effects of the Syrian civil war. By the end of 2014, Turkey hosted about a million Syrian refugees, mostly Sunnis, in a region of the country in which religious minorities are concentrated, sparking resentments within those communities. In Lebanon, no stranger to sectarian strife, the Syrian civil war sparked clashes between Hizbullah, the Shiʿi organization that supports the Assad government, and mostly Sunni supporters of the Syrian opposition. In addition, some political actors have operated in sectarian terms as a matter of policy. The Islamic State, for example, has deliberately targeted non-Sunni communities (and even Sunnis who do not practice Islam as its loyalists do) in its quest to "purify" the Islamic community and construct their caliphate. Finally, the competition for regional dominance between predominantly Sunni Saudi Arabia and predominantly Shiʿi Iran has driven sectarianism. Although the competition is geostrategic and not religious—Saudi Arabia, a status quo power, fears any shift in the regional balance of power while Iran seeks a shift in its favor—neither side has been shy about playing the sectarian card to win or maintain the support of fellow Sunnis or Shiʿis elsewhere in its attempt to outmaneuver its rival.

What does the increasing sectarianization of politics mean for the future of the region? As we have seen, once it takes root, sectarianism within an individual state has never been eradicated. Communities often separate themselves physically from each other, or sectarianism gets inscribed into the political system à la Lebanon. In the highly unlikely event of a political settlement in Syria, for example, you can bet that the Alawite minority will demand constitutional guarantees to ensure its protection and its proportional representation in the government and administration. But also as we have seen, sectarianism does not necessarily lead to secession or state fragmentation. In contemporary Yemen, for example, the state has been fighting an insurgent movement in the northern part of the country in what has been called the "Houthi Rebellion" since the early part of this century. The Houthis derive their name from a prominent Zaydi sheikh and his family (Zaydi Islam is an offshoot of Shiʿism and Zaydis constitute anywhere from 25 to 40 percent of the Yemeni population). Fueled by the government's campaign to spread a strict interpretation of Sunni Islam in the Zaydi homeland, the rebellion gained momentum. By 2013 the Houthis had built a state within a state. A year later, they crushed a Yemeni army sent north to put down the rebellion, marched on Yemen's capital, Sana, and forced Yemen's president to dismiss the government and guarantee Houthi representation in a new one. Nevertheless, they did not demand northern independence, which they might well have achieved. Similarly, during uprisings in Saudi Arabia and Bahrain, the minority Shi'i community in the former and the majority Shi'i community in the latter also demanded greater inclusion and not the severance of ties with their fellow countrymen.

This brings us to the second trend that observers of the region cite as threatening the nation-state and the current arrangement of nation-states in the Middle East: challenges to the post–World War I state system.

Recently there has been a lot of attention paid to the artificiality of the boundaries dividing states in the Middle East from each other and the question of whether the state system will hold, particularly under the stress of the increasing sectarianization of the region and the activities of spoilers like the Islamic State. The media has taken up al-Qaeda's terminology—and, in effect, is making al-Qaeda's argument—by using the phrase "Sykes-Picot" boundaries as a code that connotes the illegitimacy of the current state system, in spite of the fact that the lines drawn by Mark Sykes and François Georges-Picot during World War I bear little resemblance to current state borders (i.e., Is France in southern and central Anatolia or Britain in Iraq and eastern Arabia? Is Jerusalem internationalized?), that the borders in question affect only six of nineteen states in the region, and, when it comes down to it, all borders are artificial (although it might be argued that not all borders are drawn by far-off diplomats). As a matter of fact, instead of viewing the Middle East state system as fragile and a source of instability, the opposite argument might be made: In spite of the fact that there are currently at least eight boundary disputes among the states surrounding the Persian Gulf, that Syria never renounced its claim to the Turkish province of Hatay (although it came close), that a land-for-peace deal between Syria and Israel remains elusive, and that the Sahrawi and Palestinian questions have yet to be resolved, the state system in the Middle East has been remarkably stable for more than fifty years, or at least since the British withdrew from the Gulf in 1971. There is no reason to believe it will not remain so. With the exception of the unification of the two Yemens in 1990 and the exchange of a few Persian Gulf islands among states of the region—sometimes accomplished through negotiation, sometimes by force—most states remain pretty much as they have been for the past half century.

There are two reasons this is the case. First, although Yemen appears on the verge of disintegration while sectarian and ethnic identities compete with a national one in Syria and seem to have trumped it in Iraq, it is just as true (as a number of political scientists have argued) that national attachments have grown stronger in much of the region since the early days of state formation for reasons discussed in Chapter 13. This patriotic attachment was evident during the Arab uprisings, which targeted for removal only the regimes under which protesters lived and which were usually accompanied by conspicuous displays of national symbols. That same chapter alluded to the second reason the existing state system in the Middle East is not an endangered species as well: When push comes to shove, some power, either great (first Britain, then the United States) or regional has intervened to maintain the status quo. Hence, Iranian intervention into a rebellion in Oman (1962–1976), Syrian intervention (supported by the Arab League) into the Lebanese Civil War (1976), and decades of Saudi intervention into Yemeni affairs.

The list of great power interventions to preserve individual states and the state system is a long one. Britain twice intervened in Oman (1959, 1975) to crush rebellions that threatened to divide the country. The British again intervened in the Gulf in 1961 to protect newly independent Kuwait from its northern neighbor which claimed it as Iraq's nineteenth province. Saddam Hussein reasserted that claim in 1990. Once again foreign intervention forced an Iraqi retreat. And lest it be thought that the only motivating factor driving the great powers is oil, there have been interventions to "protect" non-oil states as well, including American and British intervention into Lebanon and Jordan, respectively, in 1958 to shore up regimes during a time of regional instability. Oil has played its part, to be sure, as has the protection of clients and fear of expanding Soviet influence during the cold war. But so has stability for its own sake—what political scientist Boaz Atzili calls the post–World War II obsession with "border fixity." So long as the Middle East remains a region of concern for the United States, the tradition of intervening to assure the stability of individual states and the regional order will continue. Even the hesitant Barack Obama, who instinctively resisted intervening into the Syrian morass for more than three years, succumbed to that tradition.

When Obama justified making war on the Islamic State in September 2014, he cited as casus belli the acts of violence committed in its name and the potential danger to Americans and the American homeland. What he did not mention was perhaps the most compelling reason behind the decision: the threat his administration believed the Islamic State posed to the regional order. Besides the potential danger to Iraq's southern neighbor, Saudi Arabia, a precedent-setting severing of territory in Syria and Iraq is in the interest of no outside power for a variety of reasons. These include the fact that a future settlement of the Israel-Syria conflict would become a dead letter (Israel and Syria were in secret negotiations up until the outbreak of the Syrian uprising) and the establishment of an independent Kurdish state—initially carved out of Iraq and Syria but with the potential to include parts of Turkey and Iran as well—would wreak havoc on the regional order. Thus, once again the United States organized an international coalition to crush the Islamic State even though "mission accomplished" might take as long as America's misadventure in Iraq (which created the Islamic State problem in the first place).

Finally, there is the threat to states in the region by movements challenging the legitimacy of states organized as national units. While al-Qaeda was not the first group in the contemporary Middle East/Islamic world to treat the idea of the nation-state as a problem—that dubious distinction probably belongs to a Palestinian group, Hizb at-Tahrir, founded in 1953—the issue lies at the core of the group's ideology. As Louis Attiya Allah, a frequent spokesman for al-Qaeda, put it,

> The (Arab) nation states . . . are a Western model that the West created to allow it to build up its general colonialist plan for the Islamic East. These countries have no religious foundation, and have neither a right to exist nor a popular base. They were forced upon the Muslim peoples, and their survival is linked to the Western forces that created them. Therefore, the general aim of the jihad and the Mujahideen is to strike at the foundations and infrastructure of the Western colonialist program or at the so-called world order—or, to put it bluntly, to defeat the Crusaders in the battle that has been going on for over a century. Their defeat means, simply, the elimination of all forms of nation-states, such that all that remains is the natural existence familiar to Islam—the regional entity under the great Islamic state.

Nevertheless, as anarchists discovered as early as the nineteenth century, in a world in which nation-states provide the gold standard for the organization of political communities it is virtually impossible to conceptualize a workable alternative, much less organize one. Al-Qaedists have struggled—and argued—about just what a future caliphate would look like. Sometimes al-Qaedists have used the term as a metaphor, as when al-Qaeda's second leader, Ayman al-Zawahiri, defined it as "Islamic rule that will respect the rights and honor of its citizens, fight corruption and spread justice and equality," a place "in whose shade will retire every Muslim—nay, every wronged one and seeker of justice on the face of this earth." Sometimes for al-Qaedists, the caliphate takes the form of a post-millenarian hallucination, as when al-Qaeda's first leader, Osama bin Laden—who rarely broached the subject—said, "The entire Islamic community has set in motion the establishment of a rightly-guided caliphate, which our prophet foretold in an authentic hadith; to wit: the rightly-guided caliphate will return, God willing." The one thing that can be said for sure is that al-Qaedists do not envision the establishment of an Islamic superstate with the disciplinary capabilities and hierarchies of a modern nation-state. Rather, in the fevered al-Qaeda imagination it seems that a caliphate might be defined as a territorial expanse freed from the constraints of the nation-state system and ordered and administered according to the precepts of Islamic law. In the meantime, al-Qaedists have kicked the can down the road, engaging merely in prep work for a future caliphate.

But something strange happened on the path to establishing al-Qaeda's caliphate: At least one of its official affiliates, a local Syrian group, Jabhat al-Nusra, and many of its imitators, like the various Ansar al-Shari'as, seem to have accepted the idea that their struggle would only be viable within the context of their particular nation-states. Thus, realizing that most Syrians who are not inclined to support the regime of Bashar al-Assad are equally not inclined to

The Caliphate of the Islamic State (according to the Islamic State) at the end of 2014.

abandon the idea that they are Syrians and their struggle is a Syrian one, Jabhat al-Nusra defines itself as a *Syrian* jihadi movement. Likewise for the various Ansar al-Shariʿas, which actually call themselves such things as *ansar al-shariʿa bi-tunis* (Ansar al-Shariʿa in Tunisia) and *ansar al-shariʿa bi-libya* (Ansar al-Shariʿa in Libya).

The proliferation of affiliates, wannabes, and copycat groups, and their expansion into new territories, thus masks a phenomenon that should be deeply troubling to al-Qaeda purists. From its inception, al-Qaeda was not big on organization. Bin Laden himself once remarked there was no such thing as al-Qaeda. The term, he claimed, merely referred to what a bunch of guys hanging out in the Afghan badlands waging jihad called their headquarters—their base (*al-qaeda* in Arabic)—a term which Westerners latched on to and endowed with substance. More important than organization was ideology—the common bond that held al-Qaeda affiliates together and united them with al-Qaeda central. But now al-Qaeda's ideological cohesion, like the authority of al-Qaeda central, has dissipated. In their current manifestation, some al-Qaeda affiliates and its imitators have given in to reality.

Enter ISIS, a.k.a. the Islamic State, which seems to have defied the nation-state system by setting up a caliphate that includes parts of Syria and Iraq. But like Mark Twain's death, reports of the death of the nation-state in the Middle East are not only grossly exaggerated, they are ludicrous. First of all, the Islamic State has yet to define what exactly its caliphate is. For the moment and in the near future, it really doesn't have to, considering its focus is on expanding and holding on to the

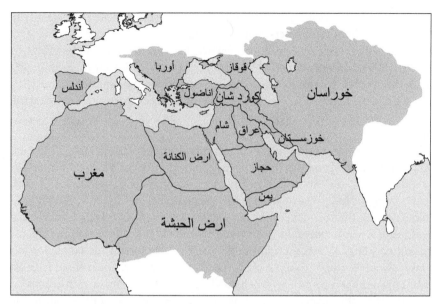

The Caliphate of the Islamic State in 2019, according to the organization's predictions.

territory under its control. But Islamic State watchers should think about other movements in the region that attempted to buck the nation-state form. The example of ʿAbd al-ʿAziz ibn al-Saʿud, who turned on the very group of fighters who led his conquests rather than let them endanger it by raiding beyond the borders of what is now Saudi Arabia, comes to mind. Rather than acting as the great purifier of Islam, ibn al-Saʿud had to accept the fact that the best he could accomplish would be to establish a nation-state. The leadership of the Islamic Republic of Iran learned the same lesson: For all its bragging about Iran's role as the vanguard of an international movement to liberate oppressed peoples from the clutches of imperialism, the regime introduced appeals to Iranian patriotism to mobilize its citizenry during the Iran–Iraq War (1980–88).

The second reason the reestablishment of a caliphate does not provide a real challenge to the nation-state form in the region is that the future of the Islamic State is not at all bright. It is small in numbers (although recent estimates of the number of its fighters vary widely, ranging from thirty-one thousand to over one hundred thousand) and it is stretched over a wide swath of territory. Its application of "Islamic punishments" and "Islamic morals" as well as its bloodlust has made it extremely unpopular wherever it has attempted to govern in Syria—so much so that it has forced rival Jabhat al-Nusra to disavow its style of rule. It is fighting on multiple fronts against multiple enemies, ranging from the Syrian government to most of the opposition in Syria to an international coalition. It has never faced an organized and equipped army in battle and is unlikely to prove any more capable of standing up to one than the coalition that faced French and

African Union forces in Mali in 2013. And it achieved its "victory" in Mosul (its four to eight hundred fighters met no resistance) and elsewhere because of its coalition with former Ba'th military men who had served under Saddam Hussein and tribal leaders—neither of which group shares its worldview (indeed, beginning in late 2014 there was already fighting among coalition members). In short, Barack Obama repeated George W. Bush's mistake by exaggerating the threat the Islamic State poses to the region and the rest of the world and thus puffing up its importance.

What further diminishes the threat posed by the Islamic State, al-Qaeda, and similar jihadi groups is that they have failed to win the battle for hearts and minds of Muslims. According to the Pew Research Global Attitudes Project, public support for al-Qaeda (that is, al-Qaeda central and its affiliates that have remained faithful to its tenets) throughout the Muslim world reached an all-time low in 2013: 57 percent of those surveyed held an unfavorable view of the organization and only 13 percent a favorable one. Support for suicide bombings followed the same trend. To top it off, 67 percent expressed concern about Islamist extremism in their countries—not a good omen for the future of such groups.

What all this seems to indicate is that despite the current upheavals in the region, the Middle East does not appear to be on the cusp of an epochal transformation. If modernity is defined by the dominance of the world economic and nation-state systems, the Middle East is firmly entrenched in its modern moment and there it is likely to stay. There does not appear to be a postmodern moment yet on the Middle Eastern horizon.

DOCUMENTS

Speech Delivered by President Gamal ͨAbd al-Nasser at Port Said on the Occasion of Victory Day on 23 December 1961

President Gamal ͨAbd al-Nasser delivered the following speech at Port Said, marking the fifth anniversary of the close of the Suez War.

In 1956, the people sacrificed—they gave their blood and there were martyrs—we did not grudge this blood or these martyrs—the people were not frightened by brute force, they were not frightened by the great powers; Britain, France and Israel did not frighten them. . . .

I am confident, fellow-brethren, that it was the great struggle that you undertook in 1956 which has opened for us the way to build the new society. I am also confident that the whole of the people of the U.A.R. have taken the same stand and fought and struggled as you did for the sake of its freedom and its independence throughout all those long years which have passed. We have fought and we have struggled. We were undaunted by imperialism and all its methods, and we were not intimidated by the tyrannical powers; neither was imperialism, with its policy which is based on sowing the seeds of dissension amongst us, able to overpower us. The proof of this is that today we are living in freedom. We are neither dominated by open imperialism nor by disguised imperialism, but we are enjoying political freedom because we have struggled to gain our political freedom. We are enjoying this political freedom because we have taken it upon ourselves to put an end to political domination. The people have risen and struggled throughout all those long years during which we suffered from imperialism, foreign domination, and occupation in order that we might be liberated. We thank God, fellow-brethren, that we are able to enjoy this freedom today. Our struggle has borne its fruits. We, our fathers and our forefathers before them, have long struggled for the sake of this freedom. We have always stood face to face with the foreign exploiting domination, and we have never wavered from our stand in any way whatsoever. . . .

Today, brethren, after this long struggle, the way has been paved for the realisation of our hopes to build the society we desire, the society in which prosperity and welfare reign supreme, the society in which class differences disappear, no masters, no slaves, but all are the sons of one nation working for the Mother-country and everyone feeling himself on an equal footing with his fellow-citizens and fellow beings. . . .

This second revolution is the people's revolution, a revolution for every son of this nation, a revolution for social justice, a revolution for the removal of class differences. By this I mean that we aim, while forging ahead with our revolution, that the society we desire, the society everyone of us desires for himself and for his children, the society in which prosperity and welfare shall reign supreme, shall be no capitalistic nor feudalistic dictatorship, no exploitation, no monopoly, but only social justice and equality of opportunity for every able-bodied son of the nation—no exploitation in any circumstances or under any condition of man by man. . . .

We say sufficiency and justice—justice is equality of distinction and not dictatorship of capital, not dictatorship of feudalism, not political nor economical nor social exploitation. Justice is that the wealth of this country be justly and equally owned by all the sons of this country each according to his work. This is justice. As to sufficiency, it is to work, strive, sweat, and build in order that we increase our national income. In order to increase our share of the wealth of this country, we nationalized the banks, the insurance companies and a number of factories and trading companies. We also nationalized all foreign trade, fifty per cent of the Anglo-Egyptian Petroleum Company, and some other companies. We also nationalized what is over L.E. 10,000 in some other industries. In this way, rights were restored. Means were restored to its owners, means of production in which they employed the worker. What does the worker have? He has his work. The capitalist? He has his money. The capitalist employs the workers. The wages of the workers were 25% of the profits whereas the few capitalists gained 75%. Is this justice? Is this the law of right, the law of God? Is this the law of justice, the law of God? Is this Islam? Is this religion? Is this Christianity in any way? This is exploitation and imperialism. This is the co-operation between imperialism, reactionism and exploitation. Who can accept this? All the profits went to a small group, while one million workers received the wages of five thousand persons, and five thousand persons got thrice as much as one million workers. This means that the capitalists, the five thousand capitalists, took thrice as much as the pay of one million workers, as profits. Is this the law of God? Can any one accept this?

President Gamal Abdel-Nasser's Speeches and Press-Interviews, January–December 1961 (Cairo: Information Department, United Arab Republic, 1962), pp. 332–43.

Zakaria Tamer: Tigers on the Tenth Day

> In his speeches, Gamal 'Abd al-Nasser presented one side of the story of the post-revolutionary Middle Eastern state. In his short story, "Tigers on the Tenth Day," Syrian writer Zakaria Tamer presents another.

The jungles had journeyed far from the tiger imprisoned in his cage, yet he was unable to forget them. He would stare angrily at men who gathered round his cage, their eyes regarding him with curiosity and without fear.

One of them would talk to him, in a voice that was quiet and yet had a commanding ring about it: 'If you really want to learn my profession, the profession of being a trainer, you must not for an instant forget that the stomach of your adversary is your first target, and you will see that the profession is both hard and easy at one and the same time.

'Look now at this tiger. He is a fierce and haughty tiger, exceedingly proud of his freedom, his strength and his courage, but he will change and become as gentle, mild and obedient as a small child. Watch what will occur between him who possesses food and him who does not, and learn.'

The men promptly said that they would be devoted students of the profession of animal training, and the trainer smiled delightedly, then addressed the tiger, enquiring of him in a sarcastic tone: 'And how is our dear guest?'

'Bring me what I eat,' said the tiger, 'for my mealtime has come.'

With feigned surprise the trainer said: 'Are you ordering me about when you are my prisoner? What an amusing tiger you are! You must realize that I am the only one here who has the right to issue orders.'

'No one gives orders to tigers,' said the tiger.

'But now you're not a tiger,' said the trainer. 'In the jungles you're a tiger, but now you're in a cage, you're just a slave who obeys orders and does what I want.'

'I shan't be anyone's slave,' said the tiger impetuously.

'You're compelled to obey me because it is I who possess the food,' said the trainer.

'I don't want your food,' said the tiger.

'Then go hungry as you wish,' said the trainer, 'for I shall not force you to do what you don't want to.'

And, addressing his pupils, he added: 'You will see how he will change, for a head held high does not gratify a hungry stomach.'

The tiger went hungry and remembered sadly the days when he would rush about, as free as the wind in pursuit of his prey.

On the second day the trainer and his pupils stood around the tiger's cage and the trainer said: 'Aren't you hungry? You're for certain so hungry it's a pain and a torture to you. Say you're hungry and you'll get what meat you want.'

The tiger remained silent, so the trainer said to him: 'Do what I say and don't be stupid. Admit you're hungry and you'll eat your fill immediately.'

'I'm hungry,' said the tiger.

The trainer laughed and said to his pupils: 'Here he is, he's fallen into a trap from which he won't escape.'

He gave orders and the tiger got a lot of meat.

On the third day, the trainer said to the tiger: 'If you want to have any food today, carry out what I ask of you.'

'I shall not obey you,' said the tiger.

'Don't be so hasty, for what I ask is very simple. You are now pacing up and down your cage; when I say to you: "Stop", you must stop.'

'That's really a trivial request,' said the tiger to himself, 'and it's not worth my being stubborn and going hungry.'

In a stern, commanding tone the trainer called out: 'Stop.'

The tiger immediately froze and the trainer said in a joyful voice, 'Well done.'

The tiger was pleased and ate greedily. Meanwhile, the trainer was saying to his pupils: 'After some days he'll become a paper tiger.'

On the fourth day the tiger said to the trainer: 'I'm hungry, so ask of me to stand still.'

The trainer said to his pupils: 'He has now begun to like my orders.'

Then, directing his words to the tiger, he said: 'You won't eat today unless you imitate the mewing of a cat.'

The tiger suppressed his anger and said to himself: 'I'll amuse myself with imitating the mewing of a cat.'

He imitated the mewing of a cat, but the trainer frowned and said disapprovingly: 'Your imitation's no good. Do you count roaring as mewing?'

So the tiger again imitated the mewing of a cat, but the trainer continued to glower and said scornfully: 'Shut up. Shut up. Your imitation is still no good. I shall leave you today to practise mewing and tomorrow I shall examine you. If you are successful you'll eat; if you're not successful you won't eat.'

The trainer moved away from the tiger's cage, walking with slow steps and followed by his pupils who were whispering among themselves and laughing. The tiger called imploringly to the jungles, but they were far distant.

On the fifth day the trainer said to the tiger: 'Come on, if you successfully imitate the mewing of a cat you'll get a large piece of fresh meat.'

The tiger imitated the mewing of a cat and the trainer clapped in applause and said joyfully: 'You're great—you mew like a cat in February,' and he threw him a large piece of meat.

On the sixth day the trainer no sooner came near the tiger than he quickly gave an imitation of a cat mewing. The trainer, however, remained silent, frowning.

'There, I've imitated a cat mewing,' said the tiger.

'Imitate the braying of a donkey,' said the trainer.

'I, the tiger who is feared by the animals of the jungles, imitate a donkey?' said the tiger indignantly. 'I'd die rather than carry out what you ask.'

The trainer moved away from the tiger's cage without uttering a word. On the seventh day he came towards the tiger's cage, with smiling face. 'Don't you want to eat?' he said to the tiger.

'I want to eat,' said the tiger.

Said the trainer: 'The meat you'll eat has a price—bray like a donkey and you'll get food.'

The tiger endeavoured to remember the jungles but failed. With closed eyes he burst forth braying. 'Your braying isn't a success,' said the trainer, 'but out of pity for you I'll give you a piece of meat.'

On the eighth day the trainer said to the tiger: 'I'll deliver a speech; when I've finished, you must clap in acclaim.'

So the trainer began to deliver his speech. 'Compatriots,' he said, 'we have previously on numerous occasions propounded our stand in relation to issues affecting our destiny, and this resolute and unequivocal stand will not change whatever hostile forces may conspire against us. With faith we shall triumph.'

'I didn't understand what you said,' said the tiger.

'It's for you to admire everything I say and to clap in acclaim,' said the trainer.

'Forgive me,' said the tiger. 'I'm ignorant and illiterate. What you say is wonderful and I shall, as you would like, clap.'

The tiger clapped and the trainer said: 'I don't like hypocrisy and hypocrites—as a punishment you will today be deprived of food.'

On the ninth day the trainer came along carrying a bundle of grass and threw it down to the tiger. 'Eat,' he said.

'What's this?' said the tiger. 'I'm a carnivore.'

'From today,' said the trainer, 'you'll eat nothing but grass.'

When the tiger's hunger became unbearable he tried to eat the grass, but he was shocked by its taste and moved away from it in disgust. However, the tiger returned to it and very gradually began to find its taste pleasant.

On the tenth day the trainer, the pupils, the tiger and the cage disappeared: The tiger became a citizen and the cage a city.

Zakaria Tamer, *Tigers on the Tenth Day and Other Stories*, trans. Denys Johnson-Davies (London: Quartet Books, 1985), pp. 13–17.

Ali Shariati: The Philosophy of History: The Story of Cain and Abel

Ali Shariati (1933–1977) received training as a sociologist at the Sorbonne and the University of Mashhad in Iran. His ideas, which drew from Islamic modernism and Marxism, gained a wide following in Iran in the decades before the revolution. In this selection, he reinterprets the story of Cain and Abel.

Now the commentators on the Qur'an and other religious scholars have said in explanation of the narrative concerning Cain and Abel that the purpose for its revelation was the condemnation of murder. But this is very superficial and oversimplifies the matter. Even if my theory is not correct, the narrative of the two brothers cannot be as slight in meaning and purpose as they hold it to be. The Abrahamic religions, especially Islam, depict this story as the first great event that occurs on the threshold of human life in this world. It is not credible that their only purpose in so doing should be the mere condemnation of murder. Whatever may be the underlying sense of the narrative, it is surely far more than a simple ethical tale, yielding the conclusion, "It has thus become clear to us now that murder is an evil deed, so we must try never to commit this shameful act. Let us avoid doing it, particularly to our brothers!"

In my opinion, the murder of Abel at the hands of Cain represents a great development, a sudden swerve in the course of history, the most important event to have occurred in all human life. It interprets and explains that event in a most profound fashion—scientifically, sociologically, and with reference to class. The story concerns the end of primitive communism, the disappearance of man's original system of equality and brotherhood, expressed in the hunting and fishing system of productivity (equated with Abel), and its replacement by agricultural production, the creation of private ownership, the formation of the first class society, the system of discrimination and exploitation, the worship of wealth and lack of true faith, the beginning of enmity, rivalry, greed, plunder, slavery, and fratricide (equated with Cain). The death of Abel and the survival of Cain are objective, historical realities, and the fact that henceforth religion, life, economy, government and the fate of men were all in the hands of Cain represents a realistic, critical, and progressive analysis of what happened. Similarly, the fact that Abel died without issue and mankind today consists of the heirs of Cain[1] also means that the society, government, religion, ethics, world-view, and conduct of Cain have become universal, so that the disequilibrium and instability of thought and morality that prevail in every society and every age derive from this fact.

The story of Cain and Abel depicts the first day in the life of the sons of Adam on this earth (their marriage with their sisters)[2] as being identical with the beginning of contradiction, conflict and ultimately warfare and fratricide. This confirms the scientific fact that life, society and history are based on contradiction and struggle, and that contrary to the belief of the idealists, the fundamental factors in all three are economics and sexuality, which come to predominate over religious faith, brotherly ties, truth and morality. . . .

My purpose in examining the story in such detail has been first, to refute the idea that it is exclusively ethical in purpose, for it treats of something far more serious than the topic for a mere essay, and secondly, to make clear that it is not the story of a dispute between two brothers. Instead, it treats two wings of human society, two modes of production; it is the story of history, the tale of bifurcated humanity in all ages, the beginning of a war that is still not concluded.

The wing represented by Abel is that of the subject and the oppressed, i.e., the people, those who throughout history have been slaughtered and enslaved by the system of Cain, the system of private ownership which has gained ascendancy over human society. The war between Cain and Abel is the permanent war of history which has been waged by every generation. The banner of Cain has always been held high by the ruling classes, and the desire to avenge the blood of Abel has been inherited by succeeding generations of his descendants—the subjected

---

[1] We mean heirs in a typological sense, not a genealogical one.
[2] Certain pious believers have invented various devices for legitimizing the marriages of Cain and Abel in order to free mankind of the blemish of bastardy. However, it is a little late for that!

people who have fought for justice, freedom and true faith in a struggle that has continued, one way or another, in every age. The weapon of Cain has been religion, and the weapon of Abel has also been religion.

It is for this reason that the war of religion against religion has also been a constant of human history. On the one hand is the religion of *shirk*, of assigning partners to God, a religion that furnishes the justification for *shirk* in society and class discrimination. On the other hand is the religion of *tauhid*, of the oneness of God, which furnishes the justification for the unity of all classes and races. The transhistorical struggle between Abel and Cain is also the struggle between *tauhid* and *shirk*, between justice and human unity on the one hand, and social and racial discrimination on the other. There has existed throughout human history, and there will continue to exist until the last day, a struggle between the religion of deceit, stupefaction and justification of the status quo and the religion of awareness, activism and revolution. The end of time will come when Cain dies and the "system of Abel" is established anew. That inevitable revolution will mean the end of the history of Cain; equality will be realized throughout the world, and human unity and brotherhood will be established, through equity and justice. This is the inevitable direction of history. A universal revolution will take place in all areas of human life; the oppressed classes of history will take their revenge. The glad tidings of God will be realized: "We have willed that We should place under obligation those who have been weakened and oppressed on the earth, by making them the leaders of men and heirs to the earth" (Qur'an, 28:5).

This inevitable revolution of the future will be the culmination of the dialectical contradiction that began with the battle of Cain and Abel and has continued to exist in all human societies, between the ruler and the ruled. The inevitable outcome of history will be the triumph of justice, equity and truth.

ʿAli Sharciati, *On the Sociology of Islam*, trans. Hamid Algar (Berkeley, Calif.: Mizan Press, 1979), pp. 103–9.

Ayatollah Khomeini: Islamic Government

In 1970, Ayatollah Khomeini delivered a series of lectures titled "Islamic Government" to religious students studying in Najaf, Iraq. In the lectures, he outlined the role he believed Islam should play in governance.

Islam is the religion of the strugglers who want right and justice, the religion of those demanding freedom and independence and those who do not want to allow the infidels to dominate the believers.

But the enemies have portrayed Islam in a different light. They have drawn from the minds of the ordinary people a distorted picture of Islam and implanted this picture even in the religious academies. The enemies' aim behind this was to extinguish the flame of Islam and to cause its vital revolutionary character to be lost so that the Moslems may not think of seeking to liberate themselves and to implement all the rules of their religion through the creation of a government that guarantees their happiness under the canopy of an honorable human life.

They have said that Islam has no relationship whatsoever with organizing life and society or with creating a government of any kind and that it only concerns itself with the rules of menstruation and childbirth. It may contain some ethics. But beyond this, it has no bearing on issues of life and of organizing society. It is regrettable that all this has had its bad effect not only on the ordinary people but also among college people and the students of theology. They misunderstand Islam and are ignorant of it. Islam has become as strange to them as alien people. It has become difficult for the Moslem missionary to familiarize people with Islam. On the other hand, there stands a line of the agents of colonialism to drown Islam with clamor and noise. . . . What we are suffering from currently is the consequence of that misleading propaganda whose perpetrators got what they wanted and which has required us to exert big efforts to prove that Islam contains principles and rules for the formation of government.

This is our situation. The enemies have implanted these falsehoods in the minds of people in cooperation with their agents, have ousted Islam's judiciary and political laws from the sphere of application and have replaced them by European laws in contempt of Islam for the purpose of driving it away from society. They have exploited every available opportunity for this end. . . .

We believe in government and we believe in the need for the prophet to appoint a caliph [successor] after him, and he did. What does the appointment of a successor mean? Does it mean a mere explanation of the laws? The mere explaining of laws does not require a successor. It would have been enough for the prophet, God's prayers be upon him, to disseminate the laws among the people and then lodge them in a book and leave it with the people to consult after him. The need for a successor is for the implementation of the laws because no law without an executor is respected. In the entire world, legislation alone is not enough and cannot secure the happiness of people. There must be an executive authority and the absence of such an authority in any nation is a factor of deficiency and weakness. This is why Islam decided to establish an executive power to implement God's laws. The prophet, may God's prayers be upon him, did. Had he not done so, he would not have conveyed his message. The appointment of a successor after him to implement and uphold the laws and to spread justice among the people was an element complementing and completing the prophet's message. In his days, the prophet, may God's prayers be upon him, was not content with explaining and conveying the laws. He also implemented them. God's prophet, may God's prayers be upon him, was the executor of the law. He punished, cut off the thief's hand, lashed and stoned and ruled justly. A successor is needed for such acts. A successor is not the conveyor of laws and not a legislator. A successor is needed for implementation. Here is where the importance of forming government and of creating and organizing executive agencies emerges. The belief is the need for forming government and for creating such agencies is an indivisible part of the belief in governance. Exerting efforts for and seeking this goal are an aspect of the belief in governance. . . .

In view of the fact that the Islamic government is a government of law, it is a must that the ruler of the Moslems be knowledgeable in the law, as the Hadith says.

The ruler must have the highest degree of faith in the creed, good ethics, the sense of justice and freedom from sins because whoever undertakes to set the strictures, to achieve the rights and to organize the revenues and expenditures of the treasury houses must not be unjust. God says in his precious book: "The unjust shall not have my support." Thus, if the ruler is not just, he cannot be trusted not to betray the trust and not to favor himself, his family and his relatives over the people.

Ayatollah Khomeini, "Islamic Government," trans. Joint Publications Research Service (Arlington, Va.: 19 January 1979).

Sayyid Qutb: Milestones

Sayyid Qutb (1906–1966) was one of Islamism's most influential theorists. A member of the Muslim Brotherhood of Egypt, Qutb was imprisoned, then executed, by the government of Gamal ᶜAbd al-Nasser. In this selection, Qutb discusses *jahiliyya*, a term that originally referred to the "period of ignorance" before Islam. Qutb redefined *jahiliyya* to mean the state of ignorance that exists wherever Muslims do not or cannot live their lives according to Islamic principles.

If we look at the sources and foundations of modern ways of living, it becomes clear that the whole world is steeped in **Jahiliyyah,** and all the marvellous material comforts and high-level inventions do not diminish this ignorance. This **Jahiliyyah** is based on rebellion against God's sovereignty on earth. It transfers to man one of the greatest attributes of God, namely sovereignty, and makes some men lords over others. It is now not in that simple and primitive form of the ancient **Jahiliyyah,** but takes the form of claiming that the right to create values, to legislate rules of collective behavior, and to choose any way of life rests with men, without regard to what God has prescribed. The result of this rebellion against the authority of God is the oppression of His creatures. . . . Only in the Islamic way of life do all men become free from the servitude of some men to others and devote themselves to the worship of God alone, deriving guidance from Him alone, and bowing before Him alone. . . .

When a person embraced Islam during the time of the Prophet—peace be on him—he would immediately cut himself off from **Jahiliyyah**. When he stepped into the circle of Islam, he would start a new life, separating himself completely from his past life under ignorance of the Divine Law. He would look upon the deeds during his life of ignorance with mistrust and fear, with a feeling that these were impure and could not be tolerated in Islam! With this feeling, he would turn toward Islam for new guidance; and if at any time temptations overpowered him, or the old habits attracted him, or if he became lax in carrying out the injunctions of Islam, he would become restless with a sense of guilt and would feel the need to purify himself of what had happened, and would turn to the Qurʾan to mold himself according to its guidance.

Thus, there would be a break between the Muslim's present Islam and his past **Jahiliyyah**, and this after a well thought out decision, as a result of which all his relationships with **Jahiliyyah** would be cut off and he would be joined completely to Islam, although there would be some give-and-take with the polytheists in commercial activity and daily business; yet relationships of understanding are one thing and daily business is something else.

This renunciation of the **jahili** environment, its customs and traditions, its ideas and concepts, proceeded from the replacement of polytheism by the concept of the Oneness of God, of the **jahili** view of life and the world by that of the Islamic view, and from absorption into the new Islamic community under a new leadership and dedication of all loyalties and commitments to this new society and new leadership.

This was the parting of the ways and the starting of a new journey, a journey free from the pressures of the values, concepts and traditions of the **jahili** society. The Muslim encountered nothing burdensome except torture and oppression; but he had already decided in the depths of his heart that he would face it with equanimity, and hence no pressure from the **jahili** society would have any effect on his continuing steadfastness.

We are also surrounded by **Jahiliyyah** today, which is of the same nature as it was during the first period of Islam, perhaps a little deeper. Our whole environment, people's beliefs and ideas, habits and art, rules and laws—is **Jahiliyyah,** even to the extent that what we consider to be Islamic culture, Islamic sources, Islamic philosophy and Islamic thought are also constructs of **Jahiliyyah!**

This is why the true Islamic values never enter our hearts, why our minds are never illuminated by Islamic concepts, and why no group of people arises among us who are of the calibre of the first generation of Islam.

It is therefore necessary—in the way of the Islamic movement—that in the early stages of our training and education we should remove ourselves from all the influences of the **Jahiliyyah** in which we live and from which we derive benefits. We must return to that pure source from which those people derived their guidance, the source which is free from any mixing or pollution. We must return to it to derive from it our concepts of the nature of the universe, the nature of human existence, and the relationship of these two with the Perfect, the Real Being, God Most High. From it we must also derive our concepts of life, our principles of government, politics, economics and all other aspects of life.

We must return to it with a sense of instruction for obedience and action, and not for academic discussion and enjoyment. We should return to it to find out what kind of person it asks us to be, and then be like that. During this process, we will also discover the artistic beauty in the Qur'an, the marvellous tales in the Qur'an, the scenes of the Day of Judgment in the Qur'an, the intuitive logic in the Qur'an, and all other such benefits which are sought in the Qur'an by academic and literary people. We will enjoy all these other aspects, but these are not the main object of our study. Our primary purpose is to know what way of life is demanded of us by the Qur'an, the total view of the universe which the Qur'an wants us to have, what is the nature of our knowledge of God taught to us by the Qur'an, the kind of morals and manners which are enjoined by it, and the kind of legal and constitutional system it asks us to establish in the world.

We must also free ourselves from the clutches of **jahili** society, **jahili** concepts, **jahili** traditions and **jahili** leadership. Our mission is not to compromise with the practices of **jahili** society, nor can we be loyal to it. **Jahili** society, because of its **jahili** characteristics, is not worthy to be compromised with. Our aim is first to change ourselves so that we may later change the society.

Our foremost objective is to change the practices of this society. Our aim is to change the **jahili** system at its very roots—this system which is fundamentally at variance with Islam and which, with the help of force and oppression, is keeping us from living the sort of life which is demanded by our Creator.

Our first step will be to raise ourselves above the **jahili** society and all its values and concepts. We will not change our own values and concepts either more or less to make a bargain with this **jahili** society. Never! We and it are on different roads, and if we take even one step in its company, we will lose our goal entirely and lose our way as well.

We know that in this we will have difficulties and trials, and we will have to make great sacrifices. But if we are to walk in the footsteps of the first generation of Muslims, through whom God established His system and gave it victory over **Jahiliyyah,** then we will not be masters of our own wills.

It is therefore desirable that we should be aware at all times of the nature of our course of action, of the nature of our position, and the nature of the road which we must traverse to come out of ignorance, as the distinguished and unique generation of the Companions of the Prophet—peace be on him—came out of it.

Sayyid Qutb, *Milestones* (Cedar Rapids, Iowa: The Mother Mosque Foundation, n.d.), pp. 10–11, 19–22.

"Statement of the April 6 Movement Regarding the Demands of the Youth and the Refusal to Negotiate with Any Side"

The April 6 Youth Movement was one of the best known groups to call for protests in Tahrir Square, Cairo, in late January 2011. The following document lists their grievances and demands.

February 6, 2011

The Egyptian Resistance Movement

The youth of Egypt have stood their ground and struggled against the tyrants. We have faced bullets against bare chests with great courage and patience. We salute the great Egyptian people, the creators of this revolution. For that reason, we affirm that victory is the fall of Mubarak and his regime.

Since the 25th of January, "The Egyptian Uprising," we have toppled the legitimacy of the dictator. Egypt is now ruled by the valiant Egyptian people. To protect the peaceful and glorious uprising, let us continue to protect ourselves and our Egyptian assets against the destruction and thuggery of the terrorist regime.

We will complete what we started on the 25th of January. We the Egyptian youth will not be deceived by Mubarak's talk, which aimed to manipulate the emotions of the Egyptian people and under-estimated their intelligence as he has become accustomed to doing for thirty years in speeches, false promises, and mock election programs that were never meant to be implemented. Mubarak resorted to this misleading talk, thinking that Egyptian people could be deceived yet more.

To all Egyptians who love their homeland, we are your children, your sons and daughters and we represent your demands and that which we have all suffered under Mubarak's rule. Mubarak pretends to fully comply with the demands of the Egyptian people, but you must understand that this is merely a maneuver by the Egyptian regime to deceive the free Egyptian people who refused to go back to their homes and end their protests. Whoever among us examines the events that have transpired in the last few days with a conscious mind, beginning with Friday's "Day of Rage", will clearly realize that the Egyptian regime implemented an evil plan to keep Mubarak in power as is the desire of those elements within the regime who want to protect their own personal security, rather than the security of Egypt.

After that, the prime minister appeared with invitations to dialogue. The first thing he did to convey his belief in the importance of dialogue, was to launch an attack by regime thugs and security people in plain clothes against the Egyptian youth, who were without weapons [to defend themselves], in Tahrir square which led to the injury of hundreds and the deaths of eleven martyrs. In addition, the regime undertook an arrest campaign of people in the April 6 Movement's operation room, many lawyers, human rights activists, and representatives of the youth groups which called for the demonstrations on January 25th. The prime minister was not satisfied with this dialogue, so he gave orders to shoot live bullets at the innocent demonstrators. The arrests and chasing down of the movement's activists is still ongoing. Is that the dialogue that Omar Suleiman and Ahmad Shafiq are calling for?

We, the youth of the April 6th Movement, announce our rejection of Omar Suleiman's (the vice president) invitation for dialogue. There can be no dialogue until the departure of President Mubarak. We insist that we intend to proceed with what we started on January 25th to restore the rights that the Mubarak regime has robbed us of during its 30 year reign.

We announce from Tahrir Square:

We will persevere until our demands are fulfilled, namely:
• Mubarak should step down from power immediately.
• Dissolving of the national assembly and the senate.
• Establish a "national salvation group" that includes all public and political personalities, intellectuals, constitutional and legal experts, and representatives of youth groups who called for the demonstrations on the 25th and 28th of January. This group is to be commissioned to form a transitional coalition government that is mandated to govern the country during a transitional period. The group should also form a transitional presidential council until the next presidential elections.
• Drafting a new constitution that guarantees the principles of freedom and social justice.
• Prosecute those responsible for the killing of hundreds of martyrs in Tahrir Square.
• The immediate release of detainees.

These demands are agreed upon by all the youth groups that called for the January 25th and 28th demonstrations.

We also announce that there is not any coordination between us and what is known as "The Committee of Wise Men" who have suggested ending the demonstrations and beginning negotiations while Mubarak is still in power.

Mubarak must leave immediately to preserve the security and stability of Egypt.

There will be no negotiations until the departure of Mubarak and any negotiations should be concerned with the transferring power.

"Statement of the April 6 Movement Regarding the Demands of the Youth and the Refusal to Negotiate with Any Side," translated by Fida Adely and Aiman Haddad. *Jadaliyya ezine*, 8 February 2011, http://www.jadaliyya.com/pages/index/579/statement-of-the-april-6-movement-regarding-the-de.

Yassir al-Manawahly: "The International Monetary Fund"

Music played an important role in the Arab uprisings, mocking the old regimes and articulating the social, economic, and political grievances of many Arabs, particularly youth. In this song, Yassir al-Manawahly, a popular Egyptian singer/songwriter, bitterly combines satire and sarcasm to criticize the effects IMF intervention has had on the lives of ordinary Egyptians. The video that accompanied the release of the song begins and ends with a boy reading from a textbook, "[The] Arab nation is blessed by . . . smart and intelligent people."

O IMF, its poison is in its honey.
Who wants to try it?
(repeat)

You build my house, O IMF.
You seed my land, O IMF.
Without you life sucks, O IMF.

Show me how to manufacture, plant, and kneel to you, O IMF.
Show me where my interest lies, O IMF.
(repeat)

O, please help me!
Bind me with your loans,
Take charge of our land,
And make yourself at home, O IMF.

If I had a Nile he would tell stories
about a plant that died, about a lost nation. (repeat)
Who could grow it but you, O IMF?

If I had a hand, my wheat would have increased
and I would have lived with dignity, my head held up high. (repeat)
Now who's going to hold it up for me, except (the) IMF?

You build my house, you share my thoughts. (repeat)
You plan my future and control my decision.

You look after my best interests, you satisfy all my needs.
You heal my wounds.
You do the impossible.
Who would do the impossible for me except the IMF, O IMF?

So why did the revolution blow up, O IMF?
And the ones who died, why?
Show us the meaning of dignity, O IMF.
What was "hold your head up" for, O IMF?
Why did we cheer, "Down, down," O IMF?
Show us how the free eat, how, how, how?

You erase our past and raise money for us. (repeat twice)
You sneak your hands into our pockets and beat us.
You are my soul mate and you set up my budget.
We are poor and you are the one that supports us
and fulfills my desires.
Who would fulfil them, but the IMF?
O Monetary Fund! (repeat)

Yassir al-Manawahly, "Sanduquh" ("The International Monetary Fund"), translated by Amr Osman, https://www.youtube.com/watch?v=kJIW4LX8Tus.

SUGGESTED READINGS

Abrahamian, Ervand. *Khomeinism: Essays on the Islamic Republic*. Berkeley: University of California Press, 1993. Wonderful collection of essays that examine just how the revolution of 1978–1979 affected Iranian politics and society.

Arjomand, Said Amir. *After Khomeini: Iran Under His Successors*. New York: Oxford University Press, 2009. Detailed account of Iranian politics and society since 1989.

Beblawi, Hazem, and Luciani, Giacomo, eds. *The Rentier State*. London: Croon Helm, 1987. Wide-ranging collection of essays discussing the economic, political, and social changes brought about by oil wealth, remittances, and foreign aid in the Middle East.

Beinin, Joel, and Vairel, Frédéric, eds. *Social Movements, Mobilization, and Contestation in the Middle East and North Africa*. Stanford, Calif.: Stanford University Press, 2011. Excellent collection that applies "social movement theory" to examine case studies of rebellion in the region.

Brownlee, Jason. *Democracy Prevention: The Politics of the US-Egyptian Alliance*. Cambridge, England: Cambridge University Press, 2012. Argues that for all its rhetoric about promoting democracy, the United States colluded with Husni Mubarak to prevent democratic transition.

Gelvin, James L. *The Arab Uprisings: What Everyone Needs to Know*. 2nd ed. New York: Oxford University Press, 2015. Follows the uprisings from their beginning through their evolution, putting them within a historical and global framework.

Gordon, Joel. *Nasser's Blessed Movement: Egypt's Free Officers and the July Revolution*. New York: Oxford University Press, 1992. Clearly written study of the political origins of the 1952 Egyptian Revolution.

Halliday, Fred. *Islam and the Myth of Confrontation: Religion and Politics in the Middle East*. London: I. B. Tauris, 1996. Critical assessment of the West's attitudes and approaches to the Middle East.

Heydemann, Steven, ed. *War, Institutions, and Social Change in the Middle East*. Berkeley: University of California Press, 2000. Excellent collection of essays on the role of war in state formation and social transformation in the Middle East in the modern period.

Jones, Toby Craig. *Desert Kingdom: How Oil and Water Forged Modern Saudi Arabia*. Cambridge, Mass.: Harvard University Press, 2010. Tells the story of the emergence of Saudi Arabia by focusing on the state's ability to tap and harness the two resources.

Khomeini, Ayatollah Ruhullah Musawi. *Islam and Revolution: Writings and Declarations*, translated by Hamid Algar. London: Routledge and Kegan Paul, 1985. Annotated collection of Khomeini's writings selected by a preeminent scholar of Iran.

Kurzman, Charles. *The Unthinkable Revolution in Iran*. Cambridge, Mass.: Harvard University Press, 2005. Explains why no one was able to predict the Iranian Revolution— and by implication the Arab uprisings.

Lesch, David W. *The Middle East and the United States: A Historical and Political Reassessment*. 5th ed. Boulder, Colo.: Westview Press, 2013. A strong collection of essays tracing U.S. policy in the region from 1919 to the present day.

Louis, William Roger. *The British Empire in the Middle East: 1945–1951: Arab Nationalism, the United States, and Postwar Imperialism*. Oxford: Clarendon Press, 1984. Narrative of postwar British diplomacy and British-American rivalry in the region.

Malley, Robert. *The Call from Algeria: Third Worldism, Revolution, and the Turn to Islam*. Berkeley: University of California Press, 1996. Highly readable intellectual history of the rise and fall of Third World movements.

Migdal, Joel S. *Strong Societies and Weak States: State-Society Relations and State Capabilities in the Third World*. Princeton, N.J.: Princeton University Press, 1988. An alternative view of the Nasser regime that stresses the regime's inefficiencies, not its power.

Mitchell, Timothy. *Carbon Democracy: Political Power in the Age of Oil*. London: Verso, 2011. Fascinating rethinking of the relationship of fossil fuels to national and global politics.

Owen, Roger. *The Rise and Fall of Arab Presidents for Life*. Cambridge, Mass.: Harvard University Press, 2012. More about the rise than the fall of Arab presidents, Owen explores the foundations for authoritarian rule in the region.

Owen, Roger, and Pamuk, Sevket. *A History of Middle East Economies in the Twentieth Century*. Cambridge, Mass.: Harvard University Press, 1999. Chronological supplement to *The Middle East in the World Economy*; uses a "national economy" approach to post–World War I economic history of the region.

Richards, Alan, and Waterbury, John. *A Political Economy of the Middle East*. Boulder, Colo.: Westview Press, 1998. Covers territory similar to Owen and Pamuk, but organizes material along conceptual, not chronological or national, lines.

Tripp, Charles. *A History of Iraq*. Cambridge, England: Cambridge University Press, 2007. Possibly the best history of the modern state of Iraq from its beginning to 2007.

Wedeen, Lisa. *The Ambiguities of Domination: Politics, Rhetoric, and Symbols in Contemporary Syria*. Chicago: University of Chicago Press, 1999. Examines jokes, spectacles, and political discourse to analyze the nature of the bargain made between Hafiz al-Assad's government and the population of Syria.

Wickham, Carrie Rosefsky. *The Muslim Brotherhood: Evolution of an Islamist Movement*. Princeton, N.J.: Princeton University Press, 2013. Based on extensive fieldwork, Wickham's book traces the brotherhood from its emergence to the eve of its dissolution.

Zubaida, Sami. *Islam, the People, and the State: Political Ideas and Movements in the Middle East*. London: I. B. Tauris, 1993. A collection of some of the best essays to date on politics and political developments in the region.

al-Zubeidi, Layla, et al., eds. *Diaries of an Unfinished Revolution: Voices from Tunis to Damascus*. New York: Penguin Books, 2013. Eyewitness accounts of the Arab uprisings told by participants.

Timeline

1453	Ottomans conquer Constantinople, effectively ending the fifteen-hundred-year-old Roman Empire.
1497	Vasco Da Gama discovers Cape route, enabling European merchants to bypass overland route through the Middle East.
1501	Shah Isma'il enters the city of Tabriz, establishing the Safavid Empire.
1517	Traditional date for the founding of the Ottoman Empire.
1517	Martin Luther tacks his 95 Theses on the door of Wittenburg Cathedral; traditional date for the beginning of the Protestant Reformation.
1519	Conquest of Mexico by Hernando Cortes; five years later, Francisco Pizarro conquers Peru.
1526	Founding of Mughul Empire.
1569	Ottoman Empire grants first successful capitulations to a European power.
1722	Collapse of Safavid Empire.
1756–1763	Seven Years' War; Britain eclipses France in the Atlantic economy and becomes the preeminent power in India.
1774	Treaty of Kuchuk Kaynarja between Ottoman Empire and Russia gives Russia a foothold on the Black Sea.
1796	Founding of Qajar Empire.
1798	Napoleon invades Egypt.
1801	Mehmet Ali (Muhammad 'Ali) seizes control over Egypt and establishes a dynasty that lasts until 1953.
1803	Muhammad ibn Sa'ud conquers Mecca and establishes the "first Saudi state."
1817	Serbian rebellion ushers in era of Balkan nationalism.
1820	Bahrain becomes first British protectorate in the Persian Gulf region; more would follow.
1821	The "Greek War of Independence" against the Ottoman Empire begins.
1830	French begin conquest of Algeria.
1831–1840	Egyptian occupation of Levant.
1838	Treaty of Balta Liman further opens the market of the Ottoman Empire to Great Britain.
1839	Ottoman sultan issues the *Hatt-i Sharif* of Gulhane, inaugurating the *tanzimat* "reform" period.

1851	Dar al-Funun, a school established to train military officers and bureaucrats, established in Persia.
1856	The *Islahat Fermani* reaffirms and expands on the principles first enunciated in the *Hatt-i Sharif* of Gulhane.
1861	First constitution in the Middle East promulgated in Tunisia.
1861–1865	American Civil War leads to the expansion of cotton cultivation in Egypt and Levant.
1869	Suez Canal opened, reducing distance ships have to travel between Britain and India by half.
1872	Persians grant Julius de Reuter concession to oversee wide range of economic activities.
1873	Onset of the first truly worldwide depression.
1876	Ottoman and Egyptian bankruptcies lead to European control over finances.
1876	Promulgation of Ottoman Constitution.
1878–1908	Hamidian period ends *tanzimat*: Sultan Abdulhamid II rules Ottoman Empire without constitution or parliament.
1881	France establishes Tunisia as a protectorate.
1881–1882	ʿUrabi Revolt in Egypt ends with British occupation.
1882	Beginning of the first wave of Jewish immigration to Palestine.
1901	Persian government grants William Knox d'Arcy first oil concession in the Middle East.
1904–1905	Russo-Japanese War, followed by Russian Constitutional Revolution.
1905	Beginning of Persian Constitutional Revolution.
1907	First nationalist party in Arab world founded in Egypt.
1908	Young Turk Revolution in Ottoman Empire restores constitution.
1911	Italy begins conquest of territory that would become Libya.
1912	Ottomans lose most of its remaining territory in Europe in First Balkan War; France and Spain establish Morocco as separate protectorates.
1914–1918	World War I changes political map of the Middle East.
1915	Amir Faysal launches "Arab Revolt" against Ottomans.
1917	Bolshevik Revolution in Russia.
1917	Great Britain issues Balfour Declaration supporting the Zionist movement.
1919	Egyptian revolt against British occupation.
1919–1922	Turkish War of Independence.
1920	Treaty of Sèvres formally severs connection between Turkish and non-Turkish regions of the Ottoman Empire; mandates system imposed in Levant and Mesopotamia.
1921	British announce formation of Trans-Jordan (later Jordan) at Cairo Conference.
1922	Egypt granted conditional independence from Great Britain.
1924	Mustafa Kemal "Ataturk" abolishes caliphate.
1925	Last Qajar shah dethroned.
1926	Reza Khan proclaimed shah of Persia.
1928	Formation of Muslim Brotherhood in Egypt, an early example of a modern Islamic political movement.
1929	Traditional date marking the onset of the Great Depression.
1932	Iraq becomes first mandated territory to receive independence; Ibn Saʿud announces creation of Saudi Arabia.

1936–1939	Palestinians launch revolt against Zionists and Great Britain.
1938	Oil discovered in Saudi Arabia.
1939–1945	World War II; under Middle East Supply Center, industrial production in Arab Middle East increases 50 percent.
1941	Allies invade Iran; replace Reza Shah with son, Muhammad Reza Shah.
1948	After First Palestine War, Israel proclaims independence.
1949	First postwar military coup d'état in Arab world launched in Syria.
1951	United Nations grants Libya independence.
1952	Free Officers' coup in Egypt; Gamal ʿAbd al-Nasser soon emerges as head of state.
1953	After the nationalization of the Anglo-Iranian Oil Company, the United States and Great Britain organize the overthrow of the Iranian government.
1954–1962	Algerian war of independence.
1955	International conference in Bandung, Indonesia, marks the beginning of the nonaligned movement.
1956	Great Britain, France, Israel launch Suez War against Egypt; France grants Tunisia and Morocco independence (Spain cedes most of its claims to Morocco as well).
1958	Overthrow of monarchy in Iraq.
1958–1961	Unification of Egypt and Syria in United Arab Republic.
1960	Venezuela, Kuwait, Saudi Arabia, Iran, and Iraq form the Organization of Petroleum Exporting Countries (OPEC).
1967	June War between Israel and Arab states; Israel occupies Egyptian, Syrian, and Jordanian territory, along with East Jerusalem, the West Bank, and the Gaza Strip.
1968	Britain announces its "East of Suez" policy, pledging to withdraw from the Gulf by 1971.
1969	Yasir Arafat takes control of the Palestine Liberation Organization.
1971	With the promulgation of the Nixon Doctrine, the United States expands support for the shah of Iran; onset of international economic crisis upends the postwar international economic order.
1973	Oil "price revolution" engineered by OPEC marks greatest triumph for Third World economic nationalism.
1974	United Nations General Assembly and Arab states recognize Palestine Liberation Organization as the "sole, legitimate representative of the Palestinian people."
1978	Camp David Peace Accords negotiated between Egypt and Israel.
1978–1979	Iranian Revolution culminates in the establishment of an "Islamic republic."
1979	Onset of debt crisis opens up an era of retrenchment for states throughout the Third World.
1980–1988	Iran-Iraq war leaves half a million to one million dead and one to two million wounded.
1982	Israeli invasion of Lebanon.
1990	Iraqi invasion of Kuwait, followed by Gulf War in 1991.
1993	Oslo Accord extending mutual recognition between Israel and the Palestine Liberation Organization.
2001	Hijacked airliners crash into World Trade Center, Pentagon, and Pennsylvania countryside; George W. Bush launches Global War on Terror.

2003	The United States and allies invade Iraq and topple the government of Saddam Hussein.
2004–2007	Insurgency, then sectarian violence wrack Iraq.
2007	Hamas takes over Gaza; Palestinian national movement confronts most serious breach since the founding of the PLO.
2010	Muhammad Bouazizi sets himself on fire in Tunisia, sparking the first of the Arab uprisings.
2011	Uprisings break out in Egypt and throughout the Arab world.
2014	The "Islamic State" (formerly the Islamic State of Iraq and Syria or ISIS), establishes a "caliphate" in parts of Syria and Iraq; United States leads international coalition to "degrade and destroy" the Islamic State.

Biographical Sketches

Shah Abbas (1571–1629) Ascending to the Safavid throne in 1588, the year of the Spanish Armada, Shah Abbas "bureaucratized" and strengthened the Persian Empire in a manner similar to his contemporaries, such as the Ottoman Sultan Suleiman the Magnificent. Shah Abbas broke the power of the Qizilbash, established an army and bureaucracy under direct imperial control, and expanded the boundaries of the empire. To pay for his projects and conquests, he confiscated lands that had previously been granted to the Qizilbash, established monopolies over silk production and weaving, and attempted to supervise trade. While Shah Abbas was able to strengthen central control to an extent previously unheard of in early modern Persia, the Safavid Empire entered into a period of crisis soon after his death.

Gamal ʿAbd al-Nasser Born in 1918 in a town outside Alexandria, Nasser was the son of a postal clerk who rose in the Egyptian military to the rank of colonel. The organizer of a clandestine group known as the Free Officers, Nasser participated in the overthrow of the Egyptian monarchy and emerged as the leader of Egypt shortly thereafter. With the rise of Third Worldism and the Suez War of 1956—known in Egypt as the Tripartite Aggression—Nasser became a hero of the nonaligned movement and put in place a populist, state-directed economic development program that provided the model for development in much of the Middle East and beyond. If Nasser's political star rose after 1956, it fell after the catastrophic 1967 war. Nasser died in 1970.

Abdulhamid II (1842–1918) Ottoman sultan from 1876 to 1909. While commonly derided as a reactionary and religious zealot (he reasserted his right to the title of caliph, a title rarely adopted by Ottoman sultans), Abdulhamid II is better viewed as the last great modernizing sultan of the Ottoman Empire. Although he came to power promising to uphold the constitution, Abdulhamid II revoked it and prorogued parliament within two years of his accession to the throne. His efforts to strengthen the empire by centralizing power, promoting an Islamic/Ottoman identity, and undertaking public works (such as the Hijaz Railway which linked Istanbul with Medina) are reminiscent of the efforts of the Russian tsars of the same period.

Jamal al-Din al-Afghani (1839–1897) In spite of his name, which signifies that he came from Afghanistan, it is more than likely that Jamal al-Din al-Afghani was born in Persia. This would make sense: While Jamal al-Din's ideas betray their Usuli roots, he sought to spread them in the Sunni Turkish and Arab worlds. Jamal al-Din al-Afghani was a salafi whose ideology combined three elements: a fierce hatred of imperialism, particularly British imperialism; the belief that the battle against imperialism would be successful only if it involved all Muslims; and the conviction that Muslims would have to adopt both the technology and scientific method of the West to defeat their enemies. More important as a political activist than as a thinker, most of Jamal al-Din's influence came through his contacts: one associate (Muhammad ʿAbduh) became mufti of Egypt, one of his students assassinated the shah of Iran, and his followers played an important role in the Persian Constitutional Revolution of 1905.

Ahmad Bey (1806–1855) Ahmad Bey was a defensive developmentalist along the lines of Mehmet Ali of Egypt. He ascended to the throne of Tunis (Tunisia), then a province of the Ottoman Empire, in 1837. Caught between an Ottoman Empire also undergoing defensive developmentalism and French ambitions in North Africa, Ahmad Bey made military reform a top priority, establishing a conscript army, buying weapons from France, and sending his officer corps to France for training. To win support from Europeans, he sent a Tunisian contingent to the Crimean War, abolished chattel slavery, and improved the conditions of Tunis's Jewish community. This worked: He was able to force the Ottomans to recognize Tunisian autonomy and the right of his family to rule Tunisia in perpetuity in 1845.

Yasir Arafat (1929–2004) Born in either Jerusalem or Cairo to a well-to-do merchant family, Arafat received an engineering degree from King Fuad University in Egypt. He reached political maturity during the golden age of secular Arab nationalism, when anti-colonialism was at its zenith internationally. Arafat founded Fatah, a Palestinian guerrilla group, in the late 1950s but kept his group outside the Palestine Liberation Organization until after the 1967 war, when it became evident to many Palestinians that neither the Arab states nor the PLO as it had been constituted could be trusted with the liberation of Palestine. Elected chairman of the PLO in 1969, he led the PLO for twenty-five years, and in 1996 he was elected the first president of the Palestinian Authority. His death in 2004 coincided with the death throes of the Oslo process.

Hassan al-Banna (1906–1949) The son of a watchmaker in the town of Mahmudiyya, Egypt, Hassan al-Banna founded what many scholars consider to be the first modern Islamic political organization, the Society of Muslim Brothers (the Muslim Brotherhood), in 1928. He attended the Teachers' Training Center, then Cairo University, before he became a teacher in 1927. He founded the Muslim Brotherhood in the Suez Canal city of Ismaʿiliyya, where he preached and recruited members in coffeehouses and similar public venues. By 1934, the brotherhood reportedly had more than fifty branches throughout Egypt. The ideology of the brotherhood combined anti-imperialism and nationalism with a call for moral and religious reconstruction. The brotherhood participated in a guerrilla campaign against the British in the Suez Canal Zone and sent volunteers to fight in the 1948 war for Palestine. Hassan al-Banna was assassinated in 1949, probably in revenge for the assassination of the Egyptian prime minister, which the government attributed to his organization.

Muhammad Bouazizi (1984–2011) Born in the town of Sidi Bouzid where he lived and died, Muhammad Bouazizi was the son of a laborer. He had to quit school to help support his family, working a variety of odd jobs including selling produce—the job he worked at at the time of his death. On 17 December 2010, he was insulted by a policewoman and his goods were confiscated. When he got no satisfaction from the local authorities, he set himself on fire in front of the local municipal building. This event set off the Tunisian uprising, which resulted in the overthrow of Tunisia's long-standing ruler, Zine al- ⁽Abidin bin ⁽Ali, and marked the beginning of the Arab uprisings.

Ibrahim Pasha (1789–1848) Son of Mehmet Ali (Muhammad ⁽Ali), Ibrahim Pasha was one of the great military leaders of the nineteenth century. Among his achievements was the defeat of the Wahhabi movement in Arabia and the restoration of Mecca and Medina to Ottoman control. Although he was unable successfully to defeat Greek separatists—his fleet was sunk by a combined British, French, and Russian fleet at the Battle of Navarino in 1827—he soon thereafter launched a campaign to bring Greater Syria under Egyptian control, where it would remain for approximately ten years. During that time, he imposed many of the same defensive developmentalist programs in the Levant that his father had pioneered in Egypt. His army was finally expelled from the region by a joint Ottoman-British campaign assisted by a local rebellion.

Shah Isma⁽il (1487–1524) Descendant of the Kurdish mystic Safi ad-Din (from whom the Safavid dynasty got its name), Isma⁽il was the leader of a group of Qizilbash ("red head") warriors who seized control of Persia in 1501. Isma⁽il was a charismatic leader who claimed to be a nearly divine being. Under his leadership, the Qizilbash conquered Azerbaijan, Western Iran, and the Tigris-Euphrates basin. They also attracted a wide following among the Turkish tribes of central and eastern Anatolia, thus posing a threat to the Ottomans in western Anatolia. At the Battle of Chaldiran in 1514, Isma⁽il engaged the Ottomans in battle, where he was decisively defeated. Nevertheless, he left an important legacy for the region: His conquests established the Ottoman-Persian boundary, which roughly coincides with the contemporary Turkish-Iranian boundary; he consolidated Safavid rule; and under his leadership Persia was converted to Shi⁽i Islam.

Mustafa Kemal "Ataturk" (1881–1938) Mustafa Kemal was the most successful Ottoman general in World War I, organizing the defense of Gallipoli against British and Commonwealth invaders. After the war, when entente nations occupied parts of Anatolia, committees of resistance sprang up throughout the peninsula. The government in Istanbul dispatched Mustafa Kemal to put down the committees. Instead, he took control of the uprising, expelled foreign forces from Anatolia, established Turkey as an independent republic, and adopted the name "Ataturk," father of the Turks. Mustafa Kemal was an unabashed Westernizer and secularist: He abolished the sultanate and caliphate, "Latinized" the Turkish alphabet, granted women the right to vote, pursued a policy of national economic development, and even regulated headgear. All this was done at a price, however: His government suppressed minorities, attempted to standardize culture, and engaged in political repression and one-party rule.

Ayatollah Ruhollah Khomeini (1899–1989) Before 1963, Ayatollah Khomeini had been a relatively unknown cleric who, trained in the city of Qom, specialized in the field of theology. But in 1963, after the shah had launched the White Revolution, had expanded women's rights, and had increased the legal privileges of Americans in Iran, Khomeini rose to fame as one of the most vociferous opponents of the shah and his American backers. For his efforts, Khomeini was sent into exile, first to Iraq, then to France. After the shah expanded his crackdown on the opposition in 1977 and the official newspaper of Iran published scurrilous attacks on Khomeini, theological students in Qom protested. The army fired on the protest, killing seventy and triggering the Iranian Revolution. Khomeini kept in touch with the revolutionaries, and his exhortations to rebellion, recorded on cassettes, received wide distribution. In 1979, he returned to Iran to establish the *velayat-e faqih*— a state under the guardianship of a jurisconsult, or, as it is more commonly known, an Islamic republic.

Mehmet Ali (Muhammad ʿAli) (1770?–1849)   Ruler of Egypt who seized control of the Ottoman province in the wake of the Napoleonic invasion and established a dynasty that would oversee Egypt until 1953. Mehmet Ali was the son of an Albanian pirate or merchant (depending on the source) who was a commander of a contingent of forces sent to Egypt by the Ottomans. As ruler, he attempted to restructure the military, the government, and economy of Egypt so that he and his family might maintain an autonomous dynasty within the Ottoman Empire. Mehmet Ali was a member of the first generation of leaders in the Middle East who realized that their survival depended upon their ability to "modernize" their domains and centralize their power. Ironically, the programs that had been intended to preserve Egyptian autonomy resulted in further integration of Egypt into the world economy, bankruptcy, and British occupation.

Muhammad Mossadegh (1882–1967)   Swiss-educated Iranian politician and prime minister from 1951 to 1953. Mossadegh rose to power on a platform to nationalize the oil industry, restore parliamentary rule, and reform and develop the economy—a program with which Nasser and many other Third World leaders of the time had much agreement. At first, Mossadegh's program received such widespread support that the shah feared for his life and fled the country. However, Mossadegh's domestic program alienated segments of the Iranian population and, spurred on by the United States and Great Britain, anti-Mossadegh fervor grew. After the army seized control and restored the shah, Mossadegh was sentenced to house arrest. He died in 1967 and has since become a central figure in the Iranian nationalist narrative.

Osman (1259–1326)   Legendary founder of the Ottoman Dynasty, Osman was a frontier warrior who waged incessant campaigns against Byzantine territory in western Anatolia. The Ottoman Empire emerged from the principality he established.

Reza Khan/Reza Shah (1878–1944)   The leader of the Cossack Brigade—a unit in the Persian army that had been established by the Russians—Reza Khan seized power after the chaos, foreign intervention, warlordism, and famine of World War I, establishing a dynasty that ruled Iran until 1979. Reza Khan first toyed with the idea of establishing a republic in Persia, but after the Persian parliament deposed the last Qajar shah he took the title himself. Like Mustafa Kemal "Ataturk," upon whom he modeled himself, Reza Shah imposed a far-reaching program for centralization and modernization. Under his direction, the power of tribes was broken, education and law were taken out of the hands of the ulama, the state played a dominant role in economic development, and the government even regulated dress and religious ritual. Because of his pro-Nazi sympathies, the Allies deposed him during World War II, replacing him with his son, Muhammad Reza, the last shah of Iran.

Suleiman the Magnificent (1494–1566)   Also known as Suleiman the Lawgiver. Suleiman was sultan of the Ottoman Empire at the same time Elizabeth I ruled Britain and Philip II ruled the Spanish Empire. Like his contemporaries, Suleiman consolidated imperial power, expanded the central bureaucracy, patronized the arts, and undertook monumental building projects. Under his leadership, the Ottoman Empire became the preeminent Muslim state of its time.

Ahmad ʿUrabi (1841–1911)   Ahmad ʿUrabi was a colonel in the Egyptian army who hailed from Egyptian peasant origins at a time when the ruling elites of Egypt were descendants of Turks, Albanians, and Circassians. By the time he became the leader of the so-called ʿUrabi Revolt (1881–1882), Egypt had declared bankruptcy and Egyptian finances had been placed under the control of European creditors. The Europeans forced the government to expand taxation and cut military spending. The latter stipulation, alongside rules that discriminated against native-born Egyptians, angered many in the military. The former stipulation ensured that the military was not alone in its dissatisfaction. Military-led demonstrations were thus joined by a host of other disaffected groups, and soon the khedive faced a full-scale revolt that demanded the end of foreign interference, a national "charter," and a curtailment of the khedive's power. The revolt had two lasting effects: The British, who invaded Egypt to put down the revolt, stayed for another three-quarters of a century, and the Egyptians got the first hero to place in their national pantheon.

    Saᶜd Zaghlul (1857–1927) Born into a mid-level peasant family in the Nile delta, Saᶜd Zaghlul studied at the Islamic university, al-Azhar, in Cairo before attending the Egyptian School of Law. After his marriage to a daughter of an Egyptian prime minister, Zaghlul secured a number of ministerial positions in government. A moderate nationalist before World War I, Zaghlul was a member of the Umma Party, a party that sought to achieve Egyptian independence from the British by demonstrating that Egyptians were "civilized" enough to merit it. On the eve of World War I, Zaghlul adopted a more radical stance, and during the war he and his colleagues used their positions to construct nationalist committees throughout the country that would prove invaluable to Zaghlul and like-minded nationalists in the postwar period. In the immediate aftermath of the war, Zaghlul petitioned the British to represent Egyptian aspirations at the Paris peace conference. For his efforts, the British exiled Zaghlul and a few of his associates, an event that sparked the Egyptian Revolution of 1919. After the British granted Egypt conditional independence in 1922, Zaghlul's party—the Wafd—won 90 percent of the seats in parliament and Zaghlul became Egypt's first post-"independence" prime minister.

Glossary

ᶜAbdallah Son of Sharif Husayn; ruler of Trans-Jordan and later first king of Jordan.

Akhbari School of Shiᶜi thought that claims that the ulama were limited in their legal and doctrinal decisions to the traditions of the prophet and the teachings of the twelve imams.

Alawi/Alawite Religious sect that holds Muhammad's son-in-law, ᶜAli, in particularly high regard; the ruling group in Syria is ᶜAlawi.

Alevi Member of minority religious sect that constitutes upwards of 20 percent of the Turkish population.

aliya (pl.: *aliyot*) Literally, ascent; wave of Jewish settlement in Palestine.

Anatolia Asia Minor, the site of the present-day Republic of Turkey.

Anglo-Persian Oil Company Company created after the British government bought William Knox d'Arcy's oil concession. At its inception, the company controlled almost every aspect of the oil business in Persia; later, Anglo-Iranian Oil Company.

Anglo-Persian Treaty (1919) Treaty negotiated between the British and Persian governments in the wake of World War I that, if enacted, would have made Persia a virtual British protectorate.

anjuman (pl.: *anjumanha*) A club or secret society in Persia; *anjumanha* were particularly active in the Persian Constitutional Revolution of 1905.

"Auspicious Incident" (1826) Massacre of janissaries ordered by Sultan Mahmud II.

ayatollah Literally, sign of God; a prominent teaching *mujtahid*.

al-Azhar Islamic university in Cairo, regarded by many as the most prestigious in the Sunni world.

Baku Capital of Azerbaijan; site of oil boom in early twentieth century.

Balfour Declaration Statement issued by the British government in 1917 that stipulated, among other things, that the British government viewed "with favor" the establishment of a Jewish home in Palestine.

Baring, Evelyn (Earl of Cromer) First British consul general in Egypt.

bast Refuge; taking refuge in a mosque or government building was a common form of protest in Persia.

bazaari Merchant who works in markets (bazaars) of Iran.

bedouin Member of nomadic tribe.

berat Certificate; in the nineteenth-century Ottoman Empire, foreign consuls granted *berat*s to Ottoman citizens, making them honorary citizens of foreign countries, entitled to privileges granted foreigners.

beratli The holder of a *berat*.

Bretton Woods System The post–World War II economic system that lasted until 1971.

Bush Doctrine American strategic doctrine announced by George W. Bush after 9/11 according to which the United States should be free to take unilateral and preemptive action against its enemies.

Cairo Conference (1921) Conference held in wake of World War I at which the British created Trans-Jordan.

Caisse de la Dette Institution created by the governments of European creditors to oversee the repayment of debts owed their citizens in the wake of the Egyptian bankruptcy of 1876.

caliph "Successor (to Muhammad)"; historically for Sunnis, the leader of the Islamic community.

caliphate Domain in which a caliph plays the leadership role.

Camp David Accords (1978) Agreement negotiated among Jimmy Carter, Menachim Begin, and Anwar al-Sadat in 1978 that, among other things, included a framework for peace between Israel and Egypt; led to Israel-Egyptian peace treaty in 1979.

Canning, Stratford British representative in Istanbul who reportedly dictated the terms of the *Islahat Fermani* to the sultan in 1856.

capitulations Clauses in treaties between European countries and empires in the Middle East granting the former privileges (trade, religious, and the like) in Middle Eastern domains.

caravansaray Resting place and trading center for caravans.

Circassian Member of an ethnic group originally from the Caucasus.

Cis-Jordan The territory between the Mediterranean Sea and the Jordan River; called Palestine after 1921.

Commercial Revolution Technological, institutional, and structural changes that took place in Europe during the sixteenth century leading to an expansion of trade and, eventually, the modern world economy.

Committee of Union and Progress Secret society established in the military of Ottoman Empire in 1889; took full power in 1913.

Comstock Lode Source of huge quantities of silver discovered in Nevada in the nineteenth century; because Persia was a "silver zone," tapping new veins of silver such as the Comstock Lode had deleterious effects on the Persian economy.

concession Agreement between a government and an entrepreneur or company granting the latter exclusive rights to build infrastructure, exploit natural resources, establish institutions, and the like; granting concessions was a favored policy to foster economic growth in nineteenth-century Persia.

consortium A company of companies established to spread risk.

consul general Highest ranking British official in Egypt between 1882 and 1922, the period of British occupation.

corvée Compulsory labor service.

Cossack Brigade Cavalry unit originally trained and equipped by the Russians but manned by Persians during the nineteenth and early twentieth centuries; Reza Khan was one of its leaders.

Crémieux Decree Decree issued by the French government in 1870 granting Algerian Jews the right to French citizenship.

Crimean War (1854–1856) War pitting the British, French, Piedmontese, and Ottomans against an expanding Russia.

Dar al-Funun School established in Persia in 1851 during a brief attempt at defensive developmentalism.

d'Arcy, William Knox British adventurer who was granted the first oil concession from the Persian government in 1901.

de Reuter, Julius Recipient of a wide-ranging concession from the Persian government in 1872.

decolonization Process by which former colonies achieved independence; the period stretching from The late 1940s through the 1970s during which this happened.

deep state The formal institutions of the state, such as the military, judiciary, and security services, that resist change.

defensive developmentalism Policy of centralization and "modernization" undertaken by governments in the Middle East to strengthen their power and promote economic activity.

département French province.

devshirme A levy exacted by the early Ottoman government on Balkan Christians to recruit for the imperial bureaucracy and janissary corps.

dey A locally chosen Ottoman governor of Algeria.

Druze A member of an esoteric religious sect, found most commonly in Lebanon and Palestine.

East of Suez British policy announced in 1968 according to which Britain would abandon its military bases east of the Suez Canal by 1971.

Eastern Question Eighteenth- and nineteenth-century competition to determine the fate of the Ottoman Empire and its provinces involving Britain, France, Russia, and later Germany.

entente powers/Central Powers Two main alliances in World War I; the entente consisted of, among others, Great Britain, France, Russia, and eventually the United States; the Central Powers included, among others, Germany, the Austro-Hungarian Empire, and the Ottoman Empire.

faqih Islamic legal expert qualified to rule on matters pertaining to the shari°a.

Faysal Son of Sharif Husayn; leader of Arab Revolt; later king of Iraq.

feddan Unit of land measurement; one feddan equals approximately one acre.

fez A brimless, conical felt hat introduced into the Ottoman Empire in the nineteenth century as a sign of the empire's "modernity."

formal empire/informal empire Formal empires are those in which an imperial power asserts direct control over a territory; in informal empires that control is asserted by economic and diplomatic means and not by annexation or occupation of territory.

Fourteen Points American aims in World War I as enunciated by Woodrow Wilson; nationalist leaders throughout the world took Wilson's seeming support for their aspirations to heart.

Free Officers Military conspirators in the Egyptian army who took power in 1952; their most famous member was Gamal °Abd al-Nasser.

Gallipoli Peninsula off western Anatolia; site of battle for the Turkish straits involving mainly British and Commonwealth forces, on the one hand, and Ottoman forces, on the other; the battle made a hero of the successful Ottoman general, Mustafa Kemal.

ghazi Frontier warrior.

ghulam (pl.: *ghilman*) Slave brought into Persia to serve in the military or bureaucracy.

"Great Game" Term popularized by Rudyard Kipling to refer to nineteenth-century British-Russian competition in Central Asia.

Great Inflation Increase in prices throughout the Eurasian continent beginning in the sixteenth century. Determining the causes of the Great Inflation has resulted in great contention among historians.

Great (Palestine) Revolt (1936–1939) Palestine-wide rebellion against Zionist immigration and British control; put down harshly by the British.

guild An organization comprising all who participate in a given profession or trade.

hadith Account of the words and acts of Muhammad and his companions.

hajj Annual pilgrimage to Mecca undertaken by Muslims.

Hamas Acronym for the Islamic Resistance Movement, founded during the first *intifada* in the occupied territories.

Hatt-i Sharif of Gulhane (1839) Decree promising, among other things, equality and rights to all Ottoman citizens; regarded as the opening salvo of the *tanzimat*.

Hemmat Persian affiliate of the Russian Social Democratic Workers Party; played a role in the Persian Constitutional Revolution of 1905.

Hijaz Western region of the Arabian peninsula; site of Mecca and Medina.

Hijazi, Salamah Influential participant in *nahda*; pioneered "neo-classicism" in Arabic music and theater.

Histadrut Trade union federation established in Palestine by Zionists during the early twentieth century.

Hizbullah Shiʿi social/political/military movement in Lebanon.

Husayn 1. Sharif Husayn: Descendant of the prophet and overseer of the two holy cities in Arabia; entered into agreement with the British during World War I to declare jihad against the Ottoman Empire in return for gold, weapons, and promises of postwar independence. 2. Imam Husayn: Son of ʿAli (Muhammad's son-in-law) and, according to Shiʿis, the third imam; led revolt against caliph but was defeated at the Battle of Karbala in A.D. 680.

ibn ʿAbd al-Wahhab, Muhammad Founder of a puritanical movement in central Arabia; Wahhabism is the official ideology of the contemporary Saudi government.

ibn Saʿud, Muhammad Tribal chieftain and follower of Muhammad ibn ʿAbd al-Wahhab; established state in Arabia that was demolished by Ibrahim Pasha in the early nineteenth century.

ijtihad The application of reason to supplement the foundational texts of Islam.

ikhwan Literally, brothers; nontribal levies and followers of ʿAbd al-ʿAziz ibn al-Saʿud; instrumental in his conquest of the Arabian peninsula.

imam In Sunni Islam, a prayer leader; in Shiʿi Islam, descendant of Muhammad's son-in-law, ʿAli, and rightful leader of the community.

Imperial Tobacco Company The recipient of a concession from the Persian government in 1889 that allowed the company to control the cultivation, sale, distribution, and export of all Persian tobacco and tobacco products; the concession was cancelled after protests.

integration and peripheralization The process whereby areas of the world are brought into a common economic system (integration) but as subsidiary units (that is, mostly raw materials suppliers) to the industrialized core (peripheralization).

International Monetary Fund (IMF) One of the institutions established as part of the Bretton Woods System, originally to ensure the stability of the global economy; later became the institution through which neoliberal economic policies were spread.

intifada The Palestinian uprising against Israeli occupation that broke out in 1987 and lasted until 1993; a second *intifada* broke out in 2000.

Iraq Petroleum Company Consortium that controlled all aspects of the petroleum industry throughout Iraq.

Islahat Fermani **(1856)** Decree promulgated by the Ottoman government that reaffirmed and expanded the rights granted Ottoman citizens by the *Hatt-i Sharif* of Gulhane.

Islamic State Group that conquered parts of Syria and Iraq in 2014 and established a caliphate there.

Islamism The doctrine that asserts that society should be ordered by Islamic law and Islamic principles.

Islamist Someone who promotes Islamism.

jihad Literally, struggle; the word has various meanings, sometimes connoting an "inner struggle" for piety, sometimes connoting combat.

Kemalism The doctrines introduced to Turkey by Mustafa Kemal "Ataturk."

khedive Ottoman viceroy of Egypt; title held by descendants of Mehmet Ali until 1914.

kibbutz (pl.: kibbutzim) Zionist/Israeli communal farm; the first kibbutz was established in 1909–1910.

Kurd Member of ethnic grouping inhabiting eastern Anatolia, western Iran, northern Iraq, and Syria.

"land for peace" Formula for establishing peace between Israel and its neighbors according to which Israel would trade off land it seized during the 1967 War in return for recognition and a cessation of hostilities.

Late Antiquity Period of history stretching from the fourth to the seventh centuries, A.D.

Law of Liquidation (1880) Law enacted by the Egyptian government that gave the Caisse de la Dette expanded powers for revenue extraction.

Lawrence, T. E. ("Lawrence of Arabia") British advisor to Arab Revolt.

Levant Region proximate to eastern Mediterranean, usually considered to comprise present-day Syria, Lebanon, Israel, Palestine, Jordan, and western Iraq.

Lord Milner British government official who led inquiry into the 1919 Egyptian Revolution. At the Milner Commission's suggestion, Britain granted Egypt conditional independence in 1922.

majlis Parliament; term is used in both the Arab world and Iran.

mamluk Slave-soldiers, originally brought into the Middle East by Arab caliphs from amongst Turkic tribes; later established their own dynasties in the region.

mandates system An administrative system established by the League of Nations whereby more "advanced" states would supervise the development of less advanced peoples to prepare them to face "the strenuous conditions of the modern world."

mandatory powers Nations that assumed control over mandated territories.

market economy Economic system that is primarily based on production for exchange.

marketplace economy Economic system that is primarily based on production for consumption.

Maronite Member of Christian sect, mainly in Lebanon.

megali idea Literally, grand idea; a doctrine associated with Greek nationalism that called for the unification of all Greek-speaking, Orthodox peoples in the Balkans, Mediterranean, and Anatolia into a single (Greek) state.

mercantilism Seventeenth-century European economic doctrine that made the accumulation of gold the primary goal of national economic policy.

military-patronage state Any one of the Turco-Mongolian states established during and after the thirteenth century in which society was divided into a ruling military class and the remainder of the population; land belonged to the chief military family or families and was leased out in exchange for services rendered by the military class; and dynastic law supplemented local customs and Islamic law.

millet system Ottoman administrative practice allowing religious minorities control over many of their own affairs, including educational, charitable, and judicial affairs, as well as representation in Istanbul.

moral reconstruction The idea that social ills could be healed through individual pious acts.

moshav **(pl.:** *moshavim***)** Cooperative village first established in Palestine by Jewish immigrants in 1921.

Mosul Northern province of Iraq; also the largest city in that province.

mufti Muslim judicial official who interprets Islamic law.

mujtahid In Shiʿi Islam, a religious scholar who can render legal opinions by use of informed reason.

Muslim Brotherhood Islamic social and political organization established by Hassan al-Banna in Egypt in 1928.

mutasarrifiya A special administrative district, established in Mount Lebanon in 1861, governed by a non-Lebanese Ottoman Christian and protected by the concert of European powers.

nahda Nineteenth-century Arabic literary renaissance that was part of a wider movement for cultural and social reform.

Najd Region in the central and eastern Arabian peninsula.

nakba Literally, disaster; word used by Palestinians to refer to the 1948 war.

narghile Water pipe; hookah.

Nasir al-Din Shah Ruler of Persia during much of the late nineteenth century; assassinated in 1896.

nativism The belief that the present social, cultural, and political order should be based on that of the past, real or imagined.

Naus, Joseph Belgian national who was hired by the Persian government to oversee collection of customs; his policies were one of the triggers for the Persian Constitutional Revolution.

neoconservatives In the wake of the cold war, those who believed that the United States should take advantage of its unique position in the world to spread "American values" and maintain that position unopposed.

neoliberalism Economic doctrine first promoted by the United States in the 1970s which seeks to allow the "free market" to govern itself with minimal interference from governments.

neo-sufism The redefinition of sufi movements, beginning in the eighteenth century, to reflect a more legalistic and scripturalist approach.

New International Economic Order Set of demands made by Third World Nations during the 1970s to offset what they believed to be the inequities of the Bretton Woods System.

New World Order Phrase used by President George H. W. Bush to describe the post–cold war environment.

nonalignment Policy followed by Third World states that advocated a political stance independent of either the Western alliance or the Soviet bloc.

occultation State of being hidden; Shiᶜis believe that the last imam (either the seventh or twelfth in the line of descent, depending on the branch of Shiᶜism) was hidden by God but will one day return to guide his community.

Organization of Petroleum Exporting Countries (OPEC) Organization founded in 1960 to coordinate petroleum policies of the major producers; OPEC became a producers' cartel in 1982.

Oslo Accord The 1993 Agreement reached between Israel and the Palestinians that included mutual recognition and established a framework for further negotiations.

osmanlilik An ideology that might loosely be called Ottoman nationalism.

Ottoman Public Debt Administration Institution created by the governments of European creditors to oversee the repayment of debts owed their citizens in the wake of the Ottoman bankruptcy of 1876.

Pahlavi Last ruling dynasty of Iran (1926–1979).

Palestinian Authority (PA) Governing body established by the Oslo Accord to rule Palestine and negotiate with Israel for an independent Palestinian state.

pan-Arabism The doctrine that Arabs constitute one people; pan-Arab nationalists believe they should be joined in a single state.

prebendalism System of Ottoman and Safavid land management wherein most land is worked by a free peasantry but belongs to the ruling dynasty; land thus cannot be bought and sold.

proletarianization The process of creating a class of people who sell their labor.

protectorate A state that is nominally independent but whose foreign policy and defense are controlled by another state.

qadi Judge working in an Islamic law court.

Qizilbash Turcomen followers of Safi al-Din's teachings and their descendants.

remittances Money sent home by guest workers working in a foreign country.

rentier state A state dependent on money derived from sources other than taxation for a significant percentage of its income.

ruling bargain Metaphor used by political scientists to describe the relationship between a population and its government.

Russian Social Democratic Workers Party Russian socialist party that was influential in Baku and northern Persia at the beginning of the twentieth century.

al-Sadat, Anwar President of Egypt after Nasser (1970–1981); noteworthy for rolling back many of the populist policies of the Nasser era, his pro-American stance, and signing a treaty with the Israelis in 1979.

Safi al-Din Legendary founder of the Safavid Dynasty; leader of Turcomen sufi order.

al-salaf al-salih The "pious ancestors"; those who made up the first Islamic community and served as a source of emulation and chroniclers of the acts and sayings of Muhammad.

salafism Method of arriving at religious truth in Islam by returning to the foundational texts of Islam and using the first Islamic community as a source of emulation.

al-Sanusi, Muhammad ibn ʿAli (1787–1859) Founder of puritanical sufi order (Sanusiyya) in North Africa that played an important role in fighting the Italians in the early twentieth century.

SAVAK The often brutal intelligence agency in pre-revolutionary Iran.

Second Serfdom The re-imposition of serfdom in Eastern Europe during the sixteenth and seventeenth centuries; in part, a response to the Great Inflation.

sectarianism The phenomenon whereby religious affiliation becomes the foundation for collective identity in a multireligious environment.

settler-colonialism A form of imperialism marked by the settlement of immigrants in a foreign territory.

shah Persian emperor.

shariʿa Islamic law.

Shiʿism One of the two main branches of Islam; predominant in Iran, Iraq, and Bahrain, with significant populations elsewhere.

shura Literally, consultation; early Islamic practice cited by Islamic modernists as precedent for parliaments.

stagflation An economic crisis marked by simultaneous inflation and lack of growth, such as what happened in the aftermath of the oil price revolution of 1973–1974.

Suez War/Tripartite Aggression War launched against Nasser's Egypt in 1956 by the British, French, and Israelis.

sufism Popular religiosity, sometimes mystical, in which the followers of a pious founder group themselves into paths or *turuq* marked by unique rituals, beliefs, etc.

sultan Title adopted by rulers, such as the head of the Ottoman Empire, in much of the Middle East.

sunna In Sunni Islam, the acts and sayings of the prophet and the acts of the prophet's companions in Medina. Shiʿis include the acts and sayings of the twelve imams as well.

Sunnism Predominant branch of Islam in most of the world, including Turkey and most of the Arab world.

Sykes-Picot Agreement One of a number of secret agreements negotiated during World War I; although never implemented, the agreement has come to symbolize the role outside powers played in determining the borders of states in the Arab Middle East.

Tabriz City in northern Iran.

takfir The practice of pronouncing someone who considers themselves part of the Islamic community a non-Muslim, thus allowing "true believers" to kill them.

tanzimat Literally, regulations; refers both to new Ottoman regulations decreed in the nineteenth century and to the period in which those regulations were decreed.

tariqa (**pl.:** *turuq*) Sufi "path."

tawula Backgammon.

tax farmer Agent who pays taxes for a given territory or industry up front; in return, he is allowed to extract surplus from that territory or industry.

timar Land grant made to the commander of a cavalry unit in the early Ottoman Empire.

tiyul Persian equivalent of *timar*.

Trans-Jordan The territory to the east of the Jordan River; currently the Hashemite Kingdom of Jordan.

Treaty of Balta Liman (1838) Treaty between Britain and the Ottoman Empire in which the Ottomans agreed to abolish monopolies in their realms and lower customs duties; for signing the treaty, the Ottomans received British assistance in removing Egyptian troops from the Levant.

tribe A group of people who claim descent from a common ancestor, whether or not they are in fact related to that common ancestor or even to each other.

Trucial States A group of small principalities on the Persian Gulf placed under the protection of Great Britain; later became the United Arab Emirates.

Tudeh The communist party of Iran.

Turkish Petroleum Company A consortium that was the recipient of the second great oil concession in the Middle East; controlled all aspects of the industry in territory that is currently most of Iraq.

ulama (**sing.:** *ᶜalim*) Muslim religious scholars.

U.N. Resolution 242 Resolution passed by the Security Council of the United Nations after the 1967 war establishing the "land for peace" formula.

U.N. Resolution 338 Resolution passed by the Security Council of the United Nations after the 1973 war that fundamentally reiterated the principles of U.N. Resolution 242.

ᶜUrabi Revolt (1881–1882) Revolt initiated by the Egyptian military to end foreign interference, domestic autocracy, and discrimination against native Egyptians. The revolt received wide support in Egypt, but was crushed by the British.

Usuli School of Shiᶜism that asserts that select religious scholars could supplement the original sources of law through the use of reason (*ijtihad*).

vali-e faqih Head of state of the Islamic Republic of Iran.

"veiled protectorate" Protectorate which remains unrecognized as such by the international community.

velayat-e faqih Literally, government of the jurisconsult; form of government of the Islamic Republic of Iran in which the head of state is a legal expert qualified to rule on matters pertaining to the shariᶜa.

wafd/**Wafd** Literally, delegation; Egyptian political party founded by Saᶜd Zaghlul.

Wahhabism Puritanical religious movement founded by Muhammad ibn ᶜAbd al-Wahhab in the eighteenth century.

Young Ottomans Diffuse group of nineteenth-century intellectuals who advocated Islamic modernism and constitutional rule in the Ottoman Empire.

Young Turks Name given to an amalgam of groups opposed to Abdulhamid II;
in 1908 the Young Turks staged a revolt and restored the Ottoman constitution.

Zionism The belief that Jews are a national community entitled to their own
independent state; most Zionists believe that such a state should be situated
in Palestine.

Credits

Page 3: "The jihadists of the Islamic State. . . ." Hisham Melham, *Politico Magazine* (September 18, 2014), http://www.politico.com/magazine/story/2014/09/the-barbarians-within-our-gates-111116.html?ml=lb_4#.VDCJ-xZ2Rk0.

Page 20–21: "Because of their distance from the circuit of the sun. . . ." Bernard Lewis, *Islam from the Prophet Muhammad to the Capture of Constantinople*, vol. 2: *Religion and Society* (New York: Oxford University Press, 1987), 122.

Page 21: "A moon arose from the holy man's breast. . . ." Cemal Kafadar, *Between Two Worlds: The Construction of the Ottoman State* (Berkeley: University of California Press, 1995), 8.

Page 25: "After a siege of forty days . . . " Edward Gibbon, *The Decline and Fall of the Roman Empire*, vol. 3 (New York: Modern Library, n.d.), 771.

Page 26: "Musitch Stefan." Helen Rootham, *Kossovo: Heroic Songs of the Serbs* (Oxford: B.H. Blackwell, 1920), 59–60.

Page 41: "The sale of Bengal opium. . . ." A.J.H. Latham, *The International Economy and the Undeveloped World, 1865–1914* (London: Croom Helm, 1978), 409–10.

Page 90: "Imperialism . . . is a process. . . ." Ronald Robinson, "Non-European Foundations of European Imperialism: Sketch for a Theory of Collaboration," *Studies in the Theory of Imperialism*, ed. Roger Owen and Bob Sutcliffe, 118–119.

Page 91: "Informally if possible. . . ." John Gallagher and Ronald Robinson, "The Imperialism of Free Trade," *The Economic History Review* 6:1 (1953), 13.

Page 92: "on the cheap." Ibid., 13.

Page 95: "The Algerians were revolutionists. . . ." http://www.americanrhetoric.com/speeches/mal-colmxgrassroots.htm.

Chapter 7: All quotes from Salim Tamari, "Jerusalem's Ottoman Modernity: The Times and Lives of Wasif Jawhariyyeh," *Jerusalem Quarterly File* 9 (2000), 5–34.

Page 159: "the word 'Constitution' was in every mouth. . . ." Bernard Lewis, *The Emergence of Modern Turkey* (New York: Oxford University Press, 2002), 161.

Page 165: "Imagine some five hundred illiterate young men. . . ." Elie Kedourie, *Arabic Political Memoirs* (London: Cass, 1974), 137.

Page 207: "The wave of civilization has come to us. . . ." Ibrahim Ibrahim, Ahmad Amin and 'Abbas Mahmud al-'Aqqad , "Between al-Qadim and al-Jadid: European Challenge and Islamic Response," in *Arab Civilization: Challenges and Responses*, ed. George N. Atiyeh and Ibrahim M. Oweiss (Albany: SUNY Press, 1988), 209.

Page 207: "The love for one's country. . . ." Robert P. Mitchell, *The Society of the Muslim Brothers* (New York: Oxford University Press, 1993), 265.

Page 265: "go into opposition." Daniel Patrick Moynihan, "The United States in Opposition," *Commentary* (March 1, 1975), http://www.commentarymagazine.com/article/the-united-states-in-opposition/.

Page 267: "still presumably rotting," Ibid.

Page 273: "In the future Turks must possess. . . ." Ziya Gokalp, *The Principles of Turkism*, trans. Robert Devereaux (Leiden: EJ Brill, 1968), n.p.

Page 273: "Establishing industries is a delegated duty. . . ." Jacqueline S. Ismael and Tareq Y. Ismael, "Cultural Perspectives on Social Welfare in the Emergence of Modern Arab Social Thought," *The Muslim World* LXXXV:1–2 (January–April 1995), 95.

Page 277: "The aim of the Syrian Social Nationalist Party. . . ." Labib Zuwiyya Yamak, *The Syrian Social Nationalist Party: An Ideological Analysis* (Cambridge, MA: Harvard Middle Eastern Monograph Series, 1966), 98.

Page 322: "We attacked them as the sun rose. . . ." F.E. Peters, *A Reader on Classical Islam* (Princeton: Princeton University Press, 1994), 130–31.

Page 323: "I tell you plainly. . . ." Ayatollah Khomeini, *Islam and Revolution: Writings and Declarations of Imam Khomeini*, trans. and annot. Hamid Algar (Berkeley: Mizan Press, 1981), 207.

Page 345: "There is a revolution growing. . . ." Gaza Youth Breaks Out, http://gazaybo.wordpress.com/manifesto-0-1/

Page 355: "The (Arab) nation states. . . ." Voice of Jihad (August/September 2004) in Brad K. Berner, *The World According to Al Qaeda* (n.l.: Booksurge, 2005), 147–8.

Page 355: "Islamic rule that will respect. . . ." Laura Mansfield, *Al Qaeda 2006 Yearbook: 2006 Messages from Al-Qaeda Leadership*, ed. Laura Mansfield (N.L.: TLG Publications, 2007), 61, 234.

Page 355: "The entire Islamic community. . . ." http://ar.marefa.org/sources/index.php.

Index